Walking in the Way Day by Day

Your Daily Guide to the Promise Land

Keith E. Jackson, MFT

AuthorHouse™
1663 Liberty Drive
Bloomington, IN 47403
www.authorhouse.com
Phone: 1-800-839-8640

© 2014 Keith E. Jackson, MFT. All rights reserved.

No part of this book may be reproduced, stored in a retrieval system, or transmitted by any means without the written permission of the author.

Published by AuthorHouse   10/14/2014

ISBN: 978-1-4969-4322-4 (sc)
ISBN: 978-1-4969-4321-7 (e)

Any people depicted in stock imagery provided by Thinkstock are models, and such images are being used for illustrative purposes only.
Certain stock imagery © Thinkstock.

This book is printed on acid-free paper.

Because of the dynamic nature of the Internet, any web addresses or links contained in this book may have changed since publication and may no longer be valid. The views expressed in this work are solely those of the author and do not necessarily reflect the views of the publisher, and the publisher hereby disclaims any responsibility for them.

All rights reserved. This book is protected by the copyright laws of the United States of America. This book may not be copied or reprinted for commercial gain or profit. The use of short quotations or occasional page copying for personal or group study is permitted and encouraged. Permission will be granted upon request. Unless otherwise indicated, all Scripture quotations are taken from the Holy Bible, New Living Translation, copyright 1996, 2004 by Tyndale House Publishers, Wheaton, Illinois 60189.

Scripture quotations marked AMP are from The Amplified Bible, Old Testament copyright © 1965, 1987 by the Zondervan Corporation. The Amplified Bible, New Testament copyright © 1954, 1958, 1987 by The Lockman Foundation. Used by permission. All rights reserved.

Scripture quotations marked NLT are taken from the Holy Bible, New Living Translation, copyright © 1996, 2004, 2007. Used by permission of Tyndale House Publishers, Inc. Carol Stream, Illinois 60188. All rights reserved. Website

Scripture quotations marked NIV are taken from the Holy Bible, New International Version®. NIV®. Copyright © 1973, 1978, 1984 by International Bible Society. Used by permission of Zondervan. All rights reserved. [Biblica]

In loving memory of my father
Eugene Jackson
September 7, 1931–January 8, 2014

Preface

This book would not been written if it was not inspired by the Holy Spirit. I thank God for the people who He has brought across my path, to teach me and inspire me. My children are and always will be an inspiration for what I do. It is my desire to leave them a legacy to pass on to their children. This is the mark of true prosperity (Psalm 112:1–3). Jared and Cassandra, you have been a blessing to your mother and me.

My mother, you have always had my back, and have always been there for me, thanks mom. My ex-wife, Jane: you are the mother of my children and have become a friend that I can count on, thank you.

Next are the men and women of God who have been examples to me and taught me how to be more genuine in my walk with Christ. Men like Kenneth Copeland, Charles Capps, and Bill Winston, Leroy Thompson, Al Houghton, and Henry Grover: words cannot express all that I have learned from you in word and deed. I pray that God continues to bless you in the assignment He has given you. There are many others that I have not mentioned. I could spend at least five pages listing names, so I won't.

Finally, I would like to express my gratitude to my pastors Kimberly and Stephanie Hjelt. You have been an example of how we are to love and commit to the leadership of Christ Jesus. I have seen all that you have endured and I admire you for it. You not only teach the Word of God, but you live it. This speaks volumes to me and I thank you for all that I have learned from attending your church.

I also want to thank all my friends—past, present, and future. Thanks for your prayers, support, and rebukes. I would not be where I am today without it. To all of you: be strong in the Lord and the power of His might. KJ2014

Introduction

On November 2, 2010, I woke up to find that I could not move my legs or my arms. I was paralyzed from the shoulders down. I would later learn that the paralysis was caused by a spinal infection. The doctors were not hopeful of my recovery. They thought I would be restricted to a wheelchair for the rest of my life. But the Lord spoke to me while I lay on my bed. He told me that I would recover and would not be in a wheelchair for the rest of my life.

From that moment on I kept reminding myself of the words the Lord spoke to me. When I was told anything different, I would simply discard it, choosing rather to put all of my trust in Yahweh-Rapha, my Healer. I would eventually recover. I am now back at the gym and doing all the things the doctors said I wouldn't ever be able to do again. It was during my stay in the hospital that I felt led to write a book of daily meditations. I know that beginning your day with biblically based teaching sets the stage for a prosperous day.

In this busy age we live in, some people don't have the time to sit down and read the Scriptures, but they can sit down and read a page or two of a book. Therefore, this book has 365 different readings, one for each day. That means every day you will read something different—it's like eating manna from heaven. We are all on our journey to the Promise Land, and it's good to have some manna to chew on while we travel.

I wrote this book for those who have accepted Jesus into their heart as their Lord and Savior. If you haven't done that yet, then what's stopping you? All you have to do is believe in your heart and confess with your mouth that Jesus is Lord of your life, and you are now a believer (Romans 10:9).

Next, find yourself a Bible-believing church and you will be on your way to the Promise Land.

Finally, if you are looking for a table of contents, you won't find one. I chose not to put one in because there is a page for every day of the year. I hope you get as much out of reading this book as I did writing it. My walk with the Lord has gotten so much stronger.

Be strong in the Lord always,
Keith Jackson

January 1

THE VISION GOD HAS FOR YOU

> *The Spirit of the Sovereign Lord is upon me, for the Lord has anointed me to bring good news to the poor. He has sent me to comfort the brokenhearted and proclaim that the captives will be released and the prisoners will be freed. He has sent me to tell those who mourn that the time of the Lord's favor has come, and with it, the day of God's anger against their enemies. (Isaiah 61:1–2)*

I used to read this passage of Scripture and associate it only with Jesus, until the revelation came to me that this should be my mindset also. This explains why the church as a whole is not making a bigger impact in our society today. I often wondered where the signs and wonders are that once followed the apostles in the book of Acts. There are many Christians who believe that the signs and wonders spoken of in the book of Acts left with the disciples of Jesus. However, this is simply not true.

When I became aware of Smith Wigglesworth, and read of some of the exploits of this man, I knew that it was possible to perform signs and wonders in this day and age. He did all the things the apostles did in the book of Acts. He raised at least twenty people from the dead, healed all types of illnesses and diseases—even seeing body parts grow—through the power of the Holy Spirit.

Once I read about how God used him in such powerful ways, I was convinced that it was possible to have signs and wonders following me as well. But I also knew that I had to renew my mind in order to be trusted with such power and authority. God, through the Holy Spirit, just doesn't work through anyone who desires it. A person actually has to qualify himself in order to be used by God. This means they must spend time in the Word of God every day and make God's thoughts their thoughts (Isaiah 55:8–9).

We, as children of God, should inculcate into our mind the same mindset Jesus possessed. This is the only way we will be able to do what He did (John 14:12). We cannot allow the traditional thinking of modern-day "Christendom" to rob us from what God has already provided us through Christ Jesus. We must seek God's thoughts and not follow after the thoughts of this world's system. God has called us to be the head and not the tail (Deuteronomy 28:13), so we don't have to let the enemy deceive us any longer. We can start every morning by repeating Luke 4:18–19 until it becomes part of our thought process. And then we will begin to see ourselves as Jesus sees us, and then we will start to do the things that He did. *You have to see it in order to be it!*

Scripture Readings:
Isaiah 55:8–9; 61:1–2
Luke 4:18–19

January 2

Is Doubt in Your Mind Stopping Your Faith?

Beloved, I pray that you may prosper in every way and [that your body] may keep well, even as [I know] your soul keeps well and prospers. (3 John 2 AMP)

You have made the right confessions, read Bible passages, made sure that you confessed all known sin in your life, and even fasted, but you didn't get the answer to your prayers. Maybe the reason you didn't get the answer to your prayers is not because of the amount of faith you have; it could be something else you have not considered before. It could be unbelief housed in your mind.

Some believers make the mistake by thinking that since they are born again, they do not have to attend to their cognitive processes. Some even think that psychology has no place in the church, and view it as a worldly science. But if you think about the myriad of Scriptures that make reference to the mind, you will come to the conclusion that this is myopic thinking.

The mind is the gateway to the soul. It controls what is allowed into our spirit and heart. Why does Paul say in Romans 12:2 that we must renew our minds? He knew that if we are to walk in the fullness of what God desires for us, then we are going to have to get our mind in agreement with our spirit and heart. When the spirit, heart, and soul are working together, we are unstoppable. The enemy knows this, and will go out of his way to keep division within the realm of the soul.

This explains why so many Bible-believing, tongue-talking believers are living far below what God desires for them. These believers are the ones who will run up to the altar to have hands laid on them for healing, and a day later they are complaining about not receiving it. Eventually, their heart becomes hardened and they give up. They never stopped to consider that their thoughts might be the reason for them not keeping their healing.

Mark 6:1–6 tells the story of Jesus going to His hometown. The people were amazed by His teachings, His wisdom, and His intelligence. They even marveled at the exhibitions of power from His hands. However, in spite of what they saw, He offended them, and Jesus couldn't do any major miracles there because of their unbelief.

This occurred because the people allowed their minds to dictate to them, and it ultimately hardened their hearts. The evidence was present, but it didn't matter. They reasoned among themselves, "This is the carpenter; we knew His mother and siblings. There is no way He can be the Messiah."

Their religious teachings created a stronghold in their minds that eventually hardened their hearts. That's why it is of paramount importance that we are honest with ourselves and acknowledge the strongholds that exist within us. We need to ask God to reveal those areas and He will. We also need to be mindful that the enemy wants to keep us contained, so he will go out of his way to deceive us.

Scripture Readings:
Romans 12:1–2
Mark 6:1–6

January 3

MANIFESTING THE KINGDOM OF GOD IN YOUR LIFE

Jesus replied, "The Kingdom of God can't be detected by visible signs. You won't be able to say, 'Here it is! Or it's there!' For the Kingdom of God is already among you." (Luke 17:20–21)

Some believers fail to realize that the Kingdom of God resides within them once they accept Jesus into their heart. When Jesus was questioned by the Pharisees about the location of the Kingdom of God, they were expecting Him to give them some physical location; instead, Jesus told them that the Kingdom of God was in their midst, and they didn't even realize it. Jesus was of course referring to Himself (Luke 17:21). Jesus said this because He understood that the Kingdom of God was within Him, in the spiritual realm. The same is true for anyone who receives God into his or her heart.

The Kingdom of God has come to reside in you, and in the heart of every believer. I have heard some people say that they felt like their prayers didn't go any higher than the ceiling. Well, it does not have to go any higher than the ceiling. God can hear the prayers of every individual who prays to Him. He can do this because our dimensions of time and space do not limit God. We live in a world where only four dimensions of time and space exist—time, width, length, and height. Our concept of time is linear, while God's concept of time is geometrical, which means that it is possible for God to see the beginning and the end simultaneously.[1]

The point I am getting at is that if we are to walk in the fullness of all God has available to us, then we are going to have to expand our consciousness and start thinking outside of the box. God's thoughts and ways are higher than ours, so we must learn to think and look at things from His perspective (Isaiah 55:8–9). We have to renew our minds to

---

[1] I don't have time to go into details about this subject, but I highly recommend that you read Dr. Hugh Ross's book entitled *Beyond the Cosmos*. He does an excellent job of explaining the different dimensions of time and space. He shows how it is scientifically possible for Jesus to walk through walls.

receive the insights of the Kingdom of God. We need to have the mind of Christ (1 Corinthians 2:16). We as believers have to become God-inside-minded instead of looking up to the skies or church to find God. He cannot be found in a song, but He can be found in every heart of those who believe in Him.

Scripture Readings:
Luke 17:20–21
John 17:21
Ephesians 1:4–5
1 Peter 2:9

January 4

THE HEART IS MORE THAN A BLOOD PUMP

Guard your heart above all else, for it determines the course of your life. (Proverbs 4:23)

Being involved in the field of psychology, I am always looking for more effective ways to explain human behavior. I asked the Holy Spirit to give me some insight in this area not too long ago. As I began to look into the Scriptures, I found that there was a clear distinction between the soul, spirit, and heart. I understood the difference between the soul and the human spirit, but what about the heart? Many teach that the human spirit and heart are the same, but they are in fact much different.

The heart is more than a simple pump that is responsible for sending blood throughout the body. Recent scientific research suggests that the heart has a consciousness separate from the brain or conscious mind. Neurocardiology shows that the heart is a sensory organ that has a sophisticated center for receiving and processing information. The nervous system within the heart enables us to process information and make functional decisions independent of the brain (conscious mind). Furthermore, numerous experiments have shown that the signals from the heart have an influence on the higher functioning part of our conscious mind involved in perception, cognition, and emotional processing.

With this information, we can clearly see that it is of paramount importance that we be mindful to what we expose ourselves to, for the heart determines the course of our lives (Matthew 12:34). And it is out of the heart that evil thoughts, murder, adultery, all sexual immorality, theft, lying, and slander come (Matthew 15:19). We have to remember that we are responsible for what we allow ourselves to be exposed to. Are there people in our life who have a negative impact on us? Are there things we are watching and hearing that are unhealthy? If so, this might be the reason why we are not experiencing the victorious life God has for us.

Scripture Readings:
Matthew 12:34; 15:19
Proverbs 4:20–24

January 5

The Heart

Guard your heart above all else, for it determines the course of your life. (Proverbs 4:23)

If we are to live up to our God-given potential, it is important that we tend to the matters of the heart. For the heart has a direct influence on our emotions, will, intellect, and health. There are many believers who have their spirits renewed, but they still have wounded and deceived hearts (Jeremiah 17:9). If we are to live up to our true potential in Christ Jesus, we have to have our hearts in line with our spirits. Anything less than this will cause us to be dysfunctional in our walk with the Lord. This is why the writer of Proverbs emphasizes the importance of watching and guarding our heart (Proverbs 3:1–5; 4:21–23).

I would like to give you three ways to guard your heart:

1. *You need to repair and restore your heart.* Are there some issues in your past that need to be addressed? Are there some people you need to forgive, or do you need to forgive yourself for past transgressions? If so, do it!
2. *You need to nurture your heart.* Think of your heart like soil, for it will produce whatever you plant in it. It is vital that you spend time in the Word of God on a daily basis. Pray in the Spirit and in your natural language as well. Finally, make thanksgiving and praise regular practice in your daily routine. Start your day with thanksgiving and you will end it with praise.
3. *You need to shield your heart.* It is important you know the difference between what is secular and that which is sacred. Be mindful of what you allow yourself to be exposed to because your heart will be occupied with what you treasure the most (Matthew 6:21). Many people would rather go watch a sporting event, go hiking or fishing, or watch their favorite television show, than

attend a worship service. There is nothing wrong in doing any of the aforementioned activities; we just need to make sure we have our priorities in order.

Scripture Readings:
Proverbs 3:1–5; 4:21–23
Jeremiah 17:9

January 6

CARELESS WORDS KILL

The tongue has the power of life and death, and those who love it will eat its fruit. (Proverbs 18:21 NIV)

Our words are seeds that produce whatever we speak. If we are to have a productive life, we must monitor our words carefully (Proverbs 13:3). If not, our words can bring negative consequences into our life (Proverbs 21:23). Many believers do not realize the power they possess, and they will self-sabotage themselves because of their lack of knowledge concerning the power of their words.

From the Scriptures we know that we are created in the image and likeness of God (Genesis 1:26). What does that mean? It means that God has given us the ability to function in the same manner as He functions. This furthermore means that we can speak things we desire into existence like He does (Genesis 1:3–24). I know this statement might be a little much for some of you, but it does not mean it's not true. Throughout the Bible we can see how God admonished His people to monitor what they said. One of the reasons Jesus lived a life that pleased God, and was able to perform miracles, was because He only said what God told Him to say (John 14:10).

If you are not experiencing success in your walk with God, it might not be just an issue of not spending enough time in prayer or in the Word of God. It might be because of the careless words you speak while outside of the church. Many believers will talk with their church lingo when in the presence of other believers, but speak the exact opposite when outside the church environment.

In essence, when this occurs, they have negated every positive confession they have made. That's the reason these believers don't receive what they desire from God. The sad thing is that quite often these believers will lose their faith and be quick to disregard the faith teaching, all the while not realizing that the problem was right under their nose. Jesus said that we would give an account for every idle and careless word we speak (Matthew 12:36). So it would behoove us to monitor our words.

Scripture Readings:
Genesis 1
Matthew 12:36
John 14:10

January 7

MAKING GOD'S PLAN YOUR PLAN

God's purpose in all this was to use the church to display His wisdom in its rich variety to all the unseen rulers and authorities in the heavenly places. (Ephesians 3:10)

This morning while I was doing my daily Bible reading, a verse in the book of Ephesians caught my attention. It's amazing how the Holy Spirit will breathe new life into a Scripture you have read hundreds of times before. The first Scripture was Ephesians 3:10. There the apostle Paul writes concerning the purpose God had for the church. We as a body of believers are to demonstrate the glory of God to the unseen rulers and authorities in heavenly places. As I meditated on that thought, I realized how myopic my perspective had been. God has made it possible for us to do great exploits on His behalf, not only showing the unbelieving world what a great and mighty God we serve, but the unseen world as well. We are to be examples representing the Creator and Father of all.

So many believers are satisfied with living a mediocre life. This mindset limits God's power within them. We need to raise our level of expectation and begin to see ourselves the way God sees us, and not the way the world sees us. We can't let religion or the world brainwash us into thinking that our reward is waiting for us in heaven, and we just have to struggle through this life until we receive it. Show me in the Scriptures where Jesus struggled. According to the words of Jesus Himself, we as believers can do all the things He did, and even more (John 14:12). Nothing is impossible with God, and all things are possible for those who believe in Him (Mark 9:23; Luke 1:37).

Scripture Readings:
Ephesians 1–3
John 14:12
Mark 9:23
Luke 1:37

January 8

GOOD THOUGHTS LEAD TO GOOD HEALTH

A happy heart is good medicine and a cheerful mind works healing, but a broken spirit dries up the bones. (Proverbs 17:22 AMP)

The latest studies in the field of neuropsychology indicate that 85–97 percent of physical and mental illness is due to our cognitive thoughts. In essence, we can control our health simply by changing and/or monitoring our thought life. According to Dr. Caroline Leaf, scientist and leading expert in neuropsychology, the brain can complete 400 billion actions per second. Dr. Leaf also indicates that our thoughts have the ability to build other thoughts.

Using the example of a tree, she says that when we think positive thoughts, our brain produces green leafy-like branches; however, when we think negative thoughts, we produce barren branches. If we produce green, healthy branches, we are producing a healthy disposition; conversely, if we produce negative, barren branches, we open ourselves up to disease. Negative thoughts create inflammation in the body, which can lead to illness if not corrected. It would behoove us to examine our thought life and monitor what we spend our time meditating on. How much time do you spend thinking about negative things?

Many people are prone to depression, and they either run to the pharmacy for medication or self-medicate with drugs or alcohol, when all that is really needed is to change their thought life. In Philippians 4:4–8, the apostle Paul instructs us to do the following:

- To be full of joy.
- Instead of worrying, to pray about everything (which means not praying the problem, but the answer).
- To fix our thoughts on things that are honorable, right, pure, lovely, excellent, and praiseworthy.

God has given each of us the ability to choose what we think about! We can focus on those things that are positive and produce life, or we can focus on those things that are negative and produce death. The choice is up to us—so choose life. I want to leave you with this final thought: *Your thoughts produce emotions, and your emotions create feelings. Everything begins with your thoughts.*

Scripture Readings:
Proverbs 17:22
Psalm 19:14
Philippians 4:4–8

January 9

The Choice Is Yours

Today I have given you the choice between life and death, between blessings and curses. Now I call heaven and earth to witness the choice you make. Oh, that you would choose life so that you and your descendants might live. (Deuteronomy 30:19)

Deuteronomy 30:19 is part of the final admonishment Moses gave to the children of Israel before entering the Promise Land. In this discourse, Moses reminded them of their past and how God had dealt with them. He also reminded them of all the great miracles God had performed on their behalf, and how their unbelief and rebellion had robbed them of the many blessings God wanted to give them.

The same is true for us today. We have the choice to choose if we are going to walk in the blessings of God or in the curse of this world's system. If we choose to meditate on the things of God and the precepts of His Word, then we open ourselves up to the blessings of God. However, if we choose to follow the ways of this world, we will open ourselves up to the curses of this world.

There are some people who saturate themselves with television and various types of entertainment, giving little or no time to God. It seems the only time they run to God is when they are in some kind of crisis. These same people spend many hours worrying and distressed because of the personal and financial problems they experience. This is a curse. This is not to say that we won't experience hardships from time to time. But there are some people who continually go from one crisis to another.

What do you do when hardships come your way? Do you freak out, wring your hands, and say, "What am I going to do?" Or do you turn to the Word and quote a Scripture, and go on about your business, knowing that God will make a way for you?

How you fare in times of tribulation all comes down to your thought life. Make the positive choice by spending time in the Word every day. I am not saying you should not watch television at all, but make the Word of God first priority in your day. Seek God when you first wake up, and see what your day will be like. If you start your day with praise, it will end with thanksgiving!

Scripture Readings:
Deuteronomy 30:15–19
Psalm 19:14

January 10

WHO IS IN CONTROL: YOU OR YOUR SOUL?

For you are still controlled by your sinful nature. You are jealous of one another and quarrel with each other. Doesn't that prove you are controlled by your sinful nature? Aren't you living like people of the world? (1 Corinthians 3:3)

There are far too many born-again believers who are living mediocre and defeated lives. Yet they are born again! They are going to heaven, but their lives on this planet do not reflect the greatness that resides within them. I know this is not a popular thing to say, but it is true. As child of the living God, we are to reflect His life to a dying world.

Many believers do not realize the influence their soul has on them. The enemy goes out of his way to keep them ignorant of this so he can keep them defeated and ineffective. He cannot take your salvation away from you, but he can keep you in bondage and contained.

There are five avenues Satan will use to gain access to our soul, for he knows that the soul is an integral component to us living a victorious life on this planet. Our human spirit (which is connected to the Holy Spirit) needs the cooperation of the soul to manifest its desire for our life. If the soul is not in agreement with the human spirit, it can ignore the spirit's instructions.

Carefully read Genesis 3:1–6 and you will see the strategy of the enemy. What did Satan do first? He got Eve to question God's instructions. In effect, Satan got her to use her intellect against her. Once that happened, he was then able to get her emotions involved by looking at the fruit with desire, which is in the emotional realm. Once he had gained access to the intellect and emotional realm, the spirit was then overruled, and the will became subject to the soul. And the end result was disobedience.

The enemy's methods never change, and we see this same pattern being played out today. However, if we are aware of this strategy, we can stop it from occurring in our lives.

There are five areas the enemy will use to gain access to our soul, and which we have to guard:

1. Intellect: reasoning and justification
2. Emotions: feelings and desires
3. Memories
4. Imagination
5. The will

Scripture Readings:
Genesis 3:1–6
1 Corinthians 3:1–4

January 11

LIVING IN THE FAVOR OF THE LORD

For You, Lord, will bless the [uncompromisingly] righteous [him who is upright and in right standing with You]; as with a shield. You will surround him with goodwill (pleasure and favor). (Psalm 5:12 AMP)

For the Lord God is a Sun and Shield; the Lord bestows [present] grace and favor and [future] glory (honor, splendor, and heavenly bliss)! No good thing will He withhold from those who walk uprightly. (Psalm 84:11 AMP)

Because of the finished work of Jesus Christ, we can walk in the favor of the Lord continually. Yes, it is true. We as believers have this right, but only those who expect it will walk in it. It is not something that we have to earn. Jesus paid the price for us to walk in it and experience the same favor He walked in while He was on the earth (Act 17:28).

In order to experience the favor of the Lord, we have to be aware that it is for us! I suggest you read and meditate on the above Scriptures daily in order to get them ingrained in your heart. Then they will start to produce a harvest in your life. Start every morning by thanking God for His favor.

These are some of the benefits of the favor of God that we should thank Him for:

- Supernatural increase and promotion.
- Restoration of everything that the enemy has stolen from us.
- Honor in the midst of adversity.
- Increase in assets and real estate.
- Great victories against great odds.
- Recognition from others.
- Preferential treatment.

- Granting of requests or petitions.
- Change and reversal of policies in our favor.
- Avoidance of battles, because God is fighting them on our behalf.

Scripture Readings:
Psalm 5:12; 84:11
Acts 17:28

January 12

SALVATION COMES IN MANY FORMS

What comes to your mind when you hear the word *salvation*? Like most of us, the first thought is being saved from sin and perhaps God's wrath. But salvation is much more than merely being saved from sin and wrath. The enemy of our soul would like to keep us ignorant of what God's idea of salvation is, because he can rob us of the blessings God wants to release in our life.

Many believers are not experiencing God's best because they don't understand the true meaning of the word *salvation*. If you look it up in your Bible concordance, you will see that *salvation* has several meanings. I will show you five of them today:

- Rescue from physical harm (Daniel 6:27; Matthew 8:25; Luke 23:39; Acts 27:20, 31; Hebrews 5:7).
- Healing (Mark 10:52; 6:56; Acts 14:9; James 5:15).
- Rescue from personal enemies (Psalm 18:3–6; 59:2).
- Deliverance from political oppression (Exodus 14:13, 30).
- Deliverance from sin (Psalm 39:8; 51:14; Ephesians 2:5, 8; 2 Timothy 1:9; Titus 3:5).

These are just a few Scriptures where *salvation* is used. As we can see, it is multifaceted. If we become aware of the many ways we can use God's salvation, we will truly become more than conquerors in this life and manifest the glory of God.

Scripture Readings:
Psalm 91

January 13

It's Not the Size of Your Faith

I don't know about you, but when I used to pray for something and it didn't immediately come to pass, I thought that either I didn't have enough faith or I didn't pray long or hard enough. Recently, however, God has revealed to me that sometimes this isn't the case. In Luke 7:5–10 the disciples made a request for Jesus to increase their faith. Jesus responded that if they had faith the size of a mustard seed, then they could tell a mulberry bush to be cast into the sea and it would obey them.

After reading this, I went and looked at the size of a mustard seed. It was small! As I meditated on what Jesus said to His disciples, I realized that it's not the size of our faith that guarantees that our request will be answered; rather, having faith in the finished work of our Savior is what guarantees it. Our faith should be based on the finished work of Jesus, not on our human efforts. The Word of God states that if we abide in Jesus, then we can ask for anything and it will be given to us (John 15:7). Jesus said that He would do anything we asked in His name (John 14:13). The Scriptures also state that if we ask for anything in accordance with the will of God, then He will hear us and grant our request (1 John 5:15).

When we, through our own human efforts, try to move the hand of God without resting in the finished work of Jesus, it is easy to fall into the works of the flesh. And this will inevitably lead to pride, and ultimately frustration, which the enemy wants. I am not saying that we should not pray, fast, or spend time in the Scriptures. What I am saying is that we should not do those things with the idea that if we do them then we will somehow impress God and persuade Him to give us what we want. Rather, we should put our faith in what Jesus has already accomplished on our behalf.

Scripture Readings:
Luke 7:5–10
John 14:12–13; 15:7
1 John 5:15

January 14

THE POWER OF GRACE

But whatever I am now, it is all because God poured out His special favor on me—and not without results. For I have worked harder than any of the other apostles; yet it was not I but God who was working through me by His grace. (1 Corinthians 15:10)

The apostle Paul has been credited with writing a majority of the New Testament. How could a man that once persecuted the church have such a transformation? The apostle tells us the secret to achieving God's design and best for his life, and thus for our lives—it is by relying on God's grace. It sounds so simple, but for most people it is hard. We have a tendency to be self-reliant. We, as human beings, find a certain amount of comfort in achieving things in our own effort. This is especially true in the present culture. We like to boast about what we have done and accomplished. Unfortunately, this attitude has found its way into the body of Christ as well.

All believers agree that it was by God's grace that they were saved; but from the born-again experience, most believers rely less on God's grace and more on self-effort. Clergy preach from the pulpits that we need to perform in a certain manner, and if we don't they make us feel condemned. I am not saying that we should do nothing and live any way we want. Christ shed His blood to redeem us from all of that. However, if we think that we can live the kind of life that God wants by self-effort, then we are wrong!

If we want to live a life that pleases our heavenly Father, then we need to ask for His grace to work in and through us. One of the definitions for *grace* is to empower. God's grace is sufficient enough to overcome any shortcomings we may have. His grace can create a desire in us to want to live a more holy life. Not only will grace provide the desire, but it will also give us the power to fulfill that desire.

It is important that we learn the secret Paul learned and trust in God's grace instead of trying to do it on our own. When we wake up in the morning, we should ask God to give us the grace we need for the day, and then thank Him for giving it to us. God will download all the grace we need, just like He did for the children of Israel out in the wilderness (manna). So take as much as you need today.

Scripture Readings:
1 Corinthians 15:10
2 Corinthians 12:1–10
Galatians 2:19–20

January 15

JESUS CAN AND WILL

A man with leprosy came and knelt in front of Jesus, begging to be healed. "If You are willing, You can heal me and make me clean," he said. Moved with compassion, Jesus reached out and touched him. "I am willing," He said. "Be healed!" Instantly the leprosy disappeared, and the man was healed. (Mark 1:40–42)

In this story the man with leprosy believed that Jesus had the power to heal him, but he was not sure that He was willing to. It was not until he knew for sure that Jesus was willing to heal that he received his healing. This man is like many of us today. We know and believe that Jesus can answer our prayers, but sometimes we wonder if He'll do it for us. Usually, this is due to condemnation we are feeling, or as a result of some thoughts the enemy put in our heads. That is why it is important to spend time in the Word of God daily so you will know the will of God for your life.

Not knowing the will of God can prevent Him from answering our prayers because of doubt. We must have the God kind of faith if we want our prayers to be answered. The God kind of faith is fully confident that whatever is requested will and has already been answered (Mark 11:23–24). To ensure that we know the will of God, we must seek Scriptures on the subject we are requesting God to answer. If we want to know God's will, then we need to know the Word of God and how it applies to our lives (John 1:1).

Find the promises of God relating to your need, and quote them back to God and yourself until you have no doubt that you will receive what you have requested! Then thank God for the answer and eagerly expect your request to be answered. When doubt tries to enter your mind, speak to it by quoting the promises of God, driving it away—don't tolerate it for one moment. Continue this process until you receive your manifestation. It might happen tomorrow, next week, or even next year; but know it will happen because God always keeps His Word (Hebrews 6:18).

Scripture Readings:
Mark 1:29–42; 11:23–24
Hebrews 6:18

January 16

Do You Know Your Benefits?

Bless (affectionately, gratefully praise) the Lord, O my soul, and forget not [one of] all His benefits. (Psalm 103:2 AMP)

One of the things a person wants to know from their perspective employer is what the benefit package being offered is. Besides the salary, the benefits are quite important to a lot of people. Well, did you know that God offers all those who believe in Him a benefit package as well? You might be saying, "I know that He has given me eternal life." But there is much more He offers in His benefit package.

Many believers are not aware of the benefits God has made available to them, and, as a result, the enemy of their faith is taking advantage of them. It is our responsibility to know what benefits we have as believers and take advantage of them. The Bible is packed with all the benefits Jesus has provided for each one of us, but I want to focus on Psalm 103 for a moment. I have memorized the entire chapter and recite it almost every day because I want to remember what God has provided for me.

These are some of the benefits the psalmist recorded for us:

- He forgives all of our sins.
- He provides healing for our physical bodies.
- He has redeemed us from death (spiritual).
- He has crowned us with kindness and mercy.
- He satisfies our needs and desires with good things.
- He renews our youth.
- And He vindicates us when we are treated unjustly.

I encourage you to acquaint yourself with all the benefits God has offered you and take advantage of them. Don't allow the enemy to use your ignorance against you any longer. God has provided for all that you will ever need.

Scripture Readings:
Psalm 103

January 17

POWER OR PATIENCE?

But let endurance and steadfastness and patience have full play and do a thorough work, so that you may be [people] perfectly and fully developed [with no defects], lacking nothing. (James 1:4 AMP)

As I was studying in the book of James not too long ago, I realized the importance of patience. Patience is one of the characteristics of God's nature (Galatians 5:22; 1 Corinthians 13:4), and it's God's desire that we manifest patience in our lives, reflecting His very nature. In fact, God has no pleasure when we let go of our faith due to a lack of patience. It is the essential ingredient to ensure that we receive what we ask for in prayer.

Many people start off with great faith when they believe God for something. However, when the manifestation doesn't come when they expect it, they let go of their faith and become discouraged. It is patience that gives a person the endurance to receive the manifestation they requested from God. Yes, faith and patience go together like peanut butter and jelly. Patience is a spiritual force that is often overlooked by many believers, but it is necessary to perfect us in our spiritual development. It is not passive; it is a spiritual force.

Let's look at an example of someone who exercised patience and faith in the Scriptures: Abraham. He is recognized as being the father of our faith—so let's see what he did. Romans 4:17–21 describes how Abraham believed God's promise in spite of the circumstances that were against him. He was well past the years of bearing children, and so was his wife. But Abraham didn't look at the circumstances or his natural body; instead, he trusted the promise of God. He knew that it was impossible for God to lie (Numbers 23:19), so he allowed the hope of the fulfillment of the promise to strengthen him in faith. As a result, Abraham became the father of many nations, just as God had promised.

We should bring this to remembrance when we are tempted to let go of our faith when we don't receive what we desire from God in the time that we expected. Remember, God takes no pleasure in those who let go of their faith (Hebrews 10:38). Instead, remind yourself that nothing is impossible with God, and all things are possible for those who trust in Him.

Scripture Readings:
James 1:1–4
Romans 4:17–21

January 18

Are the Cares of this World Dragging You Down?

Then Jesus said, "Come to Me, all of you who are weary and carry heavy burdens, and I will give you rest." (Matthew 11:28)

Sometimes we allow ourselves to get burdened down with the cares of this life. If we allow them, these cares can become overwhelming for us, which cause us to take our eyes off God and His promises. Instead of walking in faith, we begin to walk in doubt, which then causes fear, and fear brings distress to our lives. Finally, distress causes us to worry, which leads to disease and illness within our physical bodies. This is a deadly progression that occurs all too often in the lives of God's people.

Jesus has promised to carry our burdens for us if we would but come to Him. We are not alone. Jesus wants us to let go of those burdens and let Him carry them for us. He will show us exactly what we need to do and when we need to do it. We only have to ask and trust Him to fulfill His promise to us.

The problem with most people is that they are too self-reliant, or they do not want to trouble God with their small, insignificant problems. But nothing could be further from the truth! If God cares for the birds of the air and provides for all of their needs, will He not care for you too (Matthew 6:26)? We are not burdening God with our small requests; He delights to hear them.

We must learn to have the same mindset as Jesus had so that we can experience peace in this troubled world. We are to know who we are in Christ Jesus, and trust in the love God has for us. Finally, we must know that we are not alone in this battle. Jesus is right beside us, offering to carry our burdens for us. Turning to Him is all we have to do.

Scripture Readings:
Psalm 68:19
Matthew 11:28–30

January 19

FAITH AND WORRY CANNOT EXIST TOGETHER

And if God cares so wonderfully for wildflowers that are here today and thrown in the fire tomorrow, He will certainly care for you. Why do you have so little faith? (Matthew 6:30)

When we allow worry or the cares of this life to enter our thought process, we are short-circuiting our ability to use faith. Faith is a spiritual force, just as fear is a spiritual force too. Faith is the positive use of the force, while fear is the negative use of it. These two forces cannot coexist together. We will either operate in one or the other, but we cannot operate in both at the same time.

When we worry, we are setting the stage for fear to enter into our hearts. We all have the tendency to worry from time to time, but instead of entertaining worry, we should speak to it and tell it to go. Speaking the promises of God to it will cause it to go. It is also important to find Scriptures in the Bible in whatever area we are being tempted to worry about, and quote them to ourselves until the worry has gone away. Quoting Scripture is what Jesus did when the enemy tempted Him in the wilderness (Matthew 4:1–11).

One of the strategies the enemy uses to short-circuit our faith is the cares of this life (Luke 8:14). So instead of thinking about the cares of this world, we are to think about the provision that has been made available to us in Christ. Don't focus on the problem; look to the answer. Trust in the Holy Spirit to lead you over the obstacles that confront you. And remember that you are to walk by faith and not by sight (2 Corinthians 5:7).

Scripture Readings:
Matthew 6:25–34
Mark 4:1–20

January 20

RECEIVE THE PEACE OF JESUS AND OVERCOME

I have told you all this so that you may have peace in Me. Here on earth you will have many trials and sorrows. But take heart, because I have overcome the world. (John 16:33)

The Bible never promises that we will not experience troubles in this life. If someone tells us that life will be easy once we accept Jesus, they are doing nothing but lying to us. In fact, Jesus says that if He was persecuted, then we should expect the same treatment too. But since we are in Jesus, we have the victory because He has overcome the world (1 Corinthians 15:57).

Do you know who resides in you as a believer? God in the person of the Holy Spirit lives within you. That means you have access to the Creator of heaven and earth—He dwells within you. With this awareness, what can possibly overcome us? The distractions of this world must not be allowed to cloud our perceptions and deceive us. Rather, we need to allow our senses to control our consciousness. We should look to the Word of God and listen to the voice of the Holy Spirit instead of what is going on around us. If we do this, we will find peace in any situation we may find ourselves in. We will have peace because we know that God has our back, and greater is He who is in me than he who is in this world (1 John 4:4).

Scripture Readings:
John 6:31–33
1 Corinthians 15:57
1 John 4:4–5; 5:4

January 21

BELIEVE TO SEE

Faith is the confidence that what we hope for will actually happen; it gives assurance about the things we cannot see. (Hebrews 11:1)

Have you ever said, "I will believe it when I see it"? Well, I think all of us have said this at one time or another. It is completely logical, and there is nothing wrong with saying this from a natural perspective. But in the supernatural realm, the statement is completely false. God is a faith God, and He operates in the realm of faith. In fact, the Bible states that it is impossible to please Him without faith (Hebrews 11:6).

As children of God, we must learn to operate in the same manner as our heavenly Father. We should study the Scriptures to see how Jesus operated while He was on this earth. Jesus should be our example in all that we do, especially when it comes to faith. If you want to know how Adam operated on this earth before the fall, then look at Jesus. The Bible states that Jesus is the last Adam (Romans 5:14). Yes, when we read about the exploits Jesus did, we see how Adam operated on the earth before the fall. The good thing is that Jesus said that we could do all the works He did and even greater things if we believe in Him (John 14:12). This means that we need to change our paradigm to Christ's way of thinking (1 Corinthians 1:16).

Faith is a substance, like water in a glass. We can't detect it with our natural eyes, but it doesn't mean it's not there. Faith is the energy that produces things in this material world. God even used faith to create the cosmos (Genesis 1:1–31). It may be helpful to look at faith as an energy or force that is activated by our words. We have the power and force to create whatever we desire as we speak out in faith. Please understand there are limits to this.

We imagine and create the image of what we want. Then we believe that we will receive it, and speak it into existence (Mark 11:23–24). It might not happen immediately, but we have to know that it will happen. That's where patience comes into play. I know that this might be too much for some of you, but just allow this to marinate in your mind for a few moments. I invite you to read all the Scriptures below to see what I'm talking about.

Scripture Readings:
John 14:10–13
Genesis 1:1–30
Hebrews 11:1–6
Mark 11:23–24

January 22

THE POWER OF LOVE

God is love, and all who live in love live in God, and God lives in them. And as we live in God, our love grows more perfect. (1 John 4:16–17)

We all have heard that God is love. But have you ever thought about what that means? There wouldn't be love if God did not exist. He is the source and developer of love. There is nothing more powerful than love because love is the essence of who God is. It is the most powerful force in the universe. The reason why some of us have not received the answers to our prayers is because we are not operating in love. Without love operating in our lives, God is not present. And without God's presence, we don't have His power, which means we are operating in our own power.

I always wondered why in Mark 11:22–25 Jesus concludes by stating that if we have anything against anyone, forgive them so that God can forgive us. Jesus was talking about getting answers to our prayers just before this. What does forgiveness have to do with getting the answer to our prayers? Jesus is telling us that when we have unforgiveness in our hearts, we are not operating in love. Without love we cut off the power of God from our lives, because God is love.

We have to make sure that if we have unforgiveness or ill will toward anyone that we get rid of it or we will cut off the power of God from operating in our lives. The enemy will send people to irritate us and provoke us so we will not have access to God's power. Don't let that happen to you. Look beyond the person and see who is motivating them. As you do this you will find it much easier to forgive them and let it go.

Scripture Readings:
Mark 11:22–25
Galatians 5:22–23
1 John 4:16–17

January 23

Soul Power

My soul, wait only upon God and silently submit to Him; for my hope and expectation are from Him. (Psalm 62:5 AMP)

Humans are tripartite beings. That means that every man and woman is a spirit who has a soul and lives in a physical body. Our spirit and soul will live forever, but our physical body is subject to eventual death. When we are spiritually reborn, it is our spirit that is reconnected to the Spirit of God, but our soul is not. It is up to us to renew our mind so that it is in agreement with our born-again spirit (Romans 12:1–2).

Many believers make the mistake of overlooking the redevelopment of their soul when they are born again. The soul is not evil in and of itself, but it needs to be subjected to our re-created spirit. To put it bluntly: we will never achieve what God has planned for us unless we get our soul in one accord with our spirit. Our spirit is perfect in the sight of God because it is joined with the Holy Spirit.

Another important aspect of the soul is that it is the only area where the enemy can attack us. There are five gates the enemy will attempt to use to control us: our emotions, intellect, memory, imagination, and the will. If we are aware of how he tries to attack us, we can defeat the enemy every time he attempts to tempt us into doing something outside the will of God.

One effective way to protect our soul is through the art of meditation, or more specifically, biblical meditation. When we meditate, it causes us to grow in the mental realm, and keeps the intellect, imagination, and will in line with the Word of God (Psalm 104:34).

There are three steps to effective biblical meditation:

1. **Ponder**: this means that we think about a Scripture. We don't just read it and forget about it, but we think about the Scripture throughout the day.
2. **Muse**: this means we chew on it. Cows have two stomachs and they have the ability to regurgitate the food in one stomach and chew on it for digestion at a later time in the other stomach. We can do the same thing with the Word of God. We can think about it, digest it, then think about it some more, receiving nourishment throughout the days.
3. **Mutter**: this means that we speak the Word of God to ourselves instead of speaking what we feel.

Scripture Readings:
Romans 12:1–2
Psalm 62:1–5

January 24

The Essence of Hope

Faith is the confidence that what we hope for will actually happen; it gives us assurance about things we cannot see. (Hebrews 11:1)

According to Hebrews 11:1, faith is the substance of things hoped for. According to this verse, there is a connection between faith and hope. We know that faith is the substance of hope, which means that without faith hope has no substance. There are people who live their lives just hoping for things to come to pass, but they never receive anything because they did not apply faith to what they hoped for.

Think of hope like a pitcher and faith as the water. If you were thirsty and wanted to get a drink of water, but you went to an empty pitcher and drank from it, would your thirst be satisfied? No, of course it wouldn't. That is the way some people live their lives by just hoping for something, but never being satisfied with what they hoped for. However, if you had a pitcher and filled it with water, you would be able to quench your thirst anytime you poured a glass of water. Which person are you? Are you the person trying to drink from an empty pitcher, or are you the person who has the pitcher filled with water?

Hope is a desire with an expectation of fulfillment. It will give you a positive attitude, but it is not a guarantee that you will receive what you have hoped for. You need to acquire faith to give your desires the ability to come to pass. According to the Scripture, faith comes by hearing God's Word (Romans 10:17). So what are you listening to today?

Scripture Readings:
Romans 10:17
Hebrews 11:1

January 25

THE HOPE AND FAITH CONNECTION

And so, Lord, where do I put my hope? My only hope is in You. (Psalm 39:7)

We know that hope is the expectation for something, but without faith there is no guarantee that what we hoped for will actually come to pass. In other words, if a person merely hopes for something, they will always be expecting but never receiving it. Do you know some people like that? We need to have the substance of faith to make our desires come to pass.

A simple definition for faith is a belief or trust in something or someone. What do you have faith in? This is an important question to answer because there are many things people put their trust in. If you put your trust in people, there is the possibility that they will let you down. You can put your trust in the government, religion, media, the financial system, or the educational system, but they cannot guarantee that they will satisfy your desire either.

There is only One Being you can put your trust in, and know that He will satisfy your every desire, and that is God. God is the ultimate truth, and there is nothing false in Him (Numbers 23:19). The Word of God will give you water that will never run dry (John 4:13). So what is the source of your faith today? Is it what you hear on the news or read in the papers, or is it in one of the myriads of talking heads out there today? Or is it in your religious affiliation? All of the aforementioned fall far short of what God's Word can provide for you. Turn to Him and trust Him today.

Scripture Readings:
Psalm 39:1–11
John 4:1–26
Numbers 23:19

January 26

WHAT IS TRUTH?

Jesus told him, "I am the way, the truth, and the life. No one can come to the Father except through Me." (John 14:6)

Jesus made a very bold statement to Thomas. It seems that Jesus was preparing His disciples for His departure from this earth. He had told Thomas that He would be returning to His Father in heaven, and that He would be preparing places for them to join Him. When Thomas questioned what Jesus was saying, Jesus told him that He was the way and the truth and the life.

The dictionary offers several definitions for truth: real state of things, something that is accepted as being true, an agreement with a fact, or reality.[2] Based on those definitions, we can define truth in many ways. This is especially true in a society where truth is defined as being relative, which means a person can define truth as they see it, not as objective reality. As a result of this, their truth becomes their reality.

As a therapist I counsel people who have adapted a truth based on what they perceive as being real. They have allowed this perception to color their world experience. Do you see how powerful your definition of truth is? If a person's truth is based on something negative, they will allow their reality to be negative. If a person bases their truth on something false, then their reality will be based on deception.

Isn't that what happened in the Garden of Eden? What was eating from the tree of knowledge of good and evil all about? It was about allowing man to interpret right from wrong on his own terms instead of trusting God's interpretation. In essence, man became his own god and functioned independently from God. He defined truth as he perceived it. Can you see the problem with this? What if someone's definition of truth is different from yours—who is right? Usually, it is the one with the most power.

---

[2] *Merriam-Webster's Concise Dictionary*, 2006, "truth."

The Bible says that Jesus is the Word of God. The Word of God reflects God's will, so the Word of God and God are the same. If we make Jesus our source of truth, we are making God our truth, and He becomes our reality. And God is the highest form of reality there is.

Scripture Readings:
Genesis 3:1–7
John 14:1–7

January 27

THE SOURCE OF YOUR FAITH MATTERS

And Jesus said, "All right, receive your sight! Your faith has healed you." (Luke 18:42)

We know by now that faith is the substance of things we hope for. Now I would like to give you an example of how this works. The source of our faith is important. If we put our faith in something that is fallible, we are likely to experience disappointment. However, if our faith is based in the truth of God and His Word, then we have the assurance that our expectation will come to pass.

There is a story in the Bible about a blind beggar who heard Jesus was in town. When he heard the commotion of the crowd, he knew Jesus was near. So he started shouting in order to get Jesus's attention. When people tried to get him to stop, he shouted even louder. Finally, Jesus stopped and asked the beggar what he wanted. The beggar told Jesus that he wanted to see. He then told the beggar that his faith had healed him. Immediately, the beggar regained his sight (Luke 18:35–42).

This is just one example of how important the source of our faith is. Because the beggar's truth was based in the Truth, his faith healed him. Faith is the gateway to the supernatural blessings of God, because it is impossible to please God without it (Hebrews 11:6). Our faith will determine what we receive from God. Not our tears, our circumstances, or our religion; just our faith.

Scripture Readings:
Luke 18:35–42
Hebrews 11:1–6

January 28

How Long Are You Willing to Wait?

When Jesus saw him and knew he had been ill for a long time, He asked him, "Would you like to get well?" (John 5:6)

There are people who go through the motions to receive from God, but they get nothing. There are number of reasons for this. One could be that they are trusting in the action to bring them results instead of trusting in God. In essence, the source of their activity becomes their god, and there is assurance in that. On the surface it looks like they are making an effort and it makes them feel good because of it. But in the end they come up short. They are in a constant state of trying.

In the Bible there is a story of a man who was paralyzed and was waiting at the pool. It was believed that when the pool of water began to bubble, if an individual was to get in, they would receive healing. Because this man was paralyzed, he was never able to get to the pool when the waters were stirred. So there he was, waiting for someone to have pity on him, to pick him up and put him in the pool. This man had been paralyzed for thirty-eight years! That is a long time.

Then Jesus saw him and asked, "Did you want to be made well?" Instead of answering the question with a yes or no, he gave an excuse for his condition. Once Jesus determined that the man wanted to get well, He told him to pick up his mat and walk. The man did just that—he picked up his mat and walked. You see, this man had the faith to walk all along, but he just needed to put his faith in the right source. What are you putting your faith in today?

Scripture Readings:
John 5:1–10

January 29

Faith Is the Highway to the Supernatural

Jesus realized at once that healing power had gone out from Him, so He turned around in the crowd and asked, "Who touched My robe?" (Mark 5:30)

In the Bible there is a story of a woman who suffered from bleeding for twelve years. In fact, she had gone to a number of different doctors in order to experience some relief. Instead of her health improving, however, it only got worse. Finally, she decided to see the Great Physician. She said to herself, "If I could just touch Him, I know that I would get healed." Her faith was based on touching Jesus, not on what the doctors had told her. All those past experiences she put behind her. Her focus was on only touching Jesus's robe.

Well, she accomplished her goal. She was able to touch Jesus's robe, and she was immediately healed when she did so. The interesting thing about this is that Jesus was not aware of what the woman had done until He felt power leaving Him. This illustrates how powerful our faith is. Our faith gives us access to God's power. The only thing that moves God is our faith in Him. We can have faith in others things or people, but their power is limited and it is fallible. It is only faith in God that is limitless.

About three years ago I had a spinal infection that left me paralyzed. I had no sensory feeling or movement in my legs or arms. The doctors said that I would probably be in a wheelchair for the rest of my life. But God had spoken to me and said that I would recover from this illness. I chose to believe God rather than listen to the doctors' opinions. Well, guess what? I am not in a wheelchair! In fact, if you were to see me, you would never know I had been in a wheelchair. This is real! The Word works—put Him to work on your behalf today.

Scripture Readings:
Mark 5:24–34

January 30

WHAT ARE YOU TRUSTING IN?

Trust in the Lord with all your heart; do not depend on your own understanding. (Proverbs 3:5)

Are you allowing only your intellect to guide you? God has given you the ability to think for a reason, and you should use your intellect according to the way it is meant to be used. But there are those people who have made their intellect their god. They give no room to the things of God, and they trust only in what is logical and can be proven through empirical evidence (1 Corinthians 1:20–22). This type of wisdom is based on the natural, and thus it is limited.

God's original plan for man was to have his spirit as the dominant source of guidance, and the intellect was to function in a subordinate position. It was God's design that the spirit and intellect would work together. Since the fall of man, however, humanity has trusted in their intellect to determine actions, and pays little or no attention to their spirit. Those who have turned to the spirit have subjected themselves to demonic influences if they are not born-again believers.

There is a story most of you have heard before, which is usually heard around Christmastime. It's the story of Mary. But I want to tell you the story from a different perspective today. An angel from the Lord had contacted Mary and told her that she was to be with child. Mary asked the angel how it could be since she was a virgin—she was not mindful of the prophecy that said the Messiah would come from a virgin. So Mary had a choice: she could have trusted in the logic of the world and rejected the message of the angel, or she could trust in the things of God. Had she rejected the message, God would have chosen another virgin to fulfill His will. But Mary received what the angel told her, and the Savior of the world was born.

Sometimes God will speak to us in our spirit, and give us instructions that make no sense at all to our natural mind. That's when we have to put our trust in God. We need to seek Scriptures to verify that what we are hearing is not in conflict with the Word of God. This is very important! Our intellect will not go down quietly, so we should expect some doubts to come up from time to time.

Scripture Readings:
Luke 1:26–38

January 31

UNBELIEF CAN FRUSTRATE GOD

And because of their unbelief, He couldn't do any mighty miracles among them except to place His hands on few sick people and heal them. And He was amazed at their unbelief. (Mark 6:5–6)

Did you know that you determine how much God can work in your life? It is not up to Him but you! Some people seem to get answers from God, and there are some who receive little or nothing from Him. Does God have favorites? I used to think so for a long time. I thought the reason why some people received great things from God was because He liked them more than He liked me. But the Bible states that God is not a respecter of persons (Matthew 22:16).

Then I came to understand that these people received more from God because they trusted Him more than me. God is a faith God, and He responds to anyone who approaches Him with faith. God does not care what church we attend, what color we are, what country we live in, or how long or short our hair is. There is only one thing that pleases God and gets His attention—that's faith (Hebrews 11:6).

In one story in the Bible, Jesus could do very little in a town because of their lack of faith. Prior to coming to that town, however, Jesus had performed many miracles, but there He could do very little. Jesus had not changed or ran out of power. The only thing that was lacking was their faith. So maybe if we are not receiving as much as we would like from God, we should check to see if we have some unbelief in our heart. If so, get in the Word and get rid of it!

Scripture Readings:
Mark 5:4–6
Romans 10:17
Hebrews 11:6

February 1

WHICH PATH WILL YOU CHOOSE?

The Lord says, "I will guide you along the pathway for your life. I will advise you and watch over you." (Psalm 32:8)

Did you know that it is possible for you to access the wisdom of God? Yes, I know that the Bible provides God's wisdom in written form, but what about those personal problems there are no Scriptures for—like should I take this promotion or marry this person? God has given us an intellect to make such decisions, but we can be influenced by outside forces and make decisions not in our best interest. Wouldn't it be nice to have someone there with us who knows the beginning from the end? Wouldn't it be nice to have someone we could trust, to give us the right answer, all of the time?

Jesus promised that He would send someone to assist us in our journey—the Holy Spirit. The Holy Spirit is the Spirit of Truth who is ready to guide us into all truth (John 16:13–15). Jesus told His disciples that He would not leave them as orphans, but has assigned the Holy Spirit to guide them. Are you a follower of Jesus? Then you too have access to Him. This is a great benefit to us because the Holy Spirit can be with all of us who believe. When Jesus was still on the earth, He had a physical body so He was limited to where He could go, but the Holy Spirit can be in all believers on this planet.

All we have to do is invite the Holy Spirit to be a confidant and companion. He will not force us to accept Him; He is very gentle. He will not take over our will. If He provides us with a solution to our problem, then we have the option of either accepting or rejecting it. If we decide not to heed His advice, He won't get mad or tell us later, "I told you so." He has the same nature as Jesus.

When we first start to get acquainted with the ways of the Holy Spirit, we might miss it. But as we become more familiar with Him, we will be able to recognize His voice. Sometimes the enemy will try to mimic the

Holy Spirit, or our own spirit will do the same. But soon we will be able to distinguish His voice from other voices around us. He speaks to us from our inner being. So if we are hearing an audible voice from outside our head, it's not Him.

Take advantage of this Ally today, an Ally who is ready and willing to assist you any time you ask. Just believe and you will receive the person of the Holy Spirit.

Scripture Readings:
Psalm 33:8–9
John 14:15–18, 26; 16:12–15

February 2

FAITH AND YOUR FEELINGS

For we live by believing and not by seeing. (2 Corinthians 5:7)

When we endeavor to use the God kind of faith, it is not an unusual experience to doubt in our mind. When we make that decision to step out in the realm of faith, we are stepping into the spiritual realm, which goes beyond our five physical senses. Our mind is not acquainted with this realm, and it cannot relate in the natural sense. So it's completely natural to question oneself from time to time. Just because we doubt in our head doesn't mean we doubt in our heart (our inner man).

Jesus said in Mark 11:23 that if we believe and not doubt in our heart, we would receive what we asked for. Notice Jesus didn't say that if we doubt in our *head*. There is a difference between doubt in our heart and doubt in our head. We must always remember that we are a spirit first, who has a soul and lives in a body. Each one of us has all three components. God's design for us is to be led by our spirit, with our mind and body in agreement. But because of the fall of man, this design has been disrupted. Man, in his natural state, is led by his mind or his body. Thus, he is being ruled by his senses instead of his spirit. That's why the things of God make no sense to him (1 Corinthians 1:20).

Until we renew our mind to the things of God, we will question ourselves when believing God. That is why it's important that we spend time in the Word of God every day. Meditating on the Word until it gets inculcated into our thought processes is vital to our spiritual life. If we do this, it will eventually become easier to ignore the doubt and act in faith. Remember, it is not what we think but what we do that matters. If we believe God for something and our mind starts giving us trouble, we only need to quote the promises of God until it stops and comes into submission to our spirit.

The enemy will try to tell us that because we have doubt, we will not receive what we believe for. He will try to use Mark 11:23 against us instead of allowing it to encourage and strengthen our faith. He will try to use Scripture against those who are ignorant and lack spiritual understanding. Remember that faith is a spiritual force used to create material things (Hebrews 11:1). So don't look for a feeling as a sign of assurance that you will receive what you prayed for; rather, look to have a knowing you will receive because it is based on the Word of God.

Scripture Readings:
Mark 11:23
1 Corinthians 5:7
Hebrews 4:12

February 3

JESUS AND THE WORD ARE ONE

In the beginning the Word already existed. The Word was with God, and the Word was God. (John 1:1–2)

Jesus is depicted as being the Word of God. Because of this, we can say Jesus and the Word are the same. Since I know that it is impossible for God to lie (Numbers 23:19), it makes it easier for me to trust in the promises of God. God's will and Jesus's will are the same—they do not change with the times and seasons. It is an eternal truth that we can always believe in. Jesus had this mindset—if it was written in the Scriptures, Jesus believed and acted on it without question (John 14:10). As a result, He could say that if we had seen Him then we had seen the Father (John 14:9).

Because of the great trust that Jesus had in the Word, God was able to manifest His glory through Him. This is one of the secrets to performing great signs and wonders. Those who trust more get more. I used to wonder why some people were receiving more from God than I was. Then I came to the realization that they had more trust in God than I had. The more we trust the Lord, the more we obey and step out when He asks us to do something. The more we obey, the more confidence we have to receive even more. That is why it is important to get rid of sin in our life. If we have known sin in our life, our heart will condemn us. And thus we will not be confident in our request.

In Hebrews 4:12 it says that the Word of God is alive and active, and it explores the thoughts, desires, soul and spirit, and it discerns the attitude of our hearts. What's interesting about this Scripture is the way that it concludes: "Nothing in all creation is hidden from God. Everything is naked and exposed before His eyes, and He is the One to whom we are accountable" (Hebrews 4:13). Who is the writer talking about here? You guessed it—Jesus.

Scripture Readings:
John 1:1–4; 5:19–20; 14:9–11
Hebrews 4:12–13

February 4

THE WISDOM OF THIS AGE AND THE WISDOM OF GOD

But the wisdom from above is first pure. It is also peace loving, gentle at all times, and willing to yield to others. It is full of mercy and good deeds. It shows no favoritism and is always sincere. (James 3:17)

Did you know there are two kinds of wisdom in this world? There is a God kind of wisdom, and there is a natural type of wisdom. God's type of wisdom is based on the thoughts of God, and the natural type of wisdom is based on the thoughts of this world. Most of us have been trained in the wisdom of this world by our parents, educational system, society, and the media. Worldly wisdom is not bad in and of itself—it has its place. However, if we rely only on the wisdom of this world, then we open ourselves up to conflict.

Think for a moment about the things we see on television today. How many programs contain jealously, selfish ambition, lying, cheating, and boasting? In fact, the more the program has the aforementioned attributes, it seems like it is more popular. The world uses the media to inculcate us to their way of thinking, making selfishness and pride a badge of honor. It is hard to determine what is truly right and wrong in our society, because it has adapted a relativistic philosophy. Right and wrong are determined by the end result. If we get what we want, then that makes it right. Can you see the chaos and disorder that comes from this?

There are believers who function in the world's wisdom. Yes, they are going to heaven, but there is little or no distinction between them and an unbeliever. These types of believers are carnal or fleshly. They think like the world and talk like the world, but the glory of God is absent from their lives. They are ruled and controlled by their senses, and they are self-deceived. Their walk with God is unfruitful, and they are of little use to the Kingdom.

If you find yourself in this category, don't deny it but change it. Renew your mind to the things of God by continually praying and meditating on God's Word. Ask God to open your eyes to His wisdom. You have the choice to choose which wisdom you are going to operate in. The power of life or death is with you.

Scripture Readings:
James 3:13–18
1 Corinthians 2:13–16

February 5

As You Think, So Are You

For as [a man] thinks in his heart, so is he. (Proverbs 23:7 AMP)

We can only go as far as we can see and as high as we can think. Most people are limited in life not by outward circumstances, but by their thoughts. If a person thinks they can't, then they are right. However, if a person thinks they can, then they are right as well. Don't underestimate the power of your thought life. Every time you have a thought it changes your brain and your body, either positively or negatively. Positive thoughts produce good attitudes and health while negative thoughts create a toxic environment within us, which open the door for disease to enter our minds and body.

Remember this one thing: Our perceptions create our reality. Perception is created in our mind. We see through eyes, but we perceive with our mind. What do I mean by this? We can take two people and they can witness the same event, but each person will see the event completely differently. For example, take the Four Gospels. Each Gospel is telling us the same story, but each rendition is slightly different from the others. This is due to the fact that each writer saw the events from a different perspective.

The same is also true with us. It's not what happens to us that is important, but how we react to what happens to us. Our reaction will be based on beliefs, and our beliefs create our perceptions. Some people's thoughts are predominately negative, and, as a result, they will filter out the positive and focus on the negative. Likewise, if a person's thoughts are mostly positive, they will filter out the negative and focus on the positive. Two people can be exposed to the same environment, and one will fall apart and the other will survive.

What we expose ourselves to is what is going to influence our thoughts. If we are exposed to negative people, watch negative programs, read negative material, listen to negative words, then we can't be surprised if we develop a negative outlook on life. On the other hand, if we expose ourselves to positive things, read positive material, and hang around positive people, then our outlook on life will be more positive.

Make it a practice to monitor what you expose yourself to today. If you find yourself being more exposed to the negative than the positive, make a conscious effort to expose yourself to a more positive environment and people. You have the power of choice, so choose life rather death.

Scripture Readings:
Proverbs 4:20–23; 23:7

February 6

YOU ARE WONDERFULLY MADE

He has made everything beautiful in its time. He also has planted eternity in men's hearts and minds [a divinely implanted sense of a purpose working through the ages which nothing under the sun but God alone can satisfy], yet so that men cannot find out what God has done from the beginning to the end. (Ecclesiastes 3:11 AMP)

Did you know that God created you with a purpose and a destiny? You were created for a specific reason; it is up to you to find out what that reason is. Many people allow the world's system to dictate to them what they are to be and do. The world's system promotes conformity to its standards and practices. It wants everyone to think the same thing so that society can be controlled. Our educational system is used to achieve this, and the media will use propaganda to influence the way we think. Power defines influence. If I can get you to see the world from my perspective, then I have gained power over you.

Each person is created with uniqueness. There is not another person who is like you. We all have different ways we process thoughts—no two people process the same way. It is good for parents to realize this and not try to compare one child to another. Though children are raised in the same household, they will often process things very differently, thus, they perceive and act differently. Instead of comparing our children to each other, recognize the glory in their uniqueness. Doing this removes pressure and resentment between siblings and parents.

Conformity can produce pressure and resentment. Let me give you an example. I like playing guitar. So I took lessons for years, and I got frustrated because I was trying to play like my guitar heroes. I would play the same licks as they played, but it didn't sound the same. I finally realized with the help of the Holy Spirit that I could never sound exactly like them because I am not them. Their perception is different than mine, and that is what makes them unique. Once I realized this, I decided that no one can play the guitar like I can. Now I enjoy playing because I have developed my own unique style of playing.

I encourage you to enjoy who you are instead of looking at other people and comparing yourself to them. There is no one else like you! So be the best you God created you to be.

Scripture Readings:
Ecclesiastes 3:11

February 7

Don't Let Others Define Your Reality

And Jesus said, [You say to Me], If you can do anything? [Why,] all things can be (are possible) to him who believes! (Mark 9:23 AMP)

According to the words of Jesus, the only thing that can limit us is our beliefs. If we can conceive it and believe it, we will eventually receive it. This is a spiritual principle that actually works! God has given us the ability to create things through the use of our imagination. If we imagine something long enough through meditation, it becomes a reality in our unconscious mind. Once the thought gains entrance into our unconscious mind, it becomes a reality to us.

Have you ever had a dream or nightmare you thought was real when you woke up? Maybe you woke up sweating or breathing hard or sighing because you realized that you were having a dream. This is an example of the power of the unconscious mind. It is designed to create for you. That is one reason why we should monitor what we expose ourselves to. If we are exposing ourselves to negative things and people, they will get into our unconscious mind, our inner man. This occurs because we meditate on what we are exposing ourselves to. When we meditate on something for long enough, it changes our thought process and builds thoughts within our mind. Thoughts become our perceptions and perceptions become our reality.

When we let others tell us what we can or cannot do, we, in essence, are allowing them to define our reality for us. Some people never achieve their potential because they believed what someone else told them, "You don't have the talent or ability to do that," or "You are not good enough." Sometimes we tell ourselves these things. Instead of listening to these voices, we should read stories of people who overcame the odds against them.

I like listening to stories of people who were told that they would never make it only to overcome their odds and make it. Did you know that a record producer for a major record label had the opportunity to sign the Beatles, but he passed because he didn't think they were any good? Or did you know that Michael Jordan was cut from his high school basketball team because the coach didn't think he was talented enough? There are a myriad of stories of people who didn't allow the opinions of others to influence them; instead, they used it as fuel to excel. God has designed you to succeed!

Scripture Readings:
Joshua 1:8
Psalm 1:3
3 John 1:2

February 8

MEDITATION: THE KEY TO FAILURE OR SUCCESS

Study this Book of Instructions continually. Meditate on it day and night so you will be sure to obey everything written it. Only then will you prosper and succeed in all you do. (Joshua 1:8)

What do you spend your time meditating on? Do you spend your time meditating on your favorite reality show, soaps, drama series, or video games? In our society, there are many things that are vying for our attention. I encourage you to use discretion on what you choose to focus on, because what you choose to focus on will determine your destiny. Some things will give you a temporary sense of accomplishment and pleasure, but that's it. Some people spend their life following their favorite sports team. They can tell you all about the players and their histories, but little or nothing about the Word of God.

I have nothing against entertainment of any kind. In fact, I think that it is good to have outside interests and hobbies. However, we need to have balance and be able discern what is profitable and what is not. There are some things that are not worth our time or attention. They are like spiritual junk food. We can't make a constant diet of it or we will eventually suffer the consequences. Just like in the physical, if we just eat junk food, we won't feel or look as good as a person who eats healthy. The same goes in the mental and spiritual realm as well.

Many people live vicariously through the television or movies. They let the illusions on the screen become their reality and become addicted to its deceptions. They allow it to control their thoughts and imaginations; thus, they limit their ability to think outside of the box. With their creativity stifled, these people become nothing more than robots, just waiting to be told what to do. I know this may sound harsh, but it is true.

Successful people know the importance of meditation on those things that will produce success for them. The Word of God promises that if we spend time with it, we are guaranteed to be successful in whatever we do. Doesn't it make sense to spend some time in the Word of God? Make it a priority every day to set aside some time to spend with the Word. Allow the Holy Spirit to assist you in your daily routine. He will give you ideas and provide you with solutions to problems you may encounter. But this only happens if you spend quality time with Him through the Word and meditation.

Scripture Readings:
Joshua 1:1–9
Psalm 1:1–3
Matthew 12:35

February 9

DESIGNED TO LIVE FROM WITHIN

But you belong to God, my dear children. You have already won a victory over those people, because the Spirit who lives in you is greater than the spirit who lives in the world. (1 John 4:4)

In psychology I learned that people are either driven from within or from without. People who are driven from within rely on their viscera to motivate them and are driven by an internal locus of control. These types of people have the ability to motivate themselves and don't rely on their environment to motivate them. They have the ability to perform no matter the circumstances. On the other hand, people who rely on their environment or people to motivate them are externally driven, having an external locus of control. These types of people are easily controlled or manipulated by the environment surrounding them. If the people are negative and the conditions are not favorable, they also become negative.

Most people have an external locus of control. If things are good, they are happy and positive. But if things are bad, they become negative and pessimistic. But most individuals who excel in life have an internal locus of control. This is due to the fact that they don't look to others for validation. They are able to persevere in spite of the obstacles facing them. They have a focus that propels them to their goal.

Jesus is a perfect example of someone who had an internal locus of control. He knew His purpose and trusted in the power residing within Him. His faith was never shaken, no matter what He faced—sickness, storms, negative opinions, and even death. We as believers have the same ability within us now. We too walk with an internal locus of control because of who resides within us. We don't have to be a believer to do this, however. There are many successful people in the world who are not believers and who have achieved success. But they are relying on their own ability and effort to make it.

Each one of us has the power of the living God living within us, and His resources are unlimited. We just have to have the God kind of faith to release that power. However, having said that, it is necessary to meditate on the Word daily to remind ourselves who resides within us. Choose to be a world overcomer rather than being overcome by the world.

Scripture Readings:
Isaiah 43:7
John 14:12
Philippians 4:13
1 John 4:4

February 10

YOU HAVE NOT BEEN GIVEN A SPIRIT OF FEAR

And be sure of this: I am with you always, even to the end of the age. (Matthew 28:20)

Did you know that fear is a spiritual force, just like faith? The spirit of fear is the result of disobedience (Genesis 3:10), the consequences of man's willful disobedience to the commands of God in the Garden of Eden. As a result, humanity has been plagued with the spirit of fear ever since. It's interesting that the phrase "Fear not" is repeated 365 times in the Bible, which matches the days in a year. So we should daily guard ourselves from fear.

Fear comes in different shapes and sizes. Cares, worries, anxieties, stress, and concern are all cousins of fear. They are the gateways used by fear to enter our consciousness. I recall a time when I was speaking to a friend from church. She was expressing concern about her daughter's behavior and how she did not want her to follow in the steps of her older sister. I cautioned her about the power of her words and the spirit of fear. She looked at me and said, "I don't have fear; I'm just concerned." She did not realize that concern is closely related to fear. Unfortunately, what she feared eventually came to pass.

Neuroscientists have recently discovered what the Bible has warned for thousands of years: fear kills. When we are in a state of fear, chemical changes occur within our body, making us more prone to illness. The immune system is impacted when we are stressed on a constant basis. Fear causes negative thoughts, and those negative thoughts stimulate glands in our brain that secrete hormones that raise the cortisol levels in our bodies, which makes us prone to infections and depression. According to Dr. Caroline Leaf, a neuroscientist, fear triggers over 1,400 physical and chemical responses in our brain and body.

God has provided a solution to fear for us in His Word. The apostle Paul instructed Timothy not to fear because God had not given him a spirit of fear. Instead, Paul reminds Timothy that God has given him a spirit of power, love, and a sound mind (2 Timothy 1:7). You see, we have the option to choose what spirit we will operate in. This is the theme that we see through the Bible, and the theme we'll see throughout this book. It is up to us to choose how we will respond today. Will we trust in God and His Word, or trust in our feelings that are influenced by the world?

Scripture Readings:
1 John 4:4
Philippians 4:6–7
Psalm 34:7, 19

February 11

You Are God's Masterpiece

For we are God's masterpiece. He has created us anew in Christ Jesus, so we can do the good things He planned for us long ago. (Ephesians 2:10)

Did you know that God created you to magnify His glory in your life? Yes, God desires to reflect His glory in and through you. Each one of us are His chosen possession (1 Peter 2:9). All we have to do is start to see ourselves the way God sees us. In order to do this, we must renew our mind to a new way of thinking about ourselves and the world around us (Romans 12:1–2). We must allow the Spirit to speak to our conscious minds and reveal the greatness that exists within each of us (Ephesians 4:23).

Jesus prayed a prayer before He left His disciples to ascend back to His Father, which can be found in John 17:20–26. He requested that not only these disciples but all who would believe in Him would realize that they are one with God through Jesus. He prayed that they would come to the realization that God loves them as He loved Jesus. He also prayed that they would see the glory of Jesus.

What a powerful prayer! Do you think that the Father heard Jesus's prayer? Do you think that God honored His prayer? If you answered yes to these questions, then it's time you start acting like His prayer is answered. Tell yourself every morning:

- God has chosen me.
- I am royalty in Christ Jesus.
- I am holy.
- I am God's chosen possession.

Start speaking God's Word over your life today, and allow the Word to change you from the inside out. You might not feel like it at first, but as you make these confessions over yourself on a daily basis, the transformation will begin to take place in your heart. Then you will find yourself being an overcomer rather than being overcome by the circumstances of life.

Scripture Readings:
John 17:20–26
Ephesians 3:10, 20
1 Peter 2:9
Psalm 43:7

February 12

MAKE GOD'S DESIRE YOUR REALITY

But you are not like that, for you are a chosen people. You are royal priests, a holy nation, God's very own possession. As a result, you can show others the goodness of God, for He called you out of darkness into His wonderful light. (1 Peter 2:9)

Potential not realized is nothing but a waste. I used to tell my son that he had potential to achieve whatever he wanted to do in life. But there are many people who have potential living in desperate conditions. Prisons are full of people who have potential to live productive lives, but instead they are wasting them behind bars, chained to the thoughts of failure and despair, because of choices they made.

The enemy knows the potential each of us have within us, so his strategy is to keep us bound to our old ways of thinking. He will use our friends, family members, television, and the guilt of our past to keep us from becoming what God wants us to be in Him. In order to overcome the enemy, we must trust in the finished work of Jesus Christ on the cross. When the enemy reminds us of our past, or points out our weaknesses and shortcomings, we need to quote the Word of God to him. We must confess that we are a new creation in Christ Jesus, the old has passed away and the new has come (2 Corinthians 5:17).

Eventually, we will be conformed into the image of Jesus. We are a unique representation of Jesus Christ on the earth today, because there is only one of us—each one of us is unique. We are called to allow God to use our talents, abilities, and even our shortcomings to magnify His glory through us today.

Scripture Readings:
1 Peter 2:9
Galatians 2:20
Ephesians 3:20

February 13

God Can Take Your Lemons and Make Lemonade

But don't be upset, and don't be angry with yourselves for selling me to this place. It was God who sent me here ahead of you to preserve your lives. (Genesis 45:5)

One of the most inspiring characters in the Old Testament is Joseph. In spite of being despised by his brothers, betrayed, and falsely accused, Joseph didn't let go of the vision God had for his life—the dream he had when he was only seventeen. Even when he was sold into slavery and later put into prison, Joseph continued to prosper and maintain a positive attitude. I believe this was due to the strong faith he had in God. Our faith will be tested to show us what we really believe.

Many times people will make a mental assent to something and think they actually believe what they have given metal assent to. Mental assent is nothing more than agreeing with something in principle only. It is not faith. There are many people who make vows and are sincere at the time they make them; however, when the time of testing comes, they fall away. For example, if I told you there was $1 million dollars somewhere in a room, what would do? If you really believed me you would look for it—probably relentlessly—until you found it. But if you didn't find anything and quit after an hour, did you really believe me? No. You only gave mental assent to what I said.

True belief never gives up or gives in to the pressures around it. Instead, it perseveres until the end. If we truly believe in ourselves and who God has made us to be, then we won't give up in spite of the poor choices and hardships we encounter along the way. There is not one person who has achieved success in life that has not had to go through some kind of hardship in order to fulfill their dream. If we have been mistreated, lied about, or betrayed, know that we are not the first person this has happened to. We just have to believe that God can take any situation that we are in and use it for His glory.

I invite you to read about Joyce Meyers. Here is a woman who was sexually abused by her father when she was young, but now she is a world-renowned speaker, teacher, and author. Her ministry is reaching millions of people. She is just one of many examples of how God can take your lemons and make lemonade.

Scripture Readings:
Jeremiah 1:5; 29:11

February 14

CHANGING YOUR PARADIGM TO THE MIND OF CHRIST

For, "Who can know the Lord's thoughts? Who knows enough to teach Him?" But we understand these things, for we have the mind of Christ. (1 Corinthians 2:16)

When a person accepts the Lord into his or her heart, their spirit is immediately reborn and united with God. They become a new being in that very moment (2 Corinthians 5:17). However, their mind is still in its natural state and needs to be renewed. If the mind is not renewed, then there will be a conflict between the mind and the spirit. That is why the Bible repeatedly instructs us to renew our minds (Romans 12:1–2; Ephesians 4:23). Believers who do not renew their minds will find themselves responding in the natural when conflicts, temptations, and challenges come their way. The apostle Paul refers to these types of believers as being "carnal" (1 Corinthians 3:3).

There are many believers who rely on their rationalization to try to understand the things of God. However, because it does not make sense to their natural minds, they disregard many of the principles contained in the Bible. These believers try natural methods to achieve their goals and visions in life. They may achieve a certain measure of success, but it will come at a cost and fall short of what they could have done with the assistance of the Holy Spirit.

When a person allows their mind to be renewed by the Spirit of God, they are creating new thoughts in their brain. These new thoughts use proteins to build new neuropathways, which build branches of new thoughts and create a new mindset within them. So one can literally change their thought process by renewing their minds according to God's Word.

It is possible to replace old destructive thoughts with new ones. It's truly amazing to know that we can change the way we view life and ourselves by spending time renewing our mind. So remember this: If we change our thoughts, we will change our life!

Scripture Readings:
1 Corinthians 2:16
Romans 12:1–2
Ephesians 4:23

February 15

SOWING: THE KEY TO PROSPERITY

I will make you into a great nation. I will bless you and make you famous, and you will be a blessing to others. (Genesis 12:2)

God's desire is to bless us in order for us to be a blessing to others. God's blessing is never for us to hoard things for ourselves. Rather, He blesses us to give to others in need. God has a plan to ensure that we have more than enough—sowing and reaping. When we follow this God-ordained plan, He is obligated to see that all our needs are met—and not just our needs, but the needs of others through us. This plan has been evident in the earth since humanity was created. Throughout the Bible, we find that God expected humanity to give a certain amount back to Him.

When we follow the principle of giving, we will experience the same return as our predecessors did. I know to the natural mind it does not make sense. But just think about it for a moment. If a farmer planted a seed and grew a papaya tree, and that tree yielded forty-seven papayas, and he either ate or sold all the papayas, then the following year he would have only forty-seven papayas. However, if that farmer had taken forty-two of the papayas to either sell or eat, and planted five papayas for the following year, then he would have 282 papayas at harvest time next year. If that same farmer took twenty-eight papaya seeds and planted them, he could expect a harvest of 1,363 papayas the following year. You get the picture. This is the principle of sowing and reaping in action. It is a universal principle that works because God designed and instituted it.

So if you want to increase financially, use the principle of sowing and reaping in your life. Go to God and ask where He wants you to give and give with a cheerful heart (2 Corinthians 9:5). God does not accept our gift if we do not have the right attitude when giving it. Why do you think God did not accept Cain's offering (Genesis 4:4–5)? He didn't have the right attitude. God also will not accept gifts that are given in response to pressure. If someone is pressuring us to give, then know that we will not receive a return on that gift (2 Corinthians 9:7). It is important to make sure that when we give, we give with expectancy to receive a harvest on what we have sown. As we thank God in advance for the harvest, it will come back to us ten-, thirty-, or a hundred-fold.

Scripture Readings:
2 Corinthians 9:1–15
Ecclesiastes 11:4–6

February 16

KNOWING YOUR ROOTS

What are mere mortals that You should think about them, human beings that You should care for them? Yet You made them only a little lower than God and crowned them with glory and honor. You gave them charge of everything You made, putting all things under their authority. (Psalm 8:4–6)

Family reunions are great because they give us the opportunity to learn about our family roots. I know for me that it has empowered me to know how my family began and see how we have prospered. My father was one of ten children raised by a father who made his living doing yard work and other odd jobs. My grandmother was a stay-at-home mom. They were both involved in the church, my grandfather being a deacon. Because of his faith, he saw his children rise to a higher level, educationally, financially, and socially. Three of his children received their doctoral degrees, and several of his children were successful in their field of business. I know that my grandfather looks down from heaven with a smile on his face.

We too should look back to see where we come from. No matter the color of our skin or the language we speak, we all have the same parents. According to the Scriptures, God created Adam and Eve in His image and likeness, and it was from them that all humanity came into being (Genesis 1:26–28). Adam, in his original state, operated on the earth like Jesus did (Romans 5:14). But now Jesus has made it possible for us to walk in that original design for mankind. We can once again walk in authority and dominion, subjecting the earth. We can speak the Word of God to the circumstances we face and overcome them with the power of the Word of God. We can operate just like Jesus did (John 14:12), but it requires that we have the same mindset Jesus had. This is the only way God will trust us with that kind of power.

Scripture Readings:
Genesis 1:26–28
Psalm 8:4–6
Isaiah 43:7
Romans 5:12–17

February 17

VISION GIVES YOU PURPOSE

Where there is no vision [no redemptive revelation of God], the people perish; but he who keeps the law [of God, which includes that of man]—blessed (happy, fortunate, and enviable) is he. (Proverbs 29:18)

What determines if we will succeed in life is our ability to develop a vision or goal to live by. There are many people with great potential and ability who are living unsatisfied lives because they have no sense of purpose. As a correctional counselor and probation officer, I have seen the results of people who didn't have a real purpose for their lives. Some of these people were intelligent, likeable, and charismatic, but for some reason they stumbled through life. The sad thing is that they will have to give an account for squandering the gifts God gave to them.

But on the other hand, there are people who despite little talent or ability achieve greatness. What was the difference? There could be many explanations to this question, but I want to focus on just one. They had a vision and a purpose for their lives. Having a vision or goal is paramount to achieving anything worthwhile. Having vision:

- gives us a sense of reason
- gives us focus
- energizes us
- and gives us something to look forward to.

People who have a vision have a glow about them, a positive attitude. Other people are drawn to them because of the energy that exudes from them.

God has given us the ability to image. The imagination was designed to create mental pictures we can use to create things in our life. We are created in the image and likeness of God, so we can operate as God operates, but on a lesser scale (Genesis 1:26). Jesus demonstrated this for us. The only things that limit us are not having a vision or not having the belief that the vision will come to pass. We have to have both of these in operation in order for it to work.

When I was paralyzed, I would wake up every morning and visualize myself walking and riding my bike. I would see myself back in the gym working out. That vision became so real that I was thoroughly confident it would happen. It didn't matter what the doctors or therapists told me. And guess what? I am doing all the things the doctors thought I would never be able to do. I know this works, and it will work for you too!

Scripture Readings:
Proverbs 18:29
Philippians 2:12–14

February 18

WINNING FROM WITHIN

For in Him we live and move and exist. As some of your own poets have said, "We are His offspring." (Acts 17:28)

If we are a believer, we have an Ally residing within us. But it is up to us to use this Ally. We have the option of trying to live this life on our own, or we can choose to get some assistance from the Spirit of God dwelling within us. The apostle Paul knew this truth better than anyone. Paul was responsible for writing most of the New Testament and was tasked with bringing the gospel of grace to the Gentiles. He was beaten, berated, shipwrecked, and placed in prison (among many other things) as a result.

Paul gave the explanation of why he was able to achieve so much in His life. In 1 Corinthians 15:10 Paul said that it was because of the special favor God had given him. He also stated in Galatians 2:20 that it was Christ within him that did the works. Paul learned not to trust or rely on his ability to do the work God called him to, but on the ability of Jesus within him.

We also should learn to involve Jesus in our lives too. If we have some assignment that needs to be done, we should take a moment and ask Jesus to help us to complete it. If we have a decision that needs to be made, we can ask Jesus to show us the best answer. We don't have to live this life on our own. We have Jesus and the Holy Spirit there to help us—all we have to do is ask. There is a reason why the term "in Christ" appears in the New Testament seventy-six times. It is trying to convey a message to the readers. That message is to let Jesus flow through us. This is how He is magnified in our lives!

Scripture Readings:
Acts 17:28
1 Corinthians 15:10
Galatians 2:20

February 19

HE MAY BE YOUR SAVIOR, BUT IS HE YOUR LORD?

If you confess with your mouth that Jesus is Lord and believe in your heart that God raised Him from the dead, you will be saved. (Romans 10:9)

Many believers know Jesus as their Savior, but do they know Him as their Lord? There is a difference between the two. If we know Jesus as only our Savior, we open ourselves up to compromise. There are many believers who fall into this category. They go to church and are good people, but there is little to no power in their lives. They are mediocre and are lukewarm at best. God is not happy with believers like this; in fact, He says He will spit them out of His mouth (Revelation 3:15–16). We have been given the divine nature in order to live above this world's system and escape its corruption (2 Peter 1:4).

Most churches have become nothing more than community-based organizations that are more concerned with attendance and being politically correct rather than teaching the full gospel of grace. Once I was invited by a Christian radio station to attend a large gathering of various churches in the city. Many pastors would be there, so I thought it would be good to meet some people and get my face known. I just published a book and thought it was an excellent opportunity to promote myself.

The event was held at a beautiful country club. The place was immaculate and the food and entertainment were great. The only thing that was missing was the power of God. While I was standing there, the Holy Spirit spoke to me and said, "They have a form of godliness but they have no power" (2 Timothy 3:5). I agreed with Him and have never forgotten that day. I realized at that moment I would have to compromise my message and water down what God had revealed to me. I was not willing to do that. So I just enjoyed the meal and show, then left.

To follow Jesus comes at a cost. It means that some people will not accept what we have to say, and others will even ridicule us. Our own family may think we are crazy for believing the Bible. But Jesus said that if He were persecuted, then His followers would also experience the same (John 16:33). The bottom line is this: I would rather have Jesus happy with me than anyone else. Is Jesus Lord of your life, or is He just your Savior?

Scripture Readings:
Isaiah 1:19
John 16:33
2 Peter 1:1–4

February 20

THE REAL ENEMY

For we are not fighting against flesh-and-blood enemies, but against evil rulers and authorities of the unseen world, against mighty powers in this dark world, and against evil spirits in the heavenly places. (Ephesians 6:12)

Have you ever known someone who just irritated you? It almost seemed like they were going out of their way to annoy or harass you. Maybe you tried everything to get along with them, but nothing seemed to work. Slowly, you began to feel resentment toward them. Then you began to devise ways to get even with them. Finding pleasure in those thoughts, you start to meditate about how to get back at them. Before you know it, you begin to act on those thoughts. Does this sound familiar?

Well, if that scenario sounds familiar, then you are not alone. I think all of us have been there at one time or another. But God showed me something in the Scriptures I have never forgotten. God showed me that my fight isn't against the person who has offended me, but the spirit that is prompting and influencing them. Quite often the person who is the offender doesn't even realize that a demonic force is using them. You see, the enemy wants to destroy and discredit us any way he possibly can. He will use women, men, and even our children to bring us to our knees.

His strategy is to rob us of our peace so that we are no longer walking in love. If we are not walking in love, the power of God cannot work in our life. If we are angry with someone, and we don't resolve it in a timely manner, it will turn into resentment. And if resentment goes unabated, it will eventually turn to rage, and that's when anger will start to manifest itself in our heart. Once we know the enemy's strategy, then we see what is really going on. Then we are in a position of superiority and are able to take control of the situation rather than the situation controlling us.

Find a place to pray for the help of the Holy Spirit, then pray for the individual who has offended you. I know it might be hard at first, but it is necessary to keep your heart tender. Then let it go, and let God deal with it. When I have done this in my own life, I have found that the first person to change was me. The things the others were doing to me didn't have the same effect once I began to pray for them. I was able to ignore it. Eventually they stopped, and they even apologized for their behavior. So take it from me: this works every time. Don't play the enemy's game any longer.

Scripture Readings:
Ephesians 2:1–2; 4:26, 31
James 1:19–21

February 21

THE REAL ROOT OF EVIL

For wherever there is jealousy and selfish ambition, there you will find disorder and evil of every kind. (James 3:16)

One of the most misquoted Scriptures in the Bible is, "Money is the root of all evil." First of all, the Scripture actually says that the *love* of money is the root of all evil (1 Timothy 6:10). The real root of all evil is selfishness. When looking at the history of Lucifer some time ago, I found his downfall occurred when he was not satisfied with his God-given position in heaven. He was an anointed cherub who created and brought praises to God. He was radiant in appearance and held a position of honor in the heavenly realm. In fact, he was one of the archangels. He had continuous access to the throne of the Most High.

Yet that was not good enough for him. He began to put his desires above God's. Read Isaiah 14:12–17, and as you do you will see the phrase "I will" three times. Lucifer told himself that he would set his kingdom above God's, he would reign over the mountains of the gods, and he would climb to the highest heavens and be like God. He was blinded by his own ambition, and deceived himself into thinking he was greater than the One who actually created him. Ultimately, he lost his position and was expelled from heaven.

Think about how Satan tempted Adam and Eve in the Garden. He came to the woman and said, "Did God really say that if you ate of the fruit, you would be like God, knowing good and evil?" (Genesis 3:5). Satan has used this strategy of selfishness to create chaos on the earth and in the heavens ever since. His selfish ambition influenced a third of the angels to follow him. Today he uses the same strategy on humanity. Think of all the tragedies that have occurred on this earth that were caused by humans.

What was at the root? Selfish ambition. Selfish ambition is the seed of all discord, and it is the cause of fear, envy, jealousy, greed, and hatred. If you have some kind of conflict in your life today, just look and you will find some fruit of selfishness at its root.

Scripture Readings:
Genesis 3:1–7
Isaiah 14:12–17
Ezekiel 28:13–19
James 3:13–16

February 22

WAIT BECAUSE HE IS NEVER LATE

Let all that I am wait quietly before God, for my hope is in Him. He alone is my rock and my salvation, my fortress where I will not be shaken. (Psalm 62:5–6)

Have you ever received a word from the Lord or someone prophesied something good over you? When you heard it, you got excited, you felt the adrenaline pumping through your body, and it probably energized you. As the days passed, you rehearsed that word and could actually visualize it. Then you began to make the vision happen—to put the word into practice. That's when the struggle starts.

With every passing day you get more frustrated and begin to wonder if the word you heard will come to pass. So you try even harder to make it happen, but all you get is more frustrated. The doubt becomes greater and you start to get angry, and the joy you once felt disappears. You feel like God abandoned you, that maybe His word was not true. Then you begin to doubt if that was really the word of God to begin with. Does this sound familiar?

This has happened to me on a number of occasions. What the Holy Spirit revealed to me was that I was trying to accomplish the word in my own power and might. I had gotten ahead of God and trusted in my own power and resources to make the vision or word come to pass. I didn't totally and completely trust the Lord. I created a timeline for the vision to happen, but in the process I failed to realize that God views time from a different perspective. We see time from a linear perspective, while God views it from a geometrical perspective. This means He can see the end from the beginning.

If God has spoken to us about something that will take place in our life, then take heart: it will happen! God cannot lie (Number 23:19). The process of waiting for God's word to be fulfilled is where patience and trust come into play. They are both fruits of the Spirit that are available to us. If God hasn't brought the word to pass, there is a proper reason for it. Don't take matters into your own hands and come up with the second best. If you wait, you will have God's best. For His word always comes to pass.

Scripture Readings:
Psalm 33:20–22
Isaiah 40:29–31
Colossians 1:11
James 1:3

February 23

SPEAKING WHAT YOU GET

Watch your tongue and keep your mouth shut, and you will stay out of trouble. (Proverbs 21:23)

Our words are the reflections of what we believe. As a counselor, one of the methods I use to counsel clients is simply listening to them talk, then I mirror back to them what I have heard. Some clients are amazed at the insight I provide for them, but I didn't really do anything but tell them what they told me. Our words can make us or they can break us. As I stated before, we are created in the image and likeness of God (Genesis 1:26). Part of what this means is that we have the power to speak things into existence.

Many people are unknowingly sabotaging themselves by the words they speak. For example, have you ever said or heard someone say, "If I didn't have bad luck, I wouldn't have any luck at all," "Things never work out for me," or "I knew it was too good to be true"? If we look at the people's lives who say these kinds of things on a consistent basis, we will see that they have received what they said. These same people are quick to blame others for their misfortune. What they have failed to realize is the major part they played by their careless use of words.

Our words can either build up or tear down. It's not the devil or God, but our tongue that is doing the building up and tearing down! Monitoring our speech is a good way to find out if what we are speaking truly reflects what we believe. Are the words we are speaking what we really want to come to pass? If not, then we need to change them. We even need to watch the words we speak in jest, because our spirit man does not know the difference. The power of life and death are in our tongue (Proverbs 18:21). Choose wisely what you will speak.

Scripture Readings:
Proverbs 18:21; 13:3
Matthew 12:36–37

February 24

THREE TYPES OF BELIEVERS

Dear brothers and sisters, when I was with you I couldn't talk to you as I would to spiritual people. I had to talk as though you belonged to this world or as though you were infants in the Christian life. (1 Corinthians 3:1)

The apostle Paul was addressing the believers in the Corinthian church. What a statement to make to an entire church. The Corinthian church was rich in the gifts of the Spirit, but they were a worldly group of believers. I wonder what Paul would say if he visited many churches today? From what I have seen, I think he would say much the same thing.

Since I began my walk with the Lord many years ago, I have observed three types of believers. The first type of believers have accepted Jesus as their Savior, but He is not Lord of their lives. They are what I call "Undercover Christians." They walk, talk, think, and act just like those in the world. They are in bondage to their flesh, finances, alcohol, and other substances. It is difficult to even know if they are saved because their lifestyle doesn't reflect a changed heart.

The second type of believers are the ones who are in a constant state of struggle. These are immature in their faith and are always looking for someone to pray for them. They lack a personal relationship with the Lord and rely on others to intercede for them. They seldom read their Bibles and rely solely on what they hear being preached. This makes them susceptible to all kinds of false teachings. This type of believers are always running to the altar to get hands laid on them because they are spiritually lazy and want instant success. They are living like the Hebrews did when they were in the wilderness.

The third type of believers are the ones who are mature in the faith. They have taken the time to develop a personal relationship with the Lord. Jesus is not only Savior in their lives, but He is Lord of all. They are the true disciples of Jesus who seek to follow Him in all of their ways. They find time to study the Word and apply its principles to their lives. These are the doers in the Kingdom, not the talkers. They are the ones people come to when they need godly counsel or prayer.

Which type of believer are you? Notice I didn't ask you what type of believer you would like to be. Be honest with yourself today, and take it to the next level. No one is stopping you but yourself.

Scripture Readings:
1 Corinthians 3:1–4

February 25

WHO'S IN CONTROL?

Those that are dominated by the sinful nature think about sinful things, but those controlled by the Holy Spirit think about the things that please the Spirit. So letting your sinful nature control your mind leads to death. But letting the Spirit control your mind leads to life and peace. (Romans 8:5–6)

Once a person is born again, they are faced with a conflict. That conflict is between their old nature and their new spirit. In between is their soul, which includes the mind, will, and emotions. The old nature is not willing or capable of change, so it will fight to stay in control. That's why we will see some people who were on fire for the Lord at one time eventually turn back to their old nature. They allowed themselves to be controlled by the old nature once again. Their mind or soul chose to walk in the old rather than the new nature.

We as believers have to realize that the walk of faith is not going to be easy. We have the old nature to contend with, and the pressures of the world trying to conform us to their image. That is why it is of paramount importance that the believer renews their mind to the things of God. The renewal of our mind is the key to a successful walk in the Spirit.

When the mind and spirit are working together, the flesh is under control. But if the mind and the flesh are working together, then the old nature is in control of all that we do. God has given us His Word and the Holy Spirit to ensure our victory, but we have to choose to use them on a regular basis. We have the power to choose life or death (Deuteronomy 30:19). We will find this theme repeated over and over again in the Scriptures. God has provided everything we need to live in peace and victory—all we have to do is trust and obey what He commands. Remember that greater is He who is in you than he who is in the world (1 John 4:4).

Scripture Readings:
Romans 8:1–16; 12:1–2
2 Corinthians 10:3–5
1 John 4:4

February 26

THERE IS NO TEMPTATION GREATER THAN YOU

The temptations in your life are no different from what others experience. And God is faithful. He will not allow the temptation to be more than you can stand. When you are tempted, He will show you a way out so that you can endure. (1 Corinthians 10:13)

Living in this world, it is certain we will be tempted. It's inevitable. There are those out there who think that it is a sin to be tempted. But that is just not true. Jesus faced temptation, but He overcame it and lived a perfect life. We can overcome it too. We live in a world that is currently controlled by Satan, for he is called the "prince of the power of the air" (Ephesians 2:2). This means he has dominion in the second heavens, or the atmosphere of earth. Since his fall, Satan desires to reign over the earth as a god. So no one is immune from temptation.

It is what we do when the temptation comes that matters. In order to successfully overcome temptation, we must first realize that greater is He who is within us than he who is in the world. We also have to realize that we cannot fight Satan in our own power. He is an expert in the art of deception. He can make anything look tempting. Look at what he did to Eve. The Scriptures say that once she saw that the fruit was desirable, she ate it (Genesis 3:6). This means that one time she did not find the fruit desirable, but it was only after Satan deceived her that she saw the fruit and desired it.

How many people who are addicted to drugs and alcohol started out not liking the taste, or the way the substance made them feel? How many people addicted to pornography felt guilty the first time they indulged, but after a period of time of repeated use they developed a craving they couldn't control? His methods are the same today. Why? Because it works! Once we understand the enemy's methods, however, we are one step closer to not falling into his trap.

As a counselor I tell clients who are struggling with temptation to do the following:

- Read and recite 1 Corinthians 10:13 every time the temptation comes to mind. By doing this we are submitting ourselves to God, and the devil has to flee (James 4:7). Jesus used this strategy when He was tempted in the wilderness (Matthew 4:1–10). Use the Word of God!
- Think long term rather than short term. Quite often, when we fall into temptation, we are only thinking about the short-term gratification it brings. Our perspective becomes very myopic. How many men or women would not have cheated on their spouse had they thought about the consequences of their actions?
- Finally, understand the principle of sowing and reaping. If we sow to the desire of the flesh, we will reap death, either now or later. It's a universal law that cannot and will not be ignored.

Remember that there is no temptation that cannot be overcome. So trust the One who dwells within you to give you the power to overcome.

Scripture Readings:
1 Corinthians 10:1–13
James 4:7

February 27

THE IMPORTANCE OF GUARDING YOUR HEART

A peaceful heart leads to a healthy body; jealousy is like cancer to the bones. (Proverbs 14:30)

It has been scientifically proven that there is a correlation between our heart, brain, and our health. Our heart it not just a blood pump, but it has its own brain and nervous system. According to Dr. Caroline Leaf, who is neuroscientist, there are 40,000 neurons in the heart and as many are found in the brain. In fact, the heart regulates the flow of emotions that are generated by our thoughts.

Dr. Leaf states that the heart is proving to be an intelligent force behind the intuitive thoughts and feelings we experience. It is also responsible for the production of a biochemical substance, atrial peptide (ANF), that regulates many of our brain functions and stimulates behavior. The heart also sends signals to our brain, which in turn influences our perceptions and emotions.

When someone says that their heart is broken, or that their heart was not in it, there is truth to that. The heart plays an important part in our total being, and it shouldn't be taken for granted. The Bible warns us to guard our heart, for it determines the course of our life (Proverbs 4:20). What we allow into our heart has a profound effect on how we live out our days. What we see, hear, and meditate on will get into our heart, and once it is our heart, we will act on it. Jesus said that our heart determines what we say and how we behave (Matthew 12:33–35).

It is important to spend time every morning praising and thanking God for what He has done for us. By doing this, our heart will release ANF, which will signal the brain to produce hormones that will cause a feeling of peace to come upon us. Yes, there is a reason why we should spend time praising God. It is to our benefit that we do so. When we have a peaceful heart, we think clearer and feel better. Plus, our immune system is stronger to fight off disease because our body is functioning in a positive mode (Proverbs 17:22).

So start every day with praise and you will end it with thanksgiving!

Scripture Readings:
Proverbs 4:20–23; 12:20; 14:30; 15:13; 17:22
Matthew 12:34–35

February 28

THINK, BELIEVE, AND ACT

Anyone who listens to My teaching and follows it is wise, like a person who builds a house on solid rock. (Matthew 7:24)

There are many believers who are quick to listen to the Word of God. They shout "Amen" and "Hallelujah" after hearing a motivational word from the pulpit. However, if we asked them the next day what the message was about, they probably couldn't tell us. Some people think that because they hear something it is enough. These types of believers are like the people Jesus described in the parable of the sower. Many accept the Word gladly, but when the time of trial comes they quickly fall away (Mark 4:16–17).

We should know that the enemy of our faith doesn't want the Word planted in our heart—he doesn't want it to take root. He knows that once it is planted in our heart, there will be a harvest of some kind. If he can prevent it through distractions, hardships, or persecutions, then he will do everything in his power to arrange it. We must understand that we are a threat to Satan, and he wants to contain us and make our walk of little or no effect.

There is also the element of self-deception that is involved. Some believers think that because they have listened and accepted the Word of God, then it is enough. They are satisfied with just listening and hearing. But this is nothing more than mental assent. Mental assent causes us to feel good about ourselves without having to act on what we think we believe. In cases like this, the enemy doesn't have to do anything because the person is self-deceived (James 1:22).

To ensure that we get the Word into our heart and have it start producing a harvest, I suggest that we do the following:

- Think or meditate on the Word of God. This gets our brain producing neurons that will produce new thoughts. This is what

the Bible calls renewing our mind (Romans 12:1–2), or a form of neuroplasticity (or changing thoughts).
- Once we meditate on the Word, believe it. Belief comes by repeating the Word over and over again, or muttering the Word throughout the day. This will increase our faith because faith grows through hearing something on a regular basis (Romans 10:17).
- Finally, we act on what we have heard. This will reinforce the new thought or behavior. When all three of these things are done, we are incorporating the soul, heart, and body. They are all working together to renew our mind. Didn't Jesus say that we're to love God with all our heart, mind, and soul (Matthew 22:37)?

Scripture Readings:
Matthew 7:21–27; 22:37
Mark 4:10–24
James 1:22–25
Isaiah 1:19

March 1

PUT SOME FEET TO YOUR FAITH

Send your grain across the seas, and in time, profits will flow back to you. (Ecclesiastes 11:1)

When we embark on our journey of faith, we will encounter obstacles along the way. What we do when these challenges occur will determine what we really believe. As I have stated earlier, there is a difference between mental assent to something and actual belief in that something. True belief will have an action attached to it, while mental assent will not. Many people are deceived into thinking they really believe when in reality they are merely giving mental assent to the belief.

True faith requires patience and perseverance. For example, Abraham waited for twenty-five years before the child God promised him was born. Twenty-three publishers rejected Dr. Seuss's first children's book before the twenty-fourth publisher sold six million copies. Henry Ford went bankrupt two times in the first three years of his business. In the first year of business Coca-Cola sold only four hundred bottles of Coke. Charles Goodyear experienced bitter disappointment, was imprisoned for bad debt, and was ridiculed by his family and friends until he experienced tremendous success. All of these experienced hardships and disappointment, but they refused to give up and the breakthrough came.

You might be going through a hard time right now; maybe you feel like giving up. Maybe it's a relationship or a business endeavor, or maybe you have been seeking employment but to no avail. No matter the challenge, don't give up! That next interview might be the one you have been waiting for your whole life. How many people have come so close to success but refused to take that final step into realizing their dreams, failing to reach the potential God created in them because they didn't persevere just a little bit longer? It has been reported that Thomas Edison experimented 10,000 times before he finally achieved success with the light bulb. Imagine if he had given up on the 9,999th time? Someone else would have come along and made it happen.

How many successes have we forfeited because we gave up way too early? How many opportunities have we let slip away from us because we didn't have the perseverance to finish the race? As a believer, we have the Word of God to strengthen us when we feel like giving up. We have the power of the Almighty God within us. When we are weak, we only need to allow God to make us strong! Charles Kettering said, "Keep going and the chances are you will stumble on something, perhaps when you are least expecting it. I never heard of anyone stumbling on something sitting down."

Scripture Readings:
Isaiah 40:29–31; 41:10
2 Corinthians 12:9

March 2

WALKING BY WHAT YOU BELIEVE, NOT BY WHAT YOU SEE

When you go out to fight your enemies and you face horses and chariots and an army greater than your own, do not be afraid. The Lord your God, who brought you out of the land of Egypt, is with you! (Deuteronomy 20:1)

Life can be quite intimidating at times. This is especially true in our society. It oftentimes seems overwhelming with the media that strives on creating fear and dissension within our culture. No wonder so many people turn to drugs, alcohol, and entertainment to pacify them and bring peace to their hearts, though it is not real peace. It is so easy to go with the flow and not step outside of the boundaries. Sometimes I think this is what is expected of us in the culture we live in. Conformity equals control. Well, our heavenly Father has called us to be the leaders and not the followers (Deuteronomy 28:13).

In the book of Joshua, the Lord instructed Joshua to lead the children of Israel into the Promise Land. Moses had recently died, thereby leaving Joshua in charge. This was overwhelming for him and he wondered if could do it. But God instructed him to meditate on the Word and speak it out of his mouth. If Joshua would follow these instructions, he was guaranteed success (Joshua 1:1–9).

Joshua encountered his first big challenge—the city of Jericho. Jericho had great walls and it was believed that no one could enter this city to take it. But God told Joshua to look beyond those walls and see that He had given the city to him (Joshua 6:1). In the natural it looked impossible; but nothing is impossible with God. Joshua had a choice to make: he could believe God and follow His instructions, or he could walk away in unbelief. Joshua chose the former and the walls of Jericho came tumbling down. Because Joshua walked by faith rather than by sight, he achieved great success.

Each of us can do the same thing today if we continually walk by faith and not by sight. We only need to find the promise in the Word of God and stand on it until we see our walls come tumbling down.

Scripture Readings:
Joshua 1:5–9
Isaiah 41:10; 43:1–2
1 John 4:4

March 3

God Is Not Limited by Your Failures

Three different times I begged the Lord to take it away. Each time He said, "My grace is all you need. My power works best in weakness." So now I am glad to boast about my weakness, so that the power of Christ can work through me. (2 Corinthians 12:8–9)

We have all missed the mark and failed at some time in our lives. Maybe we have let someone down or betrayed someone we deeply loved. Maybe we let ourselves down by giving in to that bad habit once again. Maybe we have stolen something or acted in a manner that doesn't represent who we truly are. We all have been there at one time or another. We have showered ourselves in guilt and shame; we ran and hid from God because we thought He was upset with us.

Well, God knew we were going to fail, and yet He still loves us even in the midst of our failure. He loves us no matter what we do in our life or what we fail to do with our life! Jesus is the same as He was yesterday, today, and forever (Hebrews 13:8). God doesn't love conditionally; His love for us is unconditional. He sees us through the finished work of Christ. Jesus bore all our sins—past, present, and future. This means there is no condemnation for those who are believers in Christ Jesus (Romans 8:1).

The apostle Paul lived this revelation. Paul had learned that when he stopped, God started. He relied on the grace of God through each situation he encountered in life. He realized that he was incapable of doing what he was called to do on his own. So he trusted God to do it through him. If we are struggling with something in our life, we only have to hand it over to God and let Him deal with it. When we feel ourselves getting weak, we can just say, "I am the righteousness of God in Christ, and He is working in me now."

So when we do fail, debrief the event, and then find out what led to the failure. Learn from it. Ask God for wisdom so we don't make the same mistake again. But if we do make the mistake again, know that God is on our side and He is not going to love us any less because of our failure. We simply forgive ourselves, put it behind us, and move on to our victory (Philippians 3:12–13).

Scripture Readings:
Romans 8:1–2
2 Corinthians 12:8–10
Philippians 3:12–13

March 4

ARE YOU CONNECTED?

But if you remain in Me and My words remain in you, you may ask for anything you want and it will be granted! When you produce much fruit, you are My true disciples. This brings great glory to My Father. (John 15:7–8)

What kind of life are you living? Are you living the kind of life that other people admire and try to emulate, or the kind of life that people just shake their heads at? Is there power in your presence? Has anyone ever come up to you and said, "There is something about you that just _____"? Are you the type of person people come to in their time of need? Are all your needs and wants taken care of?

Jesus promised in His Word that He would provide for us whatever we want. He didn't say He would only provide our needs, but our wants. There is a difference. Needs are necessities that are vital to live our lives, such as things we need to exist in this world—food, water, shelter, clothing, etc. Wants are things we desire but could live without. God wants us who are believers not only to live fruitful lives, but to live in a manner that attracts the attention of others. The world is not going to listen to someone who is broken down on the side of the road. In fact, they will laugh at a person like that.

God has called His children to be kings and priests on this earth. We are His chosen possession, His special people (1 Peter 1:9). He wants us to have what we desire! Everyone has different desires—not everyone wants to live in a big house or have a fancy sports car. Some people are happy with just the basics of life. The point is that God will provide for whatever we can believe Him to provide for us.

But this promise is contingent on us remaining in Him. By doing this, we will possess our possessions and they will not possess us. There may come a time when we will be tested and asked to give away what God has provided for us (Genesis 22:2). If we pass the test, then we know that God will give us far more. But if we fail, then we know what is the real God in our life (Mark 10:22).

Scripture Readings:
Isaiah 43:7; 61:6–7
John 14:13; 15:7; 16:23

March 5

WHO IS GREATER: HIM OR YOU?

He must become greater and greater, and I must become less and less. (John 3:30)

God wants to express His life through us. This doesn't mean that we need to become an automaton, having no thoughts of our own. God created each of us to be unique. There is no one in the entire universe who has our talents, perceptions, and thought processes. There is something God has assigned us to do, and no one can do it better than we can. Take a moment to think about that. There are people out there you can reach that I can't. You may be on the only light some people will ever see. You are awesome and special!

There is something I learned about living a victorious life in Christ that I want to pass on to you. It is simply this: I needed to do less and less and allow God to do more and more. I needed to let God flow through me, which required trust. This is especially true of us who like to be in control of situations and circumstances. I learned that if anything was going to get done, I needed to do it myself. I was self-reliant, independent, and self-controlled. These qualities proved to be an asset in this world, but not so much in the things of God.

God wants to protect us from being snared by the devil through pride, so there is no place for me or I in His Kingdom. Anything that we do that is worthy of any praise or recognition comes because of Him, and Him alone. He is the source of our strength, talent, and wisdom. If we keep this mindset, God has no problem exalting us because we are magnifying His glory. So we have a choice to make today: believe our own press and get full of ourselves, or humble ourselves and submit to God and let Him lift us higher and higher. Which will we choose?

Scripture Readings:
John 3:30; 5:19–20, 30; 14:10–14
Philippians 2:13; 4:13

March 6

HIGH EXPECTATIONS BASED ON WRONG INFORMATION

I do not treat the grace of God as meaningless. For if keeping the law could make us right with God, then there was no need for Christ to die. (Galatians 2:21)

Some believers unknowingly have mixed the grace of God with works of the law. What do I mean by this? Have you ever thought to yourself that the reason you didn't get an answer to your prayers was because of the following:

- I didn't pray enough?
- I haven't read my Bible enough?
- I haven't gone to church as regularly as I should?
- I should have fasted more?
- I should have given more financially?

Or have you ever questioned why God answers the prayers of those seemingly less righteous than us? If we answered yes to any of these questions, then we may be at risk of blending the works of the law with the grace of God. Now please don't misunderstand me here. I am not saying we should stop reading our Bible, praying, attending church, giving financially, or living a sanctified life. All of those things should be part of our lifestyle because we love God and want to do what pleases Him. But what is our motivation in doing them?

Are we doing those disciplines because we want to earn merit with God, or are we doing them as the result of the grace of God living in us? If we are doing them because we think we are earning brownie points with God, we are mistaken! By doing this, we are telling God that the death of Jesus on the cross was not enough, that we need to put our own two cents in. That is nothing more than an insult to the precious blood of our Savior, and it is an affront to God. I know that this is strong language, but it's the truth.

If we are basing our faith on anything other than the blood of Jesus Christ and His Word, then our expectation is based on wrong information. We are setting ourselves up for disappointment. Our answered prayer should be based on the finished work of Christ Jesus, and that alone. He bore our afflictions and diseases on the cross, so why do we feel the need to add to it? Do we not trust in the grace and Word of God? Think about that as you go about your day today.

Scripture Readings:
Galatians 2:20–21
Colossians 2:20–23
1 Samuel 16:7

March 7

JESUS HEALS

And you know that God anointed Jesus of Nazareth with the Holy Spirit and with power. Then Jesus went around doing good and healing all who were oppressed by the devil, for God was with Him. (Acts 10:38)

Jesus is the same today as He was yesterday. In fact, He will be the same forever (Hebrews 13:8). If Jesus healed people in the past, then why can't He heal you today? It is God's will that we be free of all sickness and disease because Jesus bore that on the cross for us! The reason God anointed Jesus to heal all who were oppressed was to demonstrate that it was not Him who brings sickness and disease, but rather that sickness and disease are the result of sin.

We were originally created to live harmoniously with God. God is positive and He created us in His image and likeness, so we were created to be positive as well. When we sin, we are in the negative and this creates discord within us. This discord causes our brain to react and start creating chemicals that have an adverse effect on our immune system, which makes us more prone to disease. Whenever Jesus healed anyone, He first dealt with the issue of sin. Once that person knew that they were forgiven of their sin, Jesus could then heal them.

A sin consciousness will separate us from the power of God working in our life (1 John 1:9). This separation leaves us open to the curse that is upon the earth. This is why we should be in constant fellowship with the Lord and confess all known sin whenever it comes to mind. By confessing our sins to the Lord, we are freeing ourselves from it so that we can stand boldly and be confident before God (1 John 1:7; 3:21). Once the issue of sin has been dealt with, we will have the confidence to request whatever we need from God, knowing that our request has been heard. If our request has been heard, then it will surely be answered (1 John 5:13–15).

Scripture Readings:
Isaiah 53:3–4
Mark 1:34
Luke 4:18–19
1 John 1:5–7; 3:21; 5:11–13

March 8

The Patience of God and the Hardness of the Heart

Because the sentence against an evil work is not executed speedily, the hearts of the sons of men are fully set to do evil. Though a sinner does evil a hundred times and his days [seemingly] are prolonged [in his wickedness], yet surely I know that it will be well with those who [reverently] fear God, who revere and worship Him, realizing His continual presence. (Ecclesiastes 8:11–12 AMP)

One of the main character traits of God is patience. God is patient because He hopes we will see the error of our ways and judge for ourselves, so that He won't have to do it (2 Peter 3:9). It is important to realize this because it is so easy to deceive ourselves into thinking that nothing is going to happen if we continue in our rebellious ways or in our stubborn hearts. As a probation officer, many of my clients thought like this and wound up in prison, lost their families, got strung out on drugs, and lost their self-respect. All this happened because they didn't suffer immediate consequences for their transgressions.

Satan will use the patience of God to his advantage, deceiving the individual into thinking nothing is going to happen—there will be no consequences for sin. When nothing immediately happens, it reinforces the behavior and causes the person's heart to become hardened. Once this happens, the person's conscience becomes calloused, and they feel no sense of guilt or shame. That is why it is important to listen to our conscience—it is the voice of our spirit. When we willfully ignore our conscience, we place ourselves at risk.

I remember before I suffered kidney failure, I heard my inner man telling me that I needed to rest and change my lifestyle. For years I ignored the voice from within. Doctors even told me that I needed to slow down, but I failed to adhere to their advice as well. I thought I was invincible and I was the exception to the rule. Well, it finally caught up with me. I was flat on my back in the hospital. I would eventually have to go on dialysis. Was God trying to teach me a lesson? No. In fact, He was trying to warn me, but my heart was hardened, so I suffered the consequences of my actions. It is true that we will reap what we sow (Galatians 6:7).

I hope that you will not have to learn the hard way like I did. Listen to your conscience and the advice from people you trust. More importantly, listen to the Holy Spirit because He will never lead you astray.

Scripture Readings:
Ecclesiastes 8:11–12
2 Peter 3:9

March 9

Don't Let Fear Shake Your Faith

Jesus responded, "Why are you afraid? You have so little faith!" (Matthew 8:26)

How would Jesus describe your faith? Would He marvel at your faith, as He did with the Roman officer (Matthew 8:10), or would He ask why you had so little faith (Luke 12:28)? We all have been given the same measure of faith (Romans 12:3). What we do with that measure of faith is up to us. Some people exercise their faith and build it up, and some do little with what they have been given. Our God is a faith God. He takes delight in those who operate in faith (Hebrews 11:6). Our tears do not move Him; He is moved by our faith. Faith is like money to purchase things in the spiritual realm.

There are two spiritual forces at work in the world today, faith and fear. If we are operating in faith, then we are operating in love; conversely, if we are operating in fear, then we open ourselves up to anger, rage, bitterness, anxiety, confusion, and depression. Each one of us has been given the choice to decide which one we want to operate in. This world's system promotes the spirit of fear as a means to control and entertain. Just take a moment to look at what's on television today. Some of the most popular programs are promoting hatred, rage, bitterness, and selfishness. Very few promote faith.

We as believers have to be careful not to expose ourselves to things designed to rob our faith. Without faith, we have little power. There is a story in the book of Matthew about Peter walking on the water in order to get to Jesus. When Jesus told Peter he could walk to Him, he got out of the boat in boldness. Peter was walking on the water! But once he started looking around at the waves and wind surrounding him, his faith decreased as fear increased. Peter was close enough to Jesus for Him to grab him and take him to the boat. Once in the boat, Jesus asked him why he doubted, and rebuked him for having little faith. Don't let fear rob you of your faith!

Scripture Readings:
Matthew 14:22–32

March 10

YOU ARE FREE FROM CONDEMNATION

There is no judgment against anyone who believes in Him. But anyone who does not believe in Him is already been judged for not believing in God's one and only Son. And the judgment is based on the fact: God's light came into the world, but people loved the darkness more than the light, for their actions were evil. (John 3:18–19)

There are many believers who have fallen by the wayside because of a lapse of indiscretion. They felt so ashamed for what they did, but they couldn't forgive themselves. It even got to the point where they did not feel comfortable going back to church. Those who did go back felt marginalized by the congregation and eventfully stopped going altogether. Many of these believers, once on fire for God, slipped back into the world. It has been sad to see this happen.

Had they had a better understanding of the finished work of Christ on the cross and attended a church that also understood this, many of them would be flourishing members of the body of Christ today. Instead, they remain wounded and bitter because of the treatment they experienced. This goes on all too often in churches.

There is a façade in many churches of how we are to conduct ourselves, an expectancy that is often unwritten and fosters feelings of uneasiness. Those who have personal issues are reluctant to discuss them because of the fear of not being accepted. This causes a person to be phony, not real with themselves or with others.

The issue that plagues them goes unaddressed, until it finally overwhelms them and they act out. All of this could have been avoided if they simply understood that there is no condemnation for those in Christ Jesus (Romans 8:1–2). Yes, we are free from condemnation if we are in Christ Jesus. He paid the ultimate price for all the sins you or I have or will ever commit. That doesn't mean we will escape the consequences of our actions, because we reap what we've sown (Galatians 6:7). It is a spiritual law.

Many in the pulpit are either unaware of the gospel of grace or afraid to preach it because they don't trust their congregation. They think that preaching this would be giving them a license to sin. Well, is what they don't realize is that people don't need a license if that is what they want to do.

It is my belief that most believers don't want to sin—they want to live a life that is pleasing to the Lord. We are prone to miss the mark. Instead of condemning ourselves for what we have done wrong, just repent, debrief, and get back on the horse. Know also that God has forgotten about it, so why are you repeatedly bringing it up (Isaiah 44:22)?

Scripture Readings:
John 8:1–11, 18–19
Romans 8:1–2
Isaiah 44:22

March 11

TRUST, OBEDIENCE, AND FAITH

If you love Me, obey My commandments. (John 14:15)

One of the best ways to show you trust and love someone is obedience to what they desire. As a parent, it is honoring when our children listen to us and trust what we say to them. This is a sign of their trust in us and of their love and respect for us. Well, the same is true with our heavenly Father. He takes delight when His children show their trust by obeying Him. When we are in obedience to our Father, we have confidence to ask for anything and know that it will be granted to us (John 15:7).

One of the reasons that our prayers are not being answered may be that our heart is condemning us. Is there unconfessed sin or some unforgiveness that we have not dealt with yet? If so, we need to settle the issue so that we have a clear heart before the Lord (Mark 11:25).

The more trust we have in God, the greater our faith will be. If we have trouble trusting people, then we will have problems in the area of faith. If someone has betrayed or hurt us in the past, we must forgive them. By doing this we are freeing ourselves from the hurt and pain that permeates our hearts. If we don't do it, those toxic thoughts will dominate us and prevent good, healthy thoughts from growing. In conclusion, the more we trust the easier it is to be obedient to what Jesus commands of us. The more obedient we are, the more confidence we will have. And confidence leads to stronger faith; and we know that without faith it is impossible to please God (Hebrews 11:6).

Scripture Readings:
Deuteronomy 26:18–19
John 14:15; 15:7; 16:26
1 John 3:21–22

March 12

FORGIVENESS: THE KEY TO A HEALTHIER LIFE

If you forgive those who sin against you, your heavenly Father will forgive you. But if you refuse to forgive others, your Father will not forgive your sins. (Matthew 6:14–15)

As a counselor, a majority of my clients suffer from the results of unforgiveness in their life. Those emotional wounds from the past continue to haunt them, manifesting themselves in their current relationships. Many of these clients fail to make the connection, so I take the liberty to educate them.

When we fail to forgive, we allow those toxic thoughts to remain within us. This in turn signals our amygdala, which is the portion of our brain that regulates emotions. Once this occurs, chemicals are released that cause stress hormones to be released. Subsequently, our bodies respond with an increase in blood pressure and heart rate. So every time we rehearse the past hurt or pain that someone has caused us, or even that our own actions have caused, then our body automatically reacts by stimulating the amygdala.

Over a period of time, this can be detrimental to our physical health, not to mention our mental and spiritual health. God is a God of love. In Him there is only positive—nothing negative exists. There is no resentment, rage, hatred, or distrust. When the previous attributes operate in our life, we have separated ourselves from God and what is dear to His heart. Without God there is no peace in our lives.

There is increasing scientific evidence that shows that forgiveness leads to a happier and healthier life.

When we choose to forgive past hurts, our frontal cortex link becomes active, calming the amygdala so that the toxic memory can eventually be erased, allowing a more positive memory to grow (Philippians 3:13–14). We can't change what happened to us in the past, but we can change the way we view it, reducing the negative impact on our mental and physical health.

Scripture Readings:
Matthew 6:14–15
Luke 17:4
Mark 11:25
Philippians 3:13–14

March 13

JESUS BORE IT ALL, SO WHY ARE YOU CARRYING IT?

God, for whom and through whom everything was made, chose to bring many children into glory. And it was only right that He should make Jesus, through His suffering, a perfect leader, fit to bring them into their salvation. (Hebrews 2:10)

Imagine living without the fear of rejection, shame, and guilt. Imagine how freeing that would be. Think how nice it would be to not feel guilty over past mistakes and the shame associated with them. Many people are in bondage to their past, struggling to live lives free in Christ. The painful memories of failed relationships and heartbreaks come to visit them, and they relive the event as if it just happened again. They are fearful to take a chance on another relationship because they don't want to be hurt again. Instead of taking risks, they settle to play it safe and continue to be alone. They fail to let go of those toxic thoughts that have become an active part of their memory. And that memory gets filed away in their emotional library, only to be brought back up when the emotional wound is reopened.

Human beings were designed to live in the positive. When we are in the positive, our thought processes are clear and our bodies are healthy. However, when toxic memories from the past remain in our thought processes, a negative environment is created that makes us prone to illness. There is nothing we can do about the past, but we don't have to let it control our future. God has provided a remedy for us. The finished work of Jesus took all the shame, guilt, sorrow, and rejection so that we can live lives free in Christ, cleansed by His blood (Isaiah 50:6; 53:3–6).

It is possible to erase those toxic thoughts from the past and replace them with positive thoughts by finding Scriptures in God's Word and meditating on them frequently. Whenever we feel guilt or shame, we should read Isaiah 53:3–6 out loud to ourselves. Then we can turn our hearts in praise to the Lord for the finished work of Jesus on our behalf.

Don't let the fear of rejection keep you on the sidelines any longer. Turn to Christ and allow Him to cleanse you.

Scripture Readings:
Isaiah 50:6; 53:3–6
Hebrews 2:10

March 14

THE BENEFITS OF A GOOD PRAYER LIFE

If only you would prepare your heart and lift up your hands to Him in prayer! Get rid of your sins and leave iniquity behind you. Then your face will brighten with innocence. You will be strong and free of fear. You will forget your misery; it will be like water flowing away. Your life will be brighter than the noonday. Even in darkness will be as bright as morning. (Job 11:13–17)

This Scripture was given to Job by one of his friends while he was in the midst of incredible suffering. If you're not acquainted with the story of Job, I will give you a very brief synopsis. Job was going through some tough times. He lost almost everything: his cattle were stolen, all of his children died, he was suffering physically, and his wife was not supportive in any way. As you can imagine, Job was a little upset and angry with God. The last thing Job wanted to hear was that he should turn to God in prayer.

When we are having a pity party, there is no room for prayer. That's the last thing we want to do. I have been there, so I know what I am talking about. But if we force ourselves to pray, it's more like complaining than actual prayer. We have all have been there at some time in our lives.

In times like these, the enemy likes to come in and twist the knife that is already in our back. He will accuse us of all the things we have done wrong, and he will tell us the reason that we are suffering is because God is teaching us a lesson. With these toxic thoughts rolling around in our mind, it is easy to understand why prayer is not a priority for us in these seasons.

Prayer is the best thing to do to get rid of those blues. Prayer will allow us to do the following:

- Confess our shortcomings and any known sins.
- It will restore our relationship with God.
- It will renew our spirit and our mind.

- It will cause us to forget the circumstances surrounding our lives.
- And it will cause us to look at the future with a sense of hope and optimism.

All this will happen if we will stand on the promises of God and turn to Him in prayer.

This means that we pray the answer to our problems, not the problems themselves. This is important to remember during these times! So many people will just pray about the problem instead of praying the answer found in the Word of God. We will have to do our homework—we'll have to find Scriptures that will answer our problem and meditate on them while we pray. It will work every time.

Scripture Readings:
Job 11:13–20
Philippians 4:6–7
1 John 5:14–15

March 15

ARE YOU A HEARER OR A DOER OF THE TEACHINGS OF JESUS?

So why do you keep calling Me "Lord, Lord!" when you don't do what I say? (Luke 6:46)

One of the reasons why the church is not making a bigger impact on the world is because of a lack of following through. Many believers are good listeners of the Word but not doers of what they hear. Jesus described them as a house without a solid foundation that will give way when the wind and rain comes.

I remember some really expensive houses that were built in San Diego a number of years ago. These homes were absolutely beautiful. The only problem was that they weren't built on a solid foundation, so cracks started to appear in the walls and driveways. These homes that sold for over $500,000 were almost worthless because of all the cracks in the foundation. The contractors were sued by the homeowners and eventually went out of business.

Likewise, this is true of believers who are just good listeners of the Word of God and not actually doers. They have no solid foundation and no root that goes deep into the soil of God's Word. They look good and sound good on the outside—they can quote Scriptures and recite the sermon they heard, but when trouble, temptation, or persecution comes, they fall apart. Why is this? Because that Word never went any deeper than their head. They failed to allow the Word to get into their heart and transform their lives. It is only when we allow God's Word to get into our heart that we will start acting on it, thus producing fruit.

When a person starts to act on what they have heard, a solid foundation is established. This is because they have incorporated their spirit, soul, and body into the teachings of Jesus. All three components of our being are involved in what we have heard. This reinforces the belief and causes the

Word to get inculcated into the thought processes. In essence, we grow new thoughts.

To be successful in our walk with the Lord, we must do the following:

- Come to the Word of God.
- Hear the Word of God.
- And do the Word of God.

Scripture Readings:
Luke 6:46–49
James 1:22–25

March 16

Are You Marginalizing Jesus?

Look! I stand at the door and knock. If you hear My voice and open the door, I will come in, and we will share a meal together as friends. (Revelation 3:20)

What is the first thing we do when troubles come our way? Do we call a friend or family member to bail us out? Do we find a quiet place and try to figure it out all on our own? Or do we consult the bottle or even turn to drugs? We should ask ourselves this question because it will tell us where Jesus is in our life. If we are turning to another person or thing before we turn to Jesus in prayer, then we know whom we really trust.

I am not saying anything is wrong with discussing issues with a trusted friend or relative. They can provide a different perspective and give us more of an objective view on the issue. But they are not perfect and sometimes give what is not in our best interest. Jesus, on the other hand, is the Truth (John 14:6). If we are seeking the best solution to our problem, doesn't it make sense to go to Him first? I know from my own experience, I would rather sometimes go to someone who will tell me what I want to hear rather than what I need to hear.

Sometimes we are reluctant to go to Jesus because we feel a sense of guilt and shame for the troubling circumstances we are in. We are like Adam after he disobeyed God. He and his wife ran and tried to hide themselves from God, which is a completely natural response for us as humans when we feel guilt and shame. This is because we think God's love for us is conditional, that God's love for us in contingent on our behavior. But this is not so. Jesus said that all that the Father has given Him will come to Him, and no one could snatch them away (John 10:27).

I know some believers think Jesus is not interested in their trivial problems. This couldn't be further from the truth. Jesus takes delight in those who come to Him, just like a father takes delight when his children come to him with their concerns. The problem for some people is that they didn't have that type of relationship with their earthly father, so it is hard for them to believe it when it comes to their heavenly Father. If this is the case with you, then you need to renew your mind in this area.

Jesus wants us to succeed more than we do. He understands that we will miss the mark at times. That's why He shed His blood on the cross for us. There is no condemnation for those in Christ Jesus (Romans 8:1). So don't make Jesus last on your list. How did we feel when we were a kid and we were the last to get picked for a team? It probably didn't feel good. So why would we do that to Jesus? Choose Him first whenever problems arise. He is more than faithful to meet our needs.

Scripture Readings:
John 10:22–30
Revelation 3:20
1 Peter 5:6

March 17

Are You a Pioneer of Your Future or a Prisoner of Your Past?

This means that anyone who belongs to Christ has become a new person. The old life is gone; a new life has begun! (2 Corinthians 5:17)

Is your past keeping you from your future? Are you reluctant to try again because of the past failures you may have had? Do you talk yourself out of opportunities because of the fear of rejection or failure? If you answered yes to any of the above questions, then you need to consider this: God has created you to be successful (Philippians 4:13). God has caused everything you put your hand on to prosper (Deuteronomy 28:6). The key to moving forward is forgetting the past. You can't allow past mistakes, guilt, and heartbreaks to keep you from a brighter future.

The apostle Paul is a good example of this. Before his conversion, he was responsible for persecuting the church. But when he realized that he was a new creation in Christ Jesus, he chose not to dwell on his past. Instead, he focused on the future and the purpose and plan God had for him. Many people drag themselves down because of the negative and toxic thoughts in their past, which only leads to fear and prevents them from moving forward.

In the sports world the great athletes have learned to have a short memory. This means that when they blow a play, they don't dwell on it and wonder what they could have done differently. If they did, the chances of them doing it again would be great. Instead, they immediately dismiss that negative thought and replace it with a positive one. Each of us should learn to do the same thing in our own lives. We are to forget those things in our past and look to the future before our future passes us by.

Scripture Readings:
Deuteronomy 28:6, 8
2 Corinthians 5:7
Philippians 2:12–13

March 18

THE BATTLE IS HIS, NOT YOURS

The Lord will conquer your enemies when they attack you. They will attack you from one direction, but they will scatter from you in seven! (Deuteronomy 28:7)

We have a covenant of protection with God. We have access to angels to assist us when we are under attack from the enemy. But, in order to experience this protection, we have to call upon them according to the Word of God. The angels harken to voice of God's commands (Psalm 103:20). This means that when we speak the covenant promise written in the Word of God, the angels of heaven respond. They are assigned to minister to those who are believers (Hebrews 1:14). Many believers are unaware of this covenant right and are destroyed because of their ignorance (Hosea 4:6).

When we feel threatened, our natural instinct is to lash out in the flesh. However, the Bible teaches us that our fight isn't against flesh and blood, but against spiritual forces in the heavenly realms (Ephesians 6:12). We should therefore do battle in the spiritual realm. We are called to use the Word of God to fight. We are to call on the assistance of the angels, and then stand back and watch our enemies flee from before us.

In the War of 1812 against the British, the United States was on the brink of defeat. The British troops had marched into the nation's capital, and they set fire to all of the government buildings, including the White House. Suddenly a fierce storm came in, putting the fire out at the White House. The storm was so fierce that houses were blown off their foundations, and it actually killed many of the British soldiers who sought refuge from the storm. Then several tornadoes hit, forcing the British troops out of the city. This was the turning point in the war. President James Monroe stated in his Inaugural Address, "Except the Lord keep the city, the watchman waketh in vain."

This event was unexplainable. It was in the summer. Prior to the storm coming, there was not a cloud in the sky. This is a clear example of how God intervenes in the lives of those who call upon His name. We might think that this happened coincidentally, and that's our choice to believe. However, I choose to believe that this is an example of the faithfulness of our God in keeping His covenant of protection.

Scripture Readings:
Psalm 34:6–7; 91:4; 103:20
Ephesians 6:12
Hebrews 1:14

March 19

RESPONSIBILITY AND YOUR SUCCESS

Those who hear the warnings of this curse should not congratulate themselves, thinking, "I am safe, even though I am following the desires of my own stubborn heart." This would lead to utter ruin! (Deuteronomy 29:19)

There was a man who got a dog to protect his property. He trained the dog to attack anyone who stepped within the boundaries of his property without his permission. This man made sure that there were signs on the fence that said BEWARE OF DOG. One day a man was walking home from work and it started to rain, so he decided to take a shortcut through the property. He saw the sign that warned of the dog but he thought he would take his chances just to make it home quicker. So he hopped the fence. Moments later, the dog saw the man and chased him, biting him in the butt and ripping his pants. The owner of the dog rescued the man from further injury.

Who do you think was responsible for this incident? How you answer this question tells me how responsible you are. If you answered by stating the dog, the rain, or the owner of the dog, I would know that you are a person who likes to blame others for your misfortunes. You are a person who has a victim mentality and an external locus of control. And I would furthermore think you are a person who has a tendency to be self-centered, with poor boundaries.

Are there believers who display these characteristics? Yes. Are these believers displaying the characteristics of Jesus? Of course not. Are they walking in the Spirit or in their flesh? What is the point to all of this? We can be a believer, but if we don't understand the principles of responsibility, our effectiveness in the Kingdom of God will be limited. Most people who are successful in life are people who understand what it means to be responsible. Each of us are responsible for our own thoughts, words, and actions. If we understand this, then we are on the road to empowerment.

Scripture Readings:
Deuteronomy 30:15, 19
Galatians 6:7

March 20

No Limits with God

Now all glory to God, who is able, through His mighty power at work within us, to accomplish infinitely more than we might ask or think. (Ephesians 3:20)

Sometimes we can be our own worst enemy. How often have we had a dream or vision for something we wanted to accomplish, and we talked ourselves out of it? We told ourselves that we are not talented enough, smart enough, or good looking enough. So we settled for being mediocre instead of pressing into our dreams.

We sometimes allow our parents to determine how far we can go in life as well. If our parents engrained in our thinking that we would never achieve anything in life, and we accept that, then we probably never will. Sometimes, society or culture sets how far we can go in life. We each have a choice, whether to accept the limitations that others try to impose on us or reject them.

At one time it was thought that it was physically impossible for a man to run a mile in less than four minutes. Those who accepted this as truth never attempted it and never tried to dispel the myth. However, there was one man who challenged this so-called truth. He dared to imagine outside the boundary. Roger Bannister knew a person was capable of running a mile in less than four minutes. He trained for this feat, and on May 6, 1954, he ran the mile in 3:59.4. He had broken the barrier that others thought could not be broken. His record only lasted forty-six days. Now the record for the mile is 3:43.

God has not created us to conform to being mediocre. He has given us the ability to achieve whatever we desire. There are no limits with God! The only limits that we have are the ones we place on ourselves. Did you know that your brain has the capacity of holding 300 million years of information? No computer can do that. Just image the things you are capable of. Don't disregard those visions and dreams, because maybe God has given them to you. And remember nothing is impossible for those who believe!

Scripture Readings:
Genesis 11:6
Mark 9:23
Luke 1:37

March 21

A Blessing Blocker

Oh, the joys of those who do not follow the advice of the wicked, or stand around with sinners, or join in with mockers. But they delight in the law of the Lord, meditating on it day and night. They are like trees planted along the riverbank, bearing fruit each season. Their leaves never wither, and they prosper in all they do. (Psalm 1:1–3)

How much time do we spend listening to people who are cynical and skeptical? Do we find ourselves repeating what they believe to be the truth? Maybe that's the reason we are not experiencing the blessings of the Lord in our life. It's not what we say on Sunday that counts, but what we are saying Monday–Saturday. Many believers are good at putting on a façade of spirituality, but their personal lives don't reflect the true depths of it. They say all the right things, but their lives are filled with chaos and confusion.

There is a reason for this incongruence, and it is spending more time with the world than with God. Jesus taught in the parable of the sower about how the sower sows the Word, but some seeds get choked by the weeds and never produce a crop. He later explained that the cares of the world and the lust for other things come in and stop the Word from producing fruit in their lives. In this parable, the seed is the Word of God, and the soil is our heart. It is possible for someone to accept the Word without it ever maturing if they allow themselves to be distracted.

We have to not only hear the Word but also meditate on it. This allows it to get into our heart so it can produce a great harvest. If a person spends a majority of their day listening to negative conversations, and watching shows that are contrary to what they believe, it will have an impact on their spiritual life. Their heart will be conflicted and this will cause discord within them. Ultimately, this discord will manifest in their lives.

I am not saying that we should not go to the movies, watch television, or listen to music. What I am saying is that we need to use discretion with what we are watching, and monitor how much time we spend consuming it. If it exceeds the time we spend with God, then we might want to correct that. The choice is ours.

Scripture Readings:
Proverbs 4:20–23
Mark 4:13–20
Luke 8:9–15

March 22

How Accountability Can Help

The Lord our God has secrets known to no one. We are not accountable for them, but we are and our children are accountable forever for all that He has revealed to us, so that we may obey all the terms of these instructions. (Deuteronomy 29:29)

Have you ever had urges that you find overwhelming at times? Do you find yourself giving in to them? I would like to share something I learned to combat those urges, something I taught while I was working with the correctional department. It is a simple principle the Lord showed me one day while I was preparing to teach a class to some juvenile offenders. The Lord asked me to ask a question: What does it mean to be accountable? Very few hands went up. And those who attempted to answer the question answered it incorrectly. It was in that moment that I understood why the majority of those juveniles were incarcerated.

To be accountable simply means to give an account for our actions. This is an important concept that all parents should teach their children when they are young. If we inculcate this principle into our consciousness, we have an added weapon to assist us when we are tempted. Accountability forces us to think about the consequences of our actions, and how they will impact others. When we are tempted, many times our perspective becomes very myopic. We become self-centered and only concerned with meeting our own needs.

I don't know how many people I have counseled who have told me, "If I had realized the people I was going to hurt, I would have never done what I did." With a strong sense of accountability, a person will look at the big picture and avoid making decisions that they will later regret. I used to have my kids recite to me almost every day whom they were accountable to. They would answer, "God, my parents, and my fellowman." By doing this, I know it had an impact on them and the choices they made later in life. Both of my children are living successful and prosperous lives. Remember that the stronger the sense of accountability, the more self-control we will be able to exercise.

Scripture Readings:
Deuteronomy 29:19
Matthew 12:36
Romans 14:26
1 Peter 4:5

March 23

YOU ARE THE PROPHET OF YOUR LIFE

Wise words satisfy like a good meal; the right words bring satisfaction. The tongue can bring death or life; those who love to talk will reap the consequences. (Proverbs 18:20–21)

Have you ever noticed most people who talk a lot really don't have much to say? There also seems to be a lack of power in the words they do say. Then there are other people in whose words we feel power and energy. These people have understood the power of their words. They have learned to use their words like a tool, creating what they desire.

When God created man in the Garden of Eden, He gave him the ability to speak. Speech was given for two reasons: to communicate and to create. God created the heavens and earth by speaking faith-filled words and He has given that power to us as well. He imagined what He wanted to create through His thought, and then He spoke it into existence. We have the same ability today. We obviously don't have this ability on the same scale as God, but we have been given the same ability to create through the use of our words. Words convey our thoughts and reveal what is in our hearts (Matthew 12:34). If something is in our hearts, it will eventually come out of our mouths.

Many people sabotage themselves by speaking negative statements over their life. For example, they will say things that are contrary to what they are striving for, and then they wonder why it didn't happen. Instead of looking at themselves and examining the words they have spoken, they realize it away and quit. Others blame God by saying, "I guess it just wasn't God's will for me." If we find ourselves speaking against ourselves, this is a sign that we need to renew our mind in Christ Jesus. We need to change those negative thoughts to positive ones, and start speaking what we want instead of what we fear.

Scripture Readings:
Genesis 1:1–28
Proverbs 17:27
Ecclesiastes 10:12
Matthew 12:36
James 1:26

March 24

LET YOUR SPIRIT BE YOUR GUIDE

The Lord's light penetrates the human spirit, exposing every hidden motive. (Proverbs 20:27)

Before the fall of man, Adam was one with God in spirit. God was able to speak to him directly and download information to him through his spirit. Adam had no need for an educational system because anything he wanted or needed to know came directly from God. How do you think Adam was able to name every insect, fish, mammal, and animal on the earth if this were not so? It was God revealing His knowledge to Adam.

Once the fall occurred, however, Adam became spiritually separated from God. He no longer had the ability to communicate with Him on a spiritual level. Adam was limited to his five physical senses to teach him. His ability to receive revelation from God had been short-circuited. His ability to discern was impaired. To deal with this, humanity created an educational system based on the five physical senses—on logic and empirical evidence. That's why the Bible says that we cannot understand the things of the Spirit with human wisdom, lest they seem foolishness to us (1 Corinthians 2:10–16).

Once a person has been born again, however, their spirit is once again reconnected to the Spirit of God, and they have the ability to receive from Him. The challenge for them becomes allowing their human spirit to guide them instead of their natural mind. Their mind wants to lead and make decisions based purely on the information it has received through our senses and past experiences. It feels comfortable making decisions based on logical information alone. However, when it receives information from the spirit that is contrary to logical thinking, it rebels. At that point, the believer must make a decision between following their mind and following their spirit. This decision occurs in their heart (Hebrews 4:12).

It is important that we reeducate our mind so that our spirit and mind can be in one accord. Once there is agreement between the spirit and mind, there is nothing a person cannot accomplish. We can fulfill what God has designed for us to do. We can manifest His glory so others can see Jesus in our being. I hope this motivates you today, placing a desire within you to allow your born-again spirit to guide you.

Scripture Readings:
Romans 12:1–2
1 Corinthians 2:16
Ephesians 4:23

March 25

FAITH BASED ON THE SENSES

For we live by believing and not by seeing. (2 Corinthians 5:7)

Everyone operates in faith whether they realize it or not. When a person goes to work, they go with the expectation that they will be compensated for their labor. They have faith that at the end of the pay period they will receive their salary and have money in the bank. When a person books a hotel room, they have faith that the room will be reserved and available for them when it is time to check in. What is their faith based on? In both cases their faith is based on past experience or some form of written or verbal agreement. These are examples of faith based on sense knowledge.

When Jesus performed miracles, such as feeding five thousand people with two fish and five loaves of bread, people believed because of what they saw and the food they ate. This too is faith based on the senses. When someone limits himself or herself to just having faith based on what they can see, feel, hear, or touch, they are operating in natural faith. If we are a believer, we have the capacity to operate in a much higher level of faith. As a believer we can operate in a faith that does not need information from the senses. We have the ability to operate in the God kind of faith.

The God kind of faith has no limits—the physical laws of nature do not restrict it because it operates on a higher law. Just like the laws of lift and thrust cause a plane to fly, defying the law of gravity, so the law of faith defies the laws of the natural. Jesus understood this and demonstrated what was possible for those who operated on the same principles (John 14:12). I know this may seem a little out there for some of us, but Jesus wouldn't have reprimanded His disciples on numerous occasions for their lack of faith if they weren't capable of doing what Jesus asked of them. A loving God wouldn't do that.

To operate in this kind of faith, we have to renew our mind. The Bible says that faith comes by hearing and hearing by the Word of God (Romans

10:17). I would encourage each of us to read the myriad of examples of people who operated in the God kind of faith. Read books and listen to those who operate in the God kind of faith and our faith will continue to grow. I don't know about you, but I want to operate in this level of faith and be a person who pleases God (Hebrews 11:6).

Scripture Readings:
Mark 9:23; 11:23–24
John 14:12
2 Corinthians 5:7

March 26

SLEEP AND YOUR HEALTH

In peace I will lie down and sleep, for You alone,
O Lord, will keep me safe. (Psalm 4:8)

Today I want to discuss the benefits of a good night's sleep. I will begin by telling you a story. One night I didn't sleep well. I woke up several times during the night; I was restless, so I decided to get up. I began writing this book and finished what I wanted to accomplish. Later during the day, I noticed that I felt agitated and my mood was negative. I thought that it was a satanic attack, so I got into the Word and watched some of my favorite Bible teachers on television. Instead of getting better, it only got worse. I decided that I would watch some comedy to lift my mood. That didn't work either. Suddenly, I heard a small voice within me saying, "You need to go to bed." I ignored it because I thought it was too early. But I finally gave in and went to bed.

Within moments I was fast asleep. When I woke up the next morning, I felt refreshed and energetic. It was then that I realized that what I thought was a satanic attack against me was just a lack of sleep. My mind and my body were tired, and that was the reason for my moodiness. Sometimes we give the devil too much credit. Some of the problems we experience are due to our own doings, not the devil's doings.

Sleep is vital to our health. It is during sleep that our brain releases chemicals such as growth hormones. It is during stage four sleep that our brain is revitalized and many of the issues we faced during the day are worked out. When I have something I can't figure out, I go to sleep with the expectation that I will have the answer when I wake up. And guess what? The answer will be there waiting for me when I open my eyes.

It is during sleep that our brain is able to detox itself. When we are dreaming, the brain and body are exchanging information and glial cells (support cells in the brain), and are cleaning up our memory networks. It is during this period of sleep where things we learned are ingrained in our memory, and we obtain a better understanding of the subject matter. So sleep has many benefits.

If you have problems sleeping, I would suggest you take to the Word of God. God promises that He will give His people a good night's sleep. Instead of staying up all night worrying, just go to sleep knowing that God will give you the answer when you wake up. Trust Him for He will work it all out while we rest.

Scripture Readings:
Job 4:12–13
Psalm 4:8; 127:2
Ecclesiastes 5:12

March 27

GOD WILL NOT OVERRULE YOUR DESIRE

Take delight in the Lord, and He will give you your heart's desire. (Psalm 37:4)

One day not too long ago I was reading *Foxe's Book of Martyrs*. This is a must read for anyone who is serious about their faith and wants to go deeper. It gives the reader the history of the faith from the crucifixion of Jesus up to the twentieth century, showing how the enemy through religion has compromised and secularized the gospel of Jesus Christ. It also shows the conviction of those who give their lives to ensure that the message of the gospel was not compromised but continued on throughout the centuries.

Some of these people, such as John Wycliffe, John Huss, and William Tyndale, were persecuted, tortured, and killed for the faith. Others suffered horrific deaths such as being burned on a wooden stake. I often asked God why He didn't save them. All of them had strong faith, so I know that wasn't the problem. Then God told me that it was because of their desire to die for Him. They actually considered it an honor to die for God, like Jesus did.

Then I understood that God would not overrule our desires. It is God's will that all people be saved, but He will not force us to do anything unless we choose for Him to do it. We have more power than we think. God will not stand in the way of our desire, even if it is to our detriment. If God warns us not to be involved with such and such a person, and we decide that we can't live without them, then God will not stand in our way. But know that there will be a price to pay. That price will be that we will not be in God's will.

There are many believers who have been led astray by their desires and have suffered the consequences of their choices. It does not mean that God has given up on them, but it is true that one reaps what they sow. This is a universal principle that cannot be changed. There are believers who are crippled by their addictions, living lives far below what God desires for them, because God will not overrule their desires.

What we desire is extremely important. So we need to be careful what we put before our eyes, for they are the gateway to our heart, and our heart creates our desires.

Scripture Readings:
Genesis 3:6
Psalm 1:2; 37:4; 103:5
Mark 4:19
1 Corinthians 10:6
Galatians 5:17

March 28

Your Treasure and Your Heart

Wherever your treasure is, there the desires of your heart will also be. (Matthew 6:21)

One of the reasons why some people have a distant relationship with the Lord is because there is no room for Him in their hearts. They are consumed with obtaining fame, status, wealth, and pleasure. They are like the rich young ruler who sought after Jesus and wanted be a part of His movement. However, when Jesus told him that he would have to give up his riches, he suddenly changed his mind (Mark 10:17–23). It was sad, because this man really could have been an asset to the Kingdom of God.

Like so many others who have walked away from the faith, desire for other things came in and took them away. It is important that we are careful what we place our eyes on, because we see *with* our mind but see *through* our eyes. It is our perceptions that make things attractive or repulsive to us. Have you seen someone or something that at first glance didn't attract you, but after a period of time you found it attractive? Or sometimes the very opposite happens. The object or person didn't change, but your perception changed.

The same principle applies with the Word of God. The more time we spend with it, the more we will desire that which is godly. If we treasure the Word and fellowship with God, it will eventually get into our hearts. Once this occurs, we will desire reading the Word and actually find delight in doing so.

The same goes with prayer too. I used to pray only because I knew that I should. My prayers at that time were as short as possible. But over a period of time, I have grown to enjoy prayer. In fact, I would not even consider not praying during the day. Times when I am unable to pray in the morning, I feel uneasy about my whole day. We must be careful what we place before our eyes because our heart will surely follow.

Scripture Readings:
Matthew 6:20–21; 12:35; 13:52

March 29

TAKING RELIGION OUT OF PRAYER

Don't worry about anything; instead, pray about everything. Tell God what you need, and thank Him for all He has done. Then you will experience God's peace, which exceeds anything we can understand. His peace will guard your hearts and minds as you live in Christ Jesus. (Philippians 4:6–7)

For many years I thought prayer had a certain format that had to be followed in order to be effective. When I heard people pray at church, they sounded pious and religious, so I naturally thought I was not righteous enough to pray to God. Then when I started praying, I tried to emulate what I heard at church. This made prayer uncomfortable for me. It wasn't until I read and understood the above Scripture that I began to pray with comfort and confidence.

Thanking God is important to remember as we seek to deepen our prayer life. When we pray for something, we have to believe that we receive it the moment we ask for it (Mark 11:23–24). This requires faith. As the Scripture says, it pleases God when we approach Him in faith (Hebrews 11:6). Once we ask in faith, we can't look for signs that our prayers have been answered; instead, we need to begin to thank God that He answered our prayer.

When we do this, our brain begins to release chemicals that produce a feeling of peace in our mind and body. Those anxious thoughts are erased and replaced with positive ones. Scientific studies show that prayer and being spiritually active increases frontal lobe activity, thickness, intelligence, and overall health. So there are many benefits to prayer. Prayer is simply just talking to God like we would to anyone else. Find a quiet place where you can have a one-on-one conversation with Him.

Don't make prayer a religious exercise, but talk to God like you would a trusted friend. We can pray for as long or as short as we want. I used to think that I had to pray for at least one hour until I read a book about Smith Wigglesworth, a great man of God, who only prayed for fifteen minutes at a time. So we can determine how long we should pray for on a daily basis. Since it is a relationship with Him, some days may be long and others may be short.

In conclusion, prayer is communication with God. If we have things that we need to confess, needs that we want fulfilled, or answers to a problem, then we can simply go to God with them. But we need to go with the expectation that our prayer or request will be answered because He loves to communicate with us.

Scripture Readings:
John 14:13; 15:7; 16:23–24
Mark 11:23–24
Philippians 4:6–7
1 John 5:14

March 30

SEEING IS NOT REALLY BELIEVING

So we don't look at the troubles we can see now; rather, we fix our gaze on things that cannot be seen. For the things we see now will soon be gone, but the things we cannot see will last forever. (2 Corinthians 4:18)

What do we focus on when we are faced with challenges? Do we find ourselves focusing more on the problem than the solution? When a person chooses to focus on the problem rather than the solution, they are giving the problem the control. Once this occurs, a downward spiral begins to be set in motion. Toxic thoughts are created, causing discord within the individual. The amygdala gets active and stress hormones are released, raising the blood pressure and heart rate.

Because the individual is in fight or flight mode, their limbic system requires more blood, so blood that would normally go to the brain is now diverted to the person's limbs. This causes an individual not to think clearly and poor choices are then made. This is why it is important to meditate on the promises of God daily—when trouble comes we will be prepared to fight it with the Word.

As many of us already know, as long as we are on this earth there will be challenges. No one is immune to hard times. It is not the challenge that determines our fate, however; it is our reaction to the challenge that makes the difference. When hardship comes our way, don't freak out. Instead, we are to speak to it with the authority that Christ has given to us. Find Scriptures like, "But thank God! He gives us victory over sin and death through our Lord Jesus Christ" (1 Corinthians 15:57).

By meditating on the promises of God, we develop our spiritual eyes that can see beyond the circumstances we are currently in. But if we don't spend time in the Word, we will have poor spiritual eyesight. We will only be able to see in the physical realm. That is the difference between men and women of great faith, and the average believer. God doesn't have favorites. It is us who determine how successful our walk with the Lord will be. So see your issues through the eyes of faith and get your victory today!

Scripture Readings:
Isaiah 43:1–3; 54:17
Jeremiah 17:7–8
Romans 8:31–37

March 31

ARE YOU GETTING YOUR IMAGE FROM GOD OR TELEVISION?

Your eye is a lamp that provides light for your body. When your eye is good, your whole body is filled with light. But when your eye is bad, your whole body is filled with darkness. (Matthew 6:22–23)

Did you know that the average American spends an average of five hours and eleven minutes watching television per day? It is also reported that 99 percent of American households own at least one television. On the average, a person will watch approximately nine years of television in their lifetime. Children spend approximately 1,480 hours per week in front of the television, compared to 900 hours in the classroom. What is also alarming is that by the age of eighteen our youth have witnessed more than 150,000 acts of violence on the screen. No wonder there is so much violence in our schools and society today.

Television is being used to shape our beliefs and opinions. It is an effective tool to pacify and control the masses. When a person watches television, they are induced into a state of catatonia, which is particularly true with children. I remember as a parent I would use the television as a babysitter to keep my kids occupied while I did things around the home. I didn't realize the harmful effects television had on the automatic nervous system. Because of the nature of the light that comes from the television, it causes a shift in our visual and auditory reception. This, in combination with media-induced startle effect, causes our brain to release hormones that cause the body to go into fight or flight mode. Once this happens, adrenaline and cortisol are released into the blood, causing an increase in heart rate and blood pressure.

That's why most of the television shows are so violent and scary. People are addicted. Their senses have been dulled so they need more explosions, more violence, and more suspense to satisfy their cravings. The sad thing is that most people don't even realize it. What's even sadder is that the average

American only spends twenty minutes per day reading. Do you think that might be a reason for the decline in the educational system?

I am not saying that I am against television by any means. Television can be used for good as well as for evil. There are many educational programs that can benefit our spiritual lives. It is an effective tool to get the Word of God preached to the world. What I am saying, however, is that we should consider the ratio of time we spend in front of the television to the time we spend with God. I want God to create my vision, not the television.

Scripture Readings:
Proverbs 4:20–23
Matthew 6:22
Luke 11:34

April 1

WHAT DO YOU DO WHEN YOU CAN'T TAKE ANYMORE?

David was now in great danger because all his men were very bitter about losing their sons and daughters, and they began to talk of stoning him. But David found strength in the Lord his God. (1 Samuel 30:6)

Have you ever had a time when you were just at your wits' end? Maybe it was a project you have been working on that fell apart. Or maybe it was a relationship that was not working out. Maybe you are in an abusive relationship and it doesn't seem to be getting better; or your boss or co-worker could be harassing you. I don't care who you are or what situation you are currently in, someone has been in that situation before. Did you drown your sorrows with drugs or alcohol? Did you act out by doing something outside of your character? Or did you go into a state of depression?

These are all things we tend do when we feel hopeless—it's the natural man's way of dealing with things. Each of us has another man on the inside (2 Corinthians 4:16). And it is our inner man that has the answer to our problem. In times like these, we need to remind ourselves there is no such thing as hopelessness in the Kingdom of God. If we are a believer, then we are a citizen of the Kingdom of heaven, and there is nothing impossible for those who believe. No matter what the circumstance is telling us, nothing is impossible with God (Mark 9:23).

In the book of 1 Samuel, David was in dire straits. His enemies had raided the Israelites' camp while they were away on a mission, burning it down, taking all their livestock, women, and children. David and his men were obviously distraught. David's men were so upset with him that they spoke of stoning him to death. Instead of having a pity party, however, David got away and found strength in the Lord. He reminded himself of the promises of God and his past victories.

The situation didn't change, but David did. The man who was once distraught and felt hopeless was suddenly filled with hope. His attitude completely changed. And the men who once spoke of stoning him rallied to his side. With the assistance of the Holy Spirit, David and his men were able to recover all they had lost. We should learn a lesson from this story. Sometimes we need to look with our spiritual eyes to find the answers to our problems. So strengthen yourself in the Lord today.

Scripture Readings:
John 16:33
2 Corinthians 4:16
1 John 5:4

April 2

THE HARDENED HEART

Listen! A farmer went out to plant some seeds. As he scattered them across his field, some seeds fell on a footpath, and the birds came and ate them. (Matthew 13:3–4)

One of ways Jesus taught was through the use of parables. Parables are a great way of illustrating a truth in a way people can understand, because it is something they can relate to in their everyday world. In the parable of the sower, Jesus teaches on how the condition of a person's heart determines how they will receive what was sown. This parable can be used on so many different levels. I want to look at this parable today, however, from a perspective you may not have considered before.

The farmer in this illustration is Jesus, the seeds are His teaching or the Word of God, and the soil is the human heart. For us, the farmer may be our pastor, teacher, mentor, or parent. The seed is still the Word of God, and the heart is still the same. When a person hears the Word of God, and it is something that they don't understand, there is a tendency to dismiss it. For example, there are some people who have been taught that healing stopped with the apostles in the book of Acts. If we went to a church that taught this, what do we think our response would be if we heard someone preaching that Jesus heals today? We would most likely harden our heart and not receive this Word. Or if we went to a church that taught speaking in tongues was of the devil, how would we react to someone who started speaking in tongues? We probably wouldn't receive what they had to say. Why? Because our heart would be hardened.

We can have our hearts hardened to certain aspects of the Spirit of God. Some believers don't think the prosperity message has any place in the church today, so they don't prosper on the level God has provided for them. Some believers don't think healing is available for the church today, so they don't experience the miraculous healings that are available through the finished work of Jesus.

To avoid having a hard heart, we need to search the Scriptures on our own, asking God to give us understanding if we don't understand what was said. We need to ask God to open the eyes of our understanding so that we may see all that He has made available to us through the finished work of Jesus Christ.

Scripture Readings:
Matthew 13:18
Ephesians 1:16–18; 3:16–18

April 3

ARE YOU HEARING OR LISTENING TO THE WORD?

The seed on the rocky soil represents those who hear the message and immediately receive it with joy. But since they don't have deep roots, they don't last long. They fall away as soon as they have problems or are persecuted for believing God's word. (Matthew 13:20–21)

Today we are going to discuss the second type of soil. Jesus described a soil that was rocky. He said that this type of soil is where the seed would spring up for a little while, but it would not yield a harvest because it had shallow roots. This is the category that a majority of believers fall into today. They go to church, hear the message, and are excited about it. They walk out of church feeling good about what they heard, but if we were to ask them what the message was the following day, they probably couldn't tell us.

Most of our megachurches are like this. They provide music that is entertaining and a message that is pleasant and seeker friendly. Their goal is to get as many people to attend the service as possible. There is nothing wrong with having good music or providing seeker friendly messages, doing whatever they can to get people in the door and hear the gospel, but I have noticed that this type of church demonstrates very little spiritual power. All their efforts seem to be more humanistic.

Then there are those churches that focus on the emotional needs of the congregation. They confuse emotionalism with the Holy Spirit. They work themselves up into an emotional frenzy and think that it is the Holy Spirit moving them, but there are no physical manifestations of the Spirit, just a lot of yelling, dancing, and sweating. Believers who attend this type of church are seeking an emotional high. They are like spiritual junkies looking for a fix. The preacher has become their spiritual dealer, providing them with their spiritual drug for the week. There is usually very little substance to the message, but the oratory is fantastic.

The enemy doesn't mind churches like these because they pose little threat to his kingdom. He doesn't like the fact that these churches are taking away some of his potential clientele, but he can keep them confined. Besides that, the enemy knows that because they don't develop deep roots in their beliefs, he can get most of them back with a little persecution. Just looking back on my own Christian walk, a majority of those I went to church with are no longer walking with the Lord because they had shallow roots.

How do we avoid having shallow roots? It is by not just hearing the Word of God but by actually listening to it. When we listen to something we are focusing our full attention on it; we are listening with our whole being. When we are only hearing something, we are not focusing our attention on it. Life is like being in a room of crowded people—we can hear all the conversations going on, but we are not focused on any of them. In order to determine whether we are listening or hearing the message at church, try to recall what the message was a day later. If we can't recall it, then that should tell us that we are only hearing it, not really listening to it. Let us not be hearers only, but doers of the Word too.

Scripture Readings:
James 1:22–25

April 4

Is Your Walk a Fruitful One?

The seed that fell among the thorns represents those who hear God's word, but all too quickly the message is crowded out by the worries of this life and the lure of wealth, so no fruit is produced. (Matthew 13:22)

Today we're going to talk about the seed that was planted among the thorns. Most believers fall into either the rocky soil category or the seed that fell among thorns category. The difference between the two is that those who are planted among the thorns have roots, which means they have spiritual understanding, but they don't produce much fruit because they get distracted with the cares of life.

These types of believers enjoy church and are active listeners, but they are not consistent in their attendance. They might go weeks without attending a church service or studying the Word of God for themselves because they are busy doing other things. They might allow their work schedule to get in the way, or they might have recreational events that are more of a priority for them. Some allow the anxieties of life to distract them from spending quality time with the Word of God. Others allow their community activities to get in the way.

On the surface of all these activities, there is nothing inherently wrong with any of them, as long as they are put in the right order. We need to give God and His Word first priority in our life. If He is in the first place, then all the other things will flow much more easily in our lives (Matthew 6:33). The enemy specializes in presenting things to distract our attention away from the things of God.

This world's system is designed to get and keep us in debt by creating dissatisfaction with the things we already have. Their strategy is to make us believe that the phone we have is obsolete, and we need a better one, or that television doesn't have as many pixels as the newer one, or how we need this car if we want to be noticed by the people around us. All this is designed to make our wants our needs, getting us to buy things we know we can't afford.

God is a God of abundance. If we seek His Kingdom He will make sure that all our needs and wants are taken care of without the added stress attached (Proverbs 10:22). In conclusion, put the Word of God at the top of your list as a priority for each day. Make sure you give time every day to meditate on the Word and prayer, and your walk will be a more fruitful one.

Scripture Readings:
Proverbs 10:22
Matthew 6:25–34; 13:22

April 5

Hearing with Understanding Produces a Harvest

The seed that fell on good soil represents those who truly hear and understand God's word and produce a harvest of thirty, sixty, or a hundred times as much as had been planted. (Matthew 13:23)

Yesterday we discussed the seed that fell among the weeds and thorns, which represent the distractions of this world—anxiety, concerns, pleasures, or the pursuit of wealth. All of these can be used to distract our attention away from spending quality time with God and His Word. We found that the way to prevent this is to seek the Kingdom of God first. Today we are going to look at the seed that fell on good soil.

The soil represents our heart, or our inner man. When we hear the Word and understand it, our hearts are ready to receive it. What determines the crop that will be produced depends on how much time we spend meditating on and speaking the Word of God. Meditating and speaking are like fertilizer and water to our hearts (Romans 10:17). They reinforce what we have chosen to believe and they help to keep the weeds out.

Praise and thanksgiving are a good way to ensure that our manifestation comes to fruition. It is easy to get discouraged. When this happens, there is a tendency to allow negative thoughts to enter our minds, which causes unbelief. To combat this, we need to speak to those thoughts and erase them through speaking the promises of God over our lives. We need to speak what we want to happen instead of what we fear might happen. We have to learn to see with the eyes of our faith (2 Corinthians 5:7). This is not an easy thing to do, but with practice we will develop in this area.

What is interesting is that out of all the seeds that were planted, only 25 percent produced a crop. And only 8.3 percent produced a hundred-fold return. This just shows that it is possible that out of all the believers who receive a hundred-fold return, 92 percent won't. What group do we want to be in, the 75 percent, 25 percent, or the 8.3 percent? It is up to us, the way we choose to hear and understand. According to our faith, so be it.

Scripture Readings:
Joshua 1:8
Psalm 1:2–3
Proverbs 4:20–23
2 Corinthians 5:7

April 6

A Summary of the Four Types of Soil

Jesus also said, "The Kingdom of God is like a farmer who scatters seed on the ground. Night and day, while he's asleep or awake, the seed sprouts and grows, but he does not understand how it happens." (Mark 4:26–27)

If we are honest with ourselves, we can say that we have had all the conditions of the soil present in our own hearts that are described by Jesus. There are some believers who have hardened their heart to certain doctrines taught in the Scriptures. There are some who are highly developed in sanctification, but don't believe in the message of healing. There are others who are highly developed in the gifts of the Spirit, but feel that sanctification doesn't apply to them. There are some believers who are highly developed in the prosperity message, but find no place for sanctification. Then there are those whose focus is on salvation only. In all those cases, these believers have hardened their hearts to the *full* gospel of Jesus Christ. Their spiritual walk is out of balance.

Then there are times where we have failed to allow the Word we heard to penetrate our heart. We received the Word with joy, but then we let it slip away. We all have heard a message that we enjoyed and got something out of it at the moment, but when we tried to recall the message we couldn't do it. To avoid this from happening, we should take notes on messages that apply to us. This will ensure that it will not slip away a day or two later.

There are times when we have let the cares of this life, and the pleasures of other things, crowd out of our hearts the Word of God. There is nothing wrong with enjoying this life—that's what God put us here for. But some people allow the pleasures and cares of this life to overwhelm them, and God has to take a backseat. Others allow their financial concerns to consume them. Instead of trusting God to meet their needs, they work themselves to death by working two or three jobs or look for all the overtime they can possibly get. This not only impacts their time with God, but their family suffers because of their absence in the home.

Finally, there are times when we receive the Word and meditate on it and understand it. When this occurs, the Word germinates in our hearts and produces a crop, some thirty-, some sixty-, and some a hundred-fold return, depending on how much time we spend in speaking and meditating on it. We determine our crop by the amount of Word we plant in our hearts. It is interesting that only 25 percent of the believers produced a crop, and only 8.3 percent received a hundred-fold return. God doesn't have favorites. If you want to receive God's best, make up your mind that you are going to be part of the 8.3 percent!

Scripture Readings:
Mark 4:10–29
Psalm 1:2–3
Joshua 1:8

April 7

ARE YOU LIVING IN THE LAND OF GOSHEN OR EGYPT?

> *But this time I will spare the region of Goshen, where My people live. No flies will be found there. Then you will know that I am the Lord and that I am present even in the heart of your land. I will make a clear distinction between My people and your people. (Exodus 8:22–23)*

Like in the time of Moses, God wants to make a clear distinction between those who belong to Him and those who belong to the world. God wants each of us to live in the land of Goshen. In the land of Goshen, the children of Israel were spared from the plagues the Egyptians experienced. If God was able to distinguish between the people, then He can do the same thing for us in our day. When the world is talking about recession and economic depression, we should be looking for economic opportunity.

The Scriptures say that we have overcome the world (1 John 5:4–5). God wants His people to prosper so that we can magnify His glory to the world. In the book of Joshua, it says that all the Amorite and Canaanite kings were paralyzed with fear because they heard how God had dried up the Jordan River to allow the children of Israel to cross (Joshua 5:1). These kings knew that God was with the children of Israel.

We as believers are God's children. He is with us today, and there should be a distinction in our lives as well. When everyone else is talking about lack and fear, we should be as bold as lions walking in prosperity. We should be the people the world comes to for answers. We should be the head and not the tail (Deuteronomy 28:13). This is what God desires for His people.

Don't allow the enemy to deceive you any longer. Don't accept being the tail instead of the head. Don't rationalize that you will get your rewards in heaven, but in this life you must suffer. Jesus suffered enough on the cross, so why do you think you must suffer also? Renew your mind and see yourself as more than a conqueror in Christ Jesus (John 16:33). See yourself as God sees you today, and you will be a light to others.

Scripture Readings:
Jeremiah 29:11; 33:9
Isaiah 43:7
1 Peter 2:9
1 John 5:4

April 8

THE ONLY POWER HE HAS IS DECEPTION

In this way, He disarmed the spiritual rulers and authorities. He shamed them publicly by His victory over them on the cross. (Colossians 2:15)

Folklore and Hollywood have done a great job at portraying Satan as an all-powerful ominous being. This image has been accepted as truth among many; even believers have been deceived by this depiction. Many believers walk in fear of what they think Satan can do to them. However, the Word of God gives us a different picture of our nemesis. I think Satan enjoys this image that the world has created of him because it allows him to go undetected.

According to the Scriptures, Satan's only power is that of deception. It says in the book of Revelation that he has deceived the whole world (Revelation 12:9). Deception is a powerful weapon because once it's acted upon it takes on a life of its own. It is like a snowball rolling down a hill, collecting snow and gaining momentum. All Satan wants is for us to take the bait, and once that is done, his job is finished. He can just sit back and watch the show. For example, when Eve took the fruit from the tree of knowledge of good and evil, did it stop there? No. She gave some of the fruit to her husband. As a result, Satan became the god of this world and sin has affected the whole of humanity ever since.

Was Satan directly responsible for Adam willfully violating the command God had given him? No, Adam did it on his own volition. That is how he works. He will instigate and tempt, then sit back and watch. We can see this being played out in people's lives today. Being involved in the criminal justice system, I have seen many people who have fell prey to his deceptions. The king of deception played them.

Satan can appear as an angel of light to deceive believers (2 Corinthians 11:14). He can transform himself into the best idea or experience an individual has ever seen. With his words he can seduce, making wrong seem right. He has the ability to make something look so desirable and good that a person will put up no resistance and fall into his trap. We can plainly see this in Genesis 3:6.

According to one ancient I read, the tree of knowledge of good and evil was ignored until Satan made it look attractive. His tactics haven't changed. How many people have left their spouses for someone they thought was better and later regretted it? How many people have violated their morals to pursue that brass ring that promised them happiness? We don't have to fall prey to the enemy. We only need to be aware that the only power he has is that of deception.

Scripture Readings:
Ezekiel 28:11–19
2 Corinthians 4:4; 11:14
1 John 4:4; 5:4

April 9

God's Time Is Not Your Time

And we know that God causes everything to work together for the good of those who love God and are called according to His purpose for them. (Romans 8:28)

There will be times when we will pray for something and it will appear that God has answered our prayer. However, in light of this we still find disappointment. It might be a job that we thought we were going to get. We interviewed well and it sounded like we were going to be hired, but at the last minute, due to no fault of our own, they didn't hire us and decided to go with someone else. Or it might have been a relationship we desperately wanted. We thought this was the person we had been looking for. We praised God because He answered our prayer. But all too soon we found out that they had found someone else.

In all of these scenarios, it is normal to feel disappointment and even anger. Our first response might be to point our finger at God and say, "Why did You do this to me?" I recently experienced this. I have been on a list for a kidney transplant for several years now. I had been praying that God would give me a perfectly matched kidney. Every morning I would thank Him for the kidney, and I watched my words so that I didn't contradict my prayer of thanksgiving.

Well, I finally received a call from the hospital. The transplant coordinator told me they had a possible kidney for me. I was excited to receive the good news. But I was also cautious not to say anything to anyone until I knew for certain. Later that day, I received another call from the hospital instructing me to come in and be admitted. I became excited and called my family, pastors, and friends to tell them the good news. I was finally going to get my kidney, and I would not have to do dialysis anymore!

The anticipation within me grew as I prepared for surgery. I began to visualize what life would be like without having to do dialysis. I praised

God for answering my prayer, and thanked Him for His faithfulness. I was within hours of going into the operating room when one of the doctors came in and told me that the donor kidneys were compromised, and they decided not to use them.

At first I was disappointed. I was almost willing to go through with the transplant and take my chances. But then the Holy Spirit reminded me of my prayer. I had asked for perfectly matched kidneys, and these kidneys obviously weren't perfect. I realized that God doesn't compromise in answering our prayers. Those perfect kidneys are out there and are ready for me—I just have to be patient. That's what faith is all about. It's about trusting God and having patience because His time is not always our time. His concept of time is different than ours. He sees time from a geometrical perspective, while we see it from a linear perspective. I am now more confident than ever that my perfectly matched kidney will be arriving shortly.

Scripture Readings:
James 1:3–4
1 John 5:14

April 10

How Much Time Are You Online with God?

But if you remain in Me and My words remain in you, you may ask for anything you want, and it will be granted! (John 15:7)

Do you remember the last time you tried to get on the Internet and you couldn't connect for some reason? You tried to reboot your computer, but to no avail. Then you called your service provider for assistance, where you were informed that the Internet service in your area is down. The first question you probably asked them was about how long the service was going to be down. They told you they'd have it up within the next six to eight hours. Because that is a long time, you started to get agitated because you have things to do, and you can't get them done without Internet service. That's pretty frustrating, isn't it?

Let me ask you this: How do you feel when you haven't been able to spend some quality time with God? Is there the same sense of urgency? For most people, there isn't. We have become so dependent on technology that some people wouldn't know how to live without their cell phones, laptops, or tablets. I remember when an individual had to memorize phone numbers, but nowadays it is no longer necessary. I remember being asked for my number not too long ago, and I had a problem recalling it because the cell phone does all the memorizing for me.

I recently read the Harris Interactive Poll, which reported that approximately 80 percent of adults spend at least thirteen hours a week online. And 14 percent spend twenty-four hours a week online. Contrast that to 52 percent who spend only five to thirty minutes per day reading their Bible. It seems that God is in competition with television, videos, and the Internet. There is nothing wrong with any of these things, but when we become a servant to them, that's another matter entirely. This dependency on technology can have a crippling effect upon us.

God has no problem with the use of technology. He is the One who gave us the ability to create these things. However, when this technology becomes our god, that's when the problems start. Our God is a jealous God and He does not want anyone or anything to take His place (Exodus 20:5).

Jesus said that if we remain in Him, and His words abide in us, we could ask for anything we desired and it would be granted to us. The reason why more people aren't getting their prayers answered and living the prosperous life is because they are not abiding in Jesus. They are not allowing His words to abide in them. Hearing a sermon on Sunday is not abiding and is falling far short of Jesus's intention for our lives. A branch cannot survive without being connected to the tree, and a believer cannot thrive without being connected to Jesus and His words. Being connected to Jesus through the Word of God and prayer are vital for our spiritual growth.

Scripture Readings:
Exodus 20:5
John 15:1–8

April 11

EXPECTATION: THE KEY TO MANIFESTATION

For everyone who asks, receives. Everyone who seeks, finds. And everyone who knocks, the door will be opened. (Luke 11:10)

Have you ever had someone throw you a ball you weren't expecting to catch? Most people didn't catch the ball because they were not ready to receive it. Having the expectation to receive a ball thrown to us greatly enhances our ability to catch the ball because we are prepared to receive it. When I played running back in football, every time I would get the ball I expected to gain yards, and most of the time I did.

Well, it is much the same with the things of God. When we pray for something, what is our expectation level? Are we confident that we will receive, or are we kind of ambivalent? If we are the latter, we will probably not receive what we have prayed for. This is not because God is unwilling to grant our request, but because we are not ready to receive it. Jesus said that when we ask for something in prayer, believe that we have received it, and we will have it (Mark 11:23–24). We should be expecting it to happen from that moment on. It is just like a receiver in football running his pass route. He runs the route with the expectation of receiving the pass from the quarterback. If he is just running the route not expecting to receive the ball, then the chances are that if the ball is thrown to him he will drop it.

If we are not sure if our prayer will be answered, we open the door for unbelief and doubt to enter our heart. If we have doubt in our heart, then we are like a wave in the sea being tossed from belief to unbelief. And James says this type of person should not expect to receive anything from the Lord because they are not fully trusting in the promises of God (James 1:6–7).

Our God operates on the principle of faith, and He expects His children to do the same. Not expecting our prayers to be answered is the equivalent of calling God a liar, for the promises of God are yes and amen in Christ

Jesus (2 Corinthians 1:20). Jesus told us that if we ask for anything in His name, we would receive it (John 16:23). From now on, when we ask for something in prayer, we should ask with the anticipation that we will receive it from the hand of God. It is important that we let our speech reflect our belief. Then we can begin to thank God for the answered prayer and expect to receive it!

Scripture Readings:
Mark 11:23–24
Luke 11:9–11
John 14:14; 16:23
James 1:6–7

April 12

HE HAS DONE ALL HE'S GOING TO DO, SO IT'S NOW UP TO YOU

> *All praise to God, the Father of our Lord Jesus Christ, who blessed us with every spiritual blessing in the heavenly realms because we are united with Christ. Even before He made the world, God loved us and chose us in Christ to be holy and without fault in His eyes. (Ephesians 1:3–4)*

We must understand our position in Christ Jesus. Many believers see themselves as sinners who are saved by grace. This mentality keeps them from receiving God's best because they don't think they deserve it. They see themselves as they used to be rather than seeing themselves as a new creature in Christ Jesus (2 Corinthians 5:17). Because of this, God is limited in what He can do through them. This is the main reason why the church is not making a bigger impact in our world today.

Many believers are living in the land of not enough instead of in the land of more than enough. Jesus came to the earth not only to save us, but also to show us what we are capable of doing through Him. In fact, it was Jesus who said that all the things He had done we could do now, and even greater things (John 14:12). We can perform miracles just like Jesus did, but we must have the same mindset He had (1 Corinthians 2:16). This mindset can only come by spending time in the Word of God and meditating on it daily.

Instead of looking for God to do something more for us, we need to start taking advantage of what He has already given us. We have a reborn spirit that is connected to God through Jesus Christ. We have the Holy Spirit to guide us into all truth (John 16:13). And we have His Word that has been made available to us. What else do we need?

Everything is in place for us to walk in dominion on this earth. We need to begin to use our imagination to see ourselves living a prosperous and productive life. We need to see ourselves opening blind eyes and setting the captive free, laying hands on the sick and getting them healed, and being the lender and not the borrower. All these things are possible if we believe that they will happen. The Word says so.

Scripture Readings:
John 14:12
2 Corinthians 5:17
Ephesians 1:3–5; 3:20

April 13

LOOKING AT YOURSELF THROUGH THE EYES OF FAITH

The angel of the Lord appeared to him and said, "Mighty hero, the Lord is with you!" (Judges 6:12)

The book of Judges tells the story of Gideon being visited by an angel of the Lord. At the time Gideon was threshing wheat in a winepress because he was afraid the Midianites were going to take it away from him. Gideon was surprised that the angel addressed him in this manner because he saw himself as anything but a hero. At this time, Israel was under the oppression of their enemies; they were looking for someone to deliver them, and God picked Gideon. The only problem was getting Gideon to see himself as God saw him.

Gideon saw himself as a loser. He described himself coming from the weakest tribe of Manasseh, and the least in his family (Judges 6:15). But God was looking at his heart, and what He saw was a leader and a lion. It was now up to Gideon to believe what God had told him or what others were telling him. Had Gideon chosen not to believe the Lord, someone else would have been chosen to deliver Israel.

Gideon finally accepted the call of God and received the anointing of the Lord, and he became a mighty man of valor. God was with him and Gideon delivered Israel from all their enemies. He was their judge for forty years and there was peace in the land until Gideon died. This is an example of someone who took the step of faith and stepped out of his comfort zone. Gideon could have continued to see himself as a nobody, and he could have lived the rest of his life being miserable. But he dared to believe God and with a little coaxing fulfilled his call.

God has a plan for everyone on this earth, but we have to cooperate with Him in order to fulfill it. He will not force anyone to do anything against his or her will. We might not see ourselves as someone God could use, but He sees our potential. All we have to do is believe and be willing to step out of our comfort zone. Many are called but only a few are chosen. We are the ones who determine if we are chosen or not, not God. Are you ready to accept the challenge?

Scripture Readings:
Judges 6–9

April 14

WHO IS YOUR SUPERHERO?

I will pronounce judgment on My people for all their evil—for deserting Me and burning incense to other gods. Yes, they worship idols made with their own hands! (Jeremiah 1:16)

What do Batman, Superman, and Spiderman all have in common? They all are ontological, individualistic, and loners. Most modern-day heroes fall into this category. They all have that strong individualistic persona about them that we find so attractive in our culture. Hollywood creates these characters as a means of capturing our imagination, with the purpose of having us emulate them, or at least desire to be like them.

Our culture prizes the person who is individualistic and makes his or her own rules. We can look at people like Bonnie and Clyde, which were portrayed as heroes, even though they were thieves who killed innocent people. Even today, gangsters are looked at as celebrities. Many young people try to emulate this image that is being portrayed in the media today. It seems that the more immoral a person is, the more popular they are with the masses.

An example of this is Miley Cyrus. I saw her on an awards show dancing in a provocative outfit and in a very sexual way. The reviews on her performance were outstanding. But how much talent does it take to run around a stage half naked simulating having sex? What happened to the innocent Hannah Montana that Cyrus portrayed years ago?

How many young people are going to see her doing that and think it is the way a woman should behave to get attention, and thus follow her example? How many young men will look at the images of some of the most popular rappers who flaunt their wealth, demean women, and think it is cool? We as a society have to look at what we value and compare it with what the Bible values.

The enemy is crafty in how he seduces people. He will use any method necessary to creep into our heart. He will use music to open the door and use lyrics to get his message into our mind. He will use entertainment, particularly the cinema, to create images that are pleasing to the eyes, to project his agenda into our thought life. In the 1940s and early '50s, Coca-Cola and other soft drink companies used to splice the films at movie theatres so that every forty seconds there would be an image of their product. This would happen so quickly that the audience was actually unaware of it. But their unconscious mind would see the image. Guess what happened as a result of this? The sales of Coke increased in those theatres.

All of this just goes to show us how powerful the media is in influencing our thoughts and behaviors. God has given us the ability to discern what is right and what is wrong. We are not to allow popular opinion or the media to sway us, no matter how appealing it may appear to be.

Scripture Readings:
Proverbs 4:20–23
Philippians 4:8

April 15

LOOKING BEYOND THE OBVIOUS

So the Israelites examined their food, but they did not consult the Lord. (Joshua 9:14)

I like reading the stories contained in the Old Testament, for there is such a wealth of wisdom there to be gleaned. I was reading the book of Joshua and found a story that captured my attention (Joshua 9). Joshua had led the Israelites on a string of victories. They had taken the cities of Jericho and Ai. Word had gotten out to the others kings and nations, and the fear of Israel grew because of the power of God being displayed on their behalf.

The Gibeonites knew that it was just a matter of time before they too would be defeated. So they devised a plan. They pretended that they were from a distant country. They put on old, worn-out clothes, and used old, worn-out wineskins. They even brought moldy bread with them, and sent a contingence to meet with the Israelites for the purpose of signing a treaty with them. Well, their plan worked perfectly—for a while. They fooled Joshua and the other leaders because they only examined the outside appearance and failed to consult the Lord. They made an agreement with the Gibeonites.

Later, Joshua found out that the Gibeonites were not from a distant land, but were in actuality their neighbors. Because they had made an agreement with them, the Israelites couldn't break their agreement. So they made the Gibeonites their servants, and they were responsible for chopping the wood and carrying the water of the community of Israel. There is a lesson to be learned here.

We cannot always base our decisions only on appearance. Sometimes appearances can be deceiving. How many people have gotten married to someone just based on physical appearance, or the connection they felt with that person, only to wish they had waited? They never took the time to go to the Lord and ask Him for His opinion. If they had, He would have told them that this was not the person for them. How many people have gotten involved in business deals because they looked so good and lost great sums of money because they never bothered to seek the Lord?

We cannot be in such a rush to make important decisions in our life. Taking the time to seek the Lord and involve Him in the decision-making process is so important. We will not regret it. If someone is pressuring us into making a quick decision, this should be a sign for us to wait. If they need an answer right away, then they have an agenda that is self-serving. If they are persistent in wanting an answer, just walk away—we won't regret it.

Scripture Readings:
Joshua 9:1–17
Proverbs 16:9

April 16

HOW INTIMATE ARE YOU WITH GOD?

I pray that they will be one, just as You and I are one—as You are in Me, Father, and I am in You. And may they be in Us so that the world will believe You sent Me. (John 17:21)

It is God's desire that each one of us be so intimately acquainted with Him that people will see God in our being. God wants to manifest His glory through us, just as He did with Jesus. God will not manifest His glory through a casual acquaintance. There are many people who only know God as God. What I mean is that they know all *about* God, but they don't know Him in a personal and intimate way. Even some believers fall into this category. We can read a book about someone and know where they were born, what they like to eat, and the places they like to go, but we don't know them personally.

When a person always refers to God as God, it's like referring to our father as *man*. Yes, he is a man, but that label is impersonal. God wants us to know Him more intimately than that. One of the reasons the Jews were so offended with Jesus was because He referred to God as His Father. This was a radical statement to make about God in those days. If God were His Father, then that would make Him God's Son, putting Him in the same class as God.

Jesus had a very intimate relationship with God, so much so that the two of them thought alike (John 8:28; 14:10). As a result of this intimacy, God could manifest Himself through Jesus. Jesus wants us to have the same kind of relationship with Him and the Father. He wants us to be one with Him and His Father so that the world will see God through us. Isn't that an awesome thought? We have the capacity to demonstrate the glory of God in this world. Imagine the impact the church could make if we collectively sought to have the same kind of relationship Jesus had with the Father.

One of the reasons why the church is not making a bigger impact in the world today is because we are just preaching the gospel with very little signs and wonders following. There are many religions that sound good, and that is why they are so popular. If Christianity is going to distinguish itself from the rest of the religions in the world, then we have to do more than just talk; we need some signs and wonders to follow what we preach (1 Corinthians 4:20). This can only come by having an intimate relationship with the Lord.

Scripture Readings:
John 17:20–25
1 Corinthians 4:20
Ephesians 3:10–11

April 17

ELOHIM: THE GOD OF CREATION

In the beginning God (Elohim) created the heavens and the earth. (Genesis 1:1)

To understand God, we need to know His character and nature. He has to be more than some abstract concept we have in our mind. I read a book by Dr. Hugh Ross, Ph.D., entitled *Beyond the Cosmos*. It is an excellent book that validates the biblical account of creation. Dr. Ross is an astrophysicist who became a believer once he realized that all of the new discoveries scientists are finding out about the cosmos could be found in the Bible.

One thing I found interesting while reading his book is the different dimensions of time and space, which they have found to be at least ten. We only operate in four of them—time, width, length, and height. This means there are six dimensions we are not acquainted with. But God operates in all ten of these dimensions. Our concept of time is linear, meaning there is a beginning and an end to it. But God's concept of time is geometrical, which means He has the ability to see the end from the beginning (2 Peter 3:8). Knowing this about God is important because it brings us into a deeper understanding of who He is.

We can now understand how it could be possible for God to hear the prayers of everyone at the same time. We can understand now how it was possible for Jesus to walk through walls after His death and resurrection (Luke 24:35–41). It was because He was in His glorified body that He could operate in all ten dimensions of time and space. With this understanding, it has made the Bible more real, and it has increased my faith in the supernatural. Nothing is impossible with God! So I encourage you to know God as Elohim, the Creator.

Scripture Readings:
Genesis 1:1–31
John 1:1–4
2 Peter 3:8

April 18

I Am Yahweh

And God said to Moses, "I am Yahweh—'the Lord.' I appeared to Abraham, to Isaac, and to Jacob as El-Shaddai—'God Almighty'— but I did not reveal My name, Yahweh, to them. (Exodus 6:2–3)

The way we address someone indicates the nature of our relationship with that person. For example, if a child addresses their father as sir, that would indicate their relationship with their father is formal and probably distant. Conversely, if a child refers to their father as daddy or pop, that would indicate a certain level of intimacy between the child and their father.

The same is true with our relationship with God. Jesus referred to God as His Father. By Him calling God His Father, He was implying that there was a relationship between Himself and God. The religious leaders were offended by this because they only saw God as some distant deity they needed to respect and fear. Jesus introduced a revolutionary concept by referring to God as His Father.

It's God's desire for us as believers to look at Him as our heavenly Father. This is the message Jesus conveyed to His disciples and converts. This message hasn't changed over the past two thousand years. The apostle Paul wrote in the book of Romans that we have not received a spirit that makes us slaves again to fear, but we have been adopted as God's children. Now we can call Him "Abba, Father" (Romans 8:15–17). God wants us to know Him by His name and not by His title only.

When Moses embarked on the challenge of leading the Hebrews out of Egypt, God revealed Himself in a very unique way. He told him that up until then He was only known by His title, but He desired Moses to know Him by His name, Yahweh. He was establishing a different relationship with Moses. God wants to do the same thing with you and with me. He wants us to know Him in an intimate way. He wants to have the same kind of relationship with us as a father would have with his children.

For some of us who didn't have such a good relationship with our earthly fathers, this can be challenging to embrace. But God is patient. If we are willing to learn, God is more than willing to teach us how to have that kind of relationship with a lovely Father. Isn't that a comforting thought, that the God who created the cosmos wants to have a relationship with us? Meditate on that, then praise God for His loving-kindness and new mercies.

Scripture Readings:
Psalm 89:26
Matthew 5:16
Romans 8:15
2 Corinthians 6:18

April 19

Yahweh-Jireh

Look at the birds. They don't plant or harvest or store food in barns, for your heavenly Father feeds them. And aren't you far more valuable to Him than they are? (Matthew 6:26)

It is not uncommon in this day and age to experience anxiety in our daily lives. We are inundated with news of terrorist attacks, planes disappearing, earthquakes, economic woes, and violence on our streets and at our schools. As believers, we are exposed to the same things as those in this world. But there is no need to worry. If we know God as Yahweh-Jireh, we know Him as our provider who will show up whenever we need Him. The meaning of this name is "the Lord who sees," or "the Lord who will see to it." This means that God sees all our needs and will provide for each of them.

If you are looking for a good husband or wife, ask Yahweh-Jireh and He will provide one for you. You need a job or a car? Simply ask Yahweh-Jireh and He will make it happen. But you must be specific in your request and ask with the expectation to receive. Most of all, you need to be patient because God's time schedule is different than yours. It is easy to compromise and give in to unbelief when it does not happen when you think it should.

This name of God first appeared in the Bible in Genesis 22:12–14. Abraham was commanded to sacrifice his only son, but as soon as he raised the knife to kill him, an angel stopped him. Immediately, Abraham looked up and saw a ram caught in the thicket. The ram took the place of his son Isaac. God provided the sacrifice for Abraham at just the right time—not too soon and not too late. If He did it for Abraham, then He will do it for us too because we are the seed of Abraham (Galatians 3:29).

God only shows Himself as Yahweh-Jireh to those who believe and expect for Him to be their provider. There are many believers who are struggling financially because they are only trusting in their own efforts to make ends meet. They limit themselves to only natural means to get their needs met. This world's system is limited, but God has unlimited power.

Enjoy the benefits of being a child of God and cast that stress and worry to the side of the road. Instead, thank God because He is your Yahweh-Jireh, the One who will see to it. But for this to happen, we must exercise faith. Faith comes by hearing and hearing by the Word of God. If you want to know God as Yahweh-Jireh, start to meditate on some of the Scriptures below, and ask God to give you revelation on who He is.

Scripture Readings:
Genesis 22:12–14
Psalm 37:4, 25
Matthew 6:25–34
Romans 8:37
Philippians 4:19

April 20

Yahweh-Rapha

And you know that God anointed Jesus of Nazareth with the Holy Spirit and with power. Then Jesus went around doing good and healing all who were oppressed by the devil, for God was with Him. (Acts 10:38)

We live in a world that is full of stress. Every day we are faced with new challenges that stretch us beyond our comfort zone. Sometimes this load can be unbearable and many people crack under the pressure of it. But if we are a believer in the Lord Jesus Christ, then we have access to someone who can make that bitter situation sweet. He is Yahweh-Rapha, the Lord who makes bitter things sweet, or the Lord who heals. This name was first used of God in Exodus 15:26.

The children of Israel were in the wilderness and were complaining to Moses because there was no water to drink. Eventually, they came upon a pond of water, but it was not drinkable. The people complained even more. So Moses went to the Lord, and the Lord instructed him to put a stick into the water. Once Moses obeyed, the water changed from bitter to sweet. As a result, the children of Israel were able to drink the water and satisfy their thirst. God wants to do the same thing today. He wants to take the bitter situation we have and make it sweet.

There is no situation God cannot change for the good, even if we are the ones responsible for getting ourselves into that particular situation. There is no sickness that God cannot heal, if we have faith to believe. God can bring healing in many different ways and through many different means. Sometimes He will heal us miraculously while at other times He will use doctors and medicine to bring the healing about. We only have to trust and expect that He will show Himself as Yahweh-Rapha, the Lord who makes the bitter sweet.

It is important to remember that God lives in a realm where time as we know it doesn't exist. He is never in a hurry like us, so be patient and know that He is faithful to fulfill His promise. I encourage you to look up all the Scriptures you can find on healing and meditate on your favorites. Inculcate them into your thought process so that they become part of you. Then the manifestation will come. God is faithful; He is the One who heals us.

Scripture Readings:
Exodus 15:22–27
Psalm 30:2; 103:2
Matthew 4:23
1 Peter 2:24

April 21

Yahweh-Nissi

But thank God! He gives us victory over sin and death through our Lord Jesus Christ. (1 Corinthians 15:57)

As believers in Christ Jesus, we have the capacity to win every battle we face (Romans 8:37). Yes, this is true for all of those who know Yahweh-Nissi, the Lord our banner of victory. God wants to magnify Himself through our lives, so He wants us to be victorious in all our endeavors. In this world we will find ourselves in many battles, but we don't have to lose any of them with the assistance of Yahweh-Nissi.

Exodus 17:10–16 tells of the children of Israel and how they were engaged in a battle with the Amalekites. The fighting was intense. Moses went to the top of the hill and prayed to the Lord. As he raised his hands to worship God, the Israelites prevailed, but when he got tired and lowered his arms, the Amalekites prevailed. So Aaron, Moses's brother, and Hur stood beside Moses and helped him keep his hands up until Israel completely defeated their enemies.

We, like the Israelites, are involved in warfare, only ours is on a spiritual level (Ephesians 6:10–12). We also have to fight the constant cravings of our carnal nature. Just like the victory with the Israelites against the Amalekites, we too must stand before God in prayer and ask for Yahweh-Nissi to be our banner of victory. This is something we need to do on a daily basis—our enemy is looking for every opportunity to attack. He will use people and situations that seem insurmountable to discourage and defeat us. But if we know Yahweh-Nissi, we will be empowered to prevail against all the odds.

In order to prevail, however, we will have to do our homework. I suggest that you read Exodus 17:10–16 in preparation for the battles ahead. Also read Romans 8 to get a deeper understanding of the victory Jesus has provided for you. Meditate on these Scriptures until you have renewed your mind. And then begin praising God because He is your Yahweh-Nissi. When you are facing tough times, don't stress out like the rest of the world, just look to Yahweh-Nissi, and let Him be your victory!

Scripture Readings:
Exodus 17:10–16
John 16:33
Romans 8
1 Corinthians 15:57

April 22

WITH GOD IT'S NEVER TOO LATE

I am as strong now as I was when Moses sent me on that journey, and I can still travel and fight as well as I could then. (Joshua 14:11)

One of my favorite characters in the Old Testament is Caleb. He was one of the spies who went to the Promise Land to scout it out and report back on whether or not Israel could take it. Out of the twelve spies that entered the Promise Land, only Caleb and Joshua came back with a positive report. All the other spies told the people that though the land flowed with milk and honey, there were giants in the land and they didn't think they could defeat them (Numbers 13:25–33).

Well, to make a long story short, God got upset with all the people and gave them what they expected. None of that generation made it to the Promise Land, except Joshua and Caleb. Now, forty-five years later, the children of Israel are occupying the Promise Land, and Caleb makes a request to Joshua that he be given the hill country that they spied out earlier. That land was premier property and Caleb wanted it. He didn't care that it had walled cities and the descendants still lived there, or that he was eighty-five years old. His attitude was if God is with him, then he could drive them out of the land as God promised (Joshua 14:12).

Caleb demonstrated faith that has to be admired. He didn't let the fact that he was eighty-five years old stop him from getting what God had promised him. I know that God was pleased with the attitude of Caleb's heart, and that should be an example for us today. We cannot let society dictate to us what we can and cannot do. It doesn't matter how old or young we are, it's all about how strongly we believe. There are many people who didn't achieve their dreams until later in life. Harland Sanders, the founder of Kentucky Fried Chicken, didn't become successful until he was sixty-five years old. The actor Morgan Freeman didn't make it big until he was in his fifties.

Remember, in the realm of the Spirit there is no such thing as time. If we have believed God for a promise, then we should have the same attitude as Caleb—don't give up until we see it come to fruition. God is faithful and will see to it that we receive what we are expecting because He is Yahweh-Jireh, the Lord who will see to it! So stand in faith today and don't let society create your reality. It is also important to watch your words, and never allow your age to stop you—because nothing is impossible with God.

Scripture Readings:
Joshua 14:6–15; 15:13–19
1 Corinthians 10:1–5

April 23

THE BATTLE WITHIN

I don't really understand myself, for I want to do what is right, but I don't do it. Instead, I do what I hate. (Romans 7:15)

If we are believers, then we have an outer man and an inner man, both of which are vying for dominion over us. The outer man is the man we can see and feel, the one we can touch. The inner man can only be detected with our spirit. The outer man is subject to decay and will eventually return to the earth, but the inner man will live forever (2 Corinthians 4:16). The inner man looks like the outer man, only he has a spiritual body.

Like the apostle Paul, we all have struggles with our fleshly nature. Sometimes we find ourselves doing the things that we swore we would quit doing. If we are honest with ourselves, we have all been there at some point in our lives. Sometimes we find ourselves returning to those bad habits or losing our temper when we shouldn't. We know we have the Spirit of God within us, and we shouldn't give in to our lower nature, but we still do it anyway. If that describes how you feel, then know you are not alone.

Once we are born again is when the real battle starts. Before then we lived like the world and thought like the world, but once we gave our life to Jesus, a new sheriff came to reside within us (Ephesians 2:1–2). Now we must conquer this fleshly nature in the same way the Israelites had to battle to take the Promise Land. God promised them the Promise Land, but they had to go into that land and occupy it. He was with them in the process, but they still had to step out in faith in order to possess the promise of God.

It is much the same for us today. God's Word is filled with promises, but they are not going to just fall into our lap by mere belief. There will be challenges along the way. There will be areas that are strongholds the enemy will use to keep us in bondage. But we have the Word of God, the Holy Spirit, and God's grace is evident in our lives—what else do we need? Stand on the promise that we have overcome the world (1 John 5:4–5).

We may suffer setbacks from time to time, but we can't let that stop us. The enemy will try to condemn us, but we only need to remind him of the blood of Jesus, confessing our sin to God, and then move on. We must learn from the apostle Paul who said there is nothing that can separate us from the love of God (Romans 8:35–37). Just keep in mind that no matter how you feel, in Christ Jesus you have the victory because He is Yahweh-Nissi, your banner of victory!

Scripture Readings:
Romans 7:14–25; 8:31–37
2 Corinthians 4:16–18
1 John 5:4–5

April 24

Are You Using Your Keys to the Kingdom?

And I will give you the keys of the Kingdom of Heaven. Whatever you forbid on earth will be forbidden in heaven, and whatever you permit on earth will be permitted in heaven. (Matthew 16:19)

Did you know that Jesus has given you the keys to the Kingdom of God? As a believer, we have been given access to the Kingdom of heaven while we are still living here on earth. However, there are many believers who are not aware of this fact. Because of this they are not living the kind of life God desires for them. Jesus has given us everything we need to take the Promise Land, but it is up to us to take that land. He said that the Kingdom of heaven is advancing by force, which means we cannot be passive and expect to operate in His Kingdom (Matthew 11:12).

There are three keys we should be using on a regular basis:

- Binding and loosing: Jesus has given us the power to bind and loose those things that are contrary to the Kingdom of God. In order to do this, however, we have to know God's will. We need to acquaint ourselves with the promises of God and our rights as believers. If we find something that is contrary to what we have the right to, we only need to bind it. Or if we find something that is lacking in our life, we have the right to loose it.
- We have the right to use the name of Jesus: Jesus has given us the authority to use His name (John 14:23; 16:23). Jesus's name is above all names in heaven and on earth (Philippians 2:9–11). We have the right to use the name of Jesus to rectify any situation that is contrary to the will of God.
- We also have the blood of Jesus: The precious blood of Jesus cleanses our conscience of sin and makes it possible to go before God's throne without any sense of condemnation; we have been redeemed by His precious blood (Colossians 1:14). The enemy will try to condemn us when we miss it, but all we have to do is tell

him that the blood of Jesus has cleansed us of all our sins—past, present, and future. He has no argument for that.

With these three keys there is nothing that this world can do to defeat us. Jesus came to this earth to show us how to use these keys. Those who have made an impact for the Kingdom learned to use these keys, so we must also do the same. God has done all He is going to do for us, so if we don't like the way our life is, we should start using the keys He has given us.

Scripture Readings:
Matthew 11:12
John 14:23; 16:23
Philippians 2:9–11
Colossians 1:14

April 25

WHAT ARE YOU WAITING FOR?

Then the Lord said to Moses, "Why are you crying out to Me? Tell the people to get moving!" (Exodus 14:15)

The Egyptian army was pursuing the children of Israel. The Israelites panicked and cried out to Moses so that he would do something on their behalf. In turn, Moses cried out to the Lord to do something on their behalf. And the Lord responded by asking Moses why he was crying out to Him, but he was to tell the people to get moving. God is speaking much the same thing to us today.

We go to Him in prayer and complain about what is happening to us, wanting Him to do something on our behalf. Instead, we should be utilizing what He has already provided for us in Christ Jesus. Let me explain what I mean. God had taken Moses's staff and anointed it. With that anointing, Moses was able to perform many miracles—he turned water into blood, caused frogs to come out of the streams, and turned dust into lice. Moses knew the power he held in his hand. In biblical times, the staff or rod signified power. God expected Moses to use the staff as he did with all the other miracles instead of looking to Him to solve the problem.

Jesus had the same attitude with His disciples too. On numerous occasions, Jesus questioned the disciples and asked why they had so little faith (Mark 4:35–39; Matthew 14:31). Jesus had the expectation that the disciples were capable of doing what He did (John 14:12). If it were not possible, He would not have had that expectation.

As believers, we have a spiritual staff or rod, and God expects us to use it. He has given us the keys to the Kingdom and He has empowered us with His Spirit. In addition, we have the Holy Spirit to assist us along with the angels of heaven. We are fully equipped to meet any challenge that comes our way. It does not mean that it will be easy to do so, but we must learn to walk by faith and not by sight or feelings. We have to remind ourselves constantly of who we are in Jesus and of all the allies that have our back.

So instead of praying about the problem, speak to it in faith (Mark 11:23–24). Use your staff to run those problems and cares away.

Scripture Readings:
Exodus 13:17–22; 17:5–6, 8–15
John 14:12

April 26

STRONGHOLDS ARE NOT EASY

When the Israelites grew stronger, they forced the Canaanites to work as slaves, but they never did drive them completely out of the land. (Judges 1:28)

The stories in the Old Testament are so rich with revelation concerning our spiritual walk. I have heard one preacher say that the Old Testament is the New Testament concealed, and the New Testament is the Old Testament revealed. They are both extremely relevant to us today. We can see how the hand of God moved in all the stories of both the Old and New Testaments. That means there is much to be learned in *every* book of the Bible.

Contained in the Old Testament is a story of when the Israelites finally got to the Promise Land, the Lord told Joshua that He would not abandon him and would give him the land He promised their forefathers (Joshua 1:5–6). He promised them that everywhere Joshua set his foot would be given to him. He knew that it was going to take some effort on his part to inherit the land. The Israelites, under the leadership of Joshua, were able to take most of the land; however, there were some areas that were difficult.

So instead of trusting in God and removing their enemies, they took the easy way out and compromised. They allowed their enemies to reside with them as their slaves. This displeased the Lord because He had instructed them to completely remove their enemies. Because of their failure to completely remove them, their enemies became a thorn in their flesh, and eventually caused the children of Israel to worship their gods. Before long their enemies were overtaking the Israelites.

We have inherited the Promise Land, but we like the Israelites have to be proactive in taking that land. There are going to be areas in our lives that are going to be resistant to change; there are going to be behaviors and habits that will be difficult to change; and there will be times we will want to just compromise and let those areas remain, but we need to know that it's not God's best. And eventually, like the Israelites, we will find ourselves in conflict with those areas we thought were under control.

God has given us all that we need to live a prosperous and victorious life, but it's up to us to decide to take that step of faith and not compromise. Is there someone in your life God has shown you that you need to cut ties with? Are there habits you have that you know are bad for you? Are there activities you know you shouldn't be involved in? If so, then you need to either continue to stay on the path of resistance you are on, or stand on the promises of God. As you completely drive out your enemies, God will surely bring His promises about.

Scripture Readings:
Joshua 1:3–6
Judges 2:1–4
Ephesians 1:3–5

April 27

STRONGHOLDS AND YOUR SOUL

We use God's mighty weapons, not worldly weapons, to knock down the strongholds of human reasoning and to destroy false arguments. (2 Corinthians 10:4)

Strongholds are established in the realm of the soul, which consists of the intellect, memory, will, emotions, and imagination. They will usually start in the memory or imagination, then move to the intellect and will. Memory plays an important part in either breaking down or building a stronghold. The great majority of strongholds come from unpleasant experiences we have encountered along our life's journey. It might have been from being emotionally or physically abused by someone we trusted or loved, or they may come from being betrayed. If we allow that memory to remain without letting it go through forgiveness, we will put ourselves in an emotional prison, not being able to move forward.

Many people in this category find it extremely hard to trust others and establish good, healthy relationships. They will isolate themselves emotionally, and sabotage relationships to avoid being hurt when they feel themselves getting close to someone. If you have a stronghold that is based in the realm of the memory, then it is vital that you forgive the person or persons who hurt you, letting it go.

Strongholds are difficult to remove because they involve three areas of the soul—memory, intellect, and emotions. In order to remove this stronghold, we will first have to get rid of the negative imagination and replace it with a positive one. We need to allow the Word of God to paint new images in our minds, letting our minds get renewed. Finally, we will also need to speak the Word of God to get it into our heart (will).

We have to be patient with ourselves during this process. Progress might be slow at first, but that is where faith comes in. Faith and patience produce a perfect work deep within our hearts (James 1:3).

Scripture Readings:
Matthew 18:21–35
2 Corinthians 10:4
James 1:3–4

April 28

RECEIVING GODLY IMPARTATION FROM YOUR IMAGINATION

The Lord observed the extent of human wickedness on the earth, and saw that everything they thought or imagined was consistently and totally evil. (Genesis 6:5)

I was asked to do a men's group, and after I accepted the pastor asked me what the topic was going to be about. I told him it would be on the imagination. The pastor then cautioned me to change it to *vision* because he didn't want anyone to think the church was into New Age. I immediately thought about how God spoke about the imagination long before the New Age movement was around. In fact, the word *imagination* is used fourteen times in the King James Version. It is because of this attitude that the church is playing catch-up with the world.

The imagination is one of the most important gates in the realm of the soul. It is the imagination that puts humanity in the same category as God. It can be used for the positive as well as for the negative, being the instrument that can cause a person to achieve great things in this world. The imagination is also a vehicle to accessing the spiritual realm. It is a gift from God that can take us to places we have never been, do things we have never done, and possess things we have yet to possess.

God created us in His image and likeness (Genesis 1:26), so that means we have the ability to create things like God. It is foolish then to mitigate the power of the imagination. Instead, it behooves us to embrace the imagination and learn how to use it to advance the Kingdom of God upon the earth.

Realizing the power of words is vital to understanding the imagination, because words create images. If someone said *dog,* we don't see the letters d-o-g. We see an image of a dog pictured in our minds. There was a saying from elementary school, "Sticks and stones may break my bones, but words will never harm me." That was a lie straight out of hell! Words can do damage if used improperly. How many parents have told their children that they would never amount to anything, and are currently suffering the effects of those words as adults?

God instructs us to meditate on His Word. Doing this, we can create new images in our minds so that we can begin to see ourselves as God sees us. Once we obtain this vision, it gets into our hearts and starts to influence our will and the choices we make. Once the image is in our heart, it gets into our unconscious mind (inner man), and we will begin to automatically do the things necessary to achieve our vision or dream.

Brother Leroy Thompson says that the imagination is the film of our faith. I like that definition. Our imagination and our faith can work together to achieve the impossible, or the enemy can use it to do the detestable. The choice on how you use it is completely up to you.

Scripture Readings:
Genesis 1:26; 6:5

April 29

Don't Give Up because There Is More Work to Be Done

And I am convinced and sure of this very thing, that He Who began a good work in you will continue until the day of Jesus Christ [right up to the time of His return], developing [that good work] and perfecting and bringing it to full completion in you. (Philippians 1:6 AMP)

This morning I was reading a story out of the Old Testament about the children of Israel. They had entered the Promise Land and after seven years had defeated almost all of the former inhabitants of the land. They were getting complacent, however, and Joshua admonished them about their complacency. He asked those tribes who had not received their inheritance how long they were going to wait to get it (Joshua 18:3).

The same question could be asked of many believers today. How long are we going to wait to inherit all the promises of God? Some believers are satisfied knowing that their names are written in the Lamb's Book of Life, and are just cruising through life. Others have been a little more assertive and taken some of their inheritance, but have become complacent in the process. Then there are other believers, who are like the tribes of Judah, Ruben, Gad, and Manasseh, who made sure they received their inheritance fully.

We as believers have been promised all the heavenly blessings in Christ Jesus (Ephesians 1:3–4). But many of us are not experiencing them in all their fullness. I have seen far too many believers who are still wandering in the wilderness or still in bondage in Egypt due to their reluctance to take advantage of their inheritance or their ignorance of the promises of God. And they will die in the wilderness because of it (Hosea 4:6).

Don't settle in the land of just good enough when you could be living in the land of milk and honey. Don't allow your frustrations to get the best of you. Keep pushing on until you receive the fullness of Christ who dwells within you. Stand on the promise of God that says He has made you holy (separated) and has made you whole—spirit, soul, and body (1 Thessalonians 5:23–24). If you haven't reached it yet, then you need to continue to press on until you experience the blessings of Christ in all their fullness. Don't wait for God to do it for you, because He has already given you everything you need to live a life of abundance in Him.

Scripture Readings:
Joshua 18:3
Ephesians 1:3–4
Philippians 1:6
1 Thessalonians 5:23–24
Hebrews 12:2

April 30

BIBLICAL MEDITATION TO RECEIVE MANIFESTATION

But they delight in the law of the Lord, meditating on it day and night. (Psalm 1:2)

There are many ways to meditate. Quite often after the conclusion of a yoga class the instructor will instruct everyone to meditate (empty their minds) to achieve a state of alter-consciousness. This is not the type of meditation I am referring to here. The type of meditation I am talking about here is more active than that. It means to mull over, to chew over, ruminate, or to contemplate.

A good example is the how the cow chews its food. Since they have more than one stomach, they will store some of the food in one of their stomachs and later regurgitate it up and chew on it again in order to get all the nutrients out of it. We are to do the same thing with the Word of God. We are to store it in our minds and then chew on it during the day so that we can get it into our inner man. When we meditate on the Scriptures, we are mulling it over, chewing it again and again. In essence, we are watering that Word and allowing it to take root in our inner being. Remember in the parable of the sower, there were some believers who accepted the Word but they produced no crop because that seed was either planted on stony ground or was choked out by the weeds. This would not have happened if they had meditated on that Word (seed).

There are four steps to biblical meditation:

- Meditate: be active in your listening. Take notes. Repeatedly go over that Word in your mind.
- Visualize: get your imagination involved in the process. See yourself with whatever you are meditating on.
- Actualize: once you have visualized, the promise has become real to you. Speak like you have received what you've been meditating

on because the meditation has become so real to you (Romans 4:17).
- Manifestation: this is the conclusion of the process, when you receive what you have been meditating on.

Scripture Readings:
Joshua 1:8–9
Psalm 1:1–3; 19:14
Luke 8:11–18

May 1

IF YOU DON'T LIKE THE STORY OF YOUR LIFE, CHANGE THE SCRIPT

I tell you the truth, you can say to this mountain, "May you be lifted up and thrown into the sea," and it will happen. But you must really believe it will happen and have no doubt in your heart. (Mark 11:23)

One good thing about this life is that there is always tomorrow, and tomorrow can always be better than today. As long as we have life in our body, we can change our present situation. We have the power to make changes in our life if we don't like where we are. The only thing that can stop us is our belief that it can't be changed. Jesus said there is nothing impossible for those who believe (Mark 9:23).

I am reminded of a story about a woman named Cupcake Brown. Cupcake got her name because her mother craved cupcakes during her pregnancy. She never knew her real father but was raised by her mother and stepfather. Life was good for Cupcake until her mother died from cancer when she was just eleven years old. After her mother's death, her stepfather decided not to take guardianship of Cupcake, so she drifted from relative to relative and finally wound up in the foster care system. Cupcake experienced physical and emotional abuse in foster homes, so she ran away and lived on the streets.

There Cupcake got involved in drugs and other illegal activities. Things got pretty bad for her—drug dealers were after her because she owed them money; she was attacked by gang members and was on the run. She found herself living behind a dumpster. Her drug use increased to the point that she turned to prostitution. She recalls that she would break off car antennas and use them to smoke rock-cocaine. One day Cupcake saw her reflection in a window, and she did not like what she saw. She knew that she was better than that and decided to make a change.

She went back to school and obtained her GED, later enrolling in junior college and finishing her associate's degree. From there she attended San Diego State and got a bachelor's degree. Cupcake wanted to become a lawyer so she applied to law school and was accepted. She would later graduate and pass the bar exam. Today Cupcake is a successful lawyer and a motivational speaker. She decided to rewrite the script for her life.

God has given us the power of imagination and will to determine our destiny. We only have to have the faith and the insight to use these tools to our advantage. He has provided us with His Word and given us the Holy Spirit to guide us, but we have to do our part in order to change. We don't have to live in the wilderness any longer—we can get to our Promise Land.

Scripture Readings:
Habakkuk 2:2
Proverbs 29:18
2 Corinthians 5:17

May 2

Your Body Is the Temple that God Gave You

Don't you realize that your body is the temple for the Holy Spirit, who lives in you and was given to you by God? You do not belong to yourself, for God bought you with a high price. So you must honor God with your body. (1 Corinthians 6:19–20)

Many of the health problems in this country are avoidable. Due to our lifestyle, we create many of our illnesses. According to Dr. Don Colbert, M.D., author of *Deadly Emotions*, there is a direct correlation between emotions and disease. He cites that he has found that people who suffer from chronic anxiety are more prone to mental illness, and those who are inclined to fear are more susceptible to coronary disease. There is a reason why Jesus tells us not to be afraid or worry (John 14:1).

Obesity is another major problem in this country. According to the Center for Disease Control and Prevention, 35.7 percent of the adult population is obese. Even though a large percentage of people are obese, it is one of the major causes for heart attacks, strokes, diabetes, and certain types of cancers. Sometimes we can be so heavenly minded that we neglect the practical aspects of life. Let me give you an example.

I attended a church where a majority of the congregation had serious weight problems. One of the strategies the pastor used to get people to come to Bible studies or church functions was to involve food. When food was involved, the people would show up. Well, one day during a service, the pastor was addressing the issue of health, and he told the congregation to pray to Jesus that He would take the calories out of the food they were eating so they could lose weight. I could not believe what I heard. The sad thing is that he was completely serious.

What about exercise and self-control? What about changing our lifestyle and our eating habits? These are practical solutions to address the problem, rather than just praying for Jesus to take the calories out of our food. If He were to do that for them, Jesus would be enabling them to continue their gluttonous ways. The apostle Paul stated that the people of Crete (believers) were liars, cruel animals, and lazy gluttons (Titus 1:12).

If a person is gluttonous with food, it will usually spill over into other areas of their life as well. God has given us the ability to be self-controlled, not being enslaved to our appetites (1 Corinthians 6:12). Isn't it much better to not have to pray for a miracle of healing because we were wise enough to exercise control over those areas of our life? Worry, fear, and appetite are things that we can control through the power of the Spirit. So take care of the body God has given you, and it will take care of you.

Scripture Readings:
Proverbs 17:22; 23:20
John 14:1
1 Corinthians 6:19–20
Titus 1:12

May 3

Your Body No Longer Belongs to You: Your Body Is Actually a Part of Christ

We live in a society where sex outside of marriage is not only condoned but also encouraged. Some schools actually provide their students with birth control and condoms to prevent sexually transmitted diseases and unwanted pregnancies. I remember when someone said that when they mentioned that they were a virgin, they were laughed at. There are many individuals who bow to the pressure and give in, violating their morals in order to be part of the crowd.

If we are believers, then we have now become one with Jesus (John 17:21). This means our body no longer belongs to us because it is part of Jesus's body. When we sin against our body, we are sinning against Jesus. It's not that we won't be forgiven if we sin against it, but that we will suffer the consequences of our actions. Here are just a few of the consequences we will suffer if we give into sinning against our body.

When a person chooses to engage in sexual intercourse with another individual, there is more involved than physical contact. When a person is sexually aroused, their limbic system within the brain is flooded with neurochemicals, which cause strong emotional ties and a feeling of attachment. When a sexual climax is reached, the brain releases neurohormones—oxytocin and vasopressin—which gives a person a feeling of euphoria. That is why sexual intercourse is so pleasurable. But if the people who are engaging in sexual intercourse are not married, unhealthy soul ties develop and remain long after the couple is no longer together. A person could now be married and still thinking about their ex-boyfriend or girlfriend. Sometimes these soul ties can be so strong the person gets obsessed and finds themselves stocking their former lover.

Another thing that can happen is that the person gets addicted to their partner because of the orgasmic release of oxytocin and vasopressin. There are many couples that are involved in unhealthy relationships and have settled for less than God's best because of the sexual feelings they have with their partner. There are even some people who remain in abusive relationships because of this.

There is also the spiritual aspect to all of this as well. When a person engages in sexual intercourse with another person, their spirits unite together as one (1 Corinthians 6:16–17). When a person engages in illicit sexual intercourse, they are not only sinning against their body but their spirit as well, and thereby opening themselves up to unclean spirits. I know the media makes sex look so attractive and appealing, but we have to look beyond the deception. God calls us to be holy and trust that He will send us the right partner at the right time.

Scripture Readings:
1 Corinthians 6:12–18

May 4

GOD IS FAITHFUL TO FULFILL HIS PROMISES

And the Lord gave them rest on every side, just as He had solemnly promised their ancestors. None of their enemies could stand against them, for the Lord helped them conquer all their enemies. Not a single one of all the good promises the Lord had given to the family of Israel was left unfulfilled; everything He had spoken came true. (Joshua 21:44–45)

When I read this passage of Scripture one day, I felt the power of God surge through my spirit. If you haven't already noticed at this point, I speak of the Promise Land a lot. The reason why I do this is because the Promise Land is symbolic of our inheritance that Jesus has promised us on this earth. And like the children of Israel, we have to be proactive in obtaining it. It is not going to come by just praying and waiting for God to do something. As I have already stated, God has done all He needs to do for each one of us to inherit the Promise Land.

There will be times that are going to tough, but that is when we have to use our faith and stand on the promises of God. We are going to have to use the eyes of our faith to look beyond the natural circumstances that challenge us and see the victory waiting to be obtained. We will have to remind ourselves that God is not a man that He should lie (Numbers 23:19); if the promise was made it will come to pass. It might not happen when we think it should, but it will happen nonetheless.

When times get hard and we feel like giving up, we only need to read the above Scripture and know that if God did it for Israel then He will surely do it for us too. God is not a respecter of persons. The only thing God is looking for are those who trust and have faith in Him.

Scripture Readings:
Joshua 1:5–9; 21:44–45
John 14:14; 15:7; 16:23
1 Corinthians 15:57
2 Corinthians 1:20
Ephesians 1:3–5

May 5

As You Say, So Shall It Be

The tongue can bring death or life; those who love to talk will reap the consequences. (Proverbs 18:21)

Each one of us has a spiritual weapon that we may not be aware of, and it has the power to override any device that the enemy can use against us. At the same time, if used improperly it can destroy us too. This weapon is our tongue. God has given every one of us the ability to speak words. They are not just used to communicate, but they are also used to create. Just as God used words to create the cosmos in the beginning, we can use words to create and change things in our life too.

Our words are powerful. Knowing this, we will have to give an account for every careless word we have spoken (Matthew 12:36–37). Many believers are ignorant of the power of their words and are suffering because of it (Hosea 4:6). But the Bible says that a wise man thinks before he speaks, but a foolish man doesn't (Proverbs 15:28). There are many people who have talked their way into poverty, hardships, and death because they didn't exercise control over their tongues. Elvis Presley, for example, the rock-and-roll icon of the sixties, said that he wouldn't live past the age of forty-two because his mother died at that age. Guess what? Elvis Presley died when he was forty-two years old.

In the book of Numbers, there is the story of the children of Israel about to go into the Promise Land. When they finally got to the edge of their destination, they sent spies out to see the land and they were to come back with a report. After forty days, the spies returned and told the community that the land flowed with milk and honey, as the Lord had described, and they even brought back some fruit from the land. However, they told the people that they could not take the land because of the walled cities and the giants who lived there (Numbers 13:25–33).

Now their report was factual—the walled cities did exist, and there were indeed giants who lived in the land. These giants were the descendants of the Rephaites and Nephilites, some of whom were nine feet tall. The Bible states that the King of Og's bed was eighteen feet long and six feet wide.

But the spies neglected to stand on the promise of God. God told them that He had given them this land—it was theirs for the taking. Only two spies, Joshua and Caleb, stood on the promise of God and encouraged the people to do the same. But the bad report spread throughout the community and the people rebelled against Moses and wanted to stone Joshua and Caleb. The end result was that none of those people entered the Promise Land except Joshua and Caleb. The rest of that generation died in the wilderness just like they said they would.

You see, they got exactly what they spoke. Many times we blame God or the devil for our problems, when we should look at our words. Did we speak something that opened the door to our demise? Our words are like a sword we use to do spiritual warfare with the enemy (Ephesians 6:17). When we face a situation, we need to use our words to speak the promises of God instead of speaking what we see in the natural realm. Our very life may depend on it.

Scripture Readings:
Numbers 13:25–33

May 6

THE TONGUE IS A FLAME OF FIRE THAT NEEDS TO BE QUENCHED

In the same way, the tongue is a small thing that makes grand speeches. But a tiny spark can set a great forest on fire. And the tongue is a flame of fire. It is a whole world of wickedness, corrupting your entire body. It can set your whole life on fire, for it is set on fire by hell itself. (James 3:5–6)

The tongue is vital because there is an importance our words play in the way our life is shaped. Many people mitigate the power of their words and use them carelessly. They then wonder why their life lacks power and is so chaotic. The words we speak not only have an impact on us but the people around us. As a counselor I talk with people who are still suffering the effects of what someone told them when they were children. When I worked in the correctional system, I would cringe at the verbal abuse some of the deputies used toward the inmates. I am sure it played a major part in the high recidivism rate.

In the story I shared with you yesterday, about the children of Israel going into the Promise Land, it was the negative report of those ten spies that turned the whole community of millions of people against Moses and ultimately against God. James is correct in saying that the tongue is a spark that can set a whole forest on fire. Satan will use our words to his benefit if we allow him. He has no power except that of deception, so he will deceive us into saying things that are harmful and destructive.

That's why it is important to think before we talk. Our first response might not be the best response, especially if it is coming out of the flesh. How many times have we said something we later regretted? We have to watch what we say about ourselves, about others, and also to others. This is especially true with children. They are very impressionable and things we say to them out of frustration can impact them for the rest of their lives.

God has given us the ability to speak our thoughts and give shape to the circumstances around us. What we create with our words is up to us—what we choose to speak. If we are constantly bad-mouthing ourselves, we can't blame God when we get what we have spoken. We could have easily spoken the promises of God found in the Scriptures, and gotten a different result. The power of life and death is in our tongue. It is up to us to use our words wisely.

Scripture Readings:
James 3:1–11
Psalm 39:1
Proverbs 13:3; 21:23

May 7

THE HAND OF GOD IS NEVER TOO SHORT

Then the Lord said to Moses, "Has My arm lost its power? Now you will see whether or not My word comes true!" (Numbers 11:23)

We often disqualify ourselves from some of the blessings of God because we don't understand how He could possibly fix this situation or follow through on His promise. We think that what we are going through is too much for anyone to fix. We listen to the so-called experts who tell us this situation is impossible. And it is precisely there that we make our mistake, because there is nothing impossible with God (Luke 1:37).

What happens is that we allow our logic to get in the way of our blessing. "How can God do this? I just don't see how He could possibly get me out of this situation; the doctors said there is no cure." These are all things we may have said at one time or another. I sure know I have. But after I realized that nothing is impossible with God and I began to discipline myself to not look to my logic, but rather trust God's promises and nature, I began to see the miracle-working of power of God. I still sometimes struggle, but I can now stop the struggle when it tries to enter my mind.

Moses had this type of struggle with his senses—the same Moses who saw how God acted on his behalf by parting the Red Sea. One would think that after witnessing that, Moses would have been convinced that nothing was impossible with God, but that was not the case. The children of Israel were complaining about the food they were eating. It seems they were tired of eating manna and longed for the food they ate in Egypt. The Lord told Moses to tell the people that they would eat meat for an entire month. He followed the Lord's instructions and told the people.

Moses later went to the Lord and questioned Him about how He was going to do this. They were in the middle of the wilderness and could not logically see how God could fulfill this promise. There were over 600,000 foot soldiers with their families, and there was no possible way this could be done. Even if they butchered all their livestock and caught all the fish in the sea, it would not be enough (Numbers 11:21).

But Moses forgot that God is Yahweh-Jireh, the God who will see to it. God sent a wind that brought quail from the sea and let them fall around the camp. The people were able to gather as many quail as they could catch. For miles in every direction there were quail. The people gorged themselves. Moses never thought this could happen, but nothing is impossible with God! Don't allow your thinking to put a limit on God's ability.

Scripture Readings:
Numbers 11:16–34
Mark 6:30–44
Luke 1:37
1 Corinthians 2:14

May 8

THE LORD IS YOUR STRENGTH

Don't be afraid, for I am with you. Don't be discouraged, for I am your God. I will strengthen you and help you. I will hold you up with My victorious right hand. (Isaiah 41:10)

Sometimes we can feel overwhelmed by what life throws at us. Financial worries, health problems, and family and relational issues can get to anyone. But if you are a believer, you need to remind yourself that you are not alone. God is waiting for you to call on Him for assistance, whether you think you deserve it or not. If you are anything like me, you have a tendency to isolate yourself when difficult times come your way. You think to yourself, "I can figure this thing out if I just focus." But how wrong you are.

Why put yourself through all that stress when God is ready and willing to assist you? If we really think about it for a moment, it's only our pride that keeps us locked in this mentality. Our battle is not against flesh and blood, but against principalities, powers of darkness, and wickedness in high places (Ephesians 6:12). So if we are trying to fight with our flesh alone, then we are in for an uphill battle.

Joshua's final address to the children of Israel was to recap all that God had done for them. One thing he repeatedly said was that the Lord had driven out those nations that occupied the land before them. Joshua knew that if it were not for the Lord's intervention on their behalf, they would not have been successful in their conquest (Joshua 23:9). Likewise, we are victorious in life because we are in Christ Jesus (Romans 8:31).

So when you are down and out, remind yourself that greater is He who is in you than he who is in the world (1 John 4:4). Use the Scriptures and the words of your mouth to give you the victory. Give praise and thanksgiving even though you may not feel like it. Before you know it, your whole mood will soon change. Your attitude will be more positive and you will begin to see that your victory has already been won.

Scripture Readings:
Joshua 23:9
Isaiah 41:10
1 Corinthians 15:57
1 John 4:4

May 9

A Happy Heart Makes a Healthy Body

A cheerful heart is good medicine, but a broken spirit saps a person's strength. (Proverbs 17:22)

The writer of Proverbs knew something that those in the medical field have only recently discovered: there are healing benefits in laughter. Dr. Lee Berk has found that laughter boosts the immune system and reduces dangerous stress hormones in the body. He also found in his studies conducted at Loma Linda Medical Center that the levels of cortisol, the dangerous stress hormone, fell 39 percent after a good belly laugh, while endorphin, the feel-good hormone, rose 27 percent. Not only that, but the growth hormone levels increased to 87 percent.

Cortisol can be extremely toxic to the body when it is elevated over an extended period of time. It acts like acid in the body. Dr. Berk indicated that laughter helps the immune system in very specific ways:

- It increases immunoglobulin A, which helps protect against respiratory tract infections.
- It increases gamma interferon, which is the immune system's frontline defense against viruses.
- It increases B cells that produce antibodies directly against harmful bacteria.
- It increases complement 2, a combination of proteins that act as a catalyst in antibody reactions.

In another study by Dr. William Fry Jr., it was reported that laughter caused the lungs to ventilate, leaves the muscles and nerves relaxed, and the heart becomes warm and relaxed; all of these are the very same benefits that come from aerobic exercise.

Laughter is also good for the brain because it allows a person to use both sides of their brain simultaneously. These are just some of the benefits of having a merry heart. So make it a point to have a good laugh every day, and to smile because that starts the process toward laughter. Begin and end each day with thanksgiving and praise, and you will reap the benefits. A cheerful heart is truly good like medicine.

Scripture Readings:
Proverbs 14:30; 15:13; 17:22

May 10

WHAT IS YOUR VISION FOR THE FUTURE?

And the Lord answered me and said, Write the vision and engrave it so plainly upon tablets that everyone who passes may [be able to] read [it easily and quickly] as he hastens by. (Habakkuk 2:2 AMP)

Today I want to talk about the importance of having a vision for your life, in written form. Many of us have visions or dreams we would like to accomplish, but most of us don't take the time to write them down. Most successful people write their visions down and view them at least once a day. This simple process can be the difference between us obtaining our goal or vision or just making another wish.

As a counselor I have worked with people who had great talent and ability. Some of these individuals were extremely gifted, but they floundered in life because they had no real vision. They were like a piece of driftwood floating in the ocean, being taken wherever the current decided to take them. I like what T. D. Jakes said about the importance of having a vision: "Imagine you are in a car that is fully operational, the only problem is that it is pouring rain outside and the windshield wipers don't work. Where are you going to drive? Nowhere, because you can't see." If we try to drive in such a condition, then we are certain to be a danger to others and ourselves.

As a correctional counselor I have encountered people who had all the skills to be successful and productive citizens, but they wasted their life away sitting in a jail cell because they had no real vision for their life. It was a sad thing to see. They were like the car that didn't have windshield wipers.

Having a vision is extremely important when the pressure is on. It will keep us focused and guide us through those troubled waters. Successful sports teams make it a practice to have their vision written down for all to see. Every time they walk into the locker room, they see the vision written on the walls so everyone is of one accord as they walk into the locker room.

I suggest that we do something similar. We should write out the vision we have for ourselves, the dream God has placed deep within us, and review it daily. Making sure that we write out our short-term goals and our long-term goals are also important. That way we can celebrate when we accomplish our short-term goals, as this will encourage us to continue to achieve our ultimate goal or vision.

Successful people are successful for a reason—they wrote out their vision and made it plain.

Scripture Readings:
Proverbs 29:18
Habakkuk 2:2

May 11

Wandering in the Wilderness of What If...

And now, dear brothers and sisters, one final thing. Fix your thoughts on what is true, and honorable, and right, and pure, and lovely, and admirable. Think about things that are excellent and worthy of praise. (Philippians 4:8)

Have you ever had a time in your life when your imagination went wild on you? It might have been with a loved one whom you couldn't get in contact with. Maybe you tried to call and text them and they didn't return your call. Because of this, your mind starts to wonder why they aren't returning your call. You hope that you didn't do anything to offend them. You go over and over in your mind your last conversation with them. Then you start to imagine that something terrible has happened to them. You create scenes of car wrecks and other calamities that could have happened.

By this time, your anxious thoughts become your reality, and your brain starts to release neurotransmitters that activate the hormonal release of adrenaline and cortisol into your limbic system, which causes you to get restless. With every passing moment you get more and more agitated. Then suddenly the phone rings and your loved one explains that they lost their phone and could not return your call. In a sigh of relief you tell them, "I knew something like that must have happened." Have you ever been there or am I the only one?

Well, the apostle Paul gave a solution for this all-too-common problem. He said that when our minds get flooded with negative thoughts, we are to replace them with positive ones. Many times we create our own problems with our thoughts. We create situations that only exist in our heads, and then we blame the devil for all the negative thoughts we've been having. We have been given the ability to control our thoughts, for they precede our emotions. If we are depressed about something, we need to look at the thought that caused our depression. If that thought doesn't align with the Word of God, then we need to get rid of it.

God has given us the ability to make choices in our everyday lives. We can choose to think thoughts that raise us up, or we can choose to think thoughts that will bring us down. I heard a story of an older gentleman who stated that he never had a down day. When questioned about this statement he said, "Either I am up or I am getting up." This is the kind of attitude I want to have in my own life. The Bible says there is no weapon formed against us that will prosper (Isaiah 54:17), and stronger is He who is within me than he who is in the world (1 John 4:4).

So when you feel yourself going in a downward spiral of wandering in the wilderness of what if, or I should have, just fix your thoughts on the positive and pull yourself up. Think on things that are good, honorable, and praiseworthy.

Scripture Readings:
Isaiah 54:17
Romans 8:31
Philippians 4:8–9
1 John 4:4

May 12

LOVING YOURSELF IS THE KEY TO LOVING OTHERS

> *A second equally important: "Love your neighbor as yourself." (Matthew 22:39)*

We can only love others if we love ourselves. One of the reasons why some people have such a hard time expressing love is because they don't love themselves. There could be many reasons for this. Maybe they were told by an authority figure that they were not worthy of love, maybe they were raised in a home where true love wasn't expressed, or maybe they were raised in a home where love was conditional.

God is love (1 John 4:16), and since we are made in His image and likeness (Genesis 1:26), we have His love present within us. We only have to allow that love to flow out of us. In order for this to happen, however, we must love ourselves. I am not talking about a prideful or boastful type of love, because true love is neither of those (1 Corinthians 13:4). What I mean is that we need to recognize our uniqueness in Christ. God created only one of us. There is not another human being like us that has ever existed before or that will ever exist after us! Just think about that for a moment. Celebrate your uniqueness. Start every day thanking God that He made you the way you are.

Sure, there are things that we would like to change about ourselves, but why do we want to change them? Is it something that doesn't represent godly character, or is it something that the world has imposed on us? Many people spend their life trying to fit an image that the world has created for them. They have defined themselves according to the world's standards rather than accepting themselves for who they really are. Many women strive to be a certain size and diet to the point of starvation in order to fit into those skinny jeans. They are trying to conform to some image that was made by some corporate executive who decided what it means to be attractive. Many men fall into the same trap.

Don't get me wrong here: there is nothing wrong with taking care of yourself. In fact, that's a part of loving yourself. But you are more than the physical image you portray to others. You can't fight time and no matter how hard you work on your body, it will eventually decay (2 Corinthians 4:16). Instead of focusing all your attention on the outer man, spend time working on the inner man.

Realize that God created you for a specific reason and purpose; seek to find it. Once you find the reason for which God created you, then you will feel better about yourself and you will begin to love yourself more. When you do this, it will be easier for you to show love to others. Stop comparing yourself to others and celebrate who you are in Christ Jesus.

Scripture Readings:
Matthew 19:19; 22:39
1 Corinthians 13
1 John 3:11, 23; 4:7

May 13

WHAT IS YOUR LANGUAGE OF LOVE?

Love is patient and kind. Love is not jealous or boastful or proud or rude. It does not demand its own way. It is not irritable, and keeps no record of being wronged. (1 Corinthians 13:4–5)

As a marriage and family therapist, I counsel many couples on this subject. I find if partners don't know their spouse's language of love, this can lead to conflicts and misunderstandings within their marriage. There are five basic languages of love, and we all have our favorites. If you know what your language of love is, you can communicate that to your spouse, and they can do the same for you. This will save you a lot of time and frustration in the communication process.

Let me give you an example. Let's say Mary's language of love is touch, followed by spending quality time with those who are important to her. Is Mary going to be completely happy if Bill, her husband, gives her gifts? Probably not. What I have seen in situations like these is that neither Mary nor Bill are happy. Mary is not happy because she really wants Bill to touch her and spend more time with her. Bill is frustrated because he has spent a great deal of money on gifts, and Mary doesn't appear to appreciate them.

It is not that the couple doesn't love each other, but they have failed to communicate to their partner their language of love. In my counseling sessions I often ask my clients to say their partner's favorite love language. It is interesting to see how accurately they guess. The more exact they are in answering the question indicates how intimate the couple is with each other. If a couple has a hard time answering that question, that's an indication the couple is not really that intimate with one another.

There are five basic languages of love:

1. Touch: this is not necessarily sexual touch either. Some people like to be touched. They like it when they are hugged, hold their hand, or sit next to them and put our arm around them.
2. Affirmation: some people like to hear that they are loved and appreciated. They like to know we care for them and are thinking of them by leaving notes, texting them, or just telling them.
3. Gifts: some people like to receive gifts as a sign that they are loved. The gifts don't necessarily have to be expensive, but the very act of receiving something from someone who loves them communicates they are loved. But when we give the gift, they feel appreciated and loved.
4. Acts of service: others feel loved when something is done for them, like the lawn is mowed, dinner is made, the laundry is done, the car is fixed, or the kids are picked up from school. When we perform a service for them, they feel loved.
5. Quality time: some people like it when we spend time with them. They equate the time we spend with them with the love we have for them. What is the main complaint that most men get from their girlfriend or wife? It's that they don't spend enough time with them. Children are much the same way. Many parents make the mistake of giving their kids material things without giving them their time and attention.

So now that we have been educated on the five languages of love, I am going to give you a homework assignment. Find out, if you don't already know what your partner, wife, husband, or child's favorite language of love is and make it a point to give it to them.

Scripture Readings:
1 Corinthians 13

May 14

THERE IS MORE THAN ONE TYPE OF LOVE

Jesus replied, "You must love the Lord your God will all your heart, all your soul, and all your mind." (Matthew 22:37)

In our culture we mainly use one word for love. This can be confusing because there are different kinds of love. Jesus instructs us to love our enemies (Matthew 5:44). Does that mean we are to love our enemies like we love our wife or children? No. When we understand that there is more than one type of love, then we will understand that it truly is possible to love our enemy.

There are five different types of love I will briefly describe below:

1. A love of pleasure. This is the type of love a person has when something gives them pleasure. For example, someone may say they love a car, a house, a city, etc. Their love is based on the pleasure that they receive from the object or person.
2. A love of family. This is a love based on close family ties—immediate family members.
3. A love of friends. This is a love that we have for our friends or close associates.
4. A romantic love. This is a love that we feel for someone who brings us pleasure. It is intoxicating and affects us like a drug. In fact, recent studies have shown this type of love affects the pleasure center of the brain like a drug. A person can literally be addicted to romantic love.
5. An unconditional love. This is the highest form of love because, unlike all the other types of love, it does not expect to receive but only gives. God so loved the world that He gave His only Son (John 3:16). This is the God kind of love. If you want a more detailed description of this type of love, then I invite you to read 1 Corinthians 13. It will show you what God's love is like, and how we can love our enemies.

One of the assignments I give couples I am working with is to read 1 Corinthians 13:4–7 daily. Those who follow these instructions find that their relationship improves because they begin to love each other as God loves them, not love based on one of the other forms of love. Just like Lucifer was corrupted by his pride, so love can be corrupted when we start to love someone or something based on our selfish desires. We must love with the God kind of love.

Scripture Readings:
1 Corinthians 13:4–7
1 John 3:11, 23; 4:7

May 15

LOVE YOURSELF BY FORGIVING YOURSELF

I—yes, I alone—will blot out your sins for My own sake and will never think of them again. (Isaiah 43:25)

One of the main reasons why some people don't feel good about themselves is because of a nagging sense of guilt. Some guilt is attributed to acts they may have done, and some is attributed to what they have imposed on themselves. When a person imposes guilt on themselves because of the actions of another person, this is an example of self-imposed guilt. For example, when a husband leaves his wife for another woman, the wife might blame herself for the actions of her husband and feel guilty as a result of it, when in reality she was not to blame. But if she doesn't correct her thinking, she will live the rest of her life carrying that guilt and shame with her.

No one is perfect except for God. We all have our imperfections and make mistakes from time to time. The difference between those who are successful and happy and those who are not is forgiveness. People who can forgive and forget their mistakes are less likely to make them again; they can move on with their life. Others who can't will wallow in self-pity and regret. These types of individuals seem to get some sort of satisfaction out of punishing themselves, thinking they are cleansing themselves. What they fail to realize, however, is that Jesus has paid the price for their sins—past, present, and future (Isaiah 53:2–5). He bore our sorrows, grief, sin, and punishment, so there is no need for us to carry them any longer.

If you find yourself feeling sorrow, grief, or guilt, repeat Isaiah 53:2–5 several times. Allow yourself to go through the grieving process and move on. It is important to grieve—it is a process that is healthy—but you don't want to get stuck there. How long you should grieve, no one can really say, because it depends on the individual and the circumstances. The important thing is that you learn to forgive yourself in the process. The easier it is for you to forgive yourself, the easier it will be to forgive others.

Scripture Readings:
Luke 6:37
1 John 1:9; 2:12

May 16

TRUST GOD TO TEACH YOU

"But this is the new covenant I will make with the people of Israel on that day," says the Lord. "I will put My instructions deep within them, and I will write them on their hearts. I will be their God, and they will be My people. And they will not need to teach their neighbors, nor will they need to teach their relatives, saying, 'You should know the Lord.' For everyone, from the least to the greatest, will know Me already," says the Lord. (Jeremiah 31:33–34)

Did you know that the Spirit of God resides in you if you are a believer (Proverbs 20:27)? Did you also know that if you accepted the Holy Spirit into your heart, you have a guide who will lead you into all truth (John 16:8–11)? This is a great benefit for those who will take advantage of it. God has given us all that we need to walk in close fellowship with Him. We don't have to rely on a pastor, priest, or clergyperson to show us the way. We can ultimately trust in Him and rely solely upon Him.

Before I go any further, I am not advocating that we don't need to get instruction from a brother or sister in the Lord who is qualified to teach us. Nor am I saying we don't need to go to church. The Bible clearly states that we should not forsake fellowshipping with each other, and that God has appointed pastors and leaders in the church for the purpose of teaching. But if we hear something that doesn't sound right, or it doesn't jive with our inner man, we are not to accept it because our pastor said it. Many false doctrines have started because of this. Instead, we should go to the Scriptures and search out what they say for ourselves, then ask the Holy Spirit to give us insight.

There are some ministers who will teach error because of what they have been taught—most of the time it is not intentional. If it something minor, just let it go because people can get stuck in their ways and they will get offended if we attempt to correct them. If it is something major, then it is up to us to approach the pastor or church leadership and get some clarification on the issue. Maybe we just misunderstood what was said. If we do choose to confront them, it is vital that we make sure we seek the guidance of the Holy Spirit and pray about it. If there is no resolution and we feel restless in our inner man, then we would be better off just leaving the church quietly rather than causing a division.

Most people never question church leadership and stop thinking for themselves. This is how the Jimmy Joneses in the world can lead an entire congregation into the middle of the jungle and introduce all kinds of perversion under the name of God. No one questioned him because they viewed him as a prophet from God, and what he was saying as the truth, no matter what. We have the Spirit inside of us, so we must learn to listen to Him and check with the Scriptures to verify that what we are feeling and hearing is true.

Scripture Readings:
Jeremiah 31:33–34
John 16:5–8
1 Corinthians 6:19

May 17

GREATER ARE THEY WHO ARE WITH YOU

When the 300 Israelites blew their rams' horns, the Lord caused the warriors in the camp to fight against each other with their swords. (Judges 7:22)

God had chosen Gideon to deliver the people from their oppressors. Even though he originally started out with 32,000 men, the Lord said it was too many. He wanted the people of Israel to know that it was His power that delivered them and not their own. Gideon then told his soldiers that if any wanted to go home they could. Immediately 10,000 left. So, with the 22,000 who were left, the Lord told Gideon to only take the men who cupped the water in their hands when they drank from the river. This left Gideon with only 300 men.

With those 300 men, the Lord provided Gideon with a strategy that caused his enemies to get into a panic and turn on themselves. The odds were against them, but nothing is impossible with God (Luke 1:37). Imagine the faith that Gideon and his men had to have to go against thousands of trained warriors. Imagine how hard it must have been for Gideon to watch his army dwindle from 32,000 to 300 men. Walking in faith is not an easy thing to do, but it is possible with God's assistance. Sometimes we have to operate in a faith that only God can give us.

Our faith can only take us so far, but with the God kind of faith we can move mountains (Mark 11:22–23). Like Gideon we sometimes try to fulfill the vision God has given us in our own power. We are limited in our own power, but with God's power nothing is impossible. Smith Wigglesworth said in *Ever Increasing Faith*, that the reason he was able to perform the miracles he did in his ministry was because he realized he needed God's faith to operate through him. We should also have this same mindset.

Jesus also said much the same thing: He could do nothing on His own, but only what He saw the Father do (John 5:30). God wants to demonstrate

His glory through us who believe, but we must be able to trust and obey Him in order for that to happen (Isaiah 1:19). Those stories of God manifesting His glory in the Bible are available to us today if we will believe and receive it. In order for it to happen, however, we have to learn how to trust and obey God. We must renew our minds by reading and meditating on the promises of God daily, and begin to take baby steps as we learn to walk by faith. Are you willing to take those steps?

Scripture Readings:
Judges 7
Isaiah 1:19
Mark 11:22–24
John 5:30

May 18

Angels Are Waiting

Therefore, angels are only servants—spirits sent to care for people who will inherit salvation. (Hebrews 1:14)

Did you know that there are angels that have been assigned to minister to you? I know you may get excited, but there is a catch here: The angels will only listen to words spoken according to God's Word (Psalm 103:20). This means they will not respond to our every whim or desire. When we speak the promises of God over our life, the angel(s) will see that they will come to pass. Through Jesus, we have the authority to speak what He has promised to us. If we have been born again, that means we have been made heirs to salvation. The Scriptures clearly state that angels are here to minister and care for us.

Many believers are unaware of this fact, and the enemy has taken advantage of it. Though we have a fleshly body and live in a material world, we face spiritual opposition throughout our days (Ephesians 6:12). When we try to fight the devil in our own strength, we are destined to lose. However, when we use the sword of the Spirit, which is the Word of God, the devil and his minions are no match for us.

That is why Jesus admonished His disciples that they should only speak His will and not involve themselves in foolish conversations (Matthew 12:34–37). Many believers have talked their way into misfortune because of the careless words they had spoken. When we say, even if it is in jest, "There are no good women or men out there," or "Things will never work out for me," we are opening the door for these things to happen. I know that we really don't mean what we said, but whatever we bind on earth shall be bound in heaven, and whatever we loose on earth shall be loosed in heaven (Matthew 16:19).

God has given us great power, and that is to speak faith-filled words. And we will be held accountable for the words we have spoken. So we should be economical in the use of our language (Proverbs 17:27). And we should remember that our angels are listening to everything we say, and they will move on our behalf when our words are in agreement with God's commands (Psalm 103:20).

Scripture Readings:
Psalm 8:6; 103:20
Hebrews 1:14

May 19

The Need to Worship

No one can serve two masters. For you will hate one and love the other; you will be devoted to one and despise the other. You cannot serve both God and money. (Matthew 6:24)

I watched a movie the other night about a guy whose desire was to become rich. So he got a job on Wall Street as a stockbroker, worked his way through the ranks, and was fairly successful. Then there was a stock market crash, and he was suddenly out of a job. He finally found another job selling penny stocks. This man had the gift to sell, and he was able to sell these worthless stocks and make a great deal of commissions off the sales.

He decided to start his own company and became very wealthy as a result. He fulfilled his dream and became a millionaire, but that wasn't enough for him. He became obsessed with money. He had forsaken all his morals—he lied, manipulated, and justified his actions because of his pursuit of wealth. His insatiable appetite for wealth turned out to be his downfall. Addicted to drugs, alcohol, and sex, this man lost his wife and family and wound up in prison. And the sad thing about all of this is that it was based on a true story.

How many people have traveled down this path and found similar results? How many of us have forsaken our morals and principles for the pursuit of wealth? We have a problem in this country with the pursuit of material things. They have become a god to many people. Our economy is primarily consumer driven, meaning it will not work unless people are buying something. The system promotes being in debt. Watch most commercials and you will see an agenda of promoting dissatisfaction. Our television, phone, and car are all out of date and obsolete before we get them home. Therefore, we need to buy the latest and greatest.

As believers, we should be aware of this tendency in our society, because it is easy to fall into worshipping the god of wealth (mammon). Many are working themselves to death in order to achieve what they feel is the American dream. Many are worshipping at the altars of the shopping malls rather than worshipping the true and living God.

We as human beings are designed to worship something. That is why God commanded that we are to worship Him alone (Exodus 20:5). We are not to worship anyone or anything other than God, the Creator of heaven and earth. Worshipping celebrities is the same as worshipping an idol. And some of these celebrities are used to promote an agenda that is contrary to a godly lifestyle.

God wants us to be prosperous. It brings glory to Him when His children have their needs met and are able to provide for the needs of others (Psalm 35:27). The rule with prosperity is this: possess your possessions, but don't let them possess you. Don't be like the rich young ruler who walked away from the opportunity of being a disciple of Jesus because he was possessed by his possessions (Mark 10:17–27).

Scripture Readings:
Exodus 20:5
Matthew 6:24–33

May 20

HELD CAPTIVE BY YOUR OWN SIN

An evil man is held captive by his own sins: they are ropes that catch and hold him. He will die for lack of self-control; he will be lost because of his great foolishness. (Proverbs 5:22–23)

Samson has been somewhat of an enigma to me. He was so strong and yet so weak, so wise and yet so naïve. We can learn a lot from his life story if we are careful to observe it. He was one of the many judges of the nation of Israel. God had set him apart from birth as a Nazarite (Judges 13:5). He had the Lord's anointing on him, and it was demonstrated in his exceptional strength. But Samson also had a weakness for foreign women, which would prove to be his downfall. However, God was able to use his weakness to confront Israel's enemies, the Philistines.

On one occasion Samson killed a thousand Philistines with the jawbone of an ass (Judges 15:15–17). In spite of the mantle God had given him, Samson continued in his wanton ways, going to brothels and wasting his time and money on prostitutes. His parents tried to warn him, but because of the anointing on his life, he thought he was invincible. He took God's patience for granted and thought he could do whatever he pleased at whatever time he wanted. Samson had a false sense of confidence the enemy used to deceive him.

When Samson met Delilah, he was enthralled with her, blinded by her beauty and intoxicated with the romantic love he had for her. He could not see what others around him saw. Delilah was using Samson for the pleasure and the status of being in his presence. That is why it was so easy for her to betray him. Three times Delilah tried to get Samson to tell her the secret to his strength, but all attempts failed. You would think that Samson would have known what she was up to, but pride comes before a fall (Proverbs 16:18). Finally, Samson broke down and told Delilah the secret to his strength. God could no longer protect him and a woman subdued him. It is kind of ironic that Samson was able to kill a thousand men by himself, but his demise came by the power of one woman.

Samson was captured and tortured by his enemies, then they poked out his eyes and made sport of him. However, once Samson repented, God's anointing came back upon him and in his final victory he killed three thousand Philistines along with himself. What a tragic way to end his life. I know that was not God's plan for Samson's life, but God has given us the ability to choose what we will do with this life. Learn a lesson from this: don't let your sins take you captive.

Scripture Readings:
Judges 15–17
Proverbs 16:18
Galatians 6:7
2 Peter 3:9

May 21

God's Word Produces

The rain and snow come down from the heavens and stay on the ground to water the earth. They cause the grain to grow, producing seed for the farmer and bread for the hungry. It is the same with My word. I send it out, and it always produces fruit. It will accomplish all I want it to. And it will prosper everywhere I send it. (Isaiah 55:10–11)

One of the keys to living the victorious Christian life is learning to speak the promises of God. For when we do this, it puts spiritual forces to work on our behalf (Psalm 103:20). Jesus constantly used the words of God to combat the enemy and to perform miracles (John 5:30; 14:11). He knew that when He spoke the words of God, it was like God Himself was speaking those words.

Since we are the children of God, we have the same ability that Jesus had in regards to speaking the promises of God (1 John 5:1). We have the confidence to know that whatever we speak, if it is in the Word of God, will come to pass in our lifetimes. We are to be confident, no matter what the circumstances look like to the natural eye. God has given us His Word that whatsoever we ask, if it is according to His will, we will receive it (1 John 5:14–15)! We need to meditate on this until it gets into our heart.

For those of us who get the revelation of this in our inner man and begin to operate in this confidence, we will walk in the power of God. No circumstance or weapon will be able to prosper against us (Isaiah 54:17). For those who grasp this truth, they will be able to speak to the mountains in their lives and see them disappear! They will see their enemies defeated. While others speak fearful words, they will speak hope. They will be the strong tower people run to in times of trouble, because the glory of God will be present with them. This power is available to anyone who chooses to be willing and obedient.

Scripture Readings:
Genesis 1:26
Isaiah 54:17
Mark 11:22–24
John 5:30; 14:12–14; 16:23
1 John 5:1, 14–15

May 22

GOD'S GOT A MANTLE FOR YOU

But you have been anointed by [you hold a sacred appointment from, you have been given an unction from] the Holy One, and you know all [the Truth] or you know all things. (1 John 2:20 AMP)

Did you know that once you are born again, God gives you a new mantle to wear? A mantle is an outer garment that was worn in Jesus's time, signifying who a person was in the community. Beggars wore a certain type of mantle, and prominent people wore a different kind. We as believers have been given a spiritual mantle to wear. Unfortunately, not all of us are living up to the mantle that has been given. Some of us have a mantle of prominence but we are living like beggars. Others of us have outgrown our mantles and refuse to accept a larger one. And still some of us are like Porky Pig, the cartoon character, walking around with a shirt way too small for us.

God has given each of us talents and abilities to be used for His glory and to benefit others, but some have hidden their talents in the sand out of selfishness or insecurity. Sometimes, it takes a step of faith to exercise our talents. God gave me the desire to write. Since my college days, I wanted to write and play guitar. Well, I took an English class my freshman year at the university and I got a D. Then years later I worked as a probation officer and I was told by one of my supervisors that I did not have good writing skills.

Being the type of person I am, I was determined to prove her wrong. I started working on my writing skills every day. A few years later I wrote my first book. Those in the probation department could not believe that I wrote it. Some of them even accused me of hiring a ghostwriter to do it for me. Needless to say, I took that as a complement.

I will tell you another story. One of my favorite things to do is to play guitar and write songs. I like playing my guitar at home and very seldom played in front of anyone. But one day the Holy Spirit challenged me to do so. I was teaching a men's meeting and the topic was about fear. I realized I had a fear of playing in front of people, so I decided to overcome it. I took my guitar and played worship songs for the men's meeting that day. All the fear left. I would later perform in front of the entire congregation.

If God has given you a talent, then let it flow and He will take care of the rest. God is not going to ask you to do something you are not equipped to do. There are some people who have the unction to street witness, and have no problem going up to complete strangers and preaching the gospel to them. I don't have that gift. If it were left up to me, a lot of people would be going to hell because I feel uncomfortable street witnessing. Thank God because He knows what you are good at and what you are gifted to do; so just let your gift flow.

Scripture Readings:
Ephesians 4:11
1 John 2:20

May 23

Repentance Is the Way to Freedom

Peter replied, "Each of you must repent of your sins and turn to God, and be baptized in the name of Jesus Christ for the forgiveness of your sins. Then you will receive the gift of the Holy Spirit." (Acts 2:38)

Repentance is a subject that isn't talked about much today, but it is something every believer should be aware of. Repentance is a gift from God that allows us to get back on course when we miss the mark destined for us. God is a forgiving God who wants everyone to repent so that they will not suffer the consequences of their actions (2 Peter 3:9). Repentance is more than saying we're sorry for our sins. Many people say they are sorry, but the only thing they are sorry for is that they got caught.

True repentance is when we not only apologize for our actions or behaviors, but we actually turn away from repeating them. Repentance is an action word, requiring movement. I have been studying the Old Testament and have found a pattern in the way God dealt with the nation of Israel. Time after time the children of Israel would disobey the commandments of the Lord. As a result, they would experience oppression from their enemies until they repented. Once they repented, however, God would send someone to deliver them.

There were other times when the children of Israel would call out to the Lord to rescue them, but He seemed to ignore them. This was because they were not truly repentant; they just wanted some relief from the oppression they were under. But when they were truly sincere and stopped their idol worship and began to worship the true God, then He delivered them once again. The same is true for us today. When we are truly repentant and turn from the behavior that got us into the situation we are in, then God will act on our behalf.

Jesus knows the temptations we go through because He lived on this planet as a man. He understands the pressures we experience. Not only that, but He has provided a way out for us when we miss it—repentance. When we truly repent of our actions, we have the power to walk away. This is a gift we need to utilize more. We don't have to be bound by our sins any longer; we only need to repent and walk away. Just admit and quit! God's grace is more than sufficient to empower us in this process.

Scripture Readings:
Matthew 3:2; 4:17; 18:3
Luke 13:3
Acts 2:38; 3:19; 8:22
1 Corinthians 10:13

May 24

THE HARDENED HEART

But you must not forget this one thing, dear friends: A day is like a thousand years to the Lord, and a thousand years is like a day. The Lord isn't really slow about His promise, as some people think. No, He is being patient for your sake. He does not want anyone to be destroyed, but wants everyone to repent. (2 Peter 3:8–9)

What happens to someone who refuses to repent? When a person refuses to repent of their actions, then their heart becomes hardened. Their conscience, or their moral voice, is silenced, freeing them to do whatever they want to do. The apostle Paul wrote to Timothy about this in 2 Timothy 3:1–5: people like this are living under the control of their fleshly nature, doing what seems right in their own eyes.

It is not that God is not willing to forgive them if they repent, but that they actually don't see the need to change their behavior. They have deceived themselves into thinking that what they are doing is right. They have insulated themselves with justification and rationalization for their actions. People with a hardened heart are dangerous because they are capable of doing anything to satisfy their own desires.

I have worked with people with antisocial personality disorders, and they are perfect examples of what can happen to someone with a hardened heart. They will lie, cheat, and steal all the while being your best friend. You wonder how someone could live with himself or herself after betraying someone's trust, but because they have silenced their conscience they no longer have a moral compass to direct them.

To have your heart hardened a person has to repeatedly ignore the voice within them. Because they refuse to repent of their actions or behavior, the process of a hardened heart begins. If it is not interrupted, the person will become entrenched in a way of thinking that is distorted. They will then have a stronghold in their thought process, which allows them to continue in this behavior. And they will suffer the consequences of their actions, never accepting responsibility for what they have chosen for their own lives. Don't let this happen to you. When your conscience convicts you of something, be quick to repent. Take advantage of the gift of repentance that God has so graciously given to us.

Scripture Readings:
1 Corinthians 10:13
2 Timothy 3:1–5
James 1:19–25
2 Peter 3:8–9

May 25

Is God's Grace Evident in Your Life?

When he arrived and saw what grace (favor) God was bestowing upon them, he was full of joy; and he continuously exhorted (warned, urged, and encouraged) them all to cleave unto and remain faithful to and devoted to the Lord with [resolute and steady] purpose of heart. (Acts 11:23 AMP)

Most of us are acquainted with the word *grace*, meaning God's unmerited favor. Grace is receiving a benefit that we did not deserve. But grace has another meaning as well. It means to be empowered to do something. We all have different assignments to fulfill for the Kingdom of God. So God, in His grace, has empowered us to complete the task. God, through the Holy Spirit, will empower every one of us to live up to our potential if we will but ask for it.

In the book of Acts, it is recorded that Stephen performed amazing miracles and signs among the people because of God's grace and power working in his life (Acts 6:8). The apostle Paul relied on God's grace to accomplish the spreading of the gospel to the Gentiles, and also in writing a majority of the New Testament (Galatians 1:15). Grace is available to all believers, but it is up to us to allow it to manifest in our lives.

I have a friend of mine who loves to serve. He volunteers for different outreaches in the community, as well as serving as an elder at his church. I look at him and wonder how he is able to do all of this. Then I realize that God has graced him to serve in those capacities. There are others who love to go street witnessing—they feel their calling is to witness to anybody and everybody. God has given them grace in that area. Others have the gift to teach, to give, or lead worship. The point is that God has provided His grace to assist us in our endeavors.

I have made it a practice to ask God to give me grace for the things I have to do for the day. He knows what lies ahead of me for that day, so I know that whatever I encounter I will overcome because of the grace of God operating in my life, empowering me to do what I need to do for that particular day. If you are having a difficult time in your life, then you need to call on the grace of God to get you through. Allow the grace of God to flow through you so that others can see God's favor operating in your life.

Scripture Readings:
Acts 6:8; 11:23
1 Corinthians 15:10
2 Corinthians 1:12; 12:9
Galatians 1:15
James 4:6

May 26

Know Your Role

However, He has given each one of us a special gift through the generosity of Christ. That is why the Scripture says, "When He ascended to the heights, He led a crowd of captives and gave gifts to His people." (Ephesians 4:7–8)

Yesterday I wrote about the grace of God, and how His grace can empower us to complete the task He has given us to do. I want to continue on this same theme by writing about some of the gifts Jesus has provided for the growth of the church.

Jesus has specifically assigned each of us a gift for the purpose of enriching the entire body of Christ. It is up to us to find out what our gift is and then run with it. Our gift is not going to be something that we do not want to do—God is going to give us the desire for what He has called us to do. God is not going to tell us to be a missionary in Africa or India if that is not what we want to do. So take a deep breath and relax.

In Ephesians 4:11, the apostle Paul lists the five-fold gifts for the body of Christ: apostles, prophets, evangelists, pastors, and teachers. These abovementioned offices are assigned to equip God's people to do His work and build up the church. It is God's desire that everyone knows their role and performs it with the grace that God has given them. This is not about what we think we're good at or what we would like to do, but about what we have been assigned to do. Like I said earlier, God is not going to put us in a position that we are not capable of doing. On the contrary, it will be something we greatly enjoy.

There is a certain kind of grace that a pastor has that a teacher doesn't have. There is a certain kind of grace that someone who wants to do missionary work has that a prophet doesn't have. If a teacher attempts to pastor a church, it will not be a good fit unless he or she has been graced to be a pastor/teacher. I have attended churches where the pastor was out of position. He only took the position because his father, who was the previous pastor, died. It didn't take long before scandal hit the church, and a once thriving congregation was on the brink of disaster.

We as the body of Christ need to know what our gifts are because everyone benefits when we are walking in what God has called us to do. If you are not sure what your gift is, simply ask God to reveal it to you. Be open to what He has to tell you. He might have called you to be involved in children's ministry because you enjoy working with children; He might have called you to be an evangelist because you enjoy preaching the gospel of salvation; or He might have called you to be teacher because you have a hunger for the Word of God and like teaching others. Each one of us are to know what we are gifted in because only then will we be happy—when we know our role.

Scripture Readings:
Ephesians 4:7–16

May 27

WHAT KIND OF FRUIT ARE YOU PRODUCING?

A tree is identified by its fruit. If a tree is good, its fruit will be good. If a tree is bad, its fruit will be bad. (Matthew 12:33)

The fruit of the Spirit is different than the gifts of the Spirit because all the fruit of the Spirit is available to any and every believer. It is the natural byproduct of being filled with the Spirit of God. Every believer should be manifesting the fruit of the Spirit in their lives, but it is up to each believer to allow the fruit to grow. The apostle Paul describes the fruit of the Spirit as being love, joy, peace, patience, kindness, goodness, faithfulness, gentleness, and self-control (Galatians 5:22–23).

When we were born again, the seed of the Spirit is planted in our hearts so that we can manifest the fruit of the Spirit in our lives. But it is up to us to allow that seed to germinate and grow within. We allow this to happen by spending time in the Word of God and meditating on the promises. By doing this, we are producing the proper climate for the seed to grow. Just like water and sunlight are necessary for a tree to produce fruit, so we need the water of the Word and the *Son*light of the Spirit to produce godly fruit in our lives.

There are some believers who are not producing any fruit in their lives. Like the fig tree Jesus cursed because it didn't produce any fruit, they are in jeopardy of dying and being thrown in a pile to be burned (Mark 11:12–14, 20; John 15:1–4). If we remain in Jesus, we will produce fruit. It will not require any effort on our part, just as it does not take effort from the tree to produce its fruit. All it takes is water and light. So make sure that you water your tree and give it the needed light so it can provide fruit for all to see.

Scripture Readings:
Matthew 12:33–34
Mark 11:12–14, 20
John 15:1–8
Galatians 5:22–23

May 28

THE PRESENCE OF GOD IN TROUBLED TIMES

In my distress I prayed to the Lord, and the Lord answered me and set me free. The Lord is for me, so I will have no fear. What can mere people do to me? (Psalm 118:5–6)

There will be times in all of our lives when the unexpected will come upon us like a flood. It is in times like these it is vital that we be conscious of the presence of God. If we allow the circumstances to overwhelm our minds, we will get flooded with negative thoughts. Those thoughts will cause stress hormones to be released, which in turn will cause a reactive response in our body. We will feel agitated and our thought process can become clouded. This is harmful to both our mind and our body.

Instead, take a moment and say to yourself, "Immanuel, God is with me." When you want to stress over the bills that need to be paid, simply say, "God is with me." When the car breaks down, say, "God is with me." When your kids are acting crazy, say, "God is with me." Make "God is with me" your mantra whenever you face life's challenges. And God will give you His peace and grace to go through that trial.

God never promised that we would not face trials in this life; in fact, He said we would (John 16:33). Yes, we as believers should have peace no matter what circumstances we face because God can make a way for us when there doesn't appear to be a way (Isaiah 43:16). Having this mindset allows us to be more attentive to the voice of our spirit rather than in tune with our flesh. When we quiet our soul, we can hear from the Lord and He will instruct us and guide us. Remember, there is no circumstance greater than God, and God resides within each one of us (1 John 4:4).

Finally, we should watch our words because they will determine our destiny. If we allow ourselves to be overwhelmed by the circumstances we face, we may say something negative, and this will hinder our deliverance. We have to keep in mind that our angels will only respond to God's commandments and fearful words. Instead, find Scriptures on deliverance and meditate on them frequently. This will cause us to produce positive thoughts that will release hormones that will activate the release of dopamine into our body, causing us to relax.

Scripture Readings:
Psalm 27:1; 118:5–11
Hebrews 13:5

May 29

Let the Lord Guide You

Trust in the Lord with all your heart; do not depend on your own understanding. Seek His will in all you do, and He will show you which path to take. (Proverbs 3:5–6)

Do you realize that God wants to have an intimate relationship with *you*? Do you know that He even knows the number of hairs on your head (Luke 12:7)? That is how much God knows about you, so why not include Him in your decision making? Some believers are reluctant to include God in their decision making because they feel they can do it on their own. Others feel like God is not really concerned with what is going on in their lives. Both of these thoughts are contrary to God's desires for us.

David wrote in Psalm 23:3 that the Lord guides him along the right paths, and brings honor to His name. When we allow God to guide us, we will always have the assurance that it is the right choice we are making. Sometimes we can make choices that seem right at the time, but later we regret that we made that particular choice. How many people have gotten married to someone whom they later realized was not the best choice for them? Had they sought God's guidance before they acted, that situation would not have happened.

How many bad business deals and transactions could have been avoided if the counsel of the Lord had been sought first? God has given us the Holy Spirit to be our consultant, giving us guidance through any situation or task at hand. All we need to do is call upon Him and He will answer. Becoming aware of the presence of God in our lives is necessary if we want to live the kind of life God has for us. Remember, not all believers are going to enter the Promise Land, only those who are willing and obedient. Let the Lord lead you into the Promise Land.

Scripture Readings:
Proverbs 3:1–8
Psalm 23

May 30

Do You Have Ears to Hear?

Anyone with ears to hear must listen to the Spirit and understand what He is saying to the churches. To everyone who is victorious I will give fruit from the tree of life in the paradise of God. (Revelation 2:7)

Jesus promises that anyone who listens to His voice will receive blessings from God. They will be victorious in life, they will eat from the fruit of the tree of life, and they will not be harmed by the second death (Revelation 2:11). Those who listen to God's voice will be dressed in white and have their names written in the Book of Life (Revelation 3:5–6). Jesus also said that those who will open the door of their hearts and listen to Him will not only be victorious in this life, but they will be able to sit down with Him and have a meal together (Revelation 3:20).

There are many believers who hear a lot that goes on around them but don't really listen. We hear with our ears but we listen with our mind. We will not receive an award for merely hearing the Word of God, but for listening to His voice and doing what He instructs us. Remember that it is only those who are doers of the Word who will be blessed; those who merely hear the Word but don't do what it says are just deceiving themselves, building a house on a faulty foundation (Matthew 7:24–25). When trials and tribulations come their way, they fall by the wayside because the Word never took root in their heart.

If we are to be victorious in this life, we need to actively seek the guidance of the Lord and allow Him to lead us. As we do this, we will have the peace that goes beyond understanding, no matter what circumstances we may find ourselves in. We have God's promise that He will never leave us or forsake us (Hebrews 13:3–6). We know that because Jesus has overcome the world, we too are world overcomers (1 John 5:4). We renew our minds daily to rehearse the promises of God and train ourselves to listen to the voice of the Spirit, allowing Him to guide us so that we can reach the Promise Land.

Scripture Readings:
Revelation 2:11; 3:5–6, 20
Matthew 7:24–25
James 1:22–25
1 John 4:4; 5:4

June 1

LET GOD'S ROD AND STAFF GUIDE YOU

Listen to me! For I have important things to tell you. Everything is right I say is right, for I speak the truth and detest every kind of deception. My advice is wholesome. There is nothing devious or crooked in it. (Proverbs 8:6–8)

God has provided us with His provisions so that we can walk in victory. He has provided us with His wisdom, of which there are two kinds—the wisdom that comes from the world, and the wisdom that comes from God (James 3:13–16). Worldly wisdom can lead to disorder and every kind of evil, but God's wisdom produces peace and goodness.

Godly wisdom comes from two sources as well: the Word of God and the Spirit of God. As we submit ourselves to the Good Shepherd and listen to His voice, we find godly wisdom to assist us in our everyday life. When we listen to godly wisdom, we find knowledge and discernment. Riches, honor, and enduring wealth are the results of those who walk in godly wisdom too (Proverbs 8:18–21). We will walk in righteousness and rule as a king/queen in this life. When we choose to walk in the wisdom of God, we are choosing to walk with Jesus because Jesus has been made our wisdom (1 Corinthians 1:30).

However, if we choose to walk in the wisdom of this world, we open ourselves up to deception, pride, arrogance, and corruption, because worldly wisdom has its roots in the prince of the power of the air (Ephesians 2:2). Though worldly wisdom can cause someone to prosper, that prosperity usually comes at a cost. How many people have sold their soul to get ahead in life? How many people have lied, cheated, stolen, and even killed to obtain what they wanted? How many movies and television programs glorify the deeds of those who would do anything to get ahead, poisoning the hearts of the simpleminded? Which wisdom will you choose to walk in today, God's wisdom or the wisdom of this world?

Scripture Readings:
Proverbs 8
James 3:13–16

June 2

LET THE WORD UNFOLD

Dear brothers and sisters, when troubles come your way, consider it an opportunity for great joy. For you know that when your faith is tested, your endurance has a chance to grow. So let it grow, for when your endurance is fully developed, you will be perfect and complete, needing nothing. (James 1:2–4)

There will be times in our life when we have prayed and made the right confession, and the manifestation of what we have requested still did not come. When this happens, we begin to question ourselves: "What am I doing wrong? Maybe I need to fast, or read my Bible more, or maybe I should have given more." All these thoughts can be running through our heads at times like these. As the days go on, we get more impatient and we attempt to make our prayer come to pass in our own power and strength. When we do this, we have left the rest of God and have gotten into human effort, which only increases anxiety and stress.

I have been down this road more times than I care to remember, trying to help God out. Well, God doesn't need my help. And you know what? He doesn't need your help either. Sometimes, it may appear that God is slow to respond because He is working things out that we are not aware of. Or maybe there are things He is working out *in us* before He gives us what we are asking for. We need to learn from Abraham what happens when we try to help God out and walk in doubt. We will only end up with an Ishmael (Genesis 16).

It is completely natural to get weary in waiting for the promise of God to manifest itself, but if we discipline ourselves to trust in the Lord, He will renew our strength (Isaiah 40:29–31). Sometimes God will test us by delaying our request to reveal if we truly trust and believe in Him alone. Other times He will allow us to be tried in order to mature and develop us.

It is like a caterpillar transforming into a butterfly. The caterpillar goes into a cocoon and struggles to escape. But the struggle must take place in order to develop the strength it needs to survive. Once it frees itself from the cocoon, it has become a beautiful butterfly. We likewise must go through struggles at times because God wants us to be His beautiful butterflies, manifesting His glory through us. Embrace the struggle and trust that God is working behind the scenes today.

Scripture Readings:
Genesis 16
Isaiah 40:28–31
James 1:2–4

June 3

LEARN TO DOUBT YOUR DOUBTS

But you must really believe it will happen and have no doubt in your heart. (Mark 11:23)

For a long time I used to pray for things and they never manifested. I thought it was because I had doubt in my head. I used to condemn myself until I heard Charles Capps say that there was a difference between having doubt in your head and doubt in your heart. He then went to talk about Mark 11:23 and pointed out that Jesus specifically said we are not to have doubt *in our heart*. I meditated on that and God gave me revelation that my prayers were not answered because of the doubt I had in my head, but for the words I spoke after condemning myself for having the doubt.

True faith is generated from the heart and not from the head (Romans 10:9). We can have faith in the mental realm, but that is only mental assent. Our heart has its own brain. In fact, our heart has 40,000 neurons that interact with our brain. So it is possible that our heart believes something and our brain is thinking entirely differently. Intuition is a good example of our heart speaking to us. Our mind might be telling us one thing, but our heart is telling us something else.

We must not condemn ourselves for having doubt in our heads. We have been brought into a world system that teaches us to be ruled by our natural senses. We have been taught to think logically, so it's natural for us to doubt when it comes to supernatural things, things that require faith. That is why it is important to renew our mind to the things of God so that we will begin to think like Jesus (1 Corinthians 2:16). If we don't renew our minds, we will always have an internal conflict going on within, one taking place between the heart and the mind (Hebrews 4:12).

Do you think that the patriarchs of the faith didn't have doubt in their minds? They were flesh and blood, just like you and me, but they didn't let their doubt stop them from believing God and acting on His Word. It is not the doubt or fear you have going on in your head, but what you do with it in your heart. Do you let it stop you or do you push through and act in faith? I suggest you begin to doubt your doubts. When doubt enters your mind, speak the Word of God to it and push on. Eventually, it will stop. Once you start getting positive results, you will convince your mind with the tangible evidence that your faith manifested.

Scripture Readings:
Mark 11:23–24
Romans 10:9

June 4

WHICH VOICE DO YOU LISTEN TO THE MOST?

The Lord's light penetrates the human spirit, exposing every hidden motive. (Proverbs 20:27)

We as human beings have three components that make us who we are—we are a spirit, and we have a soul and a body. I like to say that man is a spiritual being that has a soul and lives in a physical body. Before the fall, Adam was led by his spirit alone. He had the ability to communicate directly with God because God is Spirit. However, because of Adam's disobedience, he died spiritually the day he ate of the fruit of the tree. His spirit no longer led him, but he was led by his physical senses. His spirit took a backseat, and his soul and body were put in the driver's seat.

The man who once had close fellowship with God and communicated directly with Him was now spiritually dead, leaving the mind and the body to lead him. The man who was able to download information directly from God now had to rely on his sense knowledge (Genesis 3:17–19). He had to learn how to survive in his environment without God's Spirit to direct him. So man learned to listen to the voice of logic and reason. The natural man cannot accept the things of God because it doesn't make sense to him, because it's not logical (1 Corinthians 2:13–14).

Adam's body, which was a vehicle for him to use in this physical world, became more dominant. His physical senses became more important, and he started listening to the voice of the body, which are the emotions and logic. If something was displeasing, it was avoided; if something was pleasurable, it was sought after (Genesis 3:6). That was the way he learned to live, doing what he thought was right and logical, and living to please his flesh. The conscience was still there but it had been silenced by the voices of logic/reason and emotions.

We as believers have a reborn spirit that has been reconnected with the Spirit of God. We now have the ability to communicate directly with the Holy Spirit, and the voice of our spirit, which is the conscience, can be trusted to lead us into all truth (John 16:13). We can now be led by the Spirit and go back to God's original design. But we must reeducate ourselves and develop our mind so that it can be in agreement with our spirit instead of in conflict with it (Ephesians 4:23). We must learn to rely on the voice of our spirit man once again, and let him take the lead. I am not saying we are to ignore logic or emotions because they have their place in our lives; I am saying we should allow the spirit to once again take its place of prominence. Then we can walk like Jesus walked on this earth.

Scripture Readings:
Proverbs 20:27
John 5:30; 16:13
1 Corinthians 2:13–14

June 5

WHAT THE BLOOD OF JESUS PURCHASED FOR YOU

And they sang in a mighty chorus: "Worthy is the Lamb who was slaughtered—to receive power and riches and wisdom and strength and honor and glory and blessing." (Revelation 5:12)

Ask most believers today what the blood of Jesus provided for them and they will tell you something along the lines of redemption from their sins. And they are completely correct. But the blood of Jesus has provided so much more than only forgiveness of sins. The apostle Paul stated in the book of Ephesians that we have been given all the spiritual blessings in Christ Jesus (Ephesians 1:3). We have been given every spiritual blessing that we could ever need to live a prosperous and victorious life in Christ. It is available to us *now*, if we will but believe and receive it.

There are many believers who are unaware of this and their lives show it. They are living defeated lives, letting the enemy knock them upside the head any time he feels like it. It doesn't have to be that way. We only need to be like the children of Israel and take the Promise Land that has been given to us. We are going to have to activate our faith by meditating on the promises of God and speaking them daily. I don't care what the Dow-Jones or the news is telling us, we no longer belong to this kingdom; Jesus has made us a citizen of His Kingdom (Revelation 5:10).

We have to take the initiative to find out what God has provided and promised us in His Word. We can't rely on our pastor to do it for us, because they may not know. But we have the Bible, and that's all we really need. So start to take authority and exercise your Kingdom rights. Know all that the blood of Jesus provided for you.

Though this is not an exhaustive list, here are a few things the blood of Jesus has provided for us:

- Power: we have power to overcome any circumstance that we may be facing.
- Riches: we have been given all that we will ever need according to His riches in Christ Jesus.
- Wisdom: we can access this whenever we need it.
- Strength: to withstand anything that comes against us.
- Honor: for we are in Christ Jesus.
- Glory: because God resides in us, and He is manifesting His glory through us.
- Blessings: because we are children of the Most High God.

Scripture Readings:
Ephesians 1:3; 3:20
Revelation 5:10–13

June 6

You Have Been Made a King and a Priest

"And you will be My kingdom of priests, and My holy nation." This is the message you must give to the people of Israel. (Exodus 19:6)

It has been God's desire ever since the fall of man to reestablish His Kingdom on the earth. He expressed this to Moses while he was leading the children of Israel to the Promise Land (Exodus 19:6). His desire has not changed, even for us today. God still wants His people to be a nation of kings and priests to the world (Revelation 1:6).

Paul said that we are to be Christ's ambassadors while on this earth (2 Corinthians 5:20). An ambassador represents his or her country from which they come. We are to represent God's Kingdom to a world that is clouded in darkness. We are to be like a beacon of light to those who are looking for it. God has called us to be ministers of His Kingdom (Isaiah 61:6–7), and to live in abundance so that we can minister unto the needs of those who need assistance. But this will not happen if we don't believe and receive it.

God has not provided all this material and spiritual blessings just to satisfy our personal needs and wants. We are blessed so that we can be a blessing to others (Genesis 12:2–3). The enemy will use anything he can to keep this vision from our eyes. He will use religion to teach us that it is worldly to be prosperous and that holiness is being humble and struggling financially because our reward is ultimately in heaven. He will misinterpret Scripture by saying, "Money is the root of all evil," when the Scripture says, "The *love of money* is the root of all kinds of evil" (1 Timothy 6:10).

Take your rightful position as a king and a priest for the Kingdom of God today. Don't be like the children of Israel who disqualified themselves with their unbelief and died in the wilderness. Instead, accept the responsibility of being a priest and king, and start representing the Kingdom of God!

Scripture Readings:
Exodus 19:6
Isaiah 61:6–7
2 Corinthians 5:20
Revelation 5:10–12

June 7

What's Your Temperature?

I know all the things you do, that you are neither hot nor cold. I wish that you were one or the other! But since you are like lukewarm water, neither hot nor cold, I will spit you out of My mouth! (Revelation 3:15–16)

This morning when I woke up, I went to get a drink of water from the faucet. I have a purifier attached to the water faucet so I can look forward to drinking a cold glass of water every morning. Well, this morning I must not have turned the faucet all the way to cold, because when I drank the water it was lukewarm. I immediately spit it out of my mouth because I wanted cold water, not lukewarm water.

Immediately I thought about the above Scripture and felt led to include it in this book. It was written to the church of Laodicea, which was a prosperous church and many affluent and wealthy people attended it. Their church would be like many of the megachurches we have today. They had all the programs and were very user friendly. They were like the believers the apostle Paul spoke of in 2 Timothy 3:5, having a form of godliness but denying its power.

Jesus said that He would spit this church out of His mouth because He wanted a church that was hot or cold, not lukewarm. There is a lesson to be learned from this. We need to examine ourselves to see that we are not lukewarm in our faith. We must realize that God expects us to produce fruit in our lives, and not just occupy space on the pew once a week. Some people think that going to a church service is enough. They go only when it is convenient for them, they don't give of their finances or their time, they have a Bible but never read it outside of church, and they live a lifestyle that is similar to that of the world.

Jesus said that the branches that don't produce any fruit would be pruned and thrown into the fire (John 15:6). In order to produce fruit, we must remain united to the tree; those who are not united will stop producing fruit. The church of Laodicea at one time was on fire for God, but they allowed their hearts to cool and relied more on human effort than the Spirit of God. They became prideful of what they were able to achieve and slowly slipped away. Some of us have done the same thing. To avoid this from happening to you, take your temperature on a regular basis. Use the thermometer of the Holy Spirit so that Jesus doesn't spit you out of His mouth.

Scripture Readings:
Luke 13:6–9
John 15:1–8
Revelation 3:15–16

June 8

TWO TYPES OF FAITH

Then Peter called to Him, "Lord, if it's You, tell me to come to You, walking on the water." "Yes, come," Jesus said. (Matthew 14:28–29)

Peter is one of my favorite disciples because of his personality. I would have liked to hang out with him. One of the stories in the New Testament that has inspired me is the story of Peter walking on the water. Just imagine the faith it took to walk out on the water in the midst of a raging storm. Imagine the conversations that were going on before Peter stepped out of the boat. I can imagine some of the disciples trying to talk him out of it, and others hating him because he was bold enough to go for it.

Though Peter wasn't totally successful in his attempt, we have to give him credit because he did walk on water for a short distance, which was an accomplishment in and of itself. I haven't seen anybody else walk on water, have you? Peter didn't do this using his own faith, but he was operating in the supernatural faith that Jesus provided for him. This is very important to remember, because when we operate in supernatural faith, it's God faith that is doing the work within us, not ours. Many of us who desire to operate in supernatural faith try to use our faith, and like Peter we fall short.

If Peter had not gotten permission from Jesus, he would have sunk like a rock the moment he stepped out of that boat. But the Scripture states that Peter stepped out of the boat and was walking toward Jesus (Matthew 14:29). But what happened? When Peter took his eyes off Jesus and started looking around at the wind and the waves, he panicked and began to operate in his own faith, and his own faith was no match for the circumstances. But thank God that he was close enough for Jesus to grab him before he was totally submerged in the water.

God wants us to operate in the supernatural so that we can bring glory to His name. Signs and wonders should be a common occurrence among believers; how else is the world going to know the greatness of the power of God unless the church shows them (Ephesians 3:10)? But this will not happen until we begin to ask for it, just like Peter did. We have to be bold enough to pull away from the status quo and be willing to step out of the boat when God gives the go-ahead. Remember, God has to give you His faith to do the supernatural.

Scripture Readings:
Matthew 14:22–32

June 9

FIND YOUR RESTING PLACE IN GOD

For only we who believe can enter His rest. As for the others, God said, "In My anger I took an oath: 'They will never enter My place of rest,'" even though this rest has been ready since He made the world. (Hebrews 4:3)

It is difficult to not be anxious at times. The pressures of life can get to any believer if they look to themselves for the answers to life's challenges. Just spend an hour watching the news and anyone will find plenty of reasons to be anxious and worried. Our world is moving faster as we slowly move toward the end times. There is no place for the faint of heart, and in the coming days the shifting process will become more intense. Jesus spoke of this as He addressed His disciples in Matthew 24.

In spite of the pressures we might be facing, God has provided a resting place for us in Him. But it is only available to those who enter His rest through faith. We don't want to be like the children of Israel who frustrated God because of their unbelief and wound up wandering in the wilderness and eventually dying in the desert without reaching the Promise Land. No, we learn from their example and labor to enter the rest of God.

The labor required is not physical work to enter, but to labor to exercise our faith and believe in the promises of God. We must labor to speak the promises of God when we start to feel anxious and start doubting in our mind. To labor means that we praise God for the finished work of Christ Jesus and give thanks for the deliverance He has provided for us. We must not allow the circumstances to define our reality, but allow the Word of God to define it. This is how we enter the rest of God (Philippians 4:6–9).

Scripture Readings:
Matthew 6:33
Philippians 4:6–9
Hebrews 4:1–11

June 10

THE POWER OF BEING SINGLE-MINDED

But when you ask Him, be sure that your faith is in God alone. Do not waver, for a person with divided loyalty is as unsettled as a wave of the sea that is blown and tossed by the wind. (James 1:6–7)

There is a peace that comes to us when we are focused. When we are focused on a single thing, we are able to not allow our attention to be distracted by outside influences. When I am playing tennis, for example, my best games are when I am not thinking about anything other than hitting the ball where I want it to go. I get in a zone where everything is working toward that goal, where both mind and body are working together for that one purpose.

Well, it is much the same with the things of God. When we are single-minded, we will not allow the distractions of the world and of the flesh to interrupt our focus. Jesus operated this way while He was on the earth (John 5:30). He was committed to the Word of God and He didn't allow anyone or anything to distract Him (Matthew 16:23). How many times have we allowed someone to talk us out of walking in faith? These people are usually not our enemies, but are someone who is close to us and in whom we trust.

The enemy will use anyone to dissuade us from going after the promises of God. Peter didn't realize that he was being used by the enemy to discourage Jesus from fulfilling His call and eventual death. He thought he was being helpful, but in reality Peter was only thinking about his personal agenda. Not everyone will understand some of the decisions we make, and we don't have to explain our reasoning to them. We will have to answer to God and Him alone for the decisions we make, so we must decide for ourselves whom we will follow.

Scripture Readings:
Matthew 16:21–26
James 1:6–7
Hebrews 12:2

June 11

THE POWER OF PERCEPTION AND THE LOVE OF MAMMON

Your eye is a lamp that provides light for your body. When your eye is good, your whole body is filled with light. But when your eye is bad, your whole body is filled with darkness. And if the light you think you have is actually darkness, how deep that darkness is! (Matthew 6:22–23)

Jesus was teaching on the subject of serving God or serving the god of mammon, which is the personification of greed and arrogance. What we can learn from this is that we as believers must be mindful not to be lured by the love of money (1 Timothy 6:10). It is so easy to fall into the trap of serving mammon without even realizing it. There are many believers who love the Lord but have fallen prey, seeking and serving the god of mammon, without knowing what they were actually doing.

Because of the abundance of wealth in this country, we are even more susceptible to serving mammon rather than God. Right from the very beginning of this country, the god of mammon raised its ugly head by endorsing the institution of slavery and forcing the Native Americans to live on reservations. The Constitution of the United States, which guaranteed rights to all of its citizens, was ignored for financial gain and profit. Compromise was justified. And this trend continues today with the top 1 percent. According to a recent study conducted at the University of California, the top 1 percent of wage earners experienced 31.4 percent increase in wealth since the recession, while the other 99 percent saw an increase of just .04 percent.

This ideology is not just restricted to the secular business world, but it has made its way into the church as well. Financial decisions seem to take precedent over the Holy Spirit in most churches. Some ministers and teachers even research how well the congregation is doing financially before accepting a speaking engagement. The needs of the community are secondary to some denominations in planting churches. Some people would rather attend a church close to where they live to save some money rather than go to the church where they are being fed spiritually. And some Spirit-filled believers will compromise their morals to make a sale or get ahead financially, rather than trusting God to meet their needs.

I now understand how Satan was able to get Judas to betray Jesus. The god of mammon possessed his heart. Judas was the treasurer for Jesus's ministry team, which meant that he was in charge of the finances. He thought that once Jesus came into power, he would be in charge of the finances for the whole nation. However, when Jesus told His disciples that He was going to be crucified, Judas got upset because his dream of being in charge of finances was not going to happen. So he sold Him out. Why? It was because he was serving the god of mammon.

This was not easy for me to write because I had to examine myself first. And to be honest with you, I didn't like what I saw. But the good thing is that we serve a forgiving God, who allows us to judge ourselves so that we don't have to be judged by Him in the end. There is peace and a sense of freedom that we can experience from true repentance. I hope you examine yourself also, and let the Lord do a work of grace within you.

Scripture Readings:
Matthew 6:19–34

June 12

WHEN HARD TIMES COME, GO INSIDE

Nor will people say, Look! Here [it is]! or, See, [it is] there! For behold, the kingdom of God is within you [in your hearts] and among you [surrounding you]. (Luke 17:21 AMP)

If we are believers, then we have a distinct advantage over those in the world—we have the Spirit of God residing within us, empowering us to overcome the hard times we face. God's Kingdom resides within every believer who has accepted Jesus as his or her Lord and Savior, giving us access to the Kingdom of God (Ephesians 3:20). We only have to be conscious of this and seek revelation from God by meditating on the Scriptures.

When Jesus was on the earth operating as a man, He was aware that the Kingdom of God was within Him. He operated from an internal locus of control, which meant that He would not allow external circumstances to control Him. Rather, He controlled His circumstances by exercising the power of the Holy Spirit that resided within Him. For example, Jesus and His disciples were in a boat crossing to the other side of the lake when a terrible storm arose. The disciples began to panic because water was in the boat, and they thought they were going to drown. What was Jesus doing this time? He was asleep! If Jesus was operating as the Son of God, He would not need to sleep because God does not sleep; but this proves Jesus was operating as a man who was empowered by the Holy Spirit.

Why was Jesus able to sleep while the disciples were in a state of fear? It was because He was operating from an internal locus of control. He didn't allow the circumstances to shake Him because the Kingdom of God was within Him. He received orders from God that He was to go to the other side of the lake to minister, He spoke what He heard, and there was no way that it would not come to pass. There is no place for fear or failure in the Kingdom of God! What did Jesus do when the disciples woke Him up? He simply rebuked the wind and the sea and it became still (Mark 4:35–41).

We should learn from Jesus how to respond when hard times and difficulties come our way. Instead of being anxious and allowing ourselves to be overcome with fear, we should draw from the resources within us and speak the promises of God boldly, allowing our angels to assist us. God has made the Kingdom accessible to us, but we must exercise our faith to bring forth the manifestation. The Kingdom of God is within you.

Scripture Readings:
Luke 17:21
Mark 4:35–41
Romans 5:14

June 13

Is God's Grace Evident in Your Life?

Stephen, a man full of God's grace and power, performed amazing miracles and signs among the people. (Acts 6:8)

Stephen was one of the first believers mentioned in the book of Acts who was martyred for his faith. He was described as a man full of God's grace and power, and he demonstrated it by the signs and wonders he performed. Stephen was made of flesh and blood just like you and me, so it is possible for the same thing to be said about us. For this to happen, however, we must actualize the potential that is already within.

First, we must renew our minds and cleanse ourselves from the religious doctrines that teach that all the miracles and manifestations stopped with the death of the last apostle (Romans 12:1–2). We must search the Scriptures and allow God to paint a new image in our minds so that we start to think like Jesus (1 Corinthians 2:16). God's grace is reflected in us when we walk in a way that brings glory to Him.

Because of God's grace that is working within us, we can do exceedingly more than we can ask or imagine, because it is not our ability but God's ability operating within us (Ephesians 3:20). Make it a practice to ask God to open the eyes of your understanding and reveal to you the greatness of His power that resides within. Ask Him to provide you with the grace you need for the day at hand. If you do this, then others will see the grace of God operating in your life, and you will bring glory to the Kingdom of God in all that you do.

Scripture Readings:
John 14:12
Acts 6:8
Romans 12:1–2
1 Corinthians 2:16; 15:10
Ephesians 3:20

June 14

Diligence Is a Sign of Faith

> *But Benjamin's warriors, who were defending the town, came out and killed 22,000 Israelites on the battlefield that day. But the Israelites encouraged each other and took their positions again at the same place they fought the previous day. For they had gone up to Bethel and wept in the presence of the Lord until evening. They had asked the Lord, "Should we fight against our relatives from Benjamin again?" And the Lord had said, "Go out and fight against them." (Judges 20:21–23)*

I was reading the book of Judges and read about an incident that was both tragic and interesting. It seems that a Levite priest had moved to a remote part of Ephraim and served as a personal priest for a man named Micah. The priest had a concubine who lived with him, but she got mad and left to go back to her father's home in Bethlehem. After a period of time, the priest went to retrieve his concubine. He was successful in retrieving his wife, and after staying with his father-in-law for five days, he returned home.

On the way back to Ephraim, the priest and his concubine stopped in the town of Gibeah. It was late in the evening, so they tried to find a place to stay for the night, but no one offered them a place. So they decided to stay in the town square. An old man saw the couple in the square and encouraged them to stay at his house because he feared what would happen to them if they stayed in the town square.

Well, when the men of the town found out that the priest was staying with the old man, they came to the old man's house and demanded that the priest be given to them so that they could have sex with him. The old man offered his virgin daughter instead, but the men of the town wanted the priest. Finally, the priest put his concubine outside and the men raped her all night. Because of the abuse she endured, she died the next day. Her body was cut into twelve pieces and one piece was sent to every tribe in Israel.

All the tribes came together, and when they learned what had happened, they came against the tribe of Benjamin, where the men lived who were responsible for raping the woman. A conflict ensued, with Israel suffering a great loss of men. They could have given up, but they sought the Lord and He said they would be victorious if they persevered. In two days of battle, Israel lost 40,000 men. But on the third day, they prevailed against their enemies and destroyed their town with only 600 men from Benjamin being left.

The main lesson I learned from this story is that just because we get the go-ahead from God doesn't mean things will be easy for us. Just because God says yes doesn't mean we will not suffer loss along the way. We cannot think that because we meet some resistance that it is not God's will for our life, or that we somehow missed God's voice. We are to remember that some battles will take more than others, but we must play until we win, because we are more than conquerors in Christ Jesus.

Scripture Readings:
Judges 19–20

June 15

WITH GOD THERE IS ALWAYS HOPE

You have tested us, O God; You have purified us like silver. You have captured us in Your net and laid the burden of slavery on our backs. Then You put leaders over us. We went through fire and flood, but You brought us to a place of great abundance. (Psalm 66:10–12)

I have found this portion of Scripture comforting when I am going through a difficult time. It gives me hope because I realize that no matter how bad the circumstances may be, God is there with me and He will deliver me even if I was responsible for the situation by a choice I made (Isaiah 43:1–2). We are all prone to make mistakes and miss the mark, but we have a great High Priest who knows what it is like to live on this earth as a man (Hebrews 3:1).

We live in a world that is hostile to those who choose to follow Jesus. We have the influence of the world and our fleshly nature also, so if we are not careful we can fall into traps and be led astray. When this occurs, we must know that God will always provide a way out (1 Corinthians 10:12–13). Acknowledging that we missed the mark, we are to allow the Holy Spirit and the Word of God to show us the way out.

One thing I have found through the Bible is that God is more than willing to forgive if we will but ask for it. Read the book of Jonah and you will see why Jonah didn't want to go to Nineveh. He wanted God to destroy Nineveh because the citizens were Israel's enemies. Jonah got upset when he preached to the citizens there, and the entire town repented and God changed His mind and didn't destroy them like Jonah had hoped (Jonah 4:1–3). It is God's desire that no one is without repentance (2 Peter 3:8–9).

When we humble ourselves and trust God, we will receive forgiveness, peace of mind, and assurance that we will find deliverance from any circumstances. We cannot believe the lies of the enemy that tell us it's too late. We cannot listen to those who give us a myriad of reasons why things will never work out for us. Don't believe the gospel of this world any longer. Trust God to take you to your wealthy place, resting securely in Him.

Scripture Readings:
Psalm 66:10–12
Isaiah 43:1–2
1 Corinthians 10:12–13
2 Peter 3:8–9

June 16

SPEAKING THE PROMISES OF GOD

It is the same with My word. I send it out, and it always produces fruit. It will accomplish all I want it to, and will prosper everywhere I send it. (Isaiah 55:11)

God has made a promise to us: He guarantees that His Word will accomplish whatever it was sent out to do. He said it would not return to Him void. Jesus also said the same thing by stating that if we keep on asking, we will receive what we ask for, and that if we keep on knocking the door would be opened (Matthew 7:7). What did He mean by keep on asking and keep on seeking? I believe that we should only ask once for something if we truly believe it will be given to us.

I remember when I was young my dad would sometimes make promises to me and not keep them. This caused me to distrust what he told me. So I would constantly ask him over and over again if he intended to do what he promised. He would sometimes get upset with me for asking so much, but I learned to protect myself from disappointment by making sure he would follow through on his promise.

When I had children I made it a point not to make promises I couldn't keep because I didn't want them to experience what I did when I was a child. In spite of my best efforts, they would sometimes ask me over and over again if I was going to do what I said I was going to do. But the difference with them was that they were putting me in remembrance of what I had promised them. This is what Jesus was talking about when He said we are to keep on asking and keep on seeking. When we remind God of His promises, we are returning His Word back to Him. By doing this we are speaking the voice of His commands, which releases the angels to accomplish that which we have spoken (Psalm 103:20).

We see this same principle in the book of Isaiah, where it talks about watchmen who were on the wall and their assignment was to put God in remembrance of His promises day and night (Isaiah 62:6). When we speak God's promises back to Him as a reminder to Him, it not only increases our faith (Romans 10:17) but our words create images in our minds that cause us to have a positive outlook on the situation. Jesus used this when He was about to suffer on the cross. How was He able to withstand the torment He was about to endure? It was the joy that He had because of the vision of the outcome He would experience (Hebrews 12:2).

We too can employ the same strategy when we are going through difficult situations. Instead of taking some intoxicants and singing the blues, look through the Word and find promises that apply to your situation. Speak that Word back to God as a reminder of what He has promised to do for you. This will cause the angels of heaven to get involved in your situation, and you will get the desired result, because God's Word does not come back to Him void.

Scripture Readings:
Isaiah 55:8–13
Matthew 7:7–12

June 17

How Bad Do You Want It?

And again they wept together, and Orpah kissed her mother-in-law good-bye. But Ruth clung tightly to Naomi. "Look," Naomi said to her, "your sister-in-law has gone back to her people and to her gods. You should do the same." (Ruth 1:14–15)

In the book of Ruth we find a dire situation where three women lost their husbands. Naomi's husband and two sons died in a foreign land, and she was left with her two daughters-in-law, who were both Moabites. When Naomi decided to return back to her country, both of her daughters-in-law decided to go with her. Naomi tried to discourage them to not return with her, but to stay in their own country. One of the daughters-in-law changed her mind and stayed in her country, but Ruth clung to her mother-in-law and said she would not leave.

When I read this, I thought about many of my friends who accepted the Lord when I did, but who are no longer walking with Him today. Just like Orpah, the daughter-in-law who decided to leave Naomi and return to her country, they too did the same thing. Jesus said that many are called but only a few are chosen (Matthew 20:16). The lure of the world is strong and it is easy to look back and second-guess the decisions we have made along the way.

We will be tested to see if we are really committed to our Lord or not. If we pass the test, then we will be rewarded like Ruth eventually was by marrying Boaz, a rich farmer. If Ruth had gone back with her sister-in-law, what would her life have been like? She would have probably lived an ordinary life, got married and had some kids. But because she decided to leave the familiar and go with Naomi, she found a much better life and married into the line of King David's family.

We too have the choice of clinging to our Lord and Savior and walking away from the familiar things of this world, or to just live an ordinary life. I don't know about you, but I am going to cling to Jesus!

Scripture Readings:
Ruth 1–4
Matthew 7:13; 20:16

June 18

Forget Not His Benefits

Let all that I am praise the Lord; may I never forget the good things He does for me. (Psalm 103:2)

It is so easy to take certain things for granted. I remember when I was paralyzed in both my legs and arms and could do nothing but lay in bed all day. I had to have nurses get me out of my bed and put me in a wheelchair. They had to change me and bathe me. They even had to roll me over in my bed to prevent me from getting bedsores. It was during those times that I realized how much I had taken for granted. The ability to walk under my own power, to sit up, and to go to the bathroom on my own, were some of the basic things I never thought about before being paralyzed.

The same is true when it comes to the things of the Spirit. We can easily take for granted all the benefits that have been provided for us in Christ Jesus—especially for us who live in America. We have so much here that it is easy to take for granted all the blessings we have as a nation. I remember going to Ukraine for the first time. I could feel the spiritual oppression in the atmosphere—I could see it on the people's faces as they walked down the street. I didn't feel the presence of God like I did in the United States. It was there that I realized there was a distinct difference in countries where the gospel has been inculcated into the moral fabric of society, and nations where it hasn't.

We need to remind ourselves of all the benefits we have as believers. We should thank God every day for the grace, mercy, and faithfulness He provides (Psalm 68:19). We should constantly thank God for His angels that are here to minister for us (Hebrews 1:14), and for His Word and all the promises He has given to us (2 Corinthians 1:20).

If you are having a rough day and nothing seems to be going your way, take a moment and think about all the benefits you have in Christ. Those negative thoughts will soon disappear and you will have positive thoughts that take their place. Instead of being downtrodden, you will become an overcomer.

Scripture Readings:
Psalm 103; 68:19
2 Corinthians 1:20
Hebrews 1:14

June 19

THE LORD REWARDS THOSE WHO TAKE REFUGE IN HIM

May the Lord, the God of Israel, under whose wings you have come to take refuge, reward you fully for what you have done. (Ruth 2:12)

Whenever we do anything in obedience and act in faith, God takes note of that and rewards us. A good example of this can be found in the book of Ruth. After the death of her husband, Ruth had the choice of remaining in Moab, her country of origin, or going with her mother-in-law back to Israel. Ruth chose to go with her mother-in-law, leaving the familiar environment she was used to in order to live in a country that was foreign to her. She had to turn away from the gods of her forefathers to embrace the one true God.

It must have been tough for Ruth to be a single woman trying to make it in a culture that was different than what she was used to. But Ruth adjusted and worked gleaning in the fields. She would gather enough grain for her mother-in-law and herself. Then one day, Boaz, the landowner, took notice of her and inquired about her. When he found out that she was the daughter-in-law of a relative, he approached her and told her she could glean from his field, and she didn't have to go anywhere else. Boaz later instructed his workers to allow Ruth to work with the regular workers and that extra meals would be provided for her. Eventually, Boaz married Ruth and she became the wife of a wealthy landowner.

That would have never happened if Ruth had not taken refuge in the God of Israel. If she had not stepped out in faith and trusted in God, she would have never experienced the blessings that had been provided for her since the beginning of time. We have a part to play in whether we get blessed or not. We have the power of choice; everything is not up to God. We choose to walk in the blessings or in the curse (Deuteronomy 30:19).

In the story of the rich young ruler, he was faced with a similar situation. Jesus told him to give away all he had and follow Him. He could not let go of what was familiar to him so he could find something new and better. He walked away (Mark 10:17–27). Maybe Jesus wanted this young man to take the place of Judas Iscariot. He could have been one of the disciples and maybe even written one of the books in the New Testament, but instead he died wondering what if…

Jesus promises us that whatever we give up in this life we will receive a hundred-fold, not only in this life but in the life to come (Mark 10:29–30). Do you believe Him? If you do, what are you waiting for? Are you going to be a Ruth or an Orpah?

Scripture Readings:
Deuteronomy 30:19
Ruth 1–4
Mark 10:17–30

June 20

DELAY IS NOT DENIAL

But when Jesus heard about it He said, "Lazarus's sickness will not end in death. No, it happened for the glory of God that the Son of God will receive glory from this." (John 11:4)

Sometimes when we earnestly seek God for something in prayer, and we don't receive it when we think we should have, we begin to wonder if God has denied our request. This is what happened in the case of Lazarus. He was seriously ill and was at the point of death if he didn't receive immediate medical intervention. Since Jesus had a personal relationship with Lazarus and his two sisters, they sent a messenger to notify Him of Lazarus's illness (John 11:1–3). When the messenger returned and said that he had given Jesus the message, they were certain that He would come.

However, instead of immediately responding to the situation, Jesus waited two more days before leaving (John 11:6). The reason for the delay was because God had something greater in mind than just healing Lazarus (John 11:4). When Jesus finally arrived, Lazarus was dead and had already been buried in a cave. In fact, he had been dead for four days (John 11:39). We can imagine Lazarus's two sisters were perplexed with why Jesus didn't come when He was first informed about his illness (John 11:20–29).

In the end, Jesus raised Lazarus from the dead, something that no one had ever seen before—a man raised from the grave after four days. God received glory from the obedience and actions of Jesus, and many put their faith in Him as a result (John 11:40, 45). Had Jesus responded immediately to the situation, this would not have happened to the degree it did.

The moral of the story is that sometimes God has a bigger plan in mind for us that we can't see at the moment. Maybe He has a better offer waiting for us, or a better mate, or a better job than the one we want right now. That is where faith comes into the picture. Do we really trust that God has our best interest in mind? Are we really willing to submit our will to the will of God, or are we just giving mental assent to the thought of being submissive?

Scripture Readings:
Proverbs 3:5–6
John 11:1–53
James 1:4

June 21

God's Will Always Makes a Way

For all of God's promises have been fulfilled in Christ with a resounding "Yes!" And through Christ, our "Amen" ascends to God for His glory. (2 Corinthians 1:20)

There are times we have believed God for something that we have found a promise for in His Word. And during the course of time, while waiting for the manifestation to occur, we miss it by something we have said or done. This doesn't disqualify us from receiving the promise, but it may mean that the manifestation might be delayed because of our actions. God wanted the children of Israel to possess the Promise Land, but because of their disobedience and lack of faith it took them forty years to enter instead of the eleven-day journey it was supposed to be.

God's Word is His will and His Word will not return to Him void! His Word will be done no matter how long it takes. Remember, where God resides time does not exist as we view it (2 Peter 3:8). God promised Abraham and his wife would have a son. But they didn't see the manifestation of that promise until twenty-five years later. During that period, before the birth of Isaac, they had an Ishmael through their own efforts, which was part of the reason for the delay in the promise.

God has created us as free moral agents with the ability to make choices. Sometimes we make choices that work against us, and other times we make choices that work for us. When we make choices that work against us, it doesn't mean that we have been disqualified from obtaining the promise of God. What it means though is that because of our actions we might cause a delay in the manifestation of the promise. It is like using a GPS system in the car. We put the address in of where we want to go, and when we make a wrong turn the GPS has to recalculate and give us slightly different directions in order to get us to our final destination. Depending on how far off course we are, it might take us longer to get where we wanted to go.

The enemy likes to play with our minds when we miss what God has spoken to us. He will immediately tell us how we disappointed God and how frustrated and upset He is with us. God knew that we were going to blow it, so it does not come as a surprise to Him. This is nothing but an attempt to get us to give up, because that is the only way the enemy knows how to stop us—through lies and deception. Since the death and resurrection of Jesus, Satan has been rendered powerless (Colossians 2:14–15). When we miss the mark by making a poor decision, we need to acknowledge that we missed it and get back on course, because He is faithful to fulfill His promises found in His Word.

Scripture Readings:
2 Corinthians 1:20
Colossians 2:14–15
Hebrews 13:3–6

June 22

DON'T DESPAIR: THE WORD IS AT WORK

Then Moses went back to the Lord and protested, "Why have You brought all this trouble on Your own people, Lord? Why did You send me? Ever since I came to Pharaoh as Your spokesman, he has been even more brutal to Your people. And You have done nothing to rescue them!" (Exodus 5:22)

Have you ever felt like Moses? Have you stepped out in faith, and instead of things getting better they seemed to get worse? I don't know about you, but I know I have. When this happens, we start to wonder if we misunderstood what we have read or heard, because God seems so far away, and we question ourselves as to why God isn't doing anything about our situation. Well, my friend, welcome to the world of walking by faith. What is happening is that the enemy is trying us.

The last thing the enemy wants is for us to be successful in the assignment God has given. He knows that he is powerless to stop us from fulfilling our potential in God (Colossians 2:14), so he has to discourage us from pursing the things we believe for. He will use other people to come against us and create situations with the hopes that it will cause us to doubt ourselves and question God's ability to come through on our behalf (Ephesians 6:12).

If we read the book of Exodus, we will see how the enemy works to create unbelief in the children of Israel, even despite all the miracles they witnessed firsthand. His methods have not changed because they actually work. But as believers we can see through his schemes so we won't be detoured from getting to our Promise Land.

Jesus spoke of the five things used to get us to speak against the Word and to walk in unbelief. They are

1. persecutions (usually by people),
2. lust for other things (distractions, usually material or pleasure),

3. the cares of this life (family, finances, world events),
4. afflictions (which are demonic in nature), and
5. the deceitfulness of riches.

If we think about any time we have stopped pursuing a promise of God for our life, it was likely one or more of these that was the root cause of our decision. Our faith will be tried. The closer we get to our victory, the more intense the battle will be. But we must always remember that greater is He who is in us than he who is in the world (1 John 4:4). And Jesus will never leave us nor forsake us (Hebrews 13:5–6). So speak the promises of God today and watch the enemy flee.

Scripture Readings:
Colossians 2:14
Ephesians 6:12–13

June 23

DOING THE WORKS OF FAITH

I can do nothing on My own. I judge as God tells Me. Therefore, My judgment is just, because I carry out the will of the One who sent Me, not My own will. (John 5:30)

In the days to come I trust that believers will be called to perform signs and wonders like the apostles did in the book of Acts. This will be for the glory of God to be manifested to an unbelieving world who will need to see before they will believe in our Lord and Savior Jesus Christ. In order for that to happen, however, we need to renew our minds so that we have the same mindset Jesus had while He walked on the earth (1 Corinthians 2:16).

One man I admire and respect is Smith Wigglesworth. He lived in the early 1900s and had a profound miracle ministry. It is documented that he raised at least twenty people from the dead and performed miracles that astound the mind. I highly recommend that everyone read some books about this man of God. In one of his books, *Ever Increasing Faith*, Smith Wigglesworth reveals the secret of his ability to perform miracles. He said, "Oh, this wonderful faith of the Lord Jesus. Your faith comes to an end. How many times I have been to the place where I have had to tell the Lord, 'I have used all the faith I have,' and then He has placed His own faith within me."[3]

Wigglesworth's statement echoes that of Jesus when He said that it is the Father who does the works through Him (John 14:10). It is only when we come to the end of ourselves and realize that our faith is inadequate to accomplish what God wants that God will begin to act on our behalf. God wants us to be the vehicles He uses to manifest His glory in the earth. He is in the driver's seat and will determine when the signs and wonders will occur, not us. Once we understand this, God can trust us with the power of performing miracles.

---

[3] Smith Wigglesworth, *Ever Increasing Faith*, 102.

The ability to possess the faith to perform miracles is a gift given by the Holy Spirit (Galatians 6:22). We cannot generate it. Many people think that if they pray, fast, and recite enough Scripture, they will be able to garner enough faith to perform miracles. Though we should pray, fast, and read and recite Scripture, we should do it for obtaining a better understanding of God, not as a formula to get miracle-working faith. Motivation makes all the difference in world with God, because He looks at our heart (1 Samuel 16:7)!

Scripture Readings:
Mark 16:17–18
John 5:29–30; 14:12
Acts 2:43

June 24

You Will Only Go As Far As You Can See

"Stretch out Your hand with healing power; may miraculous signs and wonders be done through the name of Your holy servant Jesus." After this prayer, the meeting place shook, and they were all filled with the Holy Spirit. Then they preached the word of God with boldness. (Acts 4:30–31)

God put in place universal principles that will work in both the spiritual and secular worlds. Many of the success principles that are being taught today are principles that can be found in the Scriptures. I learned this when I was playing football. Many of the slogans my coach used I later learned came from the Bible. The words had been slightly changed to fit the context in which he was using them, but they were still words from the Bible.

One that stands out to me is, "Your body will achieve what your mind can conceive." My coach put that slogan everywhere and he said it repeatedly. All of us would laugh to one another and say it, but little did we realize the power contained in those words. I believe repeating that slogan over and over was the reason that we went from being in the bottom of our division (WAC) to being co-champions within one season. At one point we were ranked as high as number eight in the nation. And this was done with the same players who played the previous year.

I had a similar experience in high school too. When I first started playing football there, we would lose every game. Every team wanted to play us for their homecoming because they were guaranteed a win. Well, a new coach came in with a different vision and philosophy. He came from a winning program and he expected the same from us. The first season he was there, he took a losing team and got them to the playoffs. This again was with the same players who played the year before.

I tell you this because the same is true when it comes to the things of the Spirit. We need to look at ourselves from God's perspective rather than the how the world sees us. We need to grasp the vision that God has for us and make it our own. We have the potential to do great things, but they will not be realized unless we start seeing ourselves as God sees us. We can do all things through Christ who strengthens us (Philippians 4:13), and we are more than conquerors through Christ (Romans 8:37).

If you want to achieve greatness in your life, then you need to start seeing it in your mind first. By doing this you are creating an image of your inner man that does not know the difference between fantasy and reality. Then you will find yourself doing things that were once only a vision in your mind. You will go as far as you can see because Christ resides within you!

Scripture Readings:
Exodus 4:5
John 14:12
Acts 2:43; 4:30–31; 8:6

June 25

YOU HAVE BEEN RESCUED

For He rescued us from the kingdom of darkness and transferred us into the Kingdom of His dear Son, who purchased our freedom and forgave our sins. (Colossians 1:13)

A couple of days ago I wrote about Ruth, a Moabite woman who was married to the son of Naomi. Ruth made a decision after the death of her husband to stay with Naomi rather than return to her own people. She would later go with Naomi back to Israel and lived there with her mother-in-law. Ruth would go out every day and glean from the fields to supply for her mother-in-law and herself. She eventually got the attention of Boaz, a wealthy landowner, who favored her.

Boaz would eventually become her redeemer and marry her. Ruth became the mother of Obed, who would become the father of Jesse, who would become the father of King David. Because of the act of faith of Ruth, she went from being an ordinary citizen of Moab to being in the kingly line of David. Boaz served as a type of Christ who redeemed her from poverty and placed her in a place of prosperity.

This is a picture showing us what Jesus has done for us. When we act in faith and believe on Jesus Christ as our Lord and Savior, we are redeemed from the kingdom of darkness, and He provides us with an inheritance of spiritual blessings (Ephesians 1:3). We go from being strangers to the promises of God to being heirs to the Kingdom! This is something to shout about! We are now heirs of God and belong to the Kingdom of God!

Since we are heirs, we need to start acting like it. We need to start acquainting ourselves with our rights and the privileges that come with being citizens of the heavenly Kingdom by spending time in the Word of God and acquainting ourselves with the promises God has given us. There are many believers who still live like strangers to the promises of God and don't take advantage of what is available to them. Don't let that happen to you, because the precious blood of the Lamb of God has redeemed you.

Scripture Readings:
Ruth 4:13–16
Ephesians 1:3–6
Colossians 1:11–13

June 26

TAKE GOD'S PILL WHEN YOU CAN'T SLEEP

In peace I will lie down and sleep, for You alone,
O Lord, will keep me safe. (Psalm 4:8)

Have you ever noticed the number of commercials on television for antidepressants and sleeping pills? It seems that there is a growing number of the population who are having problems with getting a good night's sleep. There are many contributing factors for this, but I want to focus on the main culprit for sleeplessness—fear and all its relatives: anxiety, worry, and doubt. Any time I have had a problem going to sleep, it was because I was anxious or frustrated about something that had occurred during the day that I didn't let go of.

We live in a complex world that is getting smaller every day. Because of the Internet and modern technology, we are aware of issues going on around the world we would have never heard of a hundred years ago. We live in a world that thrives on feeding us bad news that generates fear and anxiety. It's no wonder that the pharmaceutical companies are a multi-billion-dollar industry. According to a report from the Center for Disease Control and Prevention National Center for Health Statistics, antidepressant use has increased 400 percent over the last two decades in the United States alone (October 25, 2011).

God has provided a remedy for anxiety. Jesus told His followers not to be anxious about anything, but to trust in God and seek His Kingdom first (Matthew 6:33). What did He mean by this? Jesus understood that we would face difficult situations in this life, but we must not allow them to dictate to us how we are to feel or the actions we are to take. Instead, we must learn to operate from an internal locus of control. We have the Spirit of the living God residing within us. When we allow the Kingdom that resides within to override the outside circumstances, we find the peace of God that transcends all understanding (Philippians 4:6–7).

We need to remind ourselves of the promises of God that state He will never leave us or forsake us (Hebrews 13:5–6). We must inculcate into our thought process Scriptures to combat the negative thoughts that arouse our limbic system and cause us to be anxious and agitated. We must also renew our minds to understand that we are greater than the circumstances; we are not powerless because we are more than victorious in Christ Jesus. Storms will come and the wind will blow, but we don't have to crumble in the midst of them. Instead, we can stand on the Rock and get a good night's sleep, resting secure in Him.

Scripture Readings:
Psalm 4:8
Ecclesiastes 5:12
Isaiah 41:10; 43:1–2
Matthew 6:25–34
Philippians 4:6–8

June 27

WHAT TO DO WHEN YOU ARE IN THE VALLEY

Even when I walk through the darkest valley, I will not be afraid, for You are close beside me. (Psalm 23:4)

Our walk is like a journey with the Holy Spirit leading us to our Promise Land. During this journey we will experience difficulties, hardships, and disappointments. But if we trust our Good Shepherd, He will lead us to green pastures. We must keep this in mind when we are having our valley experience. It is so easy to just give up and quit. But if we do we will be robbing ourselves of the blessings God has for us just around the bend.

I once heard Joyce Meyer say that some shepherds would deliberately take their sheep through the valley to strengthen them for the mountaintop experience. Well, our heavenly Father does the same with His children. He wants to refine us and strengthen us so that we can be useful for the Kingdom. It is through perseverance that we are perfected (James 1:3); it is through those valley experiences that we get a testimony to share with others, to encourage and strengthen them. We must remember there were many wealthy and established companies that went through the valley. Pepsi, Quaker Oats, and Henry Ford all went bankrupt more than once before they achieved success.

When we are in the valley, we must remember that we are not alone (1 John 4:4). We have the Spirit of the living God residing within us. And He does not know how to fail. We also have to silence our mind, because it will give us problems, especially if it is not renewed. Whenever doubt raises its ugly head and starts yelling at us, we only need to tell it to shut up and quote the Word of God, and it will eventually obey. I also like to recall to mind all the other times that God has delivered me from circumstances that seemed impossible. If we don't have any experiences of our own, then recall how others were delivered and use that until we get our own testimony.

Finally, don't listen to the lies of the enemy who will try to say that God has abandoned us, and He is not big enough to help us this time. Remember that he is the father of lies, so just believe the opposite of what he is saying.

It is important to also remember that it is always darkest before the dawn. There are many people who forfeited their blessings because they quit prematurely. I read a story about an inventor who was so close to inventing the first telephone, but he got discouraged and quit. He was just one wire away, but Alexander Graham Bell got credited for being the first one to invent the telephone. The moral of the story is that we cannot let those valley experiences take away what God has waiting for us on the mountaintop.

Scripture Readings:
Psalm 23
Isaiah 43:1–2
Hebrews 13:5–6

June 28

WHATEVER YOU GIVE TO GOD, HE WILL GIVE YOU MORE

And the Lord gave Hannah three sons and two daughters. Meanwhile, Samuel grew up in the presence of the Lord. (1 Samuel 2:21)

Hannah was one of two wives married to Elkanah. Peninnah, the first of Elkanah's wives, could have children, but Hannah could not. Because Hannah was barren, Peninnah would taunt her so bad that Hannah would go into a state of depression and cry. Year after year this continued. Hannah got to the point where she would not eat and cried all day long because she was unable to have children.

In her distress, Hannah made a vow to the Lord that if He would bless her with a child, then she would dedicate him to the Lord for all the days of his life. The Lord heard her prayer and blessed Hannah with a son, whom she named Samuel. In keeping her vow, Hannah kept Samuel until he was weaned and then took him to the tabernacle to serve the priest Eli. Imagine how hard that must have been for her. She had waited all those years for a child, and when she finally got want she wanted, she gave the child to the Lord. Hannah took her most precious possession and gave it back to the Lord in order to fulfill her vow.

In the process of time, the Lord eventually blessed Hannah with three sons and two daughters! You see, what we give to God does not go unnoticed in His sight. He will give us back more than what we gave to Him in the first place. Jesus said, "Give, and you will receive. Your gift will return to you in full—pressed down, shaken together to make room for more, running over, and poured into your lap. The amount you give will determine the amount you get back" (Luke 6:38). Sometimes it is hard to give up something that is of value to us. Our minds have been trained to do the exact opposite. But if we let go of that which is valuable to us, it frees God to give back to us a hundred-fold (Luke 17:29).

We can see this principle throughout the Bible. It demonstrates faith, honor, and love when we willingly give to God what is precious to us. When we give to God of our finances instead of spending on ourselves, it honors Him. If we think about it for a moment, He is the One responsible for us having the finances to begin with. So we are just giving back to Him what He has given to us. But the good thing is that we can't out-give God. So what we give to Him we should expect back in return, and rejoice that God will give us back more.

Scripture Readings:
1 Samuel 1:1–28; 2:21
Mark 10:29–34
Luke 6:38

June 29

THE WORLD'S SYSTEM AND THE PRINCE OF DARKNESS

You used to live in sin, just like the rest of the world, obeying the devil—the commander of the powers in the unseen world. (Ephesians 2:2)

We are living in a world that is under the influence of the enemy. That means it is imperative that we do not allow ourselves to adapt to this world's philosophies. Satan has done a good job of influencing the seven pillars of our society: religion, the family unit, education, government, media, arts and entertainment, and commerce.

When we think how much the moral fabric of this nation has changed over the last hundred years, it is easy to see that it is because the pillars have changed. Religion was the first on Satan's agenda to attack, so he went after the church centuries ago. More atrocities have been done in the name of religion than any other institution in the world. How many wars have been started in the name of religion?

Likewise, the family unit has changed with more single parent families, same sex marriages, and couples living together out of wedlock. Educational systems have changed for the worse in our country too. An educational system that was once one of the best is now one of the worst among the industrialized nations. Our government, which once relied on the Scriptures to guide their decisions, has turned away from God and become secularized.

The media seems to have more influence with the Internet and modern technology, which makes our world smaller each day. Arts and entertainment has changed drastically in what is viewed in the name of freedom of expression during daytime TV. Commerce is all about the ends justifying the means. In serving the god of mammon, business ethics are compromised if not completely ignored for the sake of profit. Therefore, we must always be mindful that we live in the world but are not of this world. We must never forget that our citizenship is in the Kingdom of God.

Scripture Readings:
John 18:36
1 John 2:15
James 4:4

June 30

DON'T GET TOO COMFORTABLE: REMEMBER LOT

You adulterers! Don't you realize that friendship with the world makes you an enemy of God? I say it again: If you want to be a friend of the world, you make yourself an enemy of God. (James 4:4)

If we are believers in the Lord Jesus Christ, then the blood of Jesus has brought us out of the kingdom of darkness and translated us into the Kingdom of Light (Colossians 1:13). We are now citizens of the Kingdom of God. It is God's intent, therefore, that we live on this earth as an ambassador for that Kingdom (2 Corinthians 5:20). We are to live in this world but not love this world or live according to its philosophies.

This does not mean that we can't enjoy what the world has to offer, and that we have to completely isolate ourselves from doing anything at all. But it does mean we should not be so consumed with this world and its distractions that we turn our affections away from God. God does not want to compete with anyone for our loyalty; He is a jealous God (Exodus 20:5). We must be mindful of God's presence always. We are not to become like Lot, who went to live in Sodom and Gomorrah, and got comfortable living in that environment. In fact, Lot was hesitant to leave the city when the angels came to rescue him and his family. Unfortunately, Lot's wife would die because she failed to follow the commands of the angels and turned to look back on the destruction of the city (Genesis 19:17, 26).

Lot almost lost his life because of his emotional ties to the cities of Sodom and Gomorrah. We should learn from this story that the same thing can happen to us if we get too comfortable in this world. We are now seated with Jesus Christ in heavenly places (Ephesians 1:4–5), so each one of us has a choice to make: we can choose to live as a citizen of this world, or we can be a citizen of the Kingdom of God and live in this world like an ambassador of that Kingdom. Which one will you choose?

Scripture Readings:
Genesis 19:12–26
2 Corinthians 5:20–21
Ephesians 1:4–5
Colossians 1:13

July 1

Don't Ask How, Just Believe and Receive

But Moses responded to the Lord, "There are 600,000 foot soldiers here with me, and yet You say, 'I will give them meat for a whole month!' Even if we butchered all our flocks and herds, would that satisfy them? Even if we caught all the fish in the sea, would that be enough?" (Numbers 11:21)

The Lord had just told Moses that He was going to feed all the people of Israel for an entire month. Moses was flabbergasted. He couldn't understand how God was going to do this. Because they were in the middle of the desert, Moses was reluctant to tell the people what the Lord had promised him because he didn't understand how God was going to fulfill His promise. The people were already upset with him, and if he said this to the people there would for sure be an uprising.

Moses was relying on his logic instead of putting his trust in the promise of God. But when God asked him the question, "Has My arm lost its power?" (Number 11:23), Moses went out and reported to the people what God had told him. Sure enough, God fulfilled His promise by providing quail for everyone. And He provided it in such a way that Moses never would have thought.

God's Word is His will, and He is incapable of lying (Numbers 23:19). We can trust that if we can find a promise from God in His Word, we can stand on that promise until it manifests itself, because the Word of God doesn't return to Him void but will accomplish what it was sent out to do (Isaiah 55:10–11). We don't need to know how God is going to accomplish what He has promised, because God's thoughts and ways are much higher than ours (Isaiah 55:8–9). Not relying on our own understanding, we are called to put our trust in the character and integrity of God (Proverbs 3:5–6).

Many believers have let go of their faith because they could not understand how God was going to deliver them. They tried to reason in their minds, trusting their own understanding and logic, which overruled their faith. If we are going to believe in the supernatural and experience miracles, we are going to still our mind by the Word of God. We remind ourselves of the promises of God by speaking them to our minds. Remember, there are times in our life when God delivered us. Has the arm of the Lord lost its power? Absolutely not.

Scripture Readings:
Numbers 11:4–6, 21–23, 31–34
Isaiah 55:8–11
Proverbs 3:5–6

July 2

HAVING PEACE IN THE MIDST OF A STORM

You will keep in perfect peace all who trust in You, all whose thoughts are fixed on You! Trust in the Lord always, for the Lord God is the eternal Rock. (Isaiah 26:3–4)

How can we find peace when we are in the midst of a storm? Is it even possible? Yes, it is possible to find peace in the midst of the storms of life. We can find peace in the most difficult situations if we put our focus on the Word of God and walk in faith. When we focus on the Word and trust in the integrity of God instead of on the circumstances, we give the presence of God domain over our situations. We are then allowing God to work on our behalf, and if God is for us then who can be against us (Romans 8:31)?

How was Jesus able to sleep during a raging storm when His disciples were freaking out and thought they were going to drown? Jesus trusted His relationship with God and knew that whatever He spoke was going to come to pass regardless of the circumstances (Mark 4:35–41). In other words, Jesus was operating from an internal locus of control, which was based on His faith, and was not controlled by the circumstances surrounding Him. We can operate on a higher level than non-believers because we are citizens of the Kingdom of God (Colossians 1:13).

We have the ability to choose how we will operate in this life. We can choose to trust in God and His Word and walk in the Spirit, or we can choose to walk in the realm of the natural. If we choose to walk after the Spirit, we are guaranteed that we will not be disappointed because we have the Word of the Almighty to stand on, and His Word does not and will not come back to Him without accomplishing what it was sent out to do (Isaiah 55:11).

Jesus told His disciples before His departure that they would experience difficulties in this life, but not to fear because He had overcome the world (John 16:33). Being mindful of this when we find ourselves in seemingly impossible situations can be life giving. We must constantly remind ourselves of the character and integrity of God while remembering the promises found in His Word. When we meditate on those promises, it will change our thought process from negative to positive. As we speak those promises, our faith will increase and those negative thoughts will leave, giving us an inner peace that transcends all human understanding (Philippians 4:6–7).

This is not an easy thing to do. That is why the Bible says that only those who operate in faith will enter God's rest (Hebrews 4:1–3). We must make up our minds to not walk by our senses but to walk by faith. This simply means that what God's Word says has final authority in everything that we do. If the doctor tells us that we have only six months to live but the Word of God says that Jesus took our sicknesses and diseases, then we must choose which word we are going to believe. If we want the peace of God operating, then we must keep our eyes fixed on God.

Scripture Readings:
Isaiah 26:3–4; 41:10
John 16:33

July 3

GOD LOVES YOU

The Lord did not set His heart on you choose you because you were more numerous than other nations, for you were the smallest of all nations! Rather, it was simply that the Lord loves you, and He was keeping the oath He had sworn to your ancestors. That is why the Lord rescued you with such a strong hand from your slavery and from the oppressive hand of Pharaoh, the king of Egypt. (Deuteronomy 7:7–9)

Have you ever taken the time to stop and think about how much God loves you? Sometimes we get caught up in everyday life and get consumed in what we are trying to accomplish that we forget that God really does love us. His love for us is unconditional and it never changes, even when we are disobedient and don't feel we deserve to be loved. God's love for us is not contingent on our behavior, for we are incapable to live up to the requirement that God demands (Romans 3:9). So He provided a remedy by giving His only Son to be our substitute. His Son willfully took our sinful nature upon Himself even when He was sinless. He bore our sins so that we could be looked upon as sinless (Romans 5:17–19).

When God now looks at us, He sees Jesus because we are in Him (John 17:21). God so loved all of humanity that He provided a way for us to be in fellowship with Him for an eternity (John 3:16). Do you realize what this means for everyday life? This means we can live the rest of our days without a sense of condemnation or guilt (Romans 8:1–2). Even when we miss it, all we have to do is confess our sins, and they are forgotten (Isaiah 43:25; 1 John 1:9). Having this awareness will give us the boldness to stand confidently before the throne of God and fellowship freely with the King of kings.

I encourage you to take a moment every day and meditate on and repeat to yourself, "God loves me!" And if God loves you, who can stand against you? No one! We need to be more mindful of God's love for us because this will assist us in not allowing toxic thoughts to enter our minds and cause discord within. Free yourself and love yourself because God truly does love you.

Scripture Readings:
Isaiah 43:25; 53:4–5
John 3:16; 17:12
Romans 5:17–19; 8:1–2
1 John 1:9

July 4

Guilt, Condemnation, and the Finished Work of Jesus

This means that everyone who belongs to Christ has become a new person. The old life is gone; a new life has begun. (2 Corinthians 5:17)

One of the things I find with the majority of my clients is their unwillingness to forgive themselves for the past mistakes and the poor decisions they have made. They refuse to see that this form of self-torture does nothing to remove the guilt they feel. Instead, it only inhibits them from moving forward. The enemy will sometimes remind us of our past mistakes in order to keep us stuck. But we have to understand what the finished work of Christ Jesus accomplished on our behalf—His blood cleanses us from the consciousness of sin—past, present, and future (1 John 1:9).

When Jesus ascended to the heavens, we ascended with Him (Ephesians 1:3). We have been adopted into the family of God and have become one of His children (Ephesians 1:5). If we truly understand and believe this, then there is no reason for us to allow ourselves to become remorseful because of our past transgressions. We have to adopt the same attitude the apostle Paul had when he no longer recognized his former self, Saul (Paul's former name), he reckoned him dead, and he was now a new creation in Christ Jesus. Saul was responsible for the persecution of the church, and he had believers put in prison and had some of them killed for their faith. Because of the revelation Jesus gave Paul on the finished work of Christ, he understood that he was free from the guilt and condemnation of his past mistakes. He was now free to live as though that old man never existed.

When I worked in corrections, one of the things I attempted to change with those I worked with was their self-image. One of the major reasons why so many former inmates return to jail and prison is because of the way they view themselves. So many of them have a problem of letting go of their past, so it robs them of their future.

If we continue to see ourselves as sinners saved by grace, then guess what? We should not be surprised if we keep having sin consciousness. Conversely, if we see ourselves as new creations in Christ Jesus and develop a righteousness consciousness, then we will walk uprightly in the ways of the Lord. As believers we need to inculcate into our thought process righteousness consciousness and start seeing ourselves the way God sees us instead of the way the enemy sees us. In order to achieve what we were designed to be and do, we need to have the same mindset Jesus did. Don't be a prisoner of your past any longer; be a pioneer of your future.

Scripture Readings:
Jeremiah 31:33–34
Romans 8:1–2
Ephesians 1:3–5
1 John 3:1

July 5

God's Wisdom Versus Your Wisdom

Lean on, trust in, and be confident in the Lord with all your heart and mind and do not rely on your own insight or understanding. In all your ways know, recognize, and acknowledge Him, and He will direct and make straight and plain your paths. Be not wise in your own eyes; reverently fear and worship the Lord and turn [entirely] away from evil. It shall be health to your nerves and sinews, and marrow and moistening to your bones. (Proverbs 3:5–8 AMP)

One of the struggles I have experienced is trusting my understanding more than the Lord's understanding in specific situations. I think those of us who have achieved a certain amount of success in this world have faced this dilemma. Moses surely did. When God called him to lead the children of Israel, Moses attempted to do it from his own understanding and power, and he failed as a result. In fact, he committed murder and was on the run for his life (Exodus 2:11–17). Moses had to learn not to lean on his own understanding, but to trust in the Lord's understanding.

We realize that God's understanding and ways are much higher than our own, and we in our finite minds cannot even begin to comprehend His thoughts. We trust in and rely on Him even when we don't understand what He telling us to do. It those times when we try to reason and ask the question of how, that stops us from complying and following the direction of the Lord.

An example of this can be found in the book of Matthew. Peter was asked if Jesus paid taxes or not. In response to this question, Jesus told Peter to go down and catch a fish and then look into its mouth, and he would find a large silver coin, enough to pay both of their taxes. How many of us would have done what Jesus told Peter to do? It sounds totally unreasonable to human logic to do such a thing. The logical thing for most of us is to have something to sell, or to get a part-time job, or even get a loan in order to pay our taxes. But God told Peter to go fishing, and then to look in the first fish's mouth to find the money they owed. That was truly supernatural indeed!

If we are to experience the supernatural in our lives, then we must be willing to fully trust in the leading and guidance of God and not on our own understanding. If we do this, we will disqualify ourselves from operating in the supernatural realm. Jesus performed miracles not because He was the Son of God, but because He was submissive to the will of God and followed what He told Him to do without question (John 5:30). There are many miracles that are waiting for those who are willing to trust in the Lord and not put their own understanding ahead of His.

Scripture Readings:
Proverbs 3:5–8
Isaiah 55:8–9
John 5:30; 14:10
1 Corinthians 2:13–14

July 6

TRYING TO FULFILL GOD'S PROMISE THROUGH SECULAR MEANS

Unless the Lord builds a house, the work of the builders is wasted. Unless the Lord protects a city, guarding it with sentries will do no good. It is useless for you to work so hard from early morning until late at night, anxiously working for food to eat; for God gives rest to His loved ones. (Psalm 127:1–2)

When I read this Scripture, I immediately thought about Abraham and Sarah and the promise that they would have a child. They both were advanced in years when God promised them a son who would carry on the family line. But when it did not happen within the time frame they thought it would, Sarah encouraged Abraham to have the child through her handmaiden Hagar. They must have thought they were doing the will of God, or at least they allowed their sense knowledge to preside over trusting and relying on God's promise.

Their planned worked (what they thought was) perfectly and they had a child. But it wasn't long before there were problems in Abraham's household. Jealousy and envy became a problem between Sarah and Hagar. It got so bad that Hagar left with her son and was in the desert, on the verge of dying of thirst, before an angel came and rescued them (Genesis 16:1–15). When Isaac, the child God promised, was born, Abraham was forced by his wife to ask Hagar and his son to leave his household (Genesis 21:8–11), which was upsetting for Abraham because he truly loved Ishmael.

Human efforts driven by secular methods cannot fulfill the will of God. If God gives us a promise and we try to fulfill that promise through our own methods without the direction of the Holy Spirit, we will not achieve the success God had planned for us. We may achieve a measure of success, but we will find hardship, anxiety, and despair along the way. Many of us have been guilty of doing what Abraham and Sarah did, and we gave birth to an Ishmael because we did not wait on the Lord and took things into our own hands. Now we are stuck with a car that keeps breaking down, a house we are struggling to pay for, or a marriage that is far from what we expected. And all of this has taken place because we did not trust God and lean entirely on Him.

I am not saying that we should not cooperate with God by doing our part. I am not saying that we will not experience difficulties along the way, even when we are walking in the center of His will. But the difference is that if God is in charge and we are following His lead, there will be a peace that will get through because we are operating within God's will. There are many churches today that are struggling financially because they have an Ishmael rather than an Isaac. Their motivation is good but they are trying to achieve God's promises through worldly means. It is important to remember that an Ishmael and an Isaac cannot exist within the same household—one of them will have to go.

Scripture Readings:
Genesis 16:1–12; 17:18–22; 21:1–5
Proverbs 3:5–6
Isaiah 40:31

July 7

GOD'S REST IS AVAILABLE TO THOSE WHO BELIEVE

For only we who believe can enter His rest. As for the others, God said, "In My anger I took an oath: 'They will never enter My place of rest,'" even though this rest has been ready since He made the world. (Hebrews 4:3)

God's rest exists for anyone who trusts and believes in Him. There are many believers who are not experiencing the rest of God because they refuse to believe His Word, choosing rather to believe what they hear on the news or what their own logic and reasoning tell them. They trust their own sense knowledge more than they trust in the promises of God. Unfortunately, they will experience the same result as the children of Israel who were in the wilderness being led by Moses. They will die and not get to the Promise Land.

Believers can experience the peace of God in the most trying situations if we will focus our attention on God and His Word, not on our circumstances. What it comes down to is a choice we have to make: Are we going to trust and believe in the Word of God, or are we going to walk in unbelief? If we walk in unbelief, we will not experience the peace of God; however, if we choose to walk in the Spirit and trust God, He will provide us with His peace that passes our understanding (Philippians 4:6–7).

We don't have to live with worry, anxiety, and fear if we are walking with God, because God knows no fear (Proverbs 1:33). Imagine what life would be like if we had no fear about anything we faced. Imagine for a moment the comfort we would experience if we knew that whatever we did would work out in our favor, no matter the circumstances. Well, that is possible for those who enter the rest of God.

Those who enter the rest of God can experience heaven on this earth, because fear does not exist in heaven. Didn't Jesus teach us to pray for His will to be done on earth as it is done in heaven (Matthew 6:10)? That means it must be God's will. And if it is God's will, then we can have it! But we will have to labor to enter God's rest (Hebrews 4:11). The labor the Lord requires for us is to walk in faith. And we all know that faith comes by hearing the Word of God and speaking it into our situations (Romans 10:9, 17). Will you enter His rest?

Scripture Readings:
Proverbs 1:33
Isaiah 40:31
Philippians 4:6–7
Hebrews 4:1–7

July 8

Your Faith Today Creates Your Substance Tomorrow

Faith is the confidence that what we hope for will actually happen; it gives us assurance about the things we cannot see. Through their faith, the people in days of old earned a good reputation. (Hebrews 11:1–2)

In order to walk in God's best, we must understand and appreciate the dynamics of faith, for it is by faith that the world we live in was created (Hebrews 11:3). God's mode of operation is through faith, and if we are to please Him we must operate in faith as well (Hebrews 11:6). Faith can work for us or it can work against us. The choice is ours to make. But no matter what, whatever we believe will be our outcome. We have the power to determine what we experience by the use of our faith (Deuteronomy 30:19).

When we use our faith in a negative way, it creates fear. Fear is the polar opposite of faith. They both work on the same principle. Many believers operate in fear without even realizing it. They unconsciously undermine their confession of faith by their careless and idle words (Matthew 12:36). Since our words reveal what is really in our heart (Matthew 12:34), many sabotage themselves by those careless and idle words they speak throughout the day. When we say things like, "Things never work out for me," or "It's too good to be true," we are speaking what we truly believe.

We can make all the positive confessions we want, but when our conversation does not reflect our confession, we are creating discord within our heart, being unstable in our faith and not fully confident that what we asked for will come to pass. We are deceived into thinking we are operating in faith when we are in a state of mental assent (James 1:6–7). Jesus said that if we ask without doubting in our heart, we would receive what we asked for (Mark 11:23–24). If we truly believe this, then there is no place for doubt to exist in our heart. We may have some in our mind because it's not completely renewed, but doubt in our mind will not nullify the faith we have in our heart, unless, of course, we let it by speaking doubt.

We are called to allow our faith to work for us (Luke 17:5–10). Realizing that we are created in the image of God and have the same ability to speak words of faith to create what we want in our life is essential if we are to catch this (Genesis 1:26). But there is a responsibility we have too, and that is to make sure we don't allow negative thoughts to enter our hearts and contaminate our faith. For what we say today will be our substance tomorrow.

Scripture Readings:
Deuteronomy 30:19
Matthew 12:34–36
Mark 11:23–24
Hebrews 11

July 9

Don't Put God in a Box

Is anything too hard for the Lord? I will return about this time next year, and Sarah will have a son. (Genesis 18:14)

The word *impossible* does not exist with God, for nothing is impossible with Him (Luke 1:37). Sometimes we have a tendency to forget this when we are in seemingly impossible circumstances. We sometimes lean on our own logic and past experiences to predict the future. When we do this, however, we unknowingly put God in a box and talk ourselves out of faith. This was what happened with Abraham and Sarah.

God told Abraham that he would be the father of a great multitude of people. This promise came at a time when he was seventy-five years old and had no children. Abraham and Sarah were well past the age of bearing children from the natural perspective. They waited for the promise to come to pass, but it didn't. So they grew impatient and decided to take matters into their own hands and had a child through a surrogate, and named him Ishmael. But this was an act of unbelief and it wasn't until thirteen years later that God appeared to Abraham again.

By this time Abraham was ninety-nine years old, and God told him he would have a child by his wife Sarah within a year's time. To human logic and reasoning this would be impossible, but nothing is impossible with God. Abraham had learned not to question God when He makes a promise because God cannot lie (Numbers 23:19). Sure enough, God's word was fulfilled, and a year later Isaac, the child of promise, was born.

The Bible contains many stories of how God did the impossible for those who would believe and receive. God wants to do the same thing for us today if we will not limit Him. When I was paralyzed, the doctors didn't think I would ever walk again. Their prognosis was based on their expertise and knowledge in past cases of a similar nature. But I said to myself, "God said I would recover and I will take His Word over the word of the physicians." There was no physical evidence for me to stand on, but I had God's Word and that was all I needed. Three months later I was walking under my own power. I am no one special. What God did for me, He will do for anyone who will trust and listen to Him. When someone tells us that a situation is impossible, we can simply respond by telling them, "Nothing is impossible for the God I serve!"

Scripture Readings:
Genesis 18:1–14
Isaiah 55:11
Luke 1:37
Mark 9:23

July 10

Take One Day at a Time and You Will Be Fine

Can all your worries add a single moment to your life? (Matthew 6:27)

One of the enemies of faith is worry. When we allow ourselves to worry, we open the door for doubt and unbelief to enter into our hearts. Many times we will hear an inspiring message and charge off with great faith, but it slowly starts to dissipate when logic and reason enter the picture. I am not saying for one moment that we are not to act on logic or reason. God has given us this ability for a reason, and it's not a sin to use logic or reason in making decisions and living life. But we also have to understand that it has its place. When we are dealing with the things of God and His Kingdom, there are rules that supersede earthly wisdom (Isaiah 55:8–9).

Whenever I try to figure out how God is going to do something He has promised me, it is easy for me to open the door for worry, doubt, and unbelief to come in. And it never turns out the way I had envisioned it when I was worried and anxious. God has unlimited access to resources that we know nothing about. So how can we figure out how God is going to fulfill His Word to us?

When God gave Joseph the vision of him ruling over his brothers (Genesis 37:8), he had no idea of what he would have to go through before that would be fulfilled. Do you think that if God told him that he would be betrayed by his brothers and thrown in a pit to die, later to be sold into slavery, to be falsely accused of rape and thrown into prison, that Joseph would have still wanted to be placed in a position of rulership over his brothers? I don't think so. That is where true faith comes in.

If we trust God, then we don't need to know exactly how it will come about. All we need to know is what our next step is to be. What do I need to do today? If we are walking in the will of God, He will make sure that all our needs are met, no matter the circumstances. Like Joseph, we will have the favor of God everywhere we go (Genesis 39:2).

Developing the mindset of Jesus requires us to totally trust in the providence of God. We are not to lean more on our own understanding and reasoning than God's word (rhema). We are to acknowledge Him in all that we do, which means we are not to put Him aside and try to figure things out independently of Him (Proverbs 3:5–6). If we do choose to trust Him through all of our circumstances, our life in Christ will become an exciting adventure of faith. We will do and experience things we never imagined because nothing is impossible with God!

Scripture Readings:
Proverbs 3:5–6
Isaiah 55:8–9
Matthew 6:25–34

July 11

YOUR WORDS HAVE DOMINION OVER YOUR LIFE

You shall also decide and decree a thing, and it shall be established for you; and the light [of God's favor] shall shine upon your ways. (Job 22:28 AMP)

If we are going to live the prosperous life God has designed for us, then we have to understand the power we possess in our words. Throughout the Scriptures this point is made over and over again. Since we are created in the image and likeness of God (Genesis 1:26), we possess the same ability He has in using our words to speak and create. The reason why some believers are struggling is because of the words they speak over their lives.

Words are the containers of our thoughts, and they reveal what is in our heart (Matthew 12:34–35). As a counselor I have listened to my clients and assisted them in resolving issues in their lives. By listening I can determine what's really in their hearts. Sometimes people will say what they want you to hear, but if you talk to them long enough you will find out what they really think about certain issues. Usually, it is the first thing they say in times of distress that really reveals what is in their hearts. What do we say when we are faced with difficult times? Do we say something like, "I don't know what to do?" Or do we quote a Scripture from God's Word? Our answer to these questions is important because it indicates what we truly believe.

Many people deceive themselves by confusing mental assent with faith. When we mentally assent to something, we are agreeing with it in principle, but that is it. When trouble comes, we falter because we only believed in our heads and not in our hearts. True faith is a heart issue, not a mind issue. We can have an intellectual understanding of faith, but unless we transfer that to our heart, it will do us no good.

Many times when we trust God for something, we might have doubt in our head. But what matters is what we have in our heart. Faith is in our heart, which is connected to our will. So when we are acting in faith, we will continue to make positive confessions in spite of what our mind is telling us. We speak what we believe and are ready to receive instead of speaking doubt. If we speak our doubt, we are allowing that to enter into our heart. It is vital that we understand that our words have dominion because they are like seeds that produce after their kind (Genesis 1:11–12).

We should think of our words as seeds in the soil of our heart. When we speak positive words, those words produce after their kind. Conversely, the opposite is true as well. Remember that the power of life and death are in your tongue (Proverbs 18:21).

Scripture Readings:
Job 22:21–30
Proverbs 18:21
Isaiah 55:10–11
Matthew 12:34–35

July 12

THE WEALTH TRANSFER IS COMING SOON

Evil people may have piles of money and may store away mounds of clothing. But the righteous will wear that clothing, and the innocent will divide that money. (Job 27:16–17)

The earth is the Lord's and He will do with it whatever He chooses (Psalm 24:1). God has the power to take wealth away from one and give it to another. This is what is called the wealth transfer. We can see this pattern in the life of Abraham. He started out with little, but because he was in covenant with God, he became very wealthy (Genesis 13:2). How did he obtain all that wealth? Abraham believed God's promise that he would be blessed and become a blessing to others (Genesis 12:2), and when opportunities were presented to him, he took advantage of them.

In the book of Exodus, we see the wealth transfer take place with the children of Israel leaving Egypt. Before they left, the children of Israel were instructed by Moses to ask their former employers for some compensation for their services. The Egyptians were more than generous and gave them clothing, silver, and gold (Exodus 11:2). Because of this, the children of Israel walked out of Egypt with great wealth. Later, when the children of Israel were going into the Promise Land, Moses told them that they would occupy a land that was plentiful (Deuteronomy 8:6–10).

God's desire is that His children have the best that this world has to offer, but it requires faith and obedience in order to obtain it. In the days to come, there will be another great transfer of wealth for the body of Jesus, but not everyone will qualify to receive it, only those who are givers and have the faith to receive. They will be the ones who experience this wealth transfer. And like the children of Israel before us, we must not let prosperity cause us to forget our God or it will be taken from us.

It would do us well to prepare ourselves for the great wealth transfer. Renew your mind to receive it, and start being a giver. Wealth is given in order that it may be used to advance the Kingdom and bless others. If this is your mindset, then God will make sure that all your needs and wants will be met. The wealth transfer is coming. Will you be ready to receive it?

Scripture Readings:
Genesis 13:2
Exodus 11:2
Deuteronomy 11:8–13
Job 27:16–17
Psalm 24:1

July 13

YOU ARE TO BE THE FRAGRANCE OF GOD

Our lives are a Christ-like fragrance rising up to God. But this fragrance is perceived differently by those who are being saved and by those who are perishing. (2 Corinthians 2:15)

I went to the Saturday Market last weekend and bought some scented oil. It smelled so good I couldn't resist buying it. A couple of days later I ran across this Scripture and I thought about how we have the fragrance of God on us because we are His children. When we are walking with Christ Jesus and being guided by the Holy Spirit, we give off a beautiful aroma of God to this world. For some the smell is beautiful, but for others it is repulsive.

We can be a pleasant fragrance to God when we are manifesting His glory, but we can also be a pleasant fragrance to this world. It is important to be conscious of this when we interact with others. Are we behaving in a manner that brings honor and glory to the Kingdom of God, or are we watering down our fragrance to conform to this world? If we are living the kind of life that pleases God, there will be people out there who will be attracted to us and there will people who will be repulsed by us.

Those who are repulsed are under the control of the kingdom of darkness and cannot stand the light that comes from our presence (Ephesians 2:2). So we can't take it personal when we encounter people like this. Rather, we need to rejoice because we are suffering persecution for Christ Jesus (Matthew 6:10).

Scripture Readings:
Matthew 6:10
2 Corinthians 2:14–16
Ephesians 1:4–5

July 14

BE WHO GOD CREATED YOU TO BE, NOT WHAT YOU THINK YOU SHOULD BE

For God knew His people in advance, and He chose them to become like His Son, so that His Son would be the firstborn among many brothers and sisters. And having chosen them, He called them to come to Him. And having called them, He gave them right standing with Himself. And having given them right standing, He gave them His glory. (Romans 8:29–30)

Have you ever been in the desert or mountains on a clear night? It seems like the stars are so bright that you could almost reach out and touch them. It seems like you can see all the constellations in the night sky and readily pick them out, which is something that is a little difficult to do when you are in the city. Have you ever watched a beautiful sunset, or a beautiful sunrise? It can be absolutely mesmerizing. All of these are physical manifestations of God's glory (Isaiah 35:2).

As believers, we also have a glory. Just like the sunset is never quite the same and has its own unique beauty, so each of us have our own unique glory as well. God has given all of us certain talents and abilities to magnify His glory while upon the earth. We will not be truly happy and satisfied with our lives until we find out what those abilities and talents are. God has designed each of us for a specific purpose, but it is up to us to listen to this calling.

Some people have several talents and might choose the one that will be the most lucrative for them rather than doing what God has called them to do. There are many great singers who started off singing in the church and left to make money in the secular market. There's nothing wrong with that, if that is what God has called you to do. But some have left of their own accord and achieved a measure of success. But many waste their talents and watch their life spiral out of control once the world is finished with them.

The world likes to see everyone conform to a specific image. It is easier to control the masses that way. Television is a great tool for that because it tells us what's in fashion and what's out. It reveals to us how we should look, how we should cut our hair, and how we should act. Most of us fall into a certain pattern of behavior without realizing why we think a certain way. We inadvertently put ourselves into a box, and live within the confines of that box for our entire lives, never realizing our true potential, and instead settle for mediocrity.

Our God does not live in a box, and as His children we shouldn't either. We are not to let the world define our reality. If we feel the calling on our life to do something, then we should by all means do it. We are not to ask others their opinion, because the only opinion we should be concerned about is that of our heavenly Father. We will not be truly happy until we do what He has created us to do.

Scripture Readings:
Isaiah 35:2
Romans 8:29–30

July 15

Divine Health Can Be Yours

Jesus traveled throughout the region of Galilee, teaching in the synagogues and announcing the Good News about the Kingdom. And He healed every kind of disease and illness. (Matthew 4:23)

Our health is a concern to God. In fact, one of God's names is Yahweh-Rapha, the God who heals. God has given us the provision for healing, but in order to see its manifestation we have to accept and receive it by faith. It is true that Jesus paid for our healing on the cross (1 Peter 2:24), and we can now enjoy divine health as a benefit of being a child of God (Psalm 103:2). However, we have to be aware of God's desire for our health and have the faith to believe and receive it. I cannot emphasize this enough. There are many believers who are suffering physical and mental infirmities who could be healed if they would receive the provision God has already made for them.

God can heal a person through many different ways. It does not have to be a miraculous healing, but He could choose to heal an individual through the use of medicine, or by the hand of a trained physician. Some believers think they are not acting in faith if they go to a doctor or take medication for their illness. This is simply not the case. If we pray to God for a healing and ask Him to use the physician to heal us, we are not acting in unbelief. Someone else's testimony about their miraculous healing should not sway us in any way. We simply can't live off someone else's testimony—we have to experience God for ourselves.

When I was first diagnosed with kidney failure, the doctor wanted to put me on chemotherapy. I refused to take the medication because I thought it was an act of unbelief. I prayed to God daily for my healing, and for a short period of time the symptoms stopped. But then they returned and I got worse by the day. I had real bad edema in both my legs, and I gained thirty pounds in a period of two days. I was crying out to God on my patio, asking why He was not healing me. Then He answered me.

God told me to read the story about Naaman, a commander who had leprosy. Naaman's servant told him that there was a prophet is Israel who could heal him. So Naaman sent for the prophet. The prophet didn't come, but he sent his servant and told Naaman to dip himself into the Pharpar River. Naaman got upset because the prophet didn't come and heal him the way he thought he would. Naaman's servant finally convinced him to do what the prophet instructed him to do. Seven times he dipped himself into the water, and on the seventh time he was completely healed! God told me that He is not limited in the ways and methods He can heal, and it was not up to me to tell Him how I should be healed. Once I understood that, I started taking my medication and, a few months later, I didn't need the chemotherapy.

As long as we are trusting in the Word of God for our healing, God will honor that. We might be healed suddenly, or we may not. We may be healed by someone laying hands on us, or we may get healed through having an operation. We cannot limit God in the way He chooses to heal us; just know it is our divine right to be healed.

Scripture Readings:
Exodus 15:26
2 Kings 5:1–19

July 16

JESUS WANTS TO HEAL YOU

And you know that God anointed Jesus of Nazareth with the Holy Spirit and with power. Then Jesus went around doing good and healing all who were oppressed by the devil, for God was with Him. (Acts 10:38)

Many believers know that God has the power to heal, but they are not convinced He is willing to heal them. They allow negative thoughts to override their ability to believe God for their healing. Some will talk themselves out of their healing by listening to others or allowing the voice of the enemy to convince them that God will not heal them, either because of past or current sin in their lives.

This was the case with a man who had leprosy and wanted Jesus to heal his body. When the man heard that Jesus was in town, he went and knelt before Him. He knew Jesus had the power to heal him, but he was not sure if He would be willing to do so. When Jesus told him that He was indeed willing to heal the man, Jesus then touched the man and he was immediately made whole (Matthew 8:1–4).

In order for us to receive our healing, we must know that it is God's will that we be healthy and well. If we question whether it is God's will to heal us or not, then the manifestation surely will not come. Because we are double-minded, it is easy to be tossed from belief to unbelief (James 1:6–7). If you are still unsure of God's will to heal, I would suggest you read and meditate on Scriptures relating to healing. As you meditate on those Scriptures, images of healing will sprout in your inner man, and you will be in a position to receive the healing power of God. You will also be used by God to heal others.

Scripture Readings:
Exodus 15:26
Psalm 103:2; 107:20
Isaiah 53:5
Matthew 4:23; 8:16–17; 9:35
Acts 10:38
1 Peter 2:24

July 17

Are You Ready to Take Your Position on the Throne?

All praise to God, the Father of our Lord Jesus Christ, who has blessed us with every spiritual blessing in the heavenly realms because we are united with Christ. (Ephesians 1:3)

Did you know that in the eyes of God you are currently seated in heaven with Jesus? Yes, we as believers are part of the royal family of our Lord and Savior Jesus Christ (1 Peter 2:9). Because of this, we are God's holy priests and ambassadors on this earth—we are God's representatives. Jesus shed His blood and died on the cross to make this happen. It is now up to us to realize the greatness of the power that is available to us (Ephesians 3:19–20).

If we walk about in ignorance to this fact, we will live a life that is ordinary at best. We will live day to day waiting for our time to be up, then we will go to heaven and find out all that God had planned for us to do during our time on the earth. This will be a heartbreaking time for some of us. I don't know about you, but I am not waiting to get to heaven to take advantage of what Jesus has made available for me here. I want to get it now! It's God desire that we manifest His glory to the world while living in our fleshly bodies. We should be demonstrating the goodness and power of God to others, for God has blessed us to be a blessing (Genesis 12:1–3).

Each of us who are born again are entitled to the same promise that God made to Abraham (Galatians 3:13–14). There is no reason why any believer should not take advantage of all the spiritual and material blessings that are contained in the covenant God has given to us. There are a myriad of promises in both the Old and New Testaments that God has made for those who are part of the covenant, but it is up to us to take those promises and apply them to our lives.

We have to use our faith, take those promises, and renew our minds in order to receive them. This is the labor the writer of Hebrews is talking about before we can enter God's rest (Hebrews 4:6–11). Don't be like the children of Israel who refused to believe the promise of God and never experienced God's best for their lives. Make a quality decision today to believe and receive all that God has provided for you, and take your rightful position on the throne today!

Scripture Readings:
Psalm 82
Isaiah 61:6–7
Ephesians 1:3–5; 3:19–20
1 Peter 2:9
Revelation 1:6

July 18

God Has No Grandkids

On judgment day many will say to Me, "Lord! Lord! We prophesied in Your name and cast out demons in Your name and performed many miracles in Your name." But I will reply, "I never knew you. Get away from Me, you who break God's law." (Matthew 7:22–23)

Some people think that being a believer is a birthright. They think that because their parents were Christians and they were raised in a Christian household, then they are automatically Christians too. But sadly this is not true. God has only children—He has no grandkids. Everyone who is part of His family has accepted the gift of salvation that is found in His Son Christ Jesus. The Bible clearly states that if a person believes in their heart and confesses with their lips that Jesus is Lord, they will be saved (Romans 10:9).

We are not born into the family of God by physical birth. We have to be born spiritually (John 3:3). This means a person has to accept Jesus into his or her heart on their own volition. We do not become a Christian because we attend church or do good deeds—it is not our works that save us; it is our confession of faith (Ephesians 2:8–9). Many people are deceived into thinking that if they are good enough, God will accept them, or because they are moral enough, that is all they need to go to heaven.

The Scriptures say something entirely different. The only way a person is accepted by God is through His Son Jesus (John 3:36). If we were to get to heaven by our own merit, an element of pride would exist, and what happened to Lucifer when he was in heaven would happen to us—our pride would get the best of us. But because of what Jesus has done for us, we have nothing to boast about. If we are going to boast, it will be in God and His Son, and in what they did for us, not for what we've done for ourselves. We will praise them, not ourselves. There is no room for pride in heaven.

Don't be like those who will appear before the judgment seat of Christ and find out they were not accepted into the Kingdom of God. Receive the gift of God, the gift of life, which is Christ Jesus, the hope of glory. Then get filled with the Holy Spirit and let Him guide you into all truth (John 16:13).

Scripture Readings:
John 3:16–18, 36; 14:6
Romans 6:23
Ephesians 2:8–9

July 19

SOMETIMES YOU HAVE TO KICK JONAH OFF THE BOAT

"Throw me into the sea," Jonah said, "and it will become calm again. I know that this terrible storm is all my fault." (Jonah 1:12)

Most people have heard or read about the story of Jonah and the whale. If not, I suggest you read it—it's a short book (just four chapters long) in the Old Testament. For those of us who are not familiar with the story, Jonah was a prophet of God who was instructed to preach to Israel's archenemies to repent or they would be destroyed. He refused to do that because he wanted God to destroy them.

Instead of going to Nineveh to preach, Jonah decided to go in the opposite direction. He boarded a ship to go to the city of Tarshish. Once the ship was out at sea, however, a terrible storm arose and everyone on the ship feared for their lives—all accept Jonah. He was asleep. The men on the ship woke him up and encouraged him to pray to his God to save them. Jonah then told the men that the storm was because of him, and if they threw him off the ship then the storm would stop. At first the men refused his request, but as the storm grew more intense, they finally threw him overboard. Suddenly, the storm stopped and the seas grew calm.

Sometimes we have people in our lives who are like Jonah. They bring chaos as we try to help them in their crisis. Because we care for them, we extend ourselves and violate boundaries, ultimately putting ourselves at risk of losing our peace. The bad thing about this is that these people could care less about the turmoil they are causing in our life. Our good intentions of helping them turn into enabling them, and then we are setting ourselves up for failure and disappointment.

Sometimes we have to kick Jonah off of our boat and let the Lord deal with them as He sees fit. Sometimes our assistance is interfering with what God wants to do in their lives. I know it is hard to watch someone we care about go under, but we are making a big mistake by playing god in their life. We will eventually regret it.

How many families have been torn apart because of a Jonah? How many relationships have been destroyed? Remember, there is a big difference between enabling and assisting someone. Enabling turns into unhealthy dependency. Sometimes the best thing we could do for a person is to pray for them and let them hit rock bottom. My dad used to tell me, "A hard head makes a soft behind."

Scripture Readings:
Jonah 1–3

July 20

Moving from Survival Mode to the Supernatural

I am doing this so all who see this miracle will understand what it means—that it is the Lord who has done this, the Holy One of Israel who created it. (Isaiah 41:20)

In these last days God wants to manifest His glory through His body, the church. This means believers will start to perform signs and wonders and experience the wealth transfer that has been prophesied in the Bible (Isaiah 61:6–7). However, it will not be for all believers to experience—only those who believe it and are ready to receive it will be the ones who will walk in the supernatural blessings of God.

Believers who are in bondage to this world have disqualified themselves because they cannot be trusted with the power of God. They are under the sway of the enemy and could be easily manipulated by him. Believers who are living in survival mode could experience the supernatural blessings of God, but they will need to not be distracted by the cares of this life.

If you are to walk in the supernatural realm of God, then God must have first priority in your life. You must spend time with Him on a daily basis in order to understand His method of operation and grasp His vision. We must spend time in the Word of God and in prayer, and meditate on the promises of God continually.

Only those who have renewed their minds to the things of God will qualify for the supernatural outpouring that is to come in the near future. We must think like Jesus if we are going to act like Jesus; it is only then that we will do the works Jesus did (John 14:12). Are you ready for the challenge?

Scripture Readings:
Isaiah 41:17–20; 61:6–7
John 14:12
Ephesians 3:19–20

July 21

Protocol for the Supernatural

He replied, "What is impossible for people is possible with God." (Luke 18:27)

Since I started reading through the Bible, I have found a pattern of how God uses people to manifest His glory. It would behoove us to learn this pattern so that we too can be used of God to manifest His glory throughout our time here on this planet. I have seen this pattern used in both the Old and New Testaments; therefore, I believe it's an established pattern that God chooses to use. There are three things that occur when miracles happen.

1. There is the rhema (a word from God).
2. There is obedience to what was spoken.
3. And there is a point of contact that was made for the miracle to occur.

It is important to understand that before a miracle can take place, we have to receive a word from God. When we receive a word from God, it is called the *rhema* of God. *Rhema* is the spoken word we receive from God. It is different than the *logos,* or the written Word. We want to get the rhema word of God, because once we get that we must act on it, doing exactly what we were instructed to do. Usually, it will make no sense to our human understanding. Our mind will give us trouble, but we have to learn to walk by our inner man, not our intellect. The natural man does not understand the things of the Spirit of God for they are foolishness to him (1 Corinthians 1:20–21).

Obedience is vital to experiencing the supernatural in our life. If we do not follow the instructions that God has given us, then we will nullify the supernatural from operating in our life. We must make a quality decision to do whatever God instructs us to do, no matter how foolish it may seem to our mind or to others around us.

Finally, we must have a point of contact to release our faith. If we believe for a financial breakthrough, then our point of contact would be the financial seed we have given. If we believe to get healed of an infirmity, then the point of contact would be the laying on of hands.

An example I like to use is taken from a story in the book of Joshua. God told Joshua that He would give him the city of Jericho (Joshua 6:1–2), whose walls were thought to be impenetrable. However, Joshua believed God and received the rhema word of God. Then He told Joshua to have the army walk around the city in silence for seven days, and on the seventh day he was to have the priests blow their horns and have the people shout (Joshua 6:3–15). On the seventh day they followed Joshua's instructions and the walls came tumbling down before them. It was a miracle! This strategy made no sense at all, but when we are walking in the supernatural, we defy logic because we are operating in a different realm altogether.

Scripture Readings:
Joshua 6:1–22
Matthew 17:24–27

July 22

What to Do with That Goliath in Your Life

David replied to the Philistine, "You come to me with a sword, spear, and javelin, but I come to you in the name of the Lord of Heaven's Armies—the God of the armies of Israel, whom you defied." (1 Samuel 17:45)

One of my favorite stories in the Old Testament is when David defeated Goliath. There are so many lessons to be learned from this story, but I want to focus on only one today. Some time in our life we will face a Goliath. It could be a circumstance or a person that is quite intimidating to us. They may want us to believe that there is no way we will ever defeat them, and they will use fear to try and control us. Most people would not even think to go out against them, because in their natural minds the situation seems impossible.

But we have a God who knows no limits. When we unite our faith and focus on Him instead of on the giant, we will come out victorious. David is a good example of this. When David heard the taunts of Goliath, he became upset because Goliath was making fun of his God. David took it personal. He loved the Lord, and he wanted to show what his God was capable of. There were others in the army who loved the Lord too, but none of them had the relationship David had with God.

There are believers who go to church and are faithful to the Lord, but they are not willing to step out of their comfort zone. They never put their faith to the test, so they don't have the victories to build stronger faith in the Lord. David had past victories that he used to increase his confidence for this new challenge (1 Samuel 17:34–37). You see, David put his faith to the test by defeating the lion and the bear while taking care of his father's flock of sheep. He knew that if God assisted him with the lion and bear, then He would surely be there for him with Goliath.

David stepped out in faith and declared before all the people what God was going to do through him (1 Samuel 17:45). He made his confession of faith and released the power of God. God needs us to cooperate with Him so that He can manifest His power through us. It is not enough to believe in our hearts, but we need to speak the words of faith in order to release God's power. He did just that, and with a single stone from his slingshot he fell the great giant Goliath—just like he said he would (1 Samuel 17:50–51).

Let us use this example as a strategy for defeating our giants. We can use our faith as a catalyst for bigger challenges that lie ahead. We are able to use our faith to defeat those lions and bears so that we can gain confidence in the power of God. Then when we face a giant, we will not focus on the circumstances that are right in front of us, but our focus will be on the God of the impossible, who always leads us in victory in Christ Jesus (2 Corinthians 2:14).

Scripture Readings:
1 Samuel 17:1–57
Romans 8:31–37
2 Corinthians 2:14

July 23

LOOKING BEYOND THE PHYSICAL

But the Lord said to Samuel, "Don't judge by his appearance or height, for I have rejected him. The Lord doesn't see things the way you see them. People judge by outward appearance, but the Lord looks at the heart." (1 Samuel 16:7)

We all have a tendency to look at the outward appearance of things. We judge people and things on how they appear to our physical eye. People who are attractive have an advantage in our society. Attractive children are more popular with their classmates and teachers, and teachers give higher evaluations and have higher expectations of students who are attractive. Attractive applicants have better chances of getting jobs. And a recent study showed that taller men earned around $600 per inch more than shorter executives. In court, attractive people are found guilty less often, and when they are found guilty they receive less severe sentences.

The bias of beauty operates in almost every social situation. Studies show that we react more favorably to attractive people. This is because we have a deep-seated belief that because something or someone is attractive, it possesses desirable characteristics. We have the tendency to think that attractive is good and ugly is bad. We have been conditioned to think this way. We only have to look at some of the fairy tale stories to have this confirmed. The good character is attractive and the bad character is ugly.

How was Lucifer described before his fall? He was described as beautiful (Ezekiel 28:12–13). His appearance was one of the reasons he was able to persuade a third of the angels to follow him. When Satan tempted Eve in the Garden of Eden to take the fruit, he made it look attractive to her (Genesis 3:6). Many have fallen because of the appearance of a person or thing. We must learn not to look at something by its appearance alone, we must look at things the way God does, asking for discernment, because all that glitters isn't gold.

We have access to the Holy Spirit, and we all have the Spirit of God residing within us if we are born again. We need to utilize these gifts in our daily interaction with others. Don't assume that because of a person's looks or mannerisms they possess good morals or character. Don't look at a person who is less attractive in an unfavorable light. Don't prejudge someone by their appearance alone; rather, give them the opportunity to expose their true character by their actions and their words.

Scripture Readings:
1 Samuel 16:7
Isaiah 55:8–9
James 2:1–4

July 24

Faith Is More than a Formula

A good person produces good things from the treasury of a good heart, and an evil person produces evil things from the treasury of an evil heart. (Matthew 12:35)

There is a big difference between understanding the principles of faith versus understanding the formula of faith. When a person hears an inspirational sermon on faith and gets excited, that doesn't necessarily mean that faith will begin to work for them. Many hear the formula of faith and think that it will automatically start working for them. They read Mark 11:23–24, and they think that all they have to do is just say what they desire and they will have it. Then they get discouraged when it doesn't work.

They are like seeds that were planted in the shallow ground (Mark 4:16–17). They hear the Word and receive it with joy, but because they didn't allow the Word to take root in the soil of their heart, the seed eventually dies. These believers only obtained head knowledge faith. For faith to effectively work, it has to get into our heart, into our inner man, which takes both time and effort. We are going to have to get that seed into the good ground of our hearts if we want it to produce fruit. If we plant that seed in stony ground, it won't be able to penetrate the ground and it will only remain on the surface.

The stony ground represents our hard heart that is full of doubt and unbelief. If we were raised to believe that being prosperous is worldly, and God does not heal anymore, how can we expect to receive healing or prosperity? We first must remove all those stones of false doctrine out of our heart by meditating on the promises of God and renewing our minds. Once that is done, we will have good ground in which to plant the seed of faith (Mark 4:20). Then we will position ourselves to receive what we have asked for in prayer because our heart will not doubt.

We know that the seed of the Word of God is designed to produce what it was sent out to do (Isaiah 55:11). So when we speak the promise of God, which is found in His Word, we are planting the seed in the soil of our heart. So it is just a matter of time until it will manifest completely in our lives. This is the confidence that we must have in order to see our prayers answered. It's more than just a formula. It's a principle and a lifestyle.

Scripture Readings:
Isaiah 55:10–11
Matthew 12:35
Mark 4:13–20; 11:23–24

July 25

Don't Get Ahead of Your Faith

The apostles said to the Lord, "Show us how to increase our faith." (Luke 17:5)

Faith is a process, which means that it is not something that will happen overnight or suddenly. The only exception to this is if God, through the Holy Spirit, chooses to perform a miracle in our hearts, or if a person has developed their faith to the point that God works through them (Mark 11:20–21). For most of us, however, we have to develop our faith, which means it takes time and practice. If you are anything like me, then you will act prematurely at times. You'll grab a promise from God and receive it, then begin to act in your own power instead of waiting for God to lead you.

We must remember that faith and patience work together to be effective (James 1:3–4). Our faith is like a seed. If we take a seed and plant it in the ground and water it, it would be foolish for us to think that it will produce fruit the next day. That seed needs to germinate, the ground needs to provide nutrients for the seed, and the seed needs to let its roots go deep in order to feed itself. All of this is a process. We must allow time for the seed of faith to grow in our heart (inner man). We need to water the seed every day by thanking God for the answer to our prayers.

It is during this time that our faith will grow and eventually manifest itself on the outside. So many times believers will grow impatient, and as soon as they see a blade break out of the ground, they pull the plant up. But it hasn't had time to get its roots established in the ground yet, so how can we expect to get any fruit from it? When we see the blade come up, we are to rejoice because it is beginning to manifest itself in our life. Let that blade strengthen us until the time comes for the harvest.

As we develop our faith, this process will go much faster because our faith will continually grow. Our mind will be renewed and get on board with the inner man, and we will not experience the inner conflict between our mind and our spirit. This is what happened to Peter when he walked on the water. His mind got in the way once he started looking at the waves and the wind (Matthew 14:29–30). So when God gives you a vision, realize that it might not happen immediately, but it will happen when you are ready for it. Don't get ahead of your faith. Wait patiently on God to give you what you desire.

Scripture Readings:
Isaiah 55:10–11
Mark 4:26–27; 11:14, 20–21
Luke 17:6–7
James 1:3–4

July 26

WATCH OUT FOR THOSE HATERS

When Saul realized that the Lord was with David and how much his daughter Michal loved him, Saul became even more afraid of him, and he remained David's enemy for the rest of his life. (1 Samuel 18:28–29)

Once we begin to experience the blessings of God in our life, we need prepare ourselves for the haters. There will be people who will not like what God is doing in our life, and they will come against us. Unfortunately, sometimes it's the people who are the closest to us who will come against us, speaking evil about us. Everything was good when they perceived that they were equal or above us, but when we began to pull ahead of them, they got upset. My dad used to say to me, "Some people are like crabs in a bucket. When one tries to crawl out of the bucket, the others drag it down."

This statement has been true in my life. I remember when I got a promotion at my job, those who didn't get the promotion started to distance themselves from me. I overheard them saying one day, "The only reason he got the promotion is because he is an ex-athlete." It used to bother me, but eventually I got over it, especially when I got my paycheck. I believe that everyone is prone to this behavior if they don't check themselves on a continual basis. I have felt a little envious at times because someone got something I thought I deserved. That is why we need to be honest with ourselves, and allow the Spirit of God to rebuke us from time to time.

A perfect example of a real hater was King Saul. Saul suffered from severe bouts of depression and anxiety, and he was only relieved when David played his harp (1 Samuel 16:14, 23). The Scriptures say that Saul loved David and made him his armor bearer (1 Samuel 16:21). But all that changed when a series of events took place. After David killed Goliath, he began to experience a series of successful victories in the field of battle. He became popular with the people. When the people started praising David more than Saul, Saul became upset and was fearful of losing the throne. The person he once loved he was now beginning to hate.

David did nothing to deserve this. In fact, he was loyal to King Saul and wanted nothing more than to serve him. But Saul didn't see it that way. His self-talk got the best of him, and he was convinced that David had ulterior motives—to take the throne away from him. Saul wouldn't listen to his son or daughter but surrounded himself with yes men who went along with whatever he said. Unfortunately, Saul chased off his greatest ally and turned him into his enemy. Don't be surprise if you find a Saul in your life.

Scripture Readings:
1 Samuel 18:1–30

July 27

TAKE REFUGE IN THE LORD

God is our refuge and strength, always ready to help in times of trouble. So we will not fear when earthquakes come and the mountains crumble into the sea. Let the oceans roar and foam. Let the mountains tremble as the waters surge! (Psalm 46:1–3)

I was watching a program on television and it showed the growing unrest taking place in the world. It showed news clips from New Guinea, where Exxon is developing new natural gas plants and destroying the environment, displacing people from their land, and giving them no financial compensation. Exxon has made a deal with the government for billions of dollars, but none of it has gotten into the people's hands. The only ones who seem to be benefitting from this deal are Exxon and a few people in the government. Then they showed the severe droughts in California and Texas and how they are affecting the communities and economies of each state. By the end of the program, I felt a bit anxious.

I had to remind myself that I have a God I can take refuge in when troubled times come. It is easy to understand why so many people are suffering from depression, anxiety, and hopelessness in the world today. This world is like a time bomb ready to explode at any moment. I can't imagine what it would be like to live this life without the comfort of God. It would be a living hell. No wonder there is so much discord and hatred in the world today. People are looking for answers and finding nothing but a temporary solution, which will only delay the inevitable.

We can't stop what is happening in the world, but we don't have to fear it because God is our refuge in times of trouble. We constantly have to remind ourselves of this truth. Jesus spoke of the times we are living in (Matthew 24), so we should not be surprised by what we read and see on the news. Rather, we should rejoice that even though we may witness these horrific events, it will not touch us if we abide in the shadow of the

Almighty (Psalm 91:1–5). God promises He will protect those who trust in Him (Isaiah 41:10).

Just like the children of Israel still in Egypt, when the Egyptians were experiencing the plagues the children of Israel were unaffected (Exodus 8:22–23). So it will be for us who believe and call upon the name of God during times of trouble. God is the same today as He was back then. Instead of being fearful, we can now rejoice because God is our refuge!

Scripture Readings:
Exodus 8:22–23; 10:23
Psalm 46:1–7; 91:1–16
Isaiah 41:10
Matthew 24:1–51

July 28

THE ONLY WORK GOD WANTS FROM YOU IS TO BELIEVE

They replied, "We want to perform God's works, too. What should we do?" Jesus told them, "This is the only work God wants from you: Believe in the One He has sent." (John 6:28–29)

This conversation took place after Jesus performed the miracle of feeding five thousand people with just five loaves of bread and two fish. The people realized that the power of God was with Him, but they didn't believe Jesus was sent from God. To them, He was someone who possessed special powers that they wanted. There are many people today who are attracted to the Christian faith for what they can get out of it. They hear the Word on prosperity and immediately are attracted to the message.

These are the same people who will later fall away when the formula they learned does not work for them. The reason why it didn't work for them is because their heart motive was all wrong. They were chasing after things rather than the Creator Himself. They were only trying to use the teaching of God to fulfill their own selfish desires (James 4:3). God is a discerner of the heart (1 Samuel 16:7)—we might be able to fool others, but we can't fool God.

If we are to operate in the realms of God, we first have to believe in Him and His Word. Then we have to allow Him to guide us by the Holy Spirit. Our motivation for receiving blessings is to be able to bless others and manifest the glory of the Kingdom of God. Jesus said that if we would seek His Kingdom first, then all the things we desire would be given to us (Matthew 6:33). Do you want to work the works of Jesus? Then you are going to have to have the same mindset He had (John 8:28–30).

Scripture Readings:
John 6:26–29; 8:28–30; 14:12; 15:7–8
James 4:3

July 29

THINGS THAT BLOCK YOUR BLESSINGS

There are six things the Lord hates—no, seven things He detests… (Proverbs 6:16)

If you have not received what you have prayed for, it might be that something in your character or behavior needs to be addressed in order for the breakthrough to come. God is a holy God, and if He is going to work through you, then you will need to be holy as well. No one is perfect; we all have our character flaws. That's where the blood of Jesus and the finished work of Christ come into play. We also have the Holy Spirit to admonish us when we fall short.

With that being said, we need to be aware of the things that upset the Lord and make an effort to remove those from our lives. Our enemy is very subtle and shrewd in influencing us. His favorite weapon he uses is the television. If we look at the most popular shows on air today, what are they about? Are they wholesome shows? Most of the popular shows are filled with lying, stealing, and killing, all the characteristics Jesus used to describe the enemy (John 10:10). Satan has a way of making all of the aforementioned attributes look attractive and intriguing. The story lines captivate our imaginations, creating images within us. And before we know it, we find ourselves tolerating this type of behavior and accepting it as normal.

This is the wisdom of the world that is described in the book of James and that creates discord and disharmony (James 3:13–16). As believers, we must be aware of the wisdom of the world, and make a distinction between the wisdom of the world and the wisdom of God. We cannot expect to receive the blessings of God using worldly wisdom. When we are convicted of using worldly wisdom, we need to repent and wash ourselves in the precious blood of Jesus.

There are seven sins we should eliminate from our lives if we are to allow the blessings of God to flow through us:

1. Being prideful.
2. Lying in all its forms.
3. Killing the innocent (including the unborn).
4. Plotting evil against others (malice).
5. Being quick to do wrong.
6. Being a false witness.
7. And sowing discord among others.

If we are involved in any of these activities, we need to admit it and quit it! God forgives, but He can't forgive what we refuse to confess. I would encourage you to confess to God today so the blessings and peace of God can flow in your life.

Scripture Readings:
Proverbs 6:16–19
James 3:13–16

July 30

THE DEVIL ONLY HAS THE POWER YOU GIVE HIM

*So humble yourselves before God. Resist the devil,
and he will flee from you. (James 4:7)*

Once a person accepts Jesus Christ as their Lord and Savior, they are immediately transferred from the kingdom of darkness into the Kingdom of Light (Colossians 1:13). Along with that transference comes a power shift. Because we are now in Christ Jesus, the devil is now under our feet. Yes, we now have authority over him and don't have to be subject to him any longer. Though he will try to use his deception to get us to use our authority against ourselves, if we are aware of this it will not happen.

The enemy must bow to the Word of God. Who is the Word of God? Jesus is the Word of God made flesh (John 1:1, 14). So when we speak the Word of God, it is like Jesus is speaking through us because He is the Word of God. Before Jesus's departure from this earth, He prayed a prayer to the heavenly Father and requested that those who believed in Him would experience the glory and unity He experienced while on this earth (John 17:20–24). Do you think that God heard and answered His prayer?

We have the same authority Adam had before the fall. We can live as Jesus did if we only believe and receive this truth (John 14:12). The only thing that is stopping us is our spiritual ignorance and unbelief. Don't let religious traditions rob you of all God has for you (Matthew 15:6). The enemy uses religion to restrict and manipulate people. How many atrocities have been acted out upon humanity in the name of religion? Who do you think is behind all that? I can tell you that it is not God.

We no longer have to put up with the devil and his schemes—we have authority over him because we are in Christ Jesus (Colossians 2:22). In the eyes of God we stand holy and blameless! In the spiritual realm we are holy and blameless. And when we speak the Word of God, it's like Jesus is speaking it through us! That is why the devil has to flee. He is a defeated foe. And the only weapon he has is deception. Don't let him deceive you any longer. Take your stand in Christ and resist the enemy's schemes.

Scripture Readings:
John 14:12; 17:20–24
Colossians 1:13–14; 2:22–24
James 4:7

July 31

God's Design for You Is Greatness

I will make you into a great nation. I will bless you and make you famous, and you will be a blessing to others. (Genesis 12:2)

Did you know that God's desire for you is that you be great? Each of us have been given a unique talent and ability that is just waiting to be harvested. It is up to us to find out what it is and get aligned with God's purpose in order to manifest that greatness. The world can try to make us great also, but it comes with a price, and it is only temporary. God's way to greatness also comes at a cost, but there are eternal rewards attached to it. The world can give us riches, but we will always have to answer to someone, and it can be taken away from us in a moment. How many "stars" are now broke and disgusted, trying to make a comeback that will never happen? How many "stars" have serious emotional and substance abuse problems?

Those of us in the Kingdom can achieve greatness and avoid all of that. We can be prosperous, enjoy our prosperity, and share it with others, all the while avoiding the drama that comes with following worldly wisdom (James 3:13–16). God has a plan for each of us if we will humble ourselves and trust Him.

I encourage you to find what your talent is, give it to God, and let Him guide you into greatness. This is what all the great patriarchs of the faith did. If it worked for them, it will work for us too, because God is the same today as He was back then (Hebrews 13:8)

Jesus taught that if we would take His yoke upon us and let Him teach us, we would find rest for our souls (Matthew 11:28–30). This means that if we allow ourselves to be led by the Holy Spirit like He was, we will get the same results He experienced while He walked on this earth. That means we will have no worries or strife. It doesn't mean there will not be challenges and disappointments along the way, but it will not impede us from getting to our destination, which is the Promise Land.

Scripture Readings:
Genesis 12:2; 13:2
Proverbs 10:22
Isaiah 43:7
Matthew 11:28–30
Mark 10:29–30
James 3:13–16

August 1

PROSPERITY WILL DESTROY A FOOL

For the simpletons turn away from me—to death. Fools are destroyed by their own complacency. (Proverbs 1:32)

One of the dangers of gaining wealth is that we can become self-sufficient and never rely on God. It is easy to forget that it was the power of God that gave us the ability to gain wealth in the first place, and not we ourselves (Deuteronomy 8:18). God repeatedly warned the children of Israel not to be consumed with the prosperity they would experience once they arrived in the Promise Land (Deuteronomy 11:16–17). Our hearts can be easily deceived by wealth, and it can easily become our god if we are not careful.

When a person attains wealth, there is a comfort that comes along with it. They no longer have to struggle over their finances; they suddenly have many more options in life. People cater to those who have wealth, and because of this a person can begin to think more highly of themselves than they ought to think, becoming prideful. Many people have sworn that this would not happen to them, but it eventually did. Some people become so consumed with mammon that they begin to worship it rather than worshipping the God who provided their wealth.

This is what happened to the children of Israel in the Old Testament. Once they experienced the prosperity God had provided for them, the spirit of mammon took them captive. We need to be mindful of this in our own lives as God transfers wealth to us in the end times. We should never forget that it is God who gives us the ability to prosper and we should honor Him with what He gives us. There are many people who came out of poverty and gained great wealth, and who are now bankrupt because they didn't honor God with what they obtained.

One person who comes to mind is Mike Tyson. Mike Tyson was the youngest Heavyweight Champion of the World. During his career, he made $500 million, yet he recently filed for bankruptcy. How could this happen? If he took the money and put it in the bank at 5 percent interest, he would receive $2.5 million a year without touching the principle. How many people could live on $2.5 million a year? But when we live foolishly and waste money on the desires of our flesh and forget God, this is what happens.

Many believers are afraid of wealth because they think it is worldly. But God delights in the prosperity of His people (Psalm 35:27). He wants to bless us so that we can be a blessing to others (Genesis 12:1–3). The bottom line is that it takes money for the gospel to be preached. It also takes money to pay bills and provide for the necessities of life. The enemy loves it when believers are struggling financially because they can't make an impact in this world. No one listens to a poor man (Proverbs 14:20), but the rich man will be in a position of influence. Which one do you want to be in today?

Scripture Readings:
Deuteronomy 8:11, 18; 18:8–16
Proverbs 1:32; 14:20

August 2

THE SPIRIT OF JEZEBEL

But I have this complaint against you. You are permitting this woman—that Jezebel who calls herself a prophet—to lead My servants astray. She teaches them to commit sexual sin and to eat food offered to idols. I gave her time to repent, but she does not want to turn away from her immortality. (Revelation 2:20–21)

I was recently watching an interview with the Los Angeles Clippers owner Donald Sterling, and the Lord spoke to me and said that the young woman involved had the spirit of Jezebel. I thought about this all night, and I realized what the Holy Spirit was saying to me. I thought to myself, "How could this man allow himself to be deceived into thinking that this woman, who was fifty-one years younger than him, was in love with him?" During the interview, Mr. Sterling described this woman as being a close friend and confidante, a person whom he trusted.

That is the way the Jezebel spirit operates. A person with the spirit of Jezebel will seek out people in positions of power and authority and get into their good graces. They will go out of their way to prove to the victim that they are loyal, and make themselves seem to be of importance. Jezebel will be quick to point out how valuable they are, and then they will slowly emotionally isolate their victim from others. Once they have isolated the victim, they will begin to manipulate them into doing their will by making it seem like it's the victim's will actually being done.

Once this process begins, Jezebel consumes her prey to the point that the victim abandons all good judgment in order to please the person with the Jezebel spirit. This spirit will make promises but never keep them. She dangles the carrot but never lets the victim taste it. She will cause the victim to ignore the advice of those who are closest to them, and make it seem that she is the only one who truly understands what the individual is going through.

If the victim does not do what Jezebel wants, then she will turn on him and betray him, leaving the victim emotionally disillusioned and distraught. Even after realizing what has occurred, the victim will still make excuses for Jezebel, and even long for the mirage Jezebel created, while they pick up the pieces of their shattered life. Beware of the spirit of Jezebel.

Scripture Readings:
1 Kings 16:30
Revelation 2:20–21

August 3

GOD'S PLAN IS MUCH BETTER THAN YOURS

"For I know the plans I have for you," declares the Lord, "plans to prosper you and not to harm you, plans to give you hope and a future." (Jeremiah 29:11 NIV)

God created humans to be free moral agents, which means that God gave each of us the ability to make choices on our own. Angels also have the ability to make choices, but they don't have the right to make choices because they were created to serve God and to fulfill His will. In God's original design, humanity was created to be in the same class as God (Genesis 1:26–27). Humans were created to be a ruler on this earth and the angels were sent here to assist us in that mission (Hebrews 1:14).

Because humanity had the ability to make choices, we chose to disobey God's commands, and therefore Satan gained authority over the earth. We are not automatons. Many times people make bad choices and reap the consequence of the choice they make, thinking God is punishing them for the bad choice they made. This is simply not true. They are only reaping the consequence of the choice they made.

With privilege comes responsibility. If we are not responsible, the privilege will be taken away from us. It is just that simple. If a person chooses to break the law repeatedly, their freedom will be taken away from them by society. They will be placed in prison, and upon their release they will be put on probation or parole, which is conditional. Until they prove that they can be responsible, they will not experience the freedoms others who are responsible experience.

It is the same in the realm of the Spirit. We have the ability to walk in the Spirit and experience the freedom and privileges that come from that walk. Or we can choose to walk in the flesh and experience the consequences from that type of lifestyle. Many believers are living a life of struggle and hardship, thinking that God is mad at them or punishing them, but in reality they are only reaping the consequences of the choices they made. Don't let that happen to you. Know that God has only good planned for you, but you have to trust Him and seek His will for your life. God's plan for your life is so much better than yours!

Scripture Readings:
Isaiah 40:31
Jeremiah 29:11
Matthew 11:28–29
Ephesians 3:19–20

August 4

WHICH CONSCIOUSNESS DO YOU HAVE: FEAR OR POWER?

For God has not given us a spirit of fear and timidity, but of power, love and self-discipline. (2 Timothy 1:7)

In this world it is easy to allow anxiety and worry to control us. Many in our society suffer from depression and anxiety because of the pressures they feel on a regular basis. Climate change, terrorism, and economic problems are broadcasted on our airways as a daily recurrence. Even our entertainment provokes anxiety and causes our limbic system to produce adrenaline and cortisol, which can be harmful and toxic to the body over a prolonged period of time. We cannot change the environment we live in, but we can choose not to allow it to affect us.

If you have been born again, you have the Spirit of God residing in you. God's Spirit gives us the ability to walk in power, love, and to have a sound mind, which means we don't have to walk around with a spirit of fear and worry. Jesus admonished us not to be anxious about anything, but to seek first His Kingdom and all our needs would be taken care of (Matthew 6:33). The apostle Paul wrote that we are to focus our attention on positive things and continually give praise and thanks to God as a remedy for anxiety and worry (Philippians 4:6–7). And the apostle Peter tells us to cast our cares and anxieties upon the Lord because He cares for us (1 Peter 5:6–7).

We don't have to carry the load by ourselves, for God has provided all we will ever need or want, if we will just humble ourselves and take His yoke upon us (Matthew 11:28–29). We need to renew our mind to think like Jesus, then we will find peace, power, and love. Having our minds renewed will also help us face any challenge that comes our way with confidence because we know that we are more than conquerors through Christ Jesus (Romans 8:37). We can start each day by telling ourselves that we have not been given a spirit of fear, but of power, love, and a sound mind!

Scripture Readings:
Matthew 6:33
Romans 8:37
Ephesians 3:19–20
Philippians 4:6–7
1 Peter 5:6–7

August 5

TAKING ON THE YOKE OF JESUS

Then Jesus said, "Come to Me, all of you who are weary and carry heavy burdens, and I will give you rest. Take My yoke upon you. Let Me teach you, because I am humble and gentle at heart, and you will find rest for your souls." (Matthew 11:28–29)

What is the yoke Jesus is referring to here? For the longest time I thought it had to do with how we conducted ourselves in our daily lives. But I now realize that He was referring to being totally immersed in trusting God. The people Jesus was talking to were burdened with following the laws of Moses, burdened down with regulations and rules, and they were depending on their own efforts to be in right standing with God.

Jesus told those people that those days were coming to an end. He was going to provide a new way to please God. A different work would be required, and that work would be the work of faith. No longer would they have to make sacrifices and do ceremonial rituals to gain God's favor. The only requirement God would require would be to believe in the Son of God, who came to the earth with the express purpose to sacrifice Himself for all humanity (John 3:16). This is the yoke Jesus was talking about. The only work that pleases the Father is that we believe in Him (John 6:29).

We please God when we trust and act on His Word (Hebrews 11:6). The writer of Hebrews also states that we must labor to enter into this rest by using our faith, not by relying on the works of faith (Hebrews 4:3). As I have said before, we cannot merit any favor with God by self-effort (Romans 3:21). It is only by faith and faith alone that we are put into right standing with God. Furthermore, any works we do should be the result of our faith in the finished work of Jesus Christ on the cross. I encourage you to take the yoke of Jesus on you, for you will find peace for your soul.

Scripture Readings:
Matthew 11:28–29
John 6:29
Hebrews 4:3; 11:6

August 6

FORGIVENESS IS MORE THAN WORDS

Make allowance for each other's faults, and forgive anyone who offends you. Remember, the Lord forgave you, so you must forgive others. (Colossians 3:13)

Sometimes when someone offends us, we may tell ourselves that we have forgiven him or her, but we really haven't done so. I had a situation where this occurred not too long ago. There was a woman at the church who was short with me. I was offended by her actions, but I never said anything to her. I thought I had let it go, but I hadn't. I still had resentment toward her, and the longer that resentment went unresolved the more negative feelings I had toward her. I was cordial toward this woman when I encountered her, but my defenses were definitely up.

Well, just recently I had the opportunity to interact with her and found out that she was not the person I had created in my mind. She was really nice and wasn't the uptight "bitch" I thought she was. I immediately had to repent of my thoughts toward her, asking God to forgive me for not truly forgiving her and for the perceived offenses that had occurred several months prior.

Sometimes, we have to make allowances for people. Maybe she was short with me because of some family issues in her home, which had nothing to do with me. Maybe she didn't even realize she was being short with me; maybe I was just projecting my beliefs about her. Whenever we interact with people, there is the possibility that someone will get offended. When this happens, we can give the person the benefit of the doubt and let it go, or we can tell the person what we were feeling when the perceived offense occurred, and give them the opportunity to validate or clarify. Sometimes the person might be unaware of their behavior, or it could only be our imagination.

But the worst thing to do is let it go unresolved, because unresolved issues turn into resentment. And resentment will eventually manifest itself. So remember that true forgiveness will let the offense go. You will know that you have let it go when you have resolved the issue either with yourself or with the person involved. If you don't, you are not walking in love and you are preventing God from working on your behalf (Mark 11:25).

Scripture Readings:
Luke 6:37
Mark 11:25
Colossians 3:13

August 7

HAVING A KINGDOM MENTALITY

Soon the world will no longer see Me, but you will see Me. Since I live, you also will live. (John 14:19)

If we have been made a believer in Jesus Christ, then we have the ability to see things the world cannot see. When the world sees lack, we see abundance. If the world is walking in fear, we should be walking in faith. When the world says there is no way, we should claim that there is a way. Why? Because we are in Christ Jesus, we are citizens of the Kingdom of God (Colossians 1:13). We live in this world but we are no longer of this world (John 18:36).

We have the choice of raising our mentality to see beyond this world and walk in the realm of the Spirit, or we can live as though we are still part of it. Many believers choose the latter and are susceptible to all the cares and worries this world offers. They are unaware that they can choose to renew their minds to the things of God and walk in their Kingdom privileges. We are ambassadors for the Kingdom of God (2 Corinthians 5:20), which means that just like an ambassador from another country, we can now live as though we are in our country of origin.

This type of Kingdom mentality does not happen automatically, but it is something we have to renew our mind to. We have to develop the same mindset that Jesus had (1 Corinthians 2:16), which can only come about by studying the Word of God and meditating on the promises of God. It is only in Christ Jesus that we live and move and have our being (Acts 17:28). We should meditate on this Scripture every day until it becomes ingrained into our consciousness. Then when times of trial come, we will not react the way the world reacts because we will be able to see things the world cannot see. We will see a different reality.

Scripture Readings:
John 14:19; 16:33; 18:36
Acts 17:28
1 Corinthians 2:16
2 Corinthians 5:20
Colossians 1:13
1 John 3:2

August 8

Actualizing the Christ Life within You

For in Him we live and move and exist. (Acts 17:28)

The reason Jesus gave His life was so that it could be duplicated here on earth through all those who would accept Him as their Lord and Savior. Jesus was the Word of God made flesh (John 1:14), and the Word is a seed that is to be planted within the heart (Mark 4:26). When Jesus died, He planted His life so that it could produce a great harvest. If every seed produces after its kind, and Jesus is the Word of God, and the Word is a seed, then when Jesus died the harvest would be more of Jesus on the earth.

It is God's desire that every believer replicates Jesus's life on the earth, which is what He told His disciples before He ascended to heaven. He told them that all the works that He did they would be able to do also, and even greater works (John 14:12). In the book of Acts the apostles demonstrated this on various occasions (Acts 2:43). Even throughout history there were those who got ahold of this revelation and actualized the life of Christ Jesus.

The reason why the church is not manifesting more of the miracles that happened in the early church is because of unbelief. This is partially due to what is being preached from the pulpit in many churches today. Teaching that says all the miracles stopped when the last apostle died and God does not heal today, and God does not want us to prosper, has had an impact on people's expectations. Though this is still widely preached, I think that most people have turned a deaf ear to it.

It is evident from the Scriptures that this is not the case. As stated earlier, Jesus told His disciples that they would do even greater works than He did because He was going to the Father. He told His followers before His ascension that they would perform miraculous signs, heal the sick, speak with new tongues, and cast out demons (Mark 16:16). The apostle Paul grasped this truth when he gave the secret to actualizing the Christ life within when he said that it's not him who lives but Christ who lives within him (Galatians 2:20). This theme is also echoed when the apostle John said we would be judged on how much we lived like Jesus on this earth (1 John 4:17).

To actualize the Christ within, we first have to realize that we cannot do it in and of ourselves. It is by the grace of God that it happens. All we have to do is believe and receive it. Thank God for the finished work of Jesus and just let that seed sprout in your inner man. Water it by reading the Word of God and meditating on it continually. Before you know it, you will renew your mind and start speaking and acting like Jesus. It's that simple. The only work you have to do is simply believe and receive.

Scripture Readings:
Acts 17:28
Galatians 2:20
1 John 4:17

August 9

BEING SORRY AND REPENTING ARE TWO DIFFERENT THINGS

As a dog returns to its vomit, so a fool repeats his foolishness. (Proverbs 26:11)

As a probation officer and correctional counselor I have witnessed many individuals who were sorry because they were incarcerated. Some of them would plead to the court to give them another chance. They would argue that their family needs them at home, and their belief that their incarceration has taught them not to violate the law again. However, many of the same individuals returned after a short period of time with the same or a similar charge. They never really repented; they were only expressing sorrow because they got caught.

There is a big difference between being sorry for something we have done, and repenting for it. When we repent for doing something, we turn away from it—we turn in the other direction and go a different way. Peter said this in the book of Acts when he made the statement, "Now repent of your sins and turn to God" (Acts 3:19). Many people just perform half the act of repentance by confessing their sins, but they don't turn away from it, so they wind up doing the same sin over and over again, creating a vicious cycle, which ultimately ends in their detriment.

This is what happened to King Saul. His life ended prematurely because he refused to truly repent of his actions toward David. After David had gained popularity with the people of Israel, King Saul viewed him as a threat and tried to kill him. During his pursuit of David, many innocent lives were lost and resources were wasted in vain. On several occasions, David had the opportunity to kill Saul, but he refused to raise a hand against him because of the anointed position Saul held. On both occasions David made known to Saul that he could have killed him but he didn't. And on both occasions Saul said he was sorry for trying to kill David, and he tried to get David to return with him. However, Saul would forget his vows and be on the hunt for David once again.

God gave Saul time to repent of his actions toward David, but he didn't take advantage of it. So he finally died in battle along with his three sons (1 Samuel 31:1–7). Because Saul never truly repented of his sin, he finally reaped the ultimate result of repeated and unrepentant sin, which is death. Learn a lesson from Saul and don't let this happen to you.

Scripture Readings:
Proverbs 26:11
1 Samuel 25–26; 31:1–7
Acts 3:19

August 10

Godly Sorry Versus Worldly Sorrow

For the kind of sorrow God wants us to experience leads us away from sin and results in salvation. There's no regret for that kind of sorrow. But worldly sorrow, which lacks repentance, results in spiritual death. (2 Corinthians 7:10)

I want to distinguish the difference between godly sorrow and worldly sorrow. Godly sorrow will cause an individual to not only evaluate their behavior but also cause them to do a 180-degree turn from their behavior or action (Acts 3:19). Worldly sorrow only consists of an apology, but there is little or no effort to change the behavior, so the same offense will most likely occur again and again.

Let me give you an example I have seen far too many times. A man or woman has a serious substance abuse problem that has not only caused them problems but has affected their family as well. Their spouse threatens to leave them if they don't quit using. The man or woman realizes the hurt and pain they have caused to their loved ones, and they feel a sense of remorse. So they discontinue the behavior for a period of time, but because they have not experienced godly sorrow, they never truly repented. As a result, they slowly return to their prior behavior. They only experienced a worldly sorrow, a sorrow that is based on the negative consequences of those around them but doesn't produce any change. In their heart they never truly repented and the only thing they are really sorry about is that they got caught. And because of this, they will have to experience some kind of consequence for their behavior.

I had a friend whom I worked with that I will call Skip. His family and mine would occasionally get together for family outings, and I liked Skip a lot. But Skip had a serious drinking problem, and he refused to get help for it. His drinking got so bad that he lost his job. You would think that he would have learned his lesson, but he didn't. Skip eventually got another job and continued his downward spiral. His wife threatened to leave him, and even kicked him out of the house at one point. Skip's friends tried to talk to him, but he refused to truly repent—he only expressed worldly sorrow. Finally, while driving in a drunken stupor, Skip ran into a fire hydrant and his car caught on fire. Because he was trapped inside the car, 85 percent of his body suffered third-degree burns. Skip is now sober and attending AA meetings, going back to church, and he is back with his family.

Because Skip didn't heed the warnings God provided, and only experienced worldly sorrow, he will live the rest of his life with the scars that come from an unrepentant heart. Had Skip experienced godly sorrow sooner in his life, none of this would have happened. God didn't do this to punish Skip. Skip did this to himself because he refused to heed the warnings given to him. Don't blame God for your misfortunes, but put the blame where it belongs—on yourself (Galatians 6:7).

Scripture Readings:
2 Corinthians 7:10
Galatians 6:7

August 11

Are You Caught in the Blame Game?

But forget all that—it is nothing compared to what I am going to do. For I am about to do something new. See, I have already begun! Do you see it? I will make a pathway through the wilderness. I will create rivers in the dry wasteland. (Isaiah 43:18–19)

During my career as both a probation officer and correctional counselor, I have found that many of my clients were truly victims. But they were also victims to the mentality of being a victim. They blamed their current problems on others: because they were raised without a father, or their mother was emotionally unavailable for them, or their parents were too busy to come to their sporting events when they were growing up, etc. They offered these reasons (and many more) for why they were in their current situation. Penal institutions across this nation are full of victims. Very few take responsibility for their actions, which is one of the main reasons why the recidivism rate in the correctional system is so high.

A victim is not responsible for the mishap that occurs to them. You lock your car, but someone breaks into it and steals it. Were you responsible for your car being stolen? No, you were victimized. You trust your stockbroker to make an investment of your life savings, and the stockbroker embezzles your money along with other clients' money he had. You and those other clients were victims. If you are truly a victim, you are not directly responsible for what has happened to you.

But if you are a person who views yourself as a victim, then you will be less likely to be motivated to make changes because it's not your fault—it's always someone else's fault. These types of people are caught playing the blame game: blaming others for their faults and poor decisions become a way of life. Playing the blame game can be quite comforting because you don't have to assume any responsibility for your actions or decisions. But the downside of playing this game is that you will never get out of the cycle you created, because it's not your fault that you are there.

Another result of playing the blame game is that you become imprisoned to your past. There are people living today who still haven't let go to what happened to them back in 1980. Every time you talk to them, they will find a way to tell you about what happened to them in 1980, and that's why they are the way they are today. It's sad because God wants to do a new work in their life. He wants to heal those emotional wounds and give them a beautiful new relationship, but He can't because they refuse to let go of the past. Don't let yourself get caught up in the blame game. Let God do a new work in your life!

Scripture Readings:
Isaiah 43:18–20
Philippians 3:13

August 12

AUTOMATIC THOUGHTS, PRESUMPTIONS, AND BELIEFS

*A good person produces good things from the treasury
of a good heart, and an evil person produces evil
things from the treasury of an evil heart. What you say
flows from what is in your heart. (Luke 6:45)*

Have you ever said something in a moment of anger or surprise that you later regretted? You apologized for the comment you made and excused yourself by saying, "I didn't really mean what I said." We all have been there and done that—at least I know I have. Well, according to Jesus, that comment or statement we made came from our heart or we would not have said it in the first place. Usually, the first thing that comes out of our mouth is the automatic thought that is within us. It was not something that just popped out of nowhere.

Automatic thoughts are based on presumptions or beliefs that we have about others and ourselves. So the core of presumptions is belief. What we believe we perceive, and what we perceive we will act upon. If we believe certain ways and things about people, it will affect the way we perceive those people and situations, and the way we perceive them will determine how we will behave. Let me give you an example.

Mary was raised in a home where her father cheated on her mother constantly. Mary's parents finally divorced because of her father's infidelities. Her mother never remarried because of the emotional hurt she suffered from her marriage. She preached to Mary that men couldn't be trusted. Mary went away to college and met Bill, who happened to be a great athlete and was on the football team, and they began to date. But after many of the football games, there would be parties where the players would go to celebrate. Bill noticed that Mary would become very anxious if he would converse with another woman, even if it were casual. Mary later accused Bill of wanting to go out with other women. Bill went out of his way to try to convince Mary he was not interested in any other woman, but to no avail.

As time went on, Mary became more controlling and wanted to know where Bill was going, and whom he was going to be with. Mary would check Bill's cellphone and monitor whom he associated with. Feeling smothered, Bill confronted Mary about her behavior. The conversation got heated between the couple and Mary blurted out, "All men are dogs and can't be trusted." Bill was hurt by this statement, and expressed his disappointment to Mary. She later apologized for her comment by saying she didn't mean what she said. Two weeks later Bill decided to terminate the relationship.

What was the reason for the break up? Was it Bill? No, it was the belief that Mary had about Bill and all men in general. Her belief about men caused her to presume that Bill was going to be unfaithful. That belief was based on what she experienced from her childhood, and what her mother taught her while growing up. What Jesus said was true—what comes out of our mouth is determined by what is in our heart. What we believe we perceive, and what we perceive we act upon.

Scripture Readings:
Matthew 12:34
Luke 6:45

August 13

Prayer Is More than a Ritual

So humble yourselves under the mighty power of God, and at the right time He will lift you up in honor. Give all your worries and cares to God, for He cares about you. (1 Peter 5:6–7)

Is your prayer life in a rut? Do you feel like your prayers are not being heard? Has your prayer life just become more of a ritual than effective communication with God? I think all believers know the importance of prayer, but many have a misconception about what prayer actually is. Prayer is simply a way of communicating with God. Many of us listen to clergy pray and we think that we must pray like them in order to be heard, so we try to remember all the phrases they use. But this only ends up in prayer that doesn't come from the heart. It's like having a conversation with someone and reading your response from a script.

With this type of prayer, you are not comfortable and God is not pleased. He will acknowledge the effort on your part, but that's about it. If you want to have an effective prayer life, however, you only have to talk to God like you would your best friend. From my experience, the best prayer times I have had are when I just unload on God. I forgot about the formalities I have been taught, and I spoke to Him and told Him what was on my heart. And guess what? He responded to me every time. When I left my prayer closet I felt like I had been heard.

When I was paralyzed, laying on the bedroom floor and couldn't move, I didn't say, "Oh, Thou heavenly Father, the God of the Most High, look down on your humble servant." No, I said, "God, according to Your Word You said that You would be with me in times of trouble. Well, I can't be in any more trouble than I am in now." And He responded to me immediately and told me that I would recover. Then He provided His peace and sent His angels to rescue me. I know prayer like this works.

God wants us to pour out our heart to Him in prayer because He cares about us. We show we have faith in Him when we cast our cares upon Him (1 Peter 5:6–7). The Holy Spirit delights in those who acknowledge His presence and talks to Him as a trusted friend and companion. Jesus promised that He would send the Holy Spirit to take His place (John 16:13). We need to take advantage of His services, so we can walk in all that God has provided for us. Make your prayer life more than a ritual today; talk to Him like a friend.

Scripture Readings:
John 14:13–14
1 Peter 5:6–7
1 John 5:14

August 14

DOING HEART SURGERY WITH THE WORD

For the word of God is alive and powerful. It is sharper than the sharpest two-edged sword, cutting between soul and spirit, between joint and marrow. It exposes our innermost thoughts and desires. Nothing in all creation is hidden from God. Everything is naked and exposed before His eyes, and He is the One to whom we are accountable. (Hebrews 4:12–13)

In our interactions with others, there will be times of conflict. Most conflicts between individuals are due to assumptions coupled with negative self-talk, which is a reflection of our core beliefs. These conflicts are created in an individual's mind and are given life through words. Or they can come simply because of misunderstandings due to poor communication. We might have expectations that others have not met and, as a result, we get disappointed with them. If we allow that disappointment to go unresolved, it will ultimately manifest itself in the form of resentment. If that resentment goes unresolved, then we can be assured that some type of acting out will occur.

The apostle Paul wrote that we should not allow anger to control our emotions (Ephesians 4:26), for when we do we are giving the enemy an avenue into our lives. How many times has someone acted totally out of character and committed adultery, acted violently, committed a criminal act, committed suicide, even murdered individuals, all because they were so filled with anger and could not control it any longer? As a counselor in the correctional system, I have worked with individuals who had no criminal history but were incarcerated for murder—all due to ongoing issues that went unresolved over an extended period of time.

We have the assistance of the Word of God to prevent this from happening. We can use the Word to dissect our soul and spirit, and to discern what is really in our heart (inner man). We will be able to see what the real source of our resentment is, and what motivated us to behave in a particular manner. Once the source of the resentment is found, we take it to the Word and let God speak to us. It is during this time that He will open our eyes to see things from His perspective and give us the needed insight (Isaiah 55:8–9). He will provide us with a solution and with peace in the midst of those situations. The conflict with the other person may still exist, but we will respond with the Spirit of love, not anger. And we know that love conquerors all, because God is love.

Scripture Readings:
Isaiah 55:8–9
Ephesians 4:26
Hebrews 4:12

August 15

MEDITATION: GOD'S WAY FOR SUCCESS

Study this Book of Instruction continually. Meditate on it day and night so you will be sure to obey everything written in it. Only then will you prosper and succeed in all you do. (Joshua 1:8)

God has given us the gift of our imagination. With our imagination we can create things in our minds that will be manifested through our words and actions. God has created us in His image and likeness so that we can create as He creates (Genesis 1:26–27). Before the fall of man, Adam took care of the Garden of Eden by speaking words of faith. And after the fall, one of the consequences was that humans would have to till the ground by the sweat of their brow (Genesis 3:19). Man could no longer speak words of faith with confidence because of the presence of sin, so he had to rely on the physical senses to provide for his needs.

Man still had the power of imagination and he used it to create. In fact, humanity got so good at using their imagination that God had to intervene to prevent them from fulfilling their desire to build a tower to the heavens (Genesis 11:6). With the imagination, humankind has accomplished great things. Conversely, the imagination of a person has been used to create destructive devices to harm others. That is why it is important we use our imagination for the positive, not the negative. There is an enemy out there who wants to use us to fulfill his will on this earth. Whether we realize it or not, we are constantly being influenced to use or imagination, for good or for evil.

When a person exposes himself to pornography, for example, what images are created in his or her mind? How many people eventually act out on those imaginations? How many people who expose themselves to violent images eventually act violently toward others? There is a reason for this and it's meditation. What we think about we eventually become. We will be controlled by our most dominant thoughts. If we think it and speak it, we will eventually be it. If a man thinks of himself as being a loser, and says that he is a loser, then he will eventually become a loser. If a woman thinks of herself as a winner, she will tell herself she is a winner, and she will eventually become a winner.

In the book of Psalms there is a promise that I committed to memory: It says that if a man would delight himself in the Word of God and meditate on it daily, then he would be like a tree planted by the riverbank. Have you ever seen a tree planted by the riverbank? It is not worried about not having enough water. And because it has enough water, it has no problem producing fruit. Our water is the Word of God, and if we meditate on the Word it will produce a harvest in our lives for all to see. Meditation on the Word of God is the key to a prosperous life.

Scripture Readings:
Joshua 1:8
Psalm 1:1–3
Jeremiah 17:7–8

August 16

You've Got to Say It to See It

I tell you the truth, you can say to this mountain, "May you be lifted up and thrown into the sea," and it will happen. But you must really believe it will happen and have no doubt in your heart. (Mark 11:23)

Because humans are a spirit who have a soul and who live in a body, we possess the ability to speak words to convey our thoughts. Our thoughts ultimately reveal what is in our heart (Matthew 15:18), and our words communicate our ideas and imaginations. They also determine our destiny, and that's why our words are so powerful. With our words we can build up and with our words we can destroy (Proverbs 18:21).

Jesus used His words wisely. He only said want He wanted to come to pass. He understood the power of words and the impact they had once they left the mouth. We should heed His example and use our words economically, because the more words we speak the more likely they will be used carelessly (Proverbs 17:27).

Our words paint pictures for our inner man. On a psychological level, our words are seeds that are planted in our unconscious mind that will produce after their kind. It doesn't discriminate. The same soil that will grow marijuana will also grow corn. Therefore, it is important to think of our words as seeds, our unconscious mind as the soil, and meditation as the water that causes everything to grow. All three are essential for producing a harvest.

If a person speaks something long enough, it will be planted in their unconscious mind. The unconscious mind does not know fantasy from reality, and it will produce whatever is planted in it. Day and night it will begin to bring to fruition what is planted therein. Through meditation, that seed is watered by the imagination. And when the image becomes actualized within the unconscious mind, it will bring forth a harvest. Jesus used the illustration of a sower sowing the Word in Mark 4:26–28.

The reason why many believers are not producing more of a crop of fruit is because of the abundance of the words they speak (Matthew 12:36–37). Usually, the more words a person speaks the more likely there will be the presence of sin (Proverbs 10:19). Some people's words have little or no impact at all; they talk loud but in reality they are saying nothing. They will have to give an account of all those unprofitable words they speak. It's like throwing money down the drain.

A wise person's words, however, are few because they know the power of their words and the impact they can have. Use your words wisely and you will live a prosperous and long life (Proverbs 13:3).

Scripture Readings:
Proverbs 10:19; 13:3; 17:27; 18:21
Matthew 12:36–37
Mark 4:26–28; 11:23

August 17

THE ART OF THE DECREE

You shall also decide and decree a thing, and it shall be established for you; and the light [of God's favor] shall shine upon your ways. (Job 22:28 AMP)

As a believer in our Lord Jesus Christ, you have been called to be a king and a priest (Revelation 1:6). One of the duties of a king is to make decrees. A decree is an official order issued by a legal authority that is pronounced over the land and which must be obeyed. Jesus has given all believers the authority to use His name to cast out evil spirits and heal every kind of sickness and disease (Matthew 10:1). In the book of Acts, we see how Peter uses the name of Jesus to heal a lame man (Acts 3:4). He clearly demonstrated how to decree a thing and have it manifest.

The art of the decree has been lost among most believers. There are many reasons for this, which I will not go into at this time. Because Jesus has given us authority to use His name, we have the right to decree things in our daily lives. Think about a police officer directing traffic. Why do we stop when he raises his hand? Can he physically stop us in our car while traveling at twenty-five miles per hour or more? No, unless of course he is Superman. But because he has the authority of the local government behind him, we obey. His power is based on the authority given to him by the government. As long as the officer acts in line with guidelines set by the government, he has the legal power to stop us.

The same is true in the realm of the Spirit. If a believer makes a decree according to the will of God, it will be done for him. The angels in heaven are to listen to the commands of God's words. Once a believer speaks the promises of God, their angel's job is to ensure that it comes to pass (Psalm 103:20). When we grab hold of the promises of God found in the Scriptures and decree those promises, we set in motion the mechanisms to make it come to pass. It is impossible for God's Word to return to Him void

(Isaiah 55:11). Jesus said on numerous occasions that if we ask anything in His name it would be done for us (John 14:14; 15:15; 16:26–27).

The enemy has no legal right to decree anything because he has been stripped of all his power (Colossians 2:15). He can only make threats and try to get us to use our authority against ourselves. Satan is the master of deceit. So don't let him deceive you any longer. Take your seat on the throne and start decreeing something according to the promises of God. If it is healing you need, find some Scriptures and meditate on them and decree them. If it finances you need, look up Scriptures on finances, meditate on them, sow a financial seed, and decree an increase on what you have sown. It may not happen overnight, but when a farmer plants a seed, he doesn't think it will be ready for harvest the next day. Know that it is coming. Until then, meditate on that promise and praise God for the answer!

Scripture Readings:
Job 28:22
John 14:14; 15:15; 16:26–27

August 18

Your Harvest Depends on Your Soil

And the seeds that fell on the good soil represent honest, good-hearted people who hear God's word, cling to it, and patiently produce a huge harvest. (Luke 8:15)

What determines our harvest is the condition of our soil. The soil is our heart or inner man. I invite you to read Luke 8:9–18 to gain a better understanding of what I am going to discuss today. Jesus gave this parable as the foundation for understanding how the Kingdom of God operates (Mark 4:13). It is imperative that we understand this concept if we are to receive from God.

In the parable of the sower, the sower sows the Word of God. Jesus describes four different types of soil. There is soil that is hardened, soil that is stony, soil that contains weeds and thorns, and soil that is good and fertile. As I said earlier, each soil represents the condition of an individual's heart. There are some people who have hardened hearts, and the Word of God cannot produce in their life because it cannot penetrate the soil. It's like planting seed on the pavement. Their heart has been hardened because of unbelief and doubt. Eventually the birds of the air eat the seed, or it dies on its own.

The next soil described is the soil that contains stones. Unlike the soil previously mentioned, the seed is able to penetrate it and produces a harvest, but because there are stones under the surface of the soil the roots can't get deep enough for the plant to grow. It lacks nutrients, so it quickly dies. This is the type of heart that quickly forgets what it heard and is easily distracted because it fails to meditate on the Word. They are expecting quick results, and when they do not happen, they fall away.

The next soil described is the soil that has weeds and thorns. This soil also produces a crop, but right along with the crop there are weeds that eventually choke it out. This represents people who hear and receive the

Word and who are producing a crop; however, it is eventually taken away because of the cares and concerns and distractions of this life. They are the type of believers who are on fire for a period of time but eventually fall away and return to their previous lifestyle.

Finally, the good soil represents people who hear and receive the Word, and have gained insight into the principles of how the Kingdom of God works through meditating on the Word. And as a result, they produce a harvest.

The key to producing a harvest is the condition of the soil. If our soil is hardened, then we need to renew our mind according to the Word of God. We will have to reeducate ourselves and soften our soil through study, prayer, and meditation. If we have stony ground, then we need to spend time meditating on the Word of God. If we have weeds and thorns in our soil, then we will have to pull those weeds and thorns out of our hearts. We can do this by spending time with the Word and meditating on it. God does not discriminate; if you are not receiving a harvest, check the condition of your soil.

Scripture Readings:
Mark 4:13–27
Luke 8:9–18

August 19

WORDS THAT HEAL AND WORDS THAT KILL

He sent out His word and healed them, snatching them from the door of death. (Psalm 107:20)

I looked up the word *heal* in the dictionary and found a definition that encapsulates it. To *heal* basically means to make whole or sound. Did you know that words can make a person sound or whole, or they can be used to tear down and destroy (Proverbs 12:6)? Satan knows this and is working overtime to get people to use their words negatively. This is something every believer should be mindful of. There is power in the words we speak!

Many believers are guilty of self-sabotage because of words they have spoken about themselves or certain situations they are facing. They spend an hour in prayer making a request before God, then spend the rest of the day speaking doubt and unbelief, wondering why what they have prayed for has not manifested. They spoke healing one minute and destruction and death the next. This type of behavior is confusing to their spirit because it doesn't know what exactly to produce.

Jesus was the Word of God manifested in the flesh (John 1:14). So we can exchange the Word for Jesus. If we do this, it becomes plain why God chose Jesus to come to the earth. He came to make humanity whole or sound again. God sent His Word to produce a crop for Himself (Isaiah 55:11). Jesus prospered everywhere He went and accomplished exactly what God sent Him to do (John 5:30). At Jesus's ascension, He gave these instructions to those who believed in Him. He told them to preach the Good News to everyone, and those who would receive the message would be able to heal the sick, cast out demons, speak in new languages, and be immune to poisonous drinks (Mark 16:15–18).

Jesus transferred His ability to speak words that healed His followers. We have the ability to speak healing and wholeness to others and ourselves. Our words can bring life and healing to someone in need. They can be an oasis to people who thirst. With our words, we can build something up or tear something down (Proverbs 12:18). How many people are suffering from poor self-esteem today because of what someone spoke to them in the past?

I have worked with victims of domestic violence and they have told me that what hurt the most was the verbal abuse they endured. The physical abuse was temporary, but the mental abuse still lingered. We have the power of life and death right under our nose (Proverbs 18:21). Choose your words wisely because you will have to give an account for every word you have spoken (Matthew 12:36). Think before you speak, and let your words be few (Proverbs 12:14).

Scripture Readings:
Psalm 107:20
Proverbs 12:6, 14, 18; 13:3; 15:4; 18:21
Isaiah 55:11
Mark 16:15–18

August 20

THE HEART, MIND, AND IMAGINATION

Because when they knew and recognized Him as God, they did not honor and glorify Him as God or give Him thanks. But instead they became futile and godless in their thinking [with vain imaginings, foolish reasoning, and stupid speculations] and their senseless minds were darkened. (Romans 1:21 AMP)

There is a strong link between the heart and the mind. An individual's heart has 40,000 neurons connecting it to their brain. In essence, the human heart has the ability to think, and it cooperates with the brain itself. I had believed that the imagination was the product of the mind, but according to the Scriptures the origin of the imagination begins in the heart (Genesis 6:5). It is the heart that creates the imagination and it's the mind that develops the image that is produced by the imagination.

The heart influences the mind. This makes sense, because the heart is the first organ that is developed in an infant. Until the brain develops in an infant, it's the heart that is in charge of the cognitive processes because of its connecting neurons. Likewise, it is in the heart where faith is generated (Romans 10:9), which is essential for answered prayer (Mark 11:23). Our heart is the catalyst of faith and imagination.

That is why the Bible instructs us to meditate on the Word of God daily. As we do this, we are creating an image in our hearts that will later be developed by our minds into an imagination. The heart and mind work together to produce the imagination. It is like developing film. A picture is taken with a camera, and then the film is taken and placed in the developer. Once the film is placed in the developer, then the image is created. Well, think of your heart as the film, your mind as the developer, and the imagination as the image that is the result of the film and the developer.

God has given us the ability to see things in two different ways. We can see with our physical eyes, and we can see with our inner eyes, or the imagination. Our inner eyes work in the spiritual realm, and are the genesis of creation. We have to conceive an image in our heart before we can bring it to birth in the physical realm. When we meditate, we are allowing the process of imagination to enter into our hearts, which creates an image in our minds. Once this process is complete, the manifestation will come.

You may have to read this several times and let it marinate in your heart and mind. Ask God to give you revelation on this because it could be the catalyst of the breakthrough you have been looking for. Once you understand this connection, then you will understand that nothing is impossible—if you can see it, it can happen for you.

Scripture Readings:
Genesis 6:5; 11:6
Deuteronomy 29:19
Luke 1:51
Romans 1:21

August 21

THE RECEIVING HEART

Then Mary said, Behold. I am the handmaiden of the Lord; let it be done to me according to what you have said. And the angel left her. (Luke 1:38 AMP)

I find that many well-meaning believers get frustrated with God because their prayers are not being answered. They begin to think that God must have favorites and they are obviously not one of them. If this thought pattern is not interrupted, they will soon give up on prayer all together. This is exactly what the enemy wants them to do. The problem is not with God, however, but with us. We might be saying to ourselves right now, "I did all the right things. I prayed the prayer of faith, meditated on the Word, tithed, and even fasted, but I got nothing for it."

The answer to your problem might be your failure to receive from God. It is not enough to study the Word and base your prayers on the promises of God. You must also position yourself to receive from God. In the first chapter of Luke, there is story about Mary when she received news from an angel that she would conceive the birth of the Messiah. Mary was between sixteen and eighteen years old and was a virgin. Can you imagine what her reaction was when she was informed that she would give birth to the Messiah, having never known a man?

It must have been overwhelming for her, to say the least. Mary asked the angel how this would come to pass, and the angel explained to her that the Holy Spirit would be responsible for impregnating her (Luke 1:34–37). Mary had the choice to not receive what the angel had told her, and she would have disqualified herself from being the mother of Jesus. God would have had to pick some other virgin that had a heart to receive what He wanted to do. But because Mary had an open and receptive heart, God was able to fulfill His desire and Jesus was born nine months later.

Believing God is only half the process. We also have to receive from Him. Have you every tried to do something nice for someone and they refused to accept your act of kindness? It gets kind of frustrating, doesn't it? That is the way God feels when His children refuse to receive from Him. To receive is to have an expectation for your prayers to be answered. Until the manifestation comes, you are giving God praise for the answered prayer. Just like a wide receiver expecting to receive the pass from the quarterback, you are ready to receive. Don't let another prayer be dropped. Be ready to receive!

Scripture Readings:
Matthew 21:22
Mark 11:23–24
Luke 1:26–37

August 22

WORRY IS NEGATIVE MEDITATION

Can all your worries add a single moment to your life? (Matthew 6:27)

I have discussed the importance of meditation, but I think I should clarify what I mean when I say we are to meditate on the Word of God. There are many forms of meditation. For most people, when you talk about meditation, they think of some Middle Eastern type of meditation where the mind is cleared of all thought and a mantra is chanted. No, biblical meditation is simply muttering the Word of God to yourself. You are thinking about the Word of God, not trying to empty your mind. Biblical meditation is where you chew on the Word like a cow chews on a cud of grass, absorbing all the nutrients out of it. When you are meditating on the Word of God, you are allowing the life of the Word to enter your inner man.

Everyone knows how to meditate, even if they have never really thought about it. If you have ever worried about something, then you were meditating on the negative. You visualized that catastrophe happening to you or a loved one, that you would not have enough or would be left behind. This meditation caused unrest within you, and then you started to feel anxious and agitated. Your inner man has already begun to react to the pending doom you created. This is negative meditation. If we just reverse what I described, that is positive meditation. Instead of your inner man reacting with anxiety, it reacts with joy because it expects that the answer is on its way.

If we read Joshua 1:8, it states that if we meditate on the Word day and night, then we will *make our way prosperous.* God doesn't do it, but we do it! How? Our inner man makes it happen. It will make sure we are at the right place at the right time, and it will make sure the right people are there. God will give us favor in every situation as we give ourselves to meditation on the Word of God.

To put it in psychological terms, when we meditate on the Word of God, it enters our conscious mind and then goes to the unconscious mind. As I said earlier, the unconscious mind is like soil, producing whatever is planted in it. The Word is the seed that we have planted by meditation. As we meditate, we are providing a climate for that seed to grow in our unconscious mind. Once we have meditated and the seed has been actualized within our unconscious (heart), it will give birth in the physical realm. When we worry, we are creating a climate for what we fear to come to pass.

Jesus admonished us not to worry or to fear for a reason. When we do, we are setting the stage for whatever we fear to come to pass. If we find ourselves starting to worry about something, we need to stop that thought and replace it with a promise from God. We are to let the Word abide in us, then we can ask God for anything and it will be granted to us (John 15:7). The choice is ours: we can walk in fear and anxiety, or we can walk in faith and prosperity.

Scripture Readings:
Joshua 1:8
Matthew 6:25–34
Philippians 4:6–7

August 23

Things to Remember When Faced with a Challenge

You will keep in perfect peace all who trust in You, all whose thoughts are fixed on You! (Isaiah 26:3)

When faced with a challenging situation, it is so easy to get distracted by the circumstances surrounding us. It is easy to forget about the power that resides within. Since we live in a physical world that we can see with our eyes, it is easy to react to circumstances in the physical or sense realm. But we are a spirit who has a soul and who lives in a physical body. We have to be mindful of this if we are to walk above the circumstances in this world. We have to become inside minded, remembering that greater is He who is within us than he who is in the world (1 John 4:4).

Jesus told His disciples that they would face hardships, trials, and tribulations while they lived on this earth, but He would give them peace because He overcame the world (John 16:33). Since we are one with Jesus in the spiritual realm, we can experience peace also. This peace comes by putting our trust and focus on God and His Word. When faced with a hardship, instead of looking at the situation, we turn our focus to the Word of God and find a promise to stand on. This will cause faith to grow and positive and uplifting thoughts to be generated. Positive thoughts will lead to praise, and we know that God inhabits the praises of His people.

God has promised us in His Word that He would strengthen us and help us (Isaiah 41:10). He also said that He would make a way for us where there seemed to be no way (Isaiah 43:19). We should use the promises of God like a shield of armor to protect us from the darts and arrows of the enemy (Psalm 91:4). With the shield of God's promises and the sword of the Spirit, which is the spoken Word, we can defeat any foe or situation that faces us. There is no weapon formed against us that shall prosper (Isaiah 54:17).

Scripture Readings:
Psalm 91:4
Isaiah 41:10; 43:18–19; 54:17
John 16:33
1 John 4:4

August 24

A Memory of a Steak Won't Satisfy

Study this Book of Instruction continually. Meditate on it day and night so you will be sure to obey everything written in it. Only then will you prosper and succeed in all you do. (Joshua 1:8)

Most people wouldn't think of eating only once a week. If they did, they would suffer from malnutrition. Well, the same is true in the spiritual realm. Many believers are suffering from spiritual malnutrition, because the only time they consume the Word for themselves is on Sundays. Just like we need to feed our outer man, we also need to feed our inner man on a consistent basis. The Word of God is food for the inner man of which Jesus spoke when He was at the well in Samaria (John 4:32).

According to Scripture, the Word of God is alive and active, and it is able to penetrate soul and spirit, bone and marrow, and it is a discerner of the intentions of the heart (Hebrews 4:12). We need to consume the Word daily to build our inner man, causing it to become strong in the Lord. It is not enough to rely on our memory—we need to eat the real thing. A memory of a steak we ate last week is not going to satisfy our hunger today. Why do we think that it would be any different in the realm of the Spirit?

My mother had a doctor's appointment not too long ago. Since she no longer drives, she needed me to give her a ride. I wrote the date on my calendar, and even put the appointment notification on my memo board. But I didn't look at it for over a week. I thought her appointment was at 2:00 p.m.—in fact, I was sure it was at 2:00 p.m. Well, the day of the appointment came and I made sure she was there on time. I was proud of myself because we even got there early. But it turned out she missed her appointment because it was at 11:40 a.m. I was sure they were the one who made the mistake, but when I got home and looked at my calendar I had the time as 11:40 a.m. Had I just looked at the calendar, I would have saw that her appointment time was in the morning, not in the afternoon. We can do the same with the Word of God. We can misread something or misinterpret something from the Bible, and misquote the Scripture, and even start a false doctrine because we did not take the time to read the Scripture.

We need the Word of God to build us up spiritually. If we have been fasting for several days and then try to workout, we will get fatigued because we will have no energy or fuel for our muscles. When we are using our faith, it takes spiritual energy, so we need to build up our reserves so that we have more than enough. We must be as well nourished in our inner man as our outer man.

Scripture Readings:
Joshua 1:8
John 4:31–38
Hebrews 4:12

August 25

God Desires Your Fellowship

Enoch lived 365 years, walking in close fellowship with God. Then one day he disappeared, because God took him. (Genesis 5:23–24)

A lot of people know God as their Savior and Lord but don't know Him as a friend. God wants to fellowship with us as we have fellowship with a good friend. God wants us to confide in Him, telling Him the most intimate desires of our heart. It thrills Him when His children come to Him and cast their cares upon Him (1 Peter 5:7). Doing this creates intimacy with God, and as we reveal what's in our heart, He will speak to us and give us insight into specific situations. We can have the same type of relationship with God the patriarchs of old had with God. I say this because the Bible clearly states that God is not a respecter of persons.

Having fellowship with God is not a difficult thing. All it takes is spending time with Him on a regular basis. When you are traveling in your car, instead of just listening to the radio, CD, or MP3, take some time to talk to the Holy Spirit. Tell Him what's on your mind and your heart. Give Him the opportunity to respond to You. It might seem strange at first, but the more you do it the more comfortable it will become. You will develop a confidence with God and you will be more acquainted with His nature. Soon, God will not only be your Lord and Savior, but your most trusted friend.

To have fellowship with someone means that we delight in his or her company. Do you know that when you delight in the Word of God, it is a form of fellowship? God's Word is His will. So when we delight ourselves in the Word of God, we are having fellowship with Him. And His fellowship comes with rewards. God will show us how to prosper in this life; He will give us discernment so that we avoid certain people and places. He will give us favor and protect us from the harm that is in the world. He will separate us from the crowd and give us the desires of our heart. Others will be drawn to us, and we will be given the opportunity to bless them. All of this comes to those who choose to fellowship with God.

Scripture Readings:
Genesis 5:23–24
Psalm 1:1–3
Isaiah 41:8; 58:11, 14
1 John 1:1–7

August 26

Have You Been Washed Ashore?

But if we confess our sins to Him, He is faithful and just to forgive us our sins and to cleanse us from all wickedness. (1 John 1:9)

My pastor told a story about a baby seal that was washed up on the shore. It was at the brink of death until my pastor and others started pouring buckets of sea water on it. Once the baby seal was revived again, it began its trek back to the water. The only problem was that the seal was going in the wrong direction. My pastor tried her best to redirect the seal back to the water. Finally, it made it back to the water, but because the tide of the ocean was coming in the seal wound up back on the beach. The mother seal was waiting patiently for her baby the whole time.

When I heard this story, I thought about believers who have been washed ashore, and have broken fellowship with God. Like that baby seal washed up on the beach, they need someone to pour water on them so they are revived. They also need someone to direct them back out to the ocean. But like that seal, even after being revived, the seal needs to go in the right direction. That seal was at jeopardy of losing its life because it was going in the wrong direction—instead of going toward the ocean it was going away from it.

It is easy for us to lose our way and wind up on the shore, but God will send someone to revive and assist us to get back into the ocean of His love. It is up to us to listen and follow the directions of those God sends to us. Don't be like that baby seal that didn't pay attention to those who were trying to help it get back into the ocean. What should have been a quick trip turned into a long one. Sometimes we can be the same way in our own lives. We can make things a lot more difficult than they need to be. But the good thing is that God is patient, and like that mother seal, He will wait until we finally get on the right track. We might have to suffer needlessly, but God will be there waiting for us to return to the ocean of His love.

God's Word is our guide to revive and strengthen us (Isaiah 58:11). When we lose our way, all we have to do is turn to the Word and let it lead us back to the Father. Let the Holy Spirit show you the quickest way back to the waters of the living Word of God. Don't jeopardize your life or suffer needlessly; humble yourself before the mighty hand of God, and let Him lift you up (1 Peter 1:5:6–7).

Scripture Readings:
John 6:39; 16:13
Hebrews 4:12

August 27

BEING GREEDY IS A FORM OF IDOLATRY

Don't be greedy, for a greedy person is an idolater, worshiping the things of this world. (Colossians 3:5)

Today I want to discuss something that most of us have been guilty of at one time or another, and that is coveting something or someone that is not ours. It was coveting that caused Eve to be deceived by Satan (Genesis 3:6). Once she saw that the tree was beautiful and the fruit looked delicious, and it would give her wisdom, she took it and ate it. Because of the strong desire that was created by Eve's lust, she was willing to step outside of the boundaries God had established to satisfy her cravings.

Isn't that true of many people today? How many people have set aside their morals to go after something to satisfy their carnal cravings? How many families have been destroyed because of coveting another's spouse, or looking outside of the marriage to satisfy a craving? How many people have willfully defrauded and cheated in order to gain wealth? How many government officials have used their political powers to gain wealth and further their political careers at the expense of others? How many corporations knowingly made deals that would be harmful to the environment and ultimately caused harmful effects to human beings because of their love for money? How many wars have been started because of the lust for land and the resources of that land?

Coveting is the genesis of all sin, and it is part of our DNA since the fall. That is why the world will never see peace as long as this aspect of the human condition is not controlled. The Word of God admonishes us not to crave things because it is a form of idolatry (Colossians 3:5). It also warns us not to love money because it is the source of all kinds of evil (1 Timothy 6:10), and it can be the cause of a believer wandering from the truth.

We have to be mindful of this tendency within us and continually question ourselves: Is our desire for something controlling us or are we controlling it? Are we allowing that craving to become an idol we worship and are willing to do almost anything for? This world likes to produce idols for us to worship, but we must not let our lusts create that desire within our heart. I heard Brother Keith Moore say something that stuck in my mind about covetousness: "Covetousness is when you desire something so much that you are willing to do too much to get it." I like that definition. Being greedy is a form of idolatry.

Scripture Readings:
Genesis 3:6
1 Corinthians 10:6
Colossians 3:5
1 Timothy 6:10

August 28

THE DANGERS OF IDOLATRY

You must not have any other god but Me. You must not make for yourself an idol of any kind or an image of anything in the heavens or on the earth or in the sea. You must not bow down to them or worship them, for I, the Lord your God, am a jealous God who will not tolerate your affection for any other gods. (Exodus 20:3–5)

We have been created with a need to worship, for that is how God created us. The enemy knows this, and he has used this tendency to take humanity away from worshipping the true God. He has influenced man to worship images and things, even other human beings, instead of the Creator of heaven and earth. Little do people realize that by worshipping these idols, they are indirectly worshipping Satan. He is the one who created the idol that is being worshipped; thus, that idol is under his control.

Many in our country do not think we have idols, but we do. There is a popular television showed called *American Idol*. Many entertainers are placed in a position of being worshipped by their fans. Sports figures are placed on a pedestal and worshipped. There is nothing wrong with admiring someone for his or her talents and creativity, but we step over the line when we begin to worship them.

Sporting events are places where people gather every week to worship. They plan their day around sports. They would rather miss church to watch their favorite team play. Many sports enthusiasts can readily tell you the statistics of their favorite player or team, but they can't quote a Scripture from the Bible. Many can recite the lyrics from their favorite song, but can't tell you five of the Ten Commandments.

I was watching a program on the cooking network not too long ago. And as I watched this program, I realized that food has become an idol to some people. People worship food. Just think about how many programs are on now that deal with food—they talk about how to prepare it, serve it, and how to eat it. There are networks on television for just about anything you can think of, and it is all a platform to make their subject matter an object to be worshipped.

There is nothing wrong with enjoying a sporting event, music, or eating a good meal, as long as we don't make it an idol. Our God is a jealous God, and He does not want to share our affections with another god. Instead, we should thank God for the ability He has given man to do all of these things. We are to thank God for the food He has provided for us to eat; we are to thank Him for the many pleasures we have in nature, and the things He has made available for us to enjoy. And we are to thank God for all our possessions while realizing that God is the source of all things, and we are to worship Him alone.

Scripture Readings:
Exodus 20:3–5
1 Corinthians 10:6
Colossians 3:5

August 29

WHAT DO YOU CONSIDER?

Pay attention to this, Job. Stop and consider the wonderful miracles of God! (Job 37:14)

When hardships and troubles come our way, what do we first consider? Do we consider the problem and put our focus on it, or do we focus on the solution? What are the first words that come out of our mouth in times of trouble and hardship? This is an important question for us to consider because it will reveal what's in our heart (inner man). It will reveal to us the most dominant thought in our heart.

If faced with a trial and our first thoughts are to turn to Jesus for the answer, then we know that we have already overcome the situation even though the present circumstances haven't changed—in the spiritual realm it has been taken care of. We have peace in the midst of the storm because Jesus is in the boat with us. He won't let us down. On the other hand, if we consider the problem and start speaking about it instead of to it, we will feel anxious and overwhelmed. Our speech will reflect our uncertainty and fear will be present. If we are operating in fear, then faith is not present. We will get what we said would happen.

The disciples had just left a huge meeting where Jesus fed four thousand people with seven loaves of bread and several fish. Afterward, Jesus and His disciples left in a boat to go to the region of Dalmanutha. On the way, they realized they had forgotten to bring some bread to eat. So they began to argue with each other and started blaming one another for not bringing bread for their journey. Jesus overheard their conversation and said, "Why are you arguing about having no bread? Don't you know or understand even yet? Are your hearts too hard to take it in? 'You have eyes—can't you see? You have ears—can't you hear?' Don't you remember anything at all? When I fed the 5,000 with five loaves of bread, how many baskets of leftovers did you pick up afterward?" (Mark 8:17–19).

Even though the disciples saw with their own eyes the miracle of Jesus feeding the multitudes, they failed to consider it when it came to their specific situation. Because they failed to consider or think on that situation where Jesus provided bread for so many, their hearts were hardened, and it was as if what they witnessed never happened. We can be the same way too. It is all too easy to allow our minds to focus on the situation at hand and not consider God's Word that has the answer to our specific situation. We can forget all the answered prayers of the past and the precious promises of God in a time of trouble and distress. Who or what do we first consider in times of trouble?

Scripture Readings:
Job 37:14–18
Mark 8:14–21
Hebrews 3:1–2

August 30

How Do You Guard Your Heart?

Guard your heart above all else, for it determines the course of your life. (Proverbs 4:23)

What determines the course we take in our life is our heart. Our heart can be called the inner man or the unconscious mind. As I stated in pervious lessons, medical science has proven that the heart has the ability to think, and has approximately 40,000 neurons that are connected to our brains. So there is a strong connection between our heart and our brain. With this information we can see that our thoughts have an influence on our heart, and our heart has an influence on our mind.

We can guard our heart by monitoring what we think about every day. On the average, a person will have anywhere from three to ten thousand thoughts per day, depending on how much a person reads and meditates. People who read or meditate generally have more thoughts than this. Some thoughts come and go, but there are those thoughts we choose to focus our attention on. It is those thoughts I want to focus on, because it is those thoughts that will ultimately have an influence on our inner man.

It is important to study the Word of God daily and meditate on it, because it will have an impact on our heart, and our heart determines the course of our life. It is in our heart where faith is generated. It is in our heart where imaginations are created and thoughts are transferred. The Bible promises that those who delight in the Word of God and meditate on it will be blessed in all they do (Psalm 1:1–3). The reason why this happens is because the heart determines the boundaries of a person's life, and it creates the spiritual force to bring it to manifestation.

The difference between a successful person and an unsuccessful person are their thoughts. A person who has a positive self-concept might experience hard times, but they won't allow themselves to remain in that condition because they see themselves as being prosperous. Their heart (inner man) will find a way to get them back to where they feel comfortable. On the other hand, a person who has a negative self-concept does not feel comfortable with being successful. Their heart or inner man will not allow them to remain successful because they will self-sabotage themselves, bringing them down to a level where they feel comfortable.

I have seen this time and time again with some of the people I have worked with. The boundaries of their heart would not allow them to succeed because of the dominant thoughts they have about themselves. This is why the Bible states that we have to renew our minds and not be conformed to the image that the world has created for us (Romans 12:1–2). The world's system wants us to conform to the image they have for us, because that is how they can control us and confine us. Learn to think about what you think about, and get rid of those thoughts that are opposed to the Word of God.

Scripture Readings:
Psalm 1:1–3
Proverbs 4:20–23

August 31

THE SURE MERCIES OF DAVID

I will be his Father, and he will be My son. If he sins, I will correct and discipline him with the rod, like any father would do. But My favor will not be taken from him as I took it from Saul, whom I removed from your sight. (2 Samuel 7:14–15)

Most believers are not aware of the sure mercies of David. Knowledge of the Davidic covenant is the platform for us to stand on when we miss the mark. All of us at some time or another have fallen into sin, and we have missed what God has destined for us to walk in. Through the grace of God, we are not disqualified from our position in Christ Jesus, or our calling. Yes, we will have to suffer the consequences of our actions, but we will not lose our office like King Saul did. Once King Saul failed to follow the instruction of Samuel, God disqualified him from the office of being king of Israel (1 Samuel 15:22–23). After this, God instructed Samuel to anoint David king of Israel. It would not be until years later that David would sit on the throne as king of Israel.

When David became king, God made a covenant with him. That covenant would make it possible for David to not lose his office of king due to indiscretions on his part. The covenant was called the sure mercies of David. Because of this covenant, when David lost his position as king for a short period of time, he regained his position back once again. He lost his position because he committed adultery, and then murdered the husband of his love interest. As a result of David's adulterous affair, a child was born, who later died. There was turmoil in David's household. One of his daughters was raped by her half-brother Ammon. Because of this, Absalom, the brother of Tamar, killed Ammon. If that was not bad enough, Absalom formed a coup to wrestle the kingdom away from his father (2 Samuel 13–18).

David suffered the consequences of the poor choices he made, but because of the covenant of sure mercies, he did not lose his office as king. It is because of this covenant the kingly line would later include our Lord and Savior Jesus Christ. The promise of God would be true, that David's throne would be secure forever (2 Samuel 7:16). We, like David, might be caught in sin and make poor choices from time to time. But because of the finished work of Jesus and the covenant of sure mercies, we can go before the throne of God and repent of our sin or transgression. We can walk away knowing that it will not be held against us. We might experience some fallout because of our indiscretion, but we will not lose our calling or position in the Kingdom of God.

The next time the devil tries to throw your shortcomings in your face, just tell him that the sure mercies of David have taken care of that, and you have been washed in the blood of Jesus. See what he has to say then.

Scripture Readings:
2 Samuel 7:14–15

September 1

UNLEASH THE POWER WITHIN YOU

Now all glory to God, who is able, through His mighty power at work within us, to accomplish infinitely more than we might ask or think. (Ephesians 3:20)

We have a reservoir of power within us that is just waiting to be unleashed. To release this power, however, we have to be aware that it is within us. Otherwise we will just have the potential to do great things, but it will remain only that—potential. I used to tell my son when he was playing sports that he had great potential, but if he didn't utilize that potential it would do him no good. There are many people who possess great potential yet are living unproductive lives. They will have to give an account for this when they stand before God. Potential not realized is potential wasted.

According to the Word of God, we have been given precious promises to share in the divine nature of God (2 Peter 1:3–4). Jesus said those who believe in Him would do even greater works than He did while on this earth (John 14:12). As I stated earlier, we will have to give an account for what we do and didn't do while living in our physical bodies. Many will be disappointed when they are shown what they could have done, had they exercised their faith and acted on the promises found in the Word of God.

In order to have access to this power, we need to get aligned with the Word of God. We have to realize that we cannot generate this power independent of God, and we cannot rely on our self-effort to accomplish anything in the Kingdom. Merely quoting Scriptures will not tap into this power. We have to go beyond the Scriptures and grasp what is within to have access to the power of God. It is the grace of God and faith that ignites this power within us. And it's obedience that keeps it flowing. Total submission to fulfill the will of God is required before God will trust us with His power, which is accomplished by renewing our minds (Romans 12:1–2), and obtaining the mind of Christ Jesus (1 Corinthians 2:16).

There is a good example of this found in the book of Acts. Peter had been arrested because of preaching the good news of the gospel. The religious institutions in the region were persecuting the church. So the believers got together and prayed to God for healing powers, miraculous signs, and wonders to be done in the name of Jesus. After they finished their prayer, they *were all filled* with the power of the Holy Spirit and preached the Word of God with boldness (Acts 4:29–31).

The same thing is possible for us today. God does not change. If He did it for the disciples in the book of Acts, He can do it for us too. We have to be aware of this power potential within us and use our faith to access it. It is always there, ready to be unleashed.

Scripture Readings:
Acts 2:42–43; 4:29–31
Ephesians 3:10, 20
2 Peter 1:3–4

September 2

PUT SOME LIFT IN YOUR PRAYER LIFE

For it is by believing in your heart you are made right with God, and it is by confessing with your mouth that you are saved. (Romans 10:10)

I use the above Scripture to illustrate the importance of making a confession of our faith. It is not enough to believe in our heart, but that belief must be expressed through the words of our mouth in order to complete the process. When we look at how the universe was created, we notice that God used His imagination to create the image and then He spoke the image into existence. It was the Word of God's power that caused the manifestation of the unseen to become seen.

The power of confession causes our faith to take flight. It gives lift to our prayers. Confession is like the wings of an airplane: if the plane is standing still, the plane will not fly, because the law of lift is not in operation. But once the plane begins to gain speed down the runway, the wind hits the wings and creates lift. Once the plane reaches a certain speed, the air that hits the wings creates low pressure on top of the wings and high pressure underneath the wings, causing the airplane to lift off the ground. This is called the law of lift and thrust. As long as that plane maintains that speed, it can supersede the law of gravity.

The same principle applies to the things of the Spirit too. We can supersede the natural by using the principles of faith and confession. When we decree and confess what we have exercised our faith for, it gives thrust to our prayers and lifts them up to the throne of God. The more we confess the promises of God, the more our faith increases. This is the principle Abraham used when he believed God to fulfill His promise that he would become the father of many nations (Genesis 12:1–3). The Bible states that Abraham grew strong in faith and hoped against hope (Romans 4:17–21). Abraham kept his faith strong by declaring that God would fulfill His promise.

As believers we can do the same thing today. When we begin to feel doubt, and we are beginning to lose altitude, we only need to make a positive confession of faith. Thank God for His faithfulness. Read those promises again and remind yourself of other times God has come through for you. If you do this, then you will gain thrust and begin to soar to your destination of an answered prayer.

Scripture Readings:
Mark 11:23–24
Romans 4:17–21; 10:10
1 John 5:14–15

September 3

WHATEVER HE SAYS TO YOU, DO IT

But His mother told the servants, "Do whatever He tells you." (John 2:5)

In order to experience the supernatural in our lives, we must be willing and obedient to what the Holy Spirit instructs us to do. It is not enough to pray the Scripture and speak the promise; we must be willing to act on what we are instructed to do. Let me warn you, however, that sometimes what you are instructed to do will make no sense to your logical thinking. But you must remember that the things of God make no sense and are even considered foolish by worldly wisdom (2 Corinthians 2:14).

The Bible is filled with instructions God gave to those who called on Him. Abraham was instructed to present his son, Isaac, as a sacrifice to God (Genesis 22:1–18). Moses was instructed to point his staff at the Red Sea in order to make a pathway for the children of Israel to cross to the other side on dry ground (Exodus 14:15–18). Joshua was instructed to march around the city of Jericho in silence for seven days, and then shout on the seventh day for the walls to fall down (Joshua 6:1–21). Gideon was instructed to reduce his army from 32,000 men to only 300. Then he was told to have his men carry lanterns in jars, and break the jars and blow their horns to defeat their enemies. Jesus told Peter to catch a fish and look in its mouth to get money to pay their taxes (Matthew 17:24–27). These are only a few of the examples where the people of God were instructed to do things that defied human logic or reasoning.

It is important to realize that none of the miracles these men experienced would have happened if they failed to follow God's instructions. It is the willing and obedient who will enjoy the fruit of the land (Isaiah 1:19). This means that we must be willing, but if we are not obedient we will disqualify ourselves from the blessings that God has for us. Many believers have prayed the prayer of faith and have not received from God because they failed to follow the instructions God gave them so they could receive their manifestation. Some of these believers rationalized that it must not have been God's will for them to receive, so they gave up.

We as believers must purpose in our hearts to complete the process by listening and obeying to what God tells us to do to in order to realize our prayers. What He instructs us to do may not make sense, but that is where faith comes in. We will have to step out in faith, not letting our senses talk us out of what God has told us to do. We have to ignore our logical mind and follow the instructions of the inner man. When we do this, God will give us a peace that defies understanding because we know that the answer to our prayers are on their way.

Scripture Readings:
Isaiah 1:19
John 2:1–11
Matthew 17:24–27

September 4

God Is Long-Suffering, but There Is a Price

So each generation should set its hope anew on God, not forgetting His glorious miracles and obeying His commands. Then they will not be like their ancestors—stubborn, rebellious, and unfaithful, refusing to give their hearts to God. (Psalm 78:7–8)

Psalm 78 should be read by every believer and shared with their family, especially their children. This psalm illustrates the patience of God and His willingness to quickly forgive His people. It also illustrates how hardhearted and stubborn the children of Israel were in spite of all the miracles they witnessed. Many people today say that if they had witnessed the miracles God performed in the Old and New Testaments, they would have strong faith. This is simply not true because the heart of man is most deceitful (Jeremiah 17:9). We need to learn to walk by the Spirit, and not by our senses or flesh, if we are to receive God's best (Romans 8:5–8).

When we read this psalm and meditate on these Scriptures, we will see how the malady of the heart was transferred from generation to generation. There is a pattern we can see. God would display His glory and the people would comply for a moment and then regress back to their sinful nature. This same pattern is true today for a majority of the church. It takes effort by faith and diligence for us to be mindful of God's presence in our lives. Every one of us should make it a practice to read Psalm 78 from beginning to end. We need to access and refresh our minds so that we don't make the same mistakes and fall into the same pitfalls the children of Israel did. We also need to share this psalm with our children so they will be mindful of the Most High God, their heavenly Father.

Scripture Readings:
Psalm 78

September 5

A Man After God's Heart Can Fall Sometimes

The Lord directs the steps of the godly. He delights in every detail of their lives. Though they stumble, they will never fall, for the Lord holds them by the hand. (Psalm 37:23–24)

Even the best of us have occasionally fallen into temptation and sin. When this happens, we need to debrief the situation leading up to the sin, and learn from it so that it is not repeated. We can learn many valuable lessons from the patriarchs of the Bible, but I would like to look at what happened to the man who has been described as "a man after God's own heart" (Acts 13:22). The man I am talking about is none other than David.

David had a major fall while he served as king of Israel. The infamous incident I am referring to involved lust, adultery, and murder, followed by a cover up. It sounds like the making of good television drama, doesn't it? It was the spring and David decided to stay at the palace instead of going to war with his men. He was relaxed and enjoying all that he had accomplished. His kingdom was united and expanding. I'm sure David was feeling pretty good about himself. His relationship with God was strong, and he was feeling invincible.

It is in moments like these when we are the most prone to fall. The enemy comes around when our guard is down, when we are feeling strong, and when things seem to be going well. David was on the roof of his palace after taking an afternoon nap, and he saw a vision that captured his attention. It was a beautiful woman bathing next door. He couldn't get that image out of his mind. The seed of lust was planted and it took on a life of its own. David made some inquiries about this woman and found out that she was married to one of his soldiers. Because he had such a strong desire for her, he ignored the fact that she was married. All that mattered to David was that he wanted her. So he summoned the woman to the palace and romanced her, and, as a result, the woman got pregnant. This is something David didn't bargain for.

So David devised a plan to cover his sin. He had Uriah, Bathsheba's husband, come in from battle. He hoped that he would take the opportunity to go home and be with his wife, then, when she informed him she was pregnant, he would think it was his child. Well, it didn't turn out that way. Uriah was a dedicated soldier and he didn't want to relax and enjoy his wife while his cohorts were in the field of battle. David even tried to get him drunk, but that didn't work either.

When David realized that his scheme to cover up his sin wouldn't work, he had Uriah placed in a position where he would be killed. It turned out that not only Uriah died, but other innocent men died as well. David got want he wanted, but it came at a price. It is good that God made a covenant of sure mercies with David because if He didn't David would have surely lost his office and position as king. God knew this would happen, and even in spite of this knowledge God still called David a man after His own heart (1 Samuel 13:14).

Scripture Readings:
2 Samuel 11:1–26

September 6

You Can't Win by Covering Your Sin

People who conceal their sins will not prosper, but if they confess and turn from them, they will receive mercy. (Proverbs 28:13)

When we are convicted by our conduct, the best thing to do is to confess our shortcomings to God (1 John 1:9). Doing this will restore our fellowship with God and resolve the internal conflict that is going on within us. It will also keep our conscience from becoming hardened. When a person's conscience becomes hardened, they have little or no remorse when they sin. With no remorse, there is no sense of repentance; with no repentance, there is no forgiveness, so the sin remains in effect.

This is what happened after David tried to cover his sin by having Bathsheba's husband killed in the field of battle. He thought he was in the clear. David married the widow of Uriah, and she gave birth to their first child. However, David's conscience bothered him. He was sensitive to all the talk going around the palace about him and Bathsheba. His conscience amplified all the whispers among those in his employment who knew what had transpired between Bathsheba, Uriah, and himself. David tried to forget and focus his attention elsewhere, but he couldn't run from God.

Had God not intervened through Nathan the prophet, David probably would have never repented of his sin. If his sin had remained, David's relationship with God would have suffered as a result. The human heart is most deceitful, and it can easily point out the sins of others while being blind to its own. This was the case when Nathan confronted David about this entire affair (2 Samuel 12:1–11). When he confessed his sin, he was forgiven, but that didn't exonerate him from the consequences of his transgression. There is a price that must be paid that comes with sin. David's reign would never be the same again. His rule as king would be beset with scandal and household unrest between family members, which would lead to the death of several of David's sons.

In spite of all of this, David would remain king of Israel and would thrive because of his restored relationship with God. He goes on to describe the joy that comes when a person confesses their sin in Psalm 32. He describes the feeling of relief that comes when the guilt of sin is lifted and the relationship with God is restored. His physical body was affected—he felt tired and was worried by the guilt of his sin. The fear of judgment weighed on him day after day. He couldn't completely enjoy himself because of his unconfessed sin. But all that changed when he confessed and acknowledged his sin before the Lord.

There is no sin too bad that you can't be forgiven. So don't spend another day carrying the weight of that sin around with you. God is waiting to take it away!

Scripture Readings:
2 Samuel 12:1–11
Psalm 32; 51
1 John 1:9

September 7

LET IT GO BECAUSE GOD HAS

I—yes, I alone—will blot out your sins for My own sake and will never think of them again. (Isaiah 43:25)

Sometimes the hardest thing for a believer to do is receive and accept that God has forgiven their sins and transgressions. God not only forgives us when we confess our sins, He actually forgets that they ever happened. This allows the believer to come before the throne of God's grace with confidence and boldness. The enemy is good at bringing our past sins to our remembrance in an attempt to condemn us when we approach God. But when this happens, we should remind him that there is no condemnation for those who are in Christ Jesus (Romans 8:1).

There is a process we should employ to cleanse our conscience from the committed sin, which is spelled out in 2 Samuel 12:13–24. The first step in this process is to acknowledge our sin. This sets the platform for God to forgive us and starts the process of restoration. Secondly, we are to accept the consequence for our sin, and *realize that God is not punishing us for our sin; we are reaping the consequences of our actions.* The third step is to put it behind us. The apostle Paul said it best when he wrote, "Forgetting the past and looking forward to what lies ahead, I press on to reach the end of the race and receive the heavenly prize for which God, through Christ Jesus, is calling us" (Philippians 3:13–14). The fourth step is to receive and accept the forgiveness of sins and the complete restoration of the relationship with God.

God loves us tremendously, and the depth of that love is unfathomable. Our focus then should be on God's love for us rather our love for Him (1 John 4:10). If we only focus on our love for Him, then we are setting the stage for the enemy to condemn us when we miss the mark and fall short of His glory. He will quickly point out that if we really loved God, then we would not have committed that sin. However, when we focus on how much God loves us, then our behavior is not based on how much we love Him or what we do for Him, but on how much He loves us. This will establish that our love is not based on our performance but on God's willingness to love us in spite of what we may say or do. His love is abundant and unconditional.

Scripture Readings:
2 Samuel 12:13–24
Isaiah 43:25
Philippians 3:13–14
1 John 1:9; 4:10

September 8

THERE ARE NO DROUGHTS IN THE KINGDOM

But blessed are those who trust in the Lord and have made the Lord their hope and confidence. They are like trees planted along a riverbank, with roots that reach deep into the water. Such trees are not bothered by the heat or worried by long months of drought. Their leaves stay green, and they never stop producing fruit. (Jeremiah 17:7–8)

We are citizens of heaven if we believe in the Lord Jesus Christ. Because of that, we are entitled to all the privileges that come with being a citizen of that realm. Jesus has given us the power to bind and loose on this earth as if it were in heaven. If it does not exist in heaven, then we have the authority to bind it here on earth. Conversely, if it does exist in heaven, we have the authority to loose it on the earth (Matthew 16:19). Is there lack in heaven? No. So that means we have been given the authority to bind lack in our life and release the abundance of God in all that we do.

You have a choice to make. You can choose to live according to the standards of this world, or you can choose to live according to the standards set in heaven. If you choose the former, then you will be susceptible to the concerns the world has. Throughout the world, nations are experiencing economic problems and governmental turmoil. The world seems to be on the brink of economic disaster. There are many people experiencing anxiety and worry about their future. Unfortunately, many believers are experiencing the same. But it doesn't have to be this way. The only reason believers suffer anxiety are because they are either ignorant of the covenant rights and privileges found in Christ or they refuse to believe and receive them.

We are called to be lights in this world, revealing the light and the life of Jesus to all we come into contact with. We are ambassadors of the Kingdom of God (2 Corinthians 5:20). We are to stand on the promises of God and take refuge in them, for they will be a shield to protect us from the plagues attacking the rest of the world (Psalm 91:4–8). Jesus never worried about lack while He was on this earth, because He realized He was a citizen of the Kingdom of God. As long as He trusted and sought the Kingdom, He knew His needs would be met (Matthew 6:33). God has a way of providing for those who trust in Him, even when there is a season of drought.

Scripture Readings:
Jeremiah 17:5–8
Psalm 91
Matthew 16:19; 18:18
Ephesians 1:3–5

September 9

SEEK HIS FACE AND NOT JUST HIS HAND

He revealed His character to Moses and His deeds to the people of Israel. (Psalm 103:7)

Moses had a special relationship with God. He was able to have intimate conversations with Him, even confronting Him and questioning God's actions at times. Their relationship was so intimate that God even revealed Himself to Moses and allowed him to look at His person (Exodus 33:12–23). It was to Moses that the Ten Commandments were given, and it was through him that the people of Israel were delivered and guided to the Promise Land. Moses had a very unique relationship with God, to say the least.

We should learn from Moses how to have the same kind of relationship with our heavenly Father. Moses wanted to know God personally and intimately. He wanted to know His name and His character. Moses didn't just want to know God as someone who just provided for his needs; he wanted to get acquainted with Him in a deeper way. As a result, God told him His name Yahweh and allowed Moses to see Him from behind (Exodus 33:18–23). Compare this with how the children of Israel responded when God came down to give them the Ten Commandments—they were afraid and didn't want God to speak to them, but chose to have Moses speak to them instead (Exodus 20:18–21).

The children of Israel only knew God by the miracles and acts He performed. They were satisfied with that type of relationship; most of them didn't want to know Him personally. They chose to let Moses be their representative between them and God. God wanted the entire nation of Israel to know Him and be His priests (Exodus 19:5). But they were satisfied with secondhand knowledge.

Many believers today seek God for what He can provide for them, and don't seek to know God personally. They let their pastors and teachers mediate between them and God. They fail to realize that God wants them to know Him in a deep and intimate way. Don't settle to know God as your provider, but get to know Him on a personal level. Know His character and learn how He thinks so that you can have the same type of relationship that Moses had with Him. He longs to have that type of relationship with you.

Scripture Readings:
Exodus 20:18–21; 33:12–23
Psalm 103:7

September 10

A Thin Line between Lust and Hate

The human heart is the most deceitful of all things, and desperately wicked. Who really knows how bad it is? But I, the Lord, search all hearts and examine secrets motives. I give all people their due rewards, according to what their actions deserve. (Jeremiah 17:9–10)

The affections of the heart can be deceiving at times. We can have a desire for something, and given enough time it will grow into an obsession. Our thoughts are occupied with this person or thing; we see images of it in our mind and fantasize about it constantly. Sometimes the desire can get so strong that it starts to affect us physically. It can even get to the point where a person is almost willing to do anything to satisfy their craving—sacrifice their morals, relationships, and self-esteem to get what they think they want.

The ironic thing is that once the person obtains what they want, they aren't satisfied with what they achieved. The fantasy they had was more satisfying than the reality. The person gets disappointed, and what they thought they loved quickly turns to discontent. This cycle occurs a lot in relationships between men and women. One person pursues the other, and when they finally get what they thought they wanted, they quickly lose interest and are ready to move on to another challenge.

This is what happened when Ammon, King David's eldest son, raped his half-sister Tamar. Tamar was a very beautiful woman, and Ammon was obsessed with her. He thought about her constantly, to point that he became physically ill. When a friend asked him what was wrong, Ammon told him how badly he wanted his half-sister. So his friend suggested that he pretend he was sick and request that Tamar come to his house so she could feed him. Ammon followed his friend's advice, and Tamar came over and fixed his favorite meal for him. Ammon had Tamar come into his bedroom, and when they were alone he forced himself on her and raped her, taking her virginity.

After Ammon was done, he quickly despised Tamar and kicked her out of his house. He refused to speak to her and ignored her. He never apologized for his actions, and Tamar lived in shame with her older brother Absalom. When King David found out about this incident, he became angry but never really addressed the issue, but Absalom would later take revenge on his half-brother by having him murdered.

The moral of the story is that we cannot allow our lusts to control us, but we need to control them. This world is good at enticing people. It creates illusions that build fantasies that are not realistic and, when people finally get the brass ring, they are disappointed because it didn't fill the empty void that was promised. Our enemy knows us well and will allure us away by any means necessary. We must be vigilant and stand our guard.

Scripture Readings:
2 Samuel 13:1–39

September 11

EVERY BELIEVER HAS BEEN GIVEN THE MEASURE OF FAITH

Because of the privilege and authority God has given me, I give each of you this warning: Don't think you are better than you really are. Be honest in your evaluation of yourself, measuring yourselves by the faith God has given us. (Romans 12:3)

God has given each of us the measure of faith if we are a believer in Jesus Christ. Notice I didn't say that God has given us *a* measure of faith. There is a difference between *a* measure of faith and *the* measure of faith. If we say *a* measure of faith, that would imply that God has given different amounts of faith to every person—some believers would receive large amounts of faith while others receive little. God does not discriminate, and He treats each believer fairly. It would be unjust for God to give one person more faith than another.

However, there are believers who do more with their faith. And because they have exercised their faith, it has grown and become strong, while others use their faith very little or not at all. Faith is like a muscle that has to be used. If we work that muscle out on a consistent basis, it will grow and become strong and tone. If we don't work that muscle, however, then it will atrophy and become flabby. If a person makes it a point to exercise daily, they will be in better shape than someone who exercises once a week. The principles of faith work in a similar way. A person who actively exercises their faith will build bigger and stronger faith.

Jesus gave a parable about three servants who were given some coins by their master. One servant was given five talents, another was given two, and the last one was given one talent. The servant who was given five talents put his talents to work and was able to double what he was given. His master commended him. The second servant put his talents to work and was able to double the amount he had. His master also commended him. However, the last servant just buried his talent in the ground and did nothing with it.

His master was upset and questioned why he didn't put his talent to work like the other servants. The servant gave some excuse that he was afraid to use the talent because he knew how hard his master was. Needless to say, that excuse was not acceptable, and his talent was taken away from him and given to another (Matthew 25:14–30).

The only servant whom the master wasn't happy with was the one who did nothing with his talent. Though we all have been given the measure of faith, some of us will do more with our faith than others. Though all believers have the same potential, it will not be realized in all equally. It is important that we do something with the faith we have been given. The worst thing we could do is sit on it and do nothing. Remember that we will all have to stand before Jesus and give an account for what we did and didn't do on this earth (2 Corinthians 5:10). This is a sobering thought, and I hope it provokes you to think about what you are doing with the measure of faith you have been given.

Scripture Readings:
Matthew 25:14–30
Luke 17:5–10
Romans 14:10
2 Corinthians 5:10

September 12

Is Jesus a Liberal or a Conservative?

"And so you cancel the word of God in order to hand down your own tradition. And this is only one example among many others." Then Jesus called to the crowd to come and hear. "All of you listen," He said, "and try to understand. It's not what goes into your body that defiles you; you are defiled by what comes out of your heart." (Mark 7:13–15)

There are some in this country who assume Jesus sides with the Republican Party, and many politicians from this party use this as a ploy to garner votes from Christians. But I don't think Jesus is riding on the back of either an elephant or a donkey. He will not lower Himself to the standards and the traditions of men. Jesus's political party is that of the Kingdom of God, where there is no warring political parties vying for power.

When Jesus was on the earth, He encountered two religious factions. The first was the Pharisees, who were similar to the conservatives. They believed in following the laws of Moses, being ultra-conservative, and very intellectual. They insisted that their followers obey all the commandments and its standards that they could not live up to. The second religious party was the Sadducees, who were the more liberal religious party. Both religious factions had problems with Jesus and His teachings. They both felt threatened by His popularity with the people.

In our day there are those who automatically think that voting for a Republican is what God would want them to do. So they blindly cast their vote for anyone who claims to be a Republican, and will scorn anyone who votes for any other party. There are pastors and clergy who use their influence in the pulpit to sway their congregation to vote for the more conservative party without really investigating the true beliefs of the candidate. It is not the political party a person should look at, but what is in that particular candidate's heart.

It is political bigotry to blindly assume that because someone is of a political party outside of being a Republican that they are anti-God and are unmoral. In our last election for president, there was a candidate who was of the Mormon faith, and many Republicans had no problem supporting him. The Mormons are considered to be a Christian cult, they have their own Bible, and their teachings are not the same as those of Jesus's. But that was ignored because he was a Republican. That is a little hypocritical, especially when the current president professes to be Christian and was accused to be of Islamic faith because of his birth name.

We need to renew our minds in this area and be more objective when we place our votes. We should vote for the candidate who best represents those values of the Kingdom of God regardless of their political affiliation. Realize that you are not a citizen of this world, and your political party is the Jesus party!

Scripture Readings:
Mark 7:1–20

September 13

RETURN GOD'S WORD TO RECEIVE

Don't you believe that I am in the Father and the Father is in Me? The words I speak are not My own, but My Father who lives in Me does His work through Me. (John 14:10)

God longs to demonstrate His power and glory on the earth, but He needs willing vessels to work through. That is where believers come into the picture. When a person accepts Jesus as their Lord and Savior, Jesus and His Father come to reside within them (John 17:20–22). This means that the person is a new creation who has never existed before (2 Corinthians 5:17), and they now have the power within them to do the same works Jesus did, and the potential to do even greater works (John 14:12).

The Scriptures are pretty clear about what is possible for what all believers are capable of experiencing, but why isn't it happening? There are very few believers who are tapping into the potential residing in them. There are three main reasons for this: spiritual ignorance, laziness, and unbelief. Many believers are unaware of the potential that resides within them because they have never been told about it. They have settled to know that their names are written in the Lamb's Book of Life, and they are just doing their time until the rapture comes. Some believers have heard the message but are too spiritually lazy to do anything about it. They have allowed the distractions of this world to take away their attention from spiritual things. They have not renewed their minds to the things of God. Then there are those believers who are in unbelief. They simply refuse to accept this message. Period.

We have to decide which category we are in if we want to experience what God has for us. He has revealed the secret to manifesting His glory on the earth—returning His Word back to Him. When we speak the promises of God back to Him, we are releasing the power of God to work on our behalf. He needs us to cooperate with Him to do His work on the planet. This is because He gave man dominion on this earth (Genesis 1:26–28), so it would be illegal for Him to intervene in the affairs of humans without being invited to do so.

In order to do this, however, we need to consistently spend time in the Word and learn God's will for our lives. It means we are to bind those things that are in our life that are not part of His will, and loose those things in our life that are His will (Matthew 16:19). This takes faith and perseverance on our part. It won't happen overnight. We have to see things with our spiritual eyes and learn to allow our inner man to rule the outer man. But our journey to the Promise Land will begin as soon as we take the first step. What are we waiting for?

Scripture Readings:
Isaiah 55:10–11
Matthew 16:19
John 14:10–14; 17:20–22

September 14

THE MOTIVATIONS OF THE HEART

For the word of God is alive and powerful. It is sharper than the sharpest two-edged sword, cutting between soul and spirit, between joint and marrow. It exposes our innermost thoughts and desires. (Hebrews 4:12)

We cannot always judge things by their appearance. Unlike God, we don't have the ability to look into the motivations of someone's heart (1 Samuel 16:7). This is one of the reasons why there is so much deception in the world today: People are masquerading to be someone they are not. They put on a façade in order to get what they want out of life. They lie, cheat, and manipulate. Every one of us has been guilty of this at one time or another. This is even what happened to David when his son Absalom displaced him as king of Israel.

Once Absalom had his half-brother Ammon murdered, he was banished from Jerusalem and lived in a neighboring country with his relatives. David missed his son but refused to reconcile with him until one of David's aides encouraged him to do so. He allowed Absalom to come back to Jerusalem, but he refused to see him. After a period of time, Absalom demanded to see his father. David finally met with his son and it appeared that they had reconciled their relationship. However, this was not the case. Absalom had strong resentment toward his father.

Absalom devised a plan over the next several years to take the throne away from his father, David. He would go out every day to the city gate with his chariot and horses and would hear the cases of the people. This was the job of the king, but Absalom was doing it to "help the king out." His motivation was not out of concern for the people or to assist his father, but it was self-serving. Absalom wanted to be king. He wanted to gain the support of the people so that when he attempted to overthrow King David all the people would follow him. After several years, Absalom decided it was time to put his plan into action, and he unseated the king for a short period of time (2 Samuel 14–15).

A person can do the right thing but have the wrong motive in doing it. There are people who will bend over backward for us, but the only reason they are doing it is because they want something in return. There are people who will befriend another because they want to gain a position of power or prestige. And there are people who will get involved in a relationship with someone because they feel this person will meet their needs. We cannot tell what really motivates a person, but God can. He knows the motivations of the heart. We need to seek God and ask Him for discernment and wisdom so we don't fall prey to the deception of others.

Scripture Readings:
2 Samuel 14–15
Proverbs 14:12; 20:27
Hebrews 4:12–13

September 15

Take Care of Those Kids

But those who won't care for their relatives, especially those in their own household, have denied the true faith. Such people are worse than unbelievers. (1 Timothy 5:8)

One of the worst feelings in the world for a father is not being able to take care of his children. This is one of the main reasons why some men use drugs, commit crimes, and are incarcerated for life. God created men to be providers for their families, so when they are not able to do that a feeling of frustration festers deep within them. The man in this situation feels inadequate, which is especially true if his wife becomes the main breadwinner. This is somewhat emasculating for the male in the household, and can be unbearable if she constantly reminds him of this.

Eventually that frustration will turn into anger, and if that anger is not addressed it will culminate in rage. I have seen this happen time and time again with many of the men I worked with in the correctional system. When they get out and can't find employment, they will either turn back to their life of crime or to drugs, both of which will get them back into the penal system. This cycle is hard to break, but it can be done through the Word of God and the power of the Spirit.

If you are a believer, you are no longer living under the curse of the law. And make no mistake about it: it is a curse not to be able to provide for your family. You need to find and meditate on Scriptures that describe the will of God for the family. Once you find those, then it's time to do some binding and loosing.

There is another type of father I want to discuss, and that is the man who refuses to take care of his children. These types of fathers are commonly called "deadbeat dads." It is hard for me to relate to this type of father because I don't understand how a man could live with himself, knowing that his children are suffering financially and he is doing nothing to help them. I have heard excuses like, "My ex was a real bitch." But what does that have to do with the kids? There is no reason for the kids to suffer because you have a beef with their mother, no matter what she has done.

What is even more confounding is when the deadbeat dad is a believer. That goes against everything biblical that I can think of. It is not a good witness for your children, and that's why many children don't want anything to do with Christianity. They see the hypocrisy in their parents and are turned off from the Christian faith. This will not go unanswered. How can a person expect God to bless them when they refuse to take care of their own family? God blesses us so that we can be a blessing to others (Genesis 12:1–3).

Scripture Readings:
Psalm 37:25; 112:1–3
1 Timothy 5:8

September 16

WHAT DO YOU SAY?

When Jesus came to the region of Caesarea Philippi, He asked His disciples, "Who do people say that the Son of Man is?" Well," they replied, "some say John the Baptist, some say Elijah, and others say Jeremiah or one of the prophets." Then He asked them, "But who do you say I am?" (Matthew 16:13–15)

In the above Scripture Jesus asked His disciples a question about who the people thought He was. The interesting thing was that once He got the answer from His disciples about what the people thought about Him, He then asked the disciples the same question—"Who do *you* think I am?" He wanted to see if they would give the same answer the people gave. Fortunately, Peter gave the answer Jesus was looking for, so Jesus immediately exclaimed that the revelation spoken by Peter didn't come from natural knowledge, but was a spiritual revelation from God.

As believers we should speak and see differently from those of this world. It is expected of us to speak based on the Word of God. Our vocabulary should be different. When the world is talking recession, depression, and oppression, we should be speaking, "God meets all my needs according to His riches and glory." When the world is talking of fear, we should be saying, "There is no weapon formed against me that will prosper." But for many of us, this is simply not the case. Many believers are speaking just like the world. There is no difference in their conversation and that of the world. This should not be.

Our words will give us away. There are many believers who will praise the Lord on Sunday and be a super-saint, but once they get in the parking lot, they are talking another language. Fear, doubt, and unbelief flow out of their mouth. Jesus reminds us that it is out of the abundance of the heart that the mouth speaks (Matthew 12:34–35). Some of these believers will sow a financial seed, then plant weeds by the words of their mouth, and then they will wonder why they have little to show at harvest time.

Jesus said that we would experience the same hardships the world would experience, but He prayed to the Father that we would be kept safe (John 17:15). He stated that we no longer belonged to this world any more than He no longer belonged to this world (John 17:16). Finally, Jesus requested that we (the believer) would be made holy and be taught the truth that comes from His Word (John 17:17).

We should base our conversations on the Word of God, making that our ultimate truth. There are many truths in the world. When the doctor tells you that you have cancer and shows you x-rays to verify what he is telling you, that is a type of truth. It is factual. But there is a greater truth that comes from the Word of God that says Jesus bore your sicknesses and diseases. Which truth are you going to choose to believe? When you look at your checking account and see you have more month than money, what truth are you going to stand on: "I am broke and don't know what I am going to do," or "God meets my needs according to His riches and glory"? The choice is yours today.

Scripture Readings:
Matthew 16:13–19
John 17:13–19

September 17

THE INNER AND OUTER MAN

That is why we never give up. Though our bodies are dying, our spirits are being renewed every day. (2 Corinthians 4:16)

Many believers don't realize that they have an inner man dwelling inside of them. This spiritual man won't be revealed until a person passes away. Everyone has an inner man, and this is the person that will live forever—the spirit of a person. This inner man has everything that the outer man has: it has eyes to see, ears to hear, it has a soul that remembers, and it can also feel. Our outer man will eventually return to the earth, but the inner man will never die, but will either exist in heaven or in hell.

In the book of Luke, Jesus spoke about two men who died. One was a poor man named Lazarus, and the other was a rich man. Jesus said that when Lazarus died the angels carried him to be with Abraham. This was a place all believers went before Jesus was crucified. Conversely, the rich man was buried in the ground and his soul went to the place of the dead (Luke 16:22). The rich man was in torment, which means that he could feel and see because he could see Lazarus with Abraham (Luke 16:23). He shouted and requested that Lazarus be allowed to dip his finger into some water and put it on his tongue (Luke 16:24), which means that not only could the rich man feel, but he could also remember and speak. And he asked if Lazarus could dip his finger in some water, which means that Lazarus also had a body.

When we die, we will have a spiritual body that looks much like the one we have now, only it will be a glorified body. If you are a believer, your body will not be limited to this four-dimensional world. We will have access to more dimensions of time and space, and we will be able to walk through walls and travel at the speed of thought. However, for those who are non-believers, they will be in a place of never-ending torment.

One night God allowed me to see what the outer regions of hell looked like. The thing I remember the most was the atmosphere of hopelessness that permeated the place. I was in a sea of humanity and everyone was moaning and groaning—it was never ending—and it was so dark because no light existed. I thought about how horrible this place was; I wouldn't send my worst enemy there. Then suddenly a huge hand came down and scooped me up. I woke up relieved. I will never forget that vision of hell.

Hell is not some place where you party and have a good time. It's the opposite of that. It's a place of misery and torment in an atmosphere of hopelessness that will exist for an eternity. All the people there will ask for forgiveness and accept Jesus as Lord, but it will be too late. They will remember all the opportunities they had to accept Jesus, and those thoughts will haunt them forever.

Scripture Readings:
Luke 16:19–31
2 Corinthians 4:7–18

September 18

GETTING IN LINE WITH THE WILL OF GOD

Only I can tell you the future before it even happens. Everything I plan will come to pass, for I do whatever I wish. I will call a swift bird of prey from the east—a leader from a distant land to come and do My bidding. I have said what I would do, and I will do it. (Isaiah 46:10–11)

I cannot overemphasize the importance of remaining in the will of God, for this was the key to Jesus performing the miracles He did. On several occasions He taught that He did nothing unless He saw His Father doing it, and He said nothing unless His Father said it (John 5:19). God is looking for vessels He can work through. Throughout the Bible we see how God took ordinary men and women and did extraordinary things through them because they aligned themselves with His will.

God has given His Word for us to learn who He is and how He thinks, thus giving us a glimpse into His will. Once a person spends enough time in the Word and meditates on it, their unconscious mind will start to assimilate the characteristics of God. They will begin to look at things from a different perspective. This will, in turn, affect their speech, for they will begin to talk differently because their speech will reflect the mind of Jesus (1 Corinthians 2:16). And once their speech is affected, signs and wonders are sure to follow. This is what the apostle Paul meant when he said to let the Spirit renew our mind and attitude so that we can put on the nature of God (Ephesians 4:23).

Believers have to rely on revelation more than education. There are many believers and non-believers who can quote Scriptures and are full of knowledge, but they lack revelation. All their knowledge comes from the natural mind, which cannot fully grasp the things of the Spirit of God (1 Corinthians 2:11). The power of God is not found by memorizing Scriptures, but it is found within the Scriptures themselves, and this can only be discovered through revelation. Satan knows the Scriptures, but he does not have the revelation to accompany them, otherwise he would have never crucified Jesus (1 Corinthians 2:8).

In the coming days there will be a mighty outpouring from heaven, and signs and wonders will be displayed like never before through the church. But God will not use everyone in the church. Only those who are in alignment with His will are the ones who are going to be used in this outpouring. Don't be left sitting on the sidelines; get yourself in spiritual shape so that you will be ready to play.

Scripture Readings:
John 5:19, 30; 14:10
1 Corinthians 2:16
Ephesians 4:23

September 19

THE POWER TO SUCCEED

The Lord was with Joseph, so he succeeded in everything he did as he served in the home of his Egyptian master. (Genesis 39:2)

Would your life be different if you knew that whatever you attempted to do would be successful? Well, if you are a believer and you have the Spirit of the living God inside of you, you have that potential. God does not know failure. In fact, I challenge you to find one Scripture about God failing at anything. It is impossible for God to fail, and as His children we should develop that same mindset also. Jesus never conceded to failure even though He had plenty of opportunities to do so. But because His walk with God was so intimate and strong, He would not allow thoughts of defeat to enter His mind.

The circumstances you find yourself in today do not matter. Joseph is a perfect example of someone who faced numerous challenges but was able to overcome them because he knew that the favor of the Lord was upon him. When he was sold into slavery, God blessed him. When he was falsely accused and thrown into prison, God was with him. Even when his brothers betrayed him and threw him into a pit to die, God's favor was with him.

We need to remind ourselves that we are more than conquerors in Christ Jesus (Romans 8:37), and that greater is He who is within us than he who is in the world (1 John 4:4). There is no weapon formed against us that can prevail, because God's favor and hand are with us. Our meditation every day should start by thanking God for His favor and the grace He provided for us to overcome any circumstances that come our way. Jesus said that we would suffer hardships and go through trials and tribulations, but we would find peace and comfort because He has overcome the world (John 16:33). Remember this the next time you feel like giving up. Just tell yourself, "I am never down. I am either up or getting up!"

Scripture Readings:
Genesis 39:2–3, 5, 21, 23
John 16:33
Romans 8:35–37
1 John 4:4

September 20

PREACHING THE FULL GOSPEL OF CHRIST

Jesus traveled throughout the region of Galilee, teaching in the synagogues and announcing the Good News about the Kingdom. And He healed every kind of disease and illness. News about Him spread as far as Syria, and people soon began bringing to Him all who were sick. And whatever their sickness or disease, or if they were demon-possessed or epileptic or paralyzed, He healed them. (Matthew 4:23–24)

More people would be drawn to the gospel of Jesus if the full gospel were actually preached. What we see today is only a partial gospel that is being preached—all teaching and preaching with little or no signs and wonders following. If we look at the times the message of the Kingdom was preached and had an impact on the culture, there were signs and wonders that accompanied the message. When Jesus came preaching and teaching, signs and wonders were visibly demonstrated. When the church was started in the book of Acts, signs and wonders were being demonstrated. Most recently, Azusa Street in the early 1900s saw signs and wonders as well.

Any great move of God will have signs and wonders accompanying it. It was prophesied by Brother William Seymour, the man credited with starting the Azusa Street Revival, that there would be an outpouring of the Holy Spirit greater than that of Azusa Street in approximately a hundred years. Well, guess what? We are living in the time period for that mighty outpouring of the Holy Spirit. The body of Christ will once again demonstrate signs and wonders, and many will be drawn into the Kingdom as a result.

Will you be ready when this outpouring comes? Only those who have the faith to believe will be used for this move of the Holy Spirit. So prepare yourself. Renew your mind and be ready to receive what Jesus promised would happen for those who call on His name. He said that they would be able to do all the works He did, and even greater works than those (John

14:12). The reason the majority of the church is not doing the works of Jesus is because of unbelief and ignorance. There are not many churches that are preaching and teaching this message. They have settled for more of an intellectual gospel, or a gospel that focuses on salvation only.

If we are going to make an impact on the culture in which we live, we need to demonstrate signs and wonders! There are many religions out there that sound good, and Christianity without the signs and wonders is no different than any other religion. God endorses the preaching of the gospel by the signs and wonders that accompany it. We as believers have to expect them to follow when we preach the good news of the Kingdom of God.

Scripture Readings:
Matthew 4:23–24
John 14:12
Acts 1:43; 4:30–31; 5:12; 6:8

September 21

THE POWER OF PSALM 91

The Lord says, "I will rescue those who love Me. I will protect those who trust in My name. When they call on Me, I will answer; I will be with them in trouble. I will rescue and honor them. I will reward them with long life and give them My salvation." (Psalm 91:14–16)

This section of Scripture has special meaning to me. This was the Scripture I quoted when I was struck with a sudden illness that left me a quadriplegic. I woke up one morning and couldn't get out of bed. I had lost feeling and movement in my legs and my arms. At first I thought I was dreaming, but then the reality of the situation set in. My first response was disbelief—I was moving around just fine the day before. Then a sense of panic gripped me. But the first words I spoke were the above portion of Scripture. Almost immediately a sense of peace came over me, and I heard the voice of the Lord tell me, "You will recover from this. As suddenly as this has come upon you, so shall it leave."

It would be seven weeks before I would be released from the hospital. In spite of the prognosis of the medical experts, I am walking and riding my bike, doing all the things they said I would probably never do again. Nothing is impossible with God! He is faithful to fulfill His promises found in His Word. This I know firsthand. There is power found in the Word of God. But that power goes beyond just memorizing Scripture. There are many who memorize Scripture and are getting no results. They think the power is in memorizing the Scripture, but the power is in the Scripture itself. To access the power, we have to go inside the Scripture, and there we will find the power of God.

I highly recommend that you spend time studying Psalm 91. You will find comfort there for the times ahead. Moses was relating what he experienced with God. So if anyone should know how to relate to God, it would be Moses. One of the parts that stick out the most for me is Psalm 91:4: "He will cover you with His feathers. He will shelter you with His wings. His faithful promises are your armor and protection." God promises us a shield of protection, which is a shield of faith to put out the fiery darts of the enemy (Ephesians 6:16).

When we are faced with difficult situations and impossible circumstances, the promises of God can shield and buffer us. We don't have to submit to fear, doubt, and anxiety. We can choose to stand on the Word of God, and let God rescue us in the midst of our storms. All we have to do is call on Him and believe that He will answer us and deliver us. God will see to it. Believe it and receive it!

Scripture Readings:
Psalm 91

September 22

FALLING AWAY FROM THE TRUE GOSPEL

They will act religious, but they will reject the power that could make them godly. Stay away from people like that! (2 Timothy 3:5)

The apostle Paul said in the last days there would be people with a form of godliness, but they would deny His power. This means there would be churches that would sing praises to God, pray and read the Bible, but they would not experience any of the power of God. Many churches fall into this category today. They have large buildings and a big following, but for most people who go, church is nothing more than a social or community event. What is being serviced from the pulpit is either spiritual pablum or a watered down version of the gospel, filled with positive thinking and political correctness.

Several years ago a popular minister was on *Larry King*. During the interview, Larry King asked the minister if Jesus was the only way to God. This minister tried to avoid answering the question, so Larry pressed the issue more. Finally, this minister said that he could not give an answer to his question. I thought to myself, "Why couldn't he answer him? All he had to do was quote John 14:6: 'I am the way, the truth, and the life. No one can come to the Father except through Me.'"

I finally asked the Holy Spirit to give me insight into this situation. I really liked listening to this minister and found his messages uplifting. Then I realized *all* his messages were uplifting and motivational, which was the reason why he was so popular. He preached a message that would encourage and give us hope, a message many would want to hear in these times. It was not offensive and all-inclusive, and this is his appeal. If he were to say that Jesus is the only way to God, it might alienate some of his listening audience, and his book sales might decrease.

The apostle Paul said that there would be different forms of the gospel that would be present (Galatians 1:6). It can appear to be the true gospel, but it was no gospel at all, only a counterfeit. Remember that the Bible says Satan can portray himself as an angel of light (2 Corinthians 11:14). I am not saying that Satan is using this minister, but one has to wonder what motivated him to not answer the question about Jesus being the only way to God. If we are attending a church where the full gospel is not being preached, then expect to attend a church where there is no power from God. We may feel good and leave the service with a positive outlook on life, but we won't walk in the power of God.

Scripture Readings:
John 3:36; 14:6
Romans 1:16
2 Corinthians 11:14
Galatians 1:6–7

September 23

Is There Room in Your Heart for the Truth?

Jesus said to the people who believed in Him, "You are truly My disciples if you remain faithful to My teachings. And you will know the truth, and the truth will set you free." (John 8:31–32)

Jesus told a group of believers that if they wanted to be His disciples, they would have to remain faithful to *all* of His teachings. He made a distinction between those who were just believers and those who were His followers. Many churches today are filled with those who are casual believers. They are satisfied with knowing that their name is written in the Lamb's Book of Life, and they live their life much like non-believers. The apostle Paul called these types of believers "carnal minded."

God is limited in what He can do in the lives of carnally-minded believers. They spend so little time in the Word of God, and prayer is only used as a last resort for most of them. And when they do pray, it is usually in fear and not out of faith. They will often rely on others to pray on their behalf and will trust what someone else tells them about the Scripture rather than taking the time to look for themselves. This is the type of church the apostle described 2 Timothy 3:5.

Each of us has to decide what kind of believer we are going to be. Do we want to be a believer who lives our life much like the world, with little to no power, or do we want to be a true disciple of Jesus? A true disciple is one who makes it a point to spend time in the Word of God every day, their prayers get results because they are based on the will of God, they are familiar with the Scriptures and will research what is taught from the pulpit, and they are the believers who others come to. Power radiates from their being, and God manifests His glory in their lives. These are the believers who are making a difference in the world today, and signs and wonders are manifested through them. Do you have room in your life for Jesus to move and take up permanent residence, or is He just a casual guest?

Scripture Readings:
John 8:31–46

September 24

God's Secret to Living a Fulfilled Life

For God wanted them to know that the riches and glory of Christ are for you Gentiles, too. And this is the secret: Christ lives in you. This gives you assurance of sharing His glory. (Colossians 1:27)

By now you should realize that there is a constant theme throughout this book. God gives each of us a message to teach others in order to strengthen the Kingdom of God. Some He gives the message of salvation, to others He gives the message of faith, and to others He gives the message of holiness. God has given to me the message of empowerment. We have a power source available to us that can overcome any situation this world can throw at us. Satan is no match for a believer who knows who they are in Christ Jesus.

Satan's only weapon against us is deception. He uses it to blind us from the truth; he also uses it to get us to work against ourselves. If he can get access to us through our soul, which includes the emotions, will, memory, intellect, and imagination, then he can control and limit our ability to manifest the glory of God in our lives. As I have said before, there are many believers who love the Lord but are living far below what God has designed for their lives. When they appear before the judgment seat of Christ, they will see what they could of done on this earth.

This should be a sobering thought and should motivate us to discover the potential that is already within us. We should read the promises from the Bible and meditate on them frequently. We should let them marinate within us until we can see ourselves living those promises. We should let that image inside us become actualized, where it seems real to our unconscious mind (inner man). Remembering our unconscious mind knows the difference between what is imagined and what is experienced in reality is important. When the image becomes actualized, we will begin to act as if it were true. We will speak like it is true and behave like it is true. We are calling those things that are not as though they are, which is what Abraham did, and was commended by God (Romans 4:17–20).

You might be in a situation right now that is far from what you desire it to be. But you have to realize that you don't have to remain in that situation long. Don't let the world define your reality. Let the Word of God define it! And the Word of God says that nothing is impossible with God, and all things are possible for those who believe in Him. This is the secret to living a fulfilled life.

Scripture Readings:
Mark 10:27; 11:23–24
Luke 1:37
John 14:12

September 25

THE POWER OF THE WORD

And now in these final days, He has spoken to us through His Son. God promised everything to the Son as an inheritance, and through the Son He created the universe. The Son radiates God's own glory and expresses the very character of God, and He sustains everything by the mighty power of His command. When He had cleansed us from our sins, He sat down in the place of honor at the right hand of the majestic God in heaven. (Hebrews 1:2–3)

God's creative power is reflected by His words. Jesus is described as the Word of God made flesh (John 1:1, 14). The Bible states that the Word existed before the universe was ever created, and the Word was used to create the world we live in today (Colossians 1:17). It is of paramount importance that we understand this, because words are a creative force that can change our world. We are created in the image and likeness of God (Genesis 1:26–27), which entitles us to use our words to create and bind things on this earth (Matthew 18:18). Many people are ignorant of the power that words contain.

The prophet Isaiah spoke of Jesus approximately seven hundred and fifty years before He became flesh. He spoke of a virgin giving birth to a child (Isaiah 7:14). Isaiah continued by saying this Child would have the government resting on His shoulders, adding that He would be called Wonderful Counselor, Mighty God, Everlasting Father, and Prince of Peace (Isaiah 9:6–7). God was using the mouth of the prophet to speak Jesus into existence. God does nothing before He speaks to release the power of His faith-filled words.

Since it has been established in the Scriptures that we are created in the image and likeness of God, we have the ability to speak things into existence. Like God, we can call things that are not as though they are, but on a much smaller scale, of course (Romans 4:17–20). Our example should be Jesus. Jesus operated as a man anointed by God. He set aside

His godly powers and humbled Himself, and became a man. It would have been illegal for Him to use His godly powers while He was living in human flesh. If He was to be a sacrifice for humanity, He needed to be fully human (Philippians 2:6–8).

Many believers think that Jesus was able to perform miracles because He was the Son of God. He was indeed the Son of God, but He didn't operate as the Son of God but as the Son of Man. Jesus Himself said that all the things He did we could do, and even greater things (John 14:12). Why did He say that? To make us feel good? No, He said it because it is true! All we have to do is change our paradigm, take the promises of God, and act on them in faith.

The problem is that most people speak what they see rather than what they want to see. Most people will speak about lack, sickness, and fear. I am not denying that we have to contend with these things, but instead of putting our focus on our problems we should find Scripture that has the answer to our problem and start speaking that instead. If we are sick, instead of speaking about how sick we are, say, "Jesus bore my sickness and disease. It is by His stripes that I have been healed." We are called to speak to what we want to happen instead of what is happening. Find the promises in the Word of God and release the power of God through faith-filled words.

Scripture Readings:
Mark 11:23–24

September 26

GOD IS NOT DONE WITH YOU YET

For God is working in you, giving you desire and the power to do what pleases Him. (Philippians 2:13)

Are there times when you feel like God must be getting tired of you? Have you fallen short of what you know to do? Has that sin you've been dealing with trapped you again? Has that habit that you swore you would never do again come to visit and try to enslave you once again? Well, I think all of us have been there and done that. Satan loves it when we fall short. He loves to have the opportunity to rub it in your face, with an extra dose of condemnation. But God already knew you would fall into that temptation well before it ever happened. Our salvation is not based on adherence to laws and regulations, but it is based on the finished work of Christ Jesus (Ephesians 2:8–9).

One of the main reasons why some believers fall away is because of self-condemnation. Some moral fault or shortcoming they have experienced convicts them, and they allow the enemy to condemn them because of it. He will even use people in the church to do his bidding for him. I am not saying it's all right to sin, but it happens from time to time. When it does happen, we need to admit it and quit it. Then we need to realize that God can take any situation and work it for His good.

There are countless examples of people who blew it throughout history, and God was able to use them mightily in spite of their mistakes. Moses murdered a man before God used him to lead the children of Israel out of Egyptian bondage. David had many moral faults and he had a man murdered so that he could marry his wife. In spite of that, God used him mightily, and he has been described as a man after God's heart (Acts 13:22). The apostle Paul persecuted the church and was responsible for at least one murder, yet we know how God used him to build the church. There is nothing that we could do to have God turn His back on us. We might turn our back on Him, but He will never turn His back on us.

What we have to remember is that when we accept Jesus as our Lord and Savior, the Spirit of God is activated within us. Our spirit has been reborn and God has found a place in our inner being to reside. From that moment on, we became God's child. Like a child, we will grow spiritually. That's why it's important to spend time in the Word of God, prayer, and fellowship with other believers so that our spirit can grow. During the growth process, we will experience ups and downs, but that's part of learning. God has promised that He would never fail us or abandon us (Hebrews 13:5). So the next time the enemy tries to condemn you, just quote Hebrews 13:5 and watch him flee.

Scripture Readings:
Ephesians 2:8–9
Philippians 2:13
Hebrews 13:5

September 27

SIN: CUT IT OFF BEFORE IT'S TOO LATE

Well then, should we keep on sinning so that God can show us more and more of His wonderful grace? Of course not! Since we have died to sin, how can we continue to live in it? (Romans 6:1–2)

The topic of sin is not too popular is some churches today. It is avoided at all costs because they don't want to offend anyone, or because it isn't politically correct to talk about it anymore. Whatever the reason may be, it is simply an affront to God not to discuss sin and why it's important to keep it out of our lives. Sin is like weeds in our garden—it can drain the life out of us and leave consequences that could be devastating in our life.

Sin starts off as a lustful thought that matures into a desire, which eventually turns into a temptation. Once that temptation has fully matured, it can be acted upon. If a person understands this process of sin, they can control the tendency if they choose to rely on the grace of God in the midst of it. James said that temptation is a result of our desires, and when those desires are fully grown, they give birth to sin (James 1:14–15).

So how do we prevent sin from happening in our heart? We stop it at its conception—the moment the thought enters our mind. We have to cut it off. Jesus used the analogy of cutting off body parts in reference to sin. He said if our foot causes us to sin, then we need to cut it off; if our eye causes us to sin, then we need to cut it off too; and if our hand causes us to sin, we must cut it off as well. He didn't mean that we are to literally do this to our body, but we are not to allow the fleshly nature to control us.

You are not your physical body. You are a spirit who has a soul and lives in a body. This means you have the ability to control the impulses of your mind and body by the grace and power of the Spirit who resides within you. You have the ability to speak to your body and tell it no when temptation comes. You can say, "I am not going to listen to you." Your body might rebel at first, especially if has been getting its way for a while, but remember that if you are led by the Spirit, sin has no power over you (Romans 8:1–2). This has tremendously helped me. When I get enticed with a thought, I take a moment to listen to my inner man, and then turn away. When I don't listen to my inner man, that is when temptation comes.

Once we allow ourselves to be tempted, the physical body gets involved by creating a craving. A craving is the result of the mind and body working together, desiring the same thing. It starts off in the mental realm, but then it's transferred to the physical realm. At this point sin is much harder to combat, so we have to use a different strategy. We have to look at the big picture.

When we fall into sin, our perspective becomes myopic. We only focus on what is desired and are not thinking about the consequences that are to follow. How many people who have fallen for a temptation wish that they never committed the act afterward? How many people regret they didn't exercise their authority over the temptation in the first place? Think about the long-term effects of your actions and how they will impact others, and the temptation will not seem so appealing. Cut it off before it's too late.

Scripture Readings:
Mark 9:43–48
Romans 6:1–2; 8:1–2
James 1:14–15

September 28

HOW SALTY ARE YOU?

Salt is good for seasoning. But if it loses its flavor, how do you make it salty again? You must have the qualities of salt among yourselves and live in peace with each other. (Mark 9:50–51)

Salt is used mostly as a seasoning in our time, but back in the time of Jesus salt was primarily used as a preservative. It was used to slow down the rotting process in meat and other foods because there was no type of refrigeration to keep meat from spoiling quickly back then. We have the Spirit of the living God within us, and we are to season this world with our presence. The apostle Paul said that we carry the aroma of Christ with us, which can be detected by those we come into contact with (2 Corinthians 2:15). To those who are being saved it's the aroma of life, but to those who are dying it is the aroma of death.

What happens to salt if it gets watered down? It is no longer good for anything—it's not good for preservation and it's not good for seasoning either. Unfortunately, there is no way to regain its mineral content once it comes into contact with water. It can only be thrown away. For some their life has reached this point. They have allowed this world to water down their testimony and they have let themselves slip back into their prior lifestyle. Their hearts have been hardened to the point that they no longer desire the things of God, and they have turned their back on Him.

In the book of Hebrews, it states that it is impossible to bring someone, who has been enlightened by the Holy Spirit and walked in the power of God, back if they walk away (Hebrews 4:4–6). It's impossible because they will not repent due to the hardness of their heart. That is the risk we run when we constantly live in sin. Our conscience will become so weak that we can no longer hear the truth of God and His Word. Without the voice of consequences, there is no motivation for repentance. So sin will carry us away unto death.

To avoid this we need to keep our conscience sensitive to the things of God. We must confess our sins quickly when we feel conviction in our hearts, which ultimately comes from the Holy Spirit. It is also important to spend time in the Word and pray regularly, for this will keep our saltiness and provide a fragrant aroma to God and the world.

Scripture Readings:
Mark 9:50–51
2 Corinthians 2:15
Hebrews 6:4–6

September 29

A Father Is More than a Provider

Now his father, King David, had never disciplined him at any time, even asking, "Why are you doing that?" Adonijah had been born next after Absalom, and was very handsome. (1 Kings 1:6)

King David may have been described as a man after God's heart, but he wasn't a very good father to his children. When Ammon raped his half-sister Tamar, David did very little other than get angry with him (2 Samuel 13:21). Because of David's passive attitude toward this incident, Absalom later had Ammon murdered and plotted to take the kingdom of Israel away from his father.

One of the reasons why David's household was out of control was because of his inattention to what was taking place within it. David was preoccupied with other things he thought were more important. His focus was on building and establishing his kingdom rather than taking care of his children. He also had too many wives and concubines to take care of. He probably thought that because he was king and could provide his family with anything they wanted, then his job as a father was done.

Many fathers today think the same way. They will provide their children with all the toys and games they want, and give them money and put a roof over their head. But being a father requires more than just being a provider for our families. A father must be willing to invest time and energy into the lives of his children. He must get involved in their lives and discipline them when necessary. In our society we have classes for almost everything and every type of person, but no classes to show men have to be effective fathers.

Many men today are being raised in fatherless homes and have no example of what being a good father looks like. Many television programs depict fathers as being spineless and weak, or immature dummies who are incapable of properly leading their families. All this is a formula for producing fatherless fathers in the home. As a juvenile probation officer, I witnessed firsthand young men and women whose lives were impaired because of the lack of a good father figure in the home—young women looking for a father's love and settling for some gangster who appeared to care for them, and young men having children out of wedlock with no intention of being a father to their child.

A father's worth should not be measured by how much money they have in the bank, or what they have accomplished in the business or professional world, but on how kind a father they were to their children. If the Bible were to describe you as a father, would it say that you never disciplined your children? Or would it say that your family was blessed because of the godly example you set in the home? Be the best father you can possibly be, asking God for guidance in the process.

Scripture Readings:
Psalm 112:1–3; 128:1–4
Proverbs 13:1, 24

September 30

KNOW THE SIGNS OF THE TIMES YOU LIVE IN

You should know this, Timothy, that in the last days there will be very difficult times. (2 Timothy 3:1)

Jesus said that the last days would be like they were in Noah's day—people would be going about their business enjoying themselves and suddenly world disaster would hit. If we look around today, there is a crisis taking place all over the planet. Unemployment rates in Greece and Spain are over 50 percent for the young adults, causing economic chaos. Both countries are on the brink of bankruptcy. In the Middle East, another Islamic extremist group called ISIS is wreaking havoc in Iraq. It has been reported that the police and some military have been beheaded in public executions. In Sudan, hundreds of thousands of refugees have fled the country and are living in camps barely able to feed themselves.

One country after another in this region is falling prey to civil unrest, economic problems, and terrorism. Iran has an epidemic of heroin use that is out of control. And the Iranian government is blaming the United States for this problem. And in our country we are seeing the unemployment rates climb, while more and more of the population are being forced to work more than one job to make ends meet.

In Camden, New Jersey, street surveillance cameras are being installed to combat crime. Right before our eyes we are seeing our nation become more of a police state in order to protect the public, and all this at the expense of the people's personal freedom. This is what happens when God is excluded from the culture. When a society forsakes an absolute value system and decides that right and wrong should be based on the perspective of the individual, then we are creating an environment for lawlessness.

Second Timothy 3:1–8 describes what is going on today. We are living in difficult times where it is the norm to put ourselves before others, where money is valued over all else, and where a majority of the population is questioning the relevance of God and His Word. Parents are either unwilling or unable to properly parent their children, causing them to be disobedient to any authority figure. Talk shows are becoming more and more popular, spreading a social gospel based on personal opinion and very little fact. Most churches stand by helpless to do anything because they lack any kind of power and are struggling to keep their doors open.

All of this is happening across the world we now live in. God is looking for those who will read the signs of the times and will get themselves ready. God wants to do more signs and wonders through His body, the church of Christ on the earth, but only a handful are ready. More are needed to come on board so that God's glory train can get running. Accept the challenge and take your banner. Don't settle for being mediocre any longer. God is ready and willing to use you for His glory.

Scripture Readings:
Matthew 24:37–39
2 Timothy 3:1–8

October 1

BE STILL AND KNOW THAT HE IS LORD

You will keep in perfect peace all who trust in You, all whose thoughts are fixed on You! Trust in the Lord always, for the Lord God is the eternal Rock. (Isaiah 26:3–4)

World events can be disturbing. But as believers, our focus should be on the Lord and His Word. It will be vital in the coming days that we are attentive to what the Lord has to say and act upon it. Throughout the Bible, we will see that God has always made a way for His people. God seems to enjoy delivering them from impossible circumstances. Nothing is impossible with God (Genesis 18:14). What God requires from us is that we trust Him and cooperate with Him during these times, for doing this demonstrates our faith.

Jeremiah 17:1–8 describes those who put their trust in the world's system and those who put their trust in the Kingdom of God. Those who put their trust in this world's system are described as stunted shrubs in the desert (Jeremiah 17:6). They have no hope for the future. Because of their hopelessness, their environment is barren, full of stress and strife, with no sense of real peace.

However, those who place their trust in the Kingdom of God are described as trees planted along the riverbank. Their leaves are green, they are not bothered when the drought comes or worried by the heat of the day (Jeremiah 17:8). In fact, in spite of the circumstances surrounding them, they continue to produce fruit through all seasons of life. All of this is possible because of their trust and reliance on God.

We have a choice to make: we can place our trust in the system of man, or we can put our trust in the Kingdom of God. The days of trying to work in both systems is slowly coming to an end. We can't have it both ways. We have to make a choice. Who are we going to place our trust in? We must not allow this world to fill us with fear and despair. Instead, we are called to place our trust in God and let Him give us peace.

Scripture Readings:
Isaiah 26:3–4
Jeremiah 17:1–8
John 16:33

October 2

FIVE MASTER PRINCIPLES FOR STAYING ABOVE THE FREY

When you go through deep waters, I will be with you. When you go through rivers of difficulty, you will not drown. When you walk through the fire of oppression, you will not be burned up; the flames will not consume you. (Isaiah 43:2)

The Bible states that God will never leave or forsake those who place their trust in Him (Hebrews 13:5). This is a foundational truth we have to stand on when we begin to feel anxious about the future. All that is happening before our eyes, Jesus predicted long ago would happen (Matthew 24:4–24), so know God is in control even though it may seem like He is not. Jesus told His disciples that these times would come, but He would give us His peace in the midst of them (John 16:33). Therefore, we should not let these times of trouble overwhelm us.

I want to give you five strategies to use in order to rise above the storm. Like an eagle soaring on the wings of the wind, we can spread our wings of faith and allow the wind to lift us above the clouds of turmoil in our life.

1. Know that God has the master plan. When Jesus turned to Phillip, one of His disciples, and asked how they could buy enough bread to feed five thousand people, Jesus already knew what He was going to do. He was testing the faith of Phillip (John 6:5–7). You might be like Phillip today. The situation you are facing may seem impossible, but you are looking at the problem in the natural—God operates in the supernatural!
2. We must allow God to give us instruction for the dilemma we are facing. We must get in our quiet place with the Lord and listen to what He is telling us to do (Acts 9:5–6).
3. Whatever He tells us, do it. Don't try to analyze or rationalize what He is saying to you, just do it. It might not make any sense to you at the moment, but that is the way God works. It didn't

make any sense to pour water into jugs and expect to get wine, but it happened (John 2:1–10).
4. Don't get impatient. Sometimes the manifestation happens instantly, and sometimes it doesn't. We must understand that patience is the byproduct of faith. In fact, patience will perfect our faith (James 1:3).
5. Prepare for the harvest. Don't say this won't work. I have tried that before and nothing came out of it. Forget those past failures and look forward to a brighter day. Many people have forfeited their blessings because they focus more on what happened in the past rather than focusing on the future (Luke 5:4–7)

Scripture Readings:
Luke 5:4–7
John 2:1–10; 6:5–7
Acts 9:5–6

October 3

WHAT STATE DO YOU LIVE IN?

For You bless the godly, O Lord; You surround them with Your shield of love. (Psalm 5:12)

What is your emotional state? One of the definitions for *state* is a condition of being, or a condition of the mind. It is the emotional condition you find yourself in often. Most people experience fear as a result of a threatening event. However, there are some people who live in a continual state of fear, who are controlled by fear, and some would even say they are paranoid. In extreme cases, some people are reluctant to leave their homes and are afraid of going outdoors. This condition is called agoraphobia.

Another emotional state some people live in is depression. We all experience depression from time to time—that is normal. But when a person is constantly depressed, they are living in a state of depression. Some people live with a constant pessimistic outlook on life and suffer from a low grade of depression, which is called dysthymia. Dysthymia is not as disabling as chronic depression, but it does affect a person's life.

Then there are people who live in a constant state of anger. We all get angry and upset from time to time, but when a person lives in a constant state of anger, they are a walking time bomb. All it takes is one wrong gesture, word, or event to set them off. People who live in a state of anger are a danger to themselves and others because they are controlled by their anger.

Well, there is a more positive emotional state to live in, and that's the state of favor. It is possible to live in a state of favor with God. According to the Bible, those who trust and believe in God can live in a continual state of God's favor. Psalm 5:12 states that God surrounds the believer with favor. Favor can be with us everywhere we go (Psalm 23:6), and it is available to anyone who expects it. The reason why some people are not experiencing the favor of God is because they are unaware of what is theirs in Christ. This is one of the privileges of being a child of God.

Every morning we should thank God for the favor He has given us, and expect to find favor everywhere we go. If we do this, God's favor will manifest itself in our lives. He is a God of abundant favor.

Scripture Readings:
Psalm 5:12; 23:6
Proverbs 3:4

October 4

SPEAK YOUR FAVOR INTO EXISTENCE

But give great joy to those who came to my defense. Let them continually say, "Great is the Lord, who delights in blessing His servant with peace!" (Psalm 35:27)

Developing a mentality of continually walking in the favor of God is a process that must be worked out in our life. We have to study Scripture related to the favor of God, and then we have to meditate on those Scriptures so that they transform themselves from information into revelation. The reason why some people don't get results from the things of the Spirit is because they know things on an intellectual basis. The information is only in the mental realm. We can memorize Scripture and be able to quote it, but unless those Scriptures get into our inner man, they won't produce any fruit. We will get some results, but not to the degree that God wants.

For years I thought all I had to do was memorize Scriptures and quote them to get the manifestation I wanted. It worked to a certain degree. I lived a prosperous life—my family was prosperous and we enjoyed the blessings of God. But one day I realized I was operating on my human faith and not the supernatural faith of God. I was using the Word of God to boost my faith instead of relying on God's faith. Once I got that revelation, I realized that the power was not in just memorizing Scripture, but the power was contained inside the Scripture itself. Our faith should be based on the finished work of Jesus, not on our human effort.

Once we understand this, we can walk in the continual favor of God. We need to speak it every day in order to get it into our heart and inner man. It is our heart that generates faith. The more we speak it, the more we believe it. The more we believe it, the more we speak it. Once we convince ourselves that we have the favor of God in our life, then we will begin to build a world of favor around us. Just like God framed the world into existence with His words, so we can frame our world with the words that we speak. God has given us the ability to operate just like He does, only on a much smaller scale.

I cannot emphasize enough that it takes more than memorizing some Scriptures for the favor of God to rest upon us, but that is a good starting point. Know that there is a reason for studying, meditating, and speaking the promises of God. We want to get revelation for the manifestation to come to pass in our lives. We cannot be sustained with mere information.

Scripture Readings:
Psalm 35:27; 84:11
Matthew 12:34–35
Hebrews 11:3

October 5

NEED WISDOM? ASK FOR IT

If you need wisdom, ask our generous God, and He will give it to you. He will not rebuke you for asking. (James 1:5)

When I was in elementary school, I was reluctant to ask the teacher questions because I didn't want to be ridiculed by classmates for being stupid. Because of this, my grades suffered and I didn't fully understand the material being taught. I think that some of us feel the same way in our Christian lives as I did when I was in school. Sometimes we don't ask questions because we are concerned about what others might think of us. The things of the Spirit have been hidden from the intellect of man, and only the Holy Spirit can reveal them to us. But in order for this revelation to happen, we have to ask Him to reveal it to us.

When King Solomon was appointed king over Israel, God visited him in a dream. God asked Solomon what he wanted from Him, and Solomon asked for understanding and wisdom. God was pleased with his request and told him that his request would be honored, and He also included riches and fame (1 Kings 3:5–14). The Bible records that during Solomon's reign as king, the nation of Israel lived in peace and prosperity, and the fame of Solomon spread to many other nations. Kings from every country sent ambassadors to listen to Solomon's wisdom (1 King 4:29–34).

God is not a respecter of persons, so if He did it for Solomon He will do it for you—if you ask. If you have a situation in your life that you don't understand, ask God for wisdom. He has promised to give it to you. Many people don't even consider going to God for wisdom or understanding, and would rather go to a therapist, counselor, or friend before going to God. I am not saying that it is wrong to go to any of the aforementioned people, because I am a therapist. God can use anyone to speak words of wisdom, but He should be sought first. And then we can allow God to choose the vessel to give us wisdom. If we have a problem on the job, with the family, or with anything, then we only need to ask God for His wisdom. Like Solomon before us, we will find ourselves being a resource for others.

Scripture Readings:
1 Kings 3:5–14; 4:29–34
Proverbs 8
James 1:5

October 6

THE GOOD NEWS WILL GET YOU THROUGH HARD TIMES

We can rejoice, too, when we run into problems and trials, for we know that they help us develop endurance. And endurance develops strength of character, and character strengthens our confident hope of salvation. (Romans 5:3–4)

A strategy for us to use when we are going through a difficult situation is that we are to remember what the finished work of Jesus has done for us. It has given us right standing with God, which means we have peace with Him. With this understanding of who we are in Christ, we can go boldly before His throne to receive from Him whatever we request. This is one of the privileges we have as a child of God. If we are a believer in Jesus Christ and have given our lives to Him, then we should have a different outlook on life than non-believers. The only resources that non-believers have exist in this world, but we have resources that are limitless, belonging to the realm of heaven.

The reason why some believers suffer from depression and anxiety is because they are either ignorant or have forgotten who they are in Christ Jesus. Jesus should be our example of how to live our life. He never worried or stressed about anything. He had opportunity to, but He didn't. Many would say, "Well, He is the Son of God." This is true, but He didn't operate as the Son of God while on the earth (Philippians 2:6–8). He operated as the Son of Man who was anointed by God. This means He operated like any believer is capable of operating today (John 14:12). He knew who He was and what privileges He had because He was a citizen of the Kingdom of God.

We should have the same mentality as that of Jesus Christ (1 Corinthians 2:16). We are not immune to hardships, trials, or tribulations. God never promised that life on this planet would be easy and problem free; in fact, He said that we would go through all the trials Jesus went through. But Jesus assured us that we would overcome this world because He is in us

(1 John 4:4). Knowing that His presence indwells us, we can face any situation with the hope and the faith necessary to be victorious. We are only to remember that God loves us, and love never fails.

Scripture Readings:
Romans 5:1–4; 8:31–37
1 John 4:4

October 7

Are You Calling God a Liar?

God is not a man, that He should tell or act a lie, neither the son of man, that He should feel repentance or compunction [for what He has promised]. Has He said and shall He not do it? Or has He spoken and shall He not make it good? (Numbers 23:19 AMP)

There are approximately 3,573 promises in the Bible. God has promises for every situation that we may have in our life. Why is it that some believers refuse to receive these promises? There can be only two reasons: either they are unaware of these promises or they don't believe they are true and for them.

If we don't believe God's promises are true, then we are indirectly calling God a liar. This might be harsh to some, but it is nevertheless true. If our parents told us that they would take us to the ball game on Friday night, and we acted as if they weren't going to do it, do we really believe what they told us? The answer is no, because if we believed their words then we would be ready to go to the ball game when Friday night rolled around.

When I was growing up, my father would sometimes make promises and not keep them. There were many times I would be waiting for him to take me somewhere he had promised, and he never showed up to do so. To this day I remember how I felt because he lied to me. So it was hard for me to trust anyone in my life. When someone told me they were going to do something on my behalf, I would not count on it. That way if they disappointed me, I wouldn't get hurt. I was skeptical of almost anyone and everyone. I was even skeptical of God. I would read all the wonderful promises contained in the Word, and in the back of my mind there was still doubt. "This is too good to be true," I would think. Then I acted like that promise didn't exist.

It wasn't until I renewed my mind that I addressed the distrust I had. I asked myself the question, "Why don't you step out on this promise?" And the bottom line was that I really didn't believe the promise would work for *me*. Because of this, I acted like I didn't even know the promise existed. I was calling God a liar. When I realized what I was doing, however, I repented and asked God to forgive me. Then I started to step out in faith and stand on the promises of God. I began to ignore the voice in my head that would tell me, "Don't do it." And I found that the more I stepped out in faith and stood on the promises of God, the more positive results I got.

Now my mind is beginning to get in line with my inner man. Soon it will be in complete alignment with the inner man. When that happens, watch out, because the supernatural will become as natural as breathing. God is not a liar; everything He said it true!

Scripture Readings:
Psalm 78
Matthew 14:27–36

October 8

Use that Gift—It's Yours

The Spirit of the Lord is upon Me, for He has anointed Me to bring Good News to the poor. He has sent Me to proclaim that the captives will be released, that the blind will set free, that the oppressed will be set free, and that the time of the Lord's favor has come. (Luke 4:18–19)

Did you know that God has given each of us a spiritual gift to be used to edify others? When we accepted Jesus as our Lord and Savior, the Holy Spirit imparted a spiritual gift to each one of us (1 Corinthians 12:7–11). To one person He may have given the gift of wisdom to offer godly counsel, to another He may have given the gift of great faith, and to another He may have given the gift to heal. The Holy Spirit may give to another person the power to perform miracles, and to another the ability to prophesy. All these gifts are given at the discretion of the Holy Spirit through God.

We have to discover what our gift is, and begin to use it for the good of the body of Christ and the world. You might wonder what your gift is. It's not really that complicated to figure out. It is probably the thing you enjoy doing. For me, I enjoy studying the Word of God, but I also enjoy teaching and counseling people. Doing those things don't seem like work to me. There are other things I enjoy as well, but I know that God has anointed me in the area of teaching and counseling. Yours might be in the area of music or business. Some people have been given the gift to make money; others have the gift to perform. God is not limited in the gifts He has given His people to use for His glory.

These gifts are not confined just to church-related activities. They can be used in the secular world as well. Imagine that if a believer were in the position of Bill Gates, what the impact would be for the advancement of the Kingdom of God. Imagine the impact a believer would have on the world if he could produce movies of the quality of Steven Spielberg?

Believers should be leaders in every area of life; this brings glory to God and His Kingdom. Strive to be the best, and give the glory to God!

The church has confined these gifts just to the body of Christ and has not expanded their use to the world. We have given ground to the enemy and then complained about the quality of entertainment in the secular world. We have to take back what we have given up through the power of God! Put your gifts to use. Don't let them sit dormant any longer.

Scripture Readings:
Luke 4:18–19
John 3:34
1 Corinthians 12:4–11

October 9

DON'T FORGET YOU ARE FAVORED

Why am I discouraged? Why is my heart so sad? I will put my hope in God! I will praise Him again—my Savior and my God! Now I am deeply discouraged, but I will remember You—even from distant Mount Hermon, the source of the Jordan, from the land of Mount Mizar. (Psalm 42:5–6)

There will be times in life where we will feel discouraged. There will be times when people we trusted disappoint us and even betray us. When times like these happen, it is so easy to allow our emotions to carry us away from the place of peace. The enemy uses this time to plant seeds of negative thoughts into our minds with the hope that they will one day blossom into depression, anger, or anxiety, all of which have a negative impact on our being. Negative thoughts are toxic to our body. They excite our limbic system, which releases hormones like cortisol that have a negative impact on the immune system. Blood proteins called cytokines are also released, which are known to cause fatigue and depression.

Humans were not created to experience negative emotions—we were created in the image and likeness of God (Genesis 1:26–28). However, because of the fall of humanity and the negative impact it has had on our world (Romans 8:19–22), we are subject to the consequences of sin. People often ask, "Why does God allow all this evil? Why doesn't He do something about it?" Because God gave man dominion over the earth (Genesis 1:26), it would be illegal for Him to intervene in the affairs of humankind without being invited. God is waiting for us to ask Him in faith to get involved in our lives.

When we are going through a difficult time or some sort of disappointment, we cannot give up or give in to it. Rather, we are to remember that God favors us—we are His children and citizens of the Kingdom of God. Remember the promise Jesus gave to His disciples, which we are, and receive the peace of God (John 16:33). We also need to remember that He who is within us is stronger than he who is in the world (1 John 4:4).

When we remember who we are in Christ, we will replace those negative thoughts with positive ones, which will cause our brain to release hormones that produce dopamine and norepinephrine, both of which are good for the body. God created us to be and think positive because He is a positive God.

Don't let this world rob you of your joy. It's all right to grieve when you experience disappointments, for this is part of the healing process. But don't stay there. Get up and remember that God favors you.

Scripture Readings:
Psalm 42:4–5; 43:1–5
John 16:33
Romans 8:19–22
1 John 4:4

October 10

Speak to the Storms in Your Life, Not about Them

When Jesus woke up, He rebuked the wind and said to the water, "Silence! Be still!" Suddenly the wind stopped, and there was a great calm. Then He asked them, "Why are you afraid? Do you still have no faith?" (Mark 4:39–40)

Do you often find yourself spending more time and energy talking about your problems than speaking directly to them? Most people are guilty of this. They spend hours, days, weeks, and even months pondering problems and negative situations in their life rather than using that energy to resolve the situations. When we focus on the problem rather than the solution, there is a tendency to develop a pessimistic attitude toward that specific situation. This can cause negative energy, which will hamper our ability to find resolution to the problem.

Rather than focus on the negative aspects, we should put our attention on the positive ones. We can recognize the problem and then seek the answer to the problem through the Word of God. Once we find the promise in the Word, we should begin speaking to that problem in faith. Exercising our authority as a child of God, and commanding that problem to stop in Jesus's name, is what we are invited to do.

A good example of this would be when Jesus and His disciples were crossing the lake and a great storm arose. The storm was fierce and the disciples began freaking out. Water was getting inside the boat, and they all thought they were going to drown. Jesus was in the boat, but He was fast asleep. So the disciples woke Him up. They didn't understand how He could be sleeping with so much commotion and chaos surrounding Him. They thought He didn't care. Jesus just woke up, spoke to the wind, and then told the water to be still. And they obeyed His command! Then Jesus asked His disciples why they were afraid.

When we look at this story, we can see two different reactions to the crisis. One reaction is based on fear, and the other is based on faith. The fear was brought on by a complete focus on the circumstances. The disciples had forgotten about who was in the boat with them, they had forgotten about the miracles they had just witnessed, and they had forgotten that Jesus said they were to go to the other side of the lake. On the other hand, Jesus knew that it was God's will for Him to go to the other side of the lake, and there was nothing that was going to stop Him in that mission. His focus was on the Word rather than on the circumstances. When He saw the resistance, He addressed it and spoke to it, commanding it to stop. Jesus expects us to do the same.

Many believers waste time praying about their problems rather than praying and declaring the answer to their problems, expecting Jesus to do something about them. He has already done all He needs to do in order for us to do it for ourselves—He has given us His grace and power. Don't be like the disciples in the boat who were rebuked for not having faith. Use the authority that Jesus has given you and speak to that storm in your life.

Scripture Readings:
Mark 4:35–41

October 11

RECIPE FOR DEPRESSION

For the despondent, every day brings trouble; for the happy heart, life is a continual feast. (Proverbs 15:15)

Most people will experience acute depression from time to time, which is completely normal. However, there are a growing number of adults who are experiencing chronic depression, which is not normal. According to statistics from the Center of Disease Control Prevention (CDC), approximately 1 in 10 adults suffer from some form of depression. It could be anything from a mild form of depression (dysthymia) to a major type of depression. The CDC classifies depression as a mental illness, which can be both costly and debilitating.

Depression has also been linked to the following illnesses: arthritis, asthma, cardiovascular disease, cancer, diabetes, and obesity. It also contributes to absenteeism in the workplace, disability, and lack of productivity. Many people who suffer from depression will choose to self-medicate, often abusing drugs and alcohol.

To understand why some people are prone to depression, we have to understand the dynamics of depression. Depression is the result of three things taking place in our lives:

1. a negative outlook on a present situation or circumstance,
2. a negative outlook on the future, or
3. a negative opinion of oneself.

When a person has all three of these working at the same time, they will experience a deeper depression than normal. If they have a positive opinion of themselves but are going through a negative time, they will bounce back because they know their situation is only temporary. They are filled with hope for a brighter tomorrow. If an individual has a negative opinion of himself but his current situation is positive, he might be pessimistic but he won't experience major depression. He will probably be more dysthymic. With this understanding we can develop strategies to combat depression.

For a believer, we have to realize who we are in Christ Jesus. We have to realize that we are a child of God and a citizen of the Kingdom of God. With this understanding of who we are, there is no room to have a negative opinion of ourselves. We are in Jesus; when God looks at us, He sees Jesus because His blood has cleansed us. We can plead the blood of Jesus over ourselves whenever we feel condemnation coming on us. We can also tell ourselves that we have been washed in the blood of Jesus, and all of our sins have been washed away; we are a new creation in Christ Jesus (2 Corinthians 5:17).

Next, we need to remind ourselves of our future. All things in this life are only temporary and subject to change. It might be pouring rain today, but the sun will come out tomorrow. Jesus, who resides in us, is greater than anything in this world. There is no weapon that can stand against us as we remain in Christ's love (Romans 8:37). Finally, we must speak the promises of God to what is depressing us. If we follow this remedy for depression, we will get results—with no side effects.

Scripture Readings:
Proverbs 14:30; 15:13, 15

October 12

GET RID OF THOSE BUTS IN YOUR SENTENCES

This was their report to Moses: "We entered the land you sent us to explore, and it is indeed a bountiful country—a land flowing with milk and honey. Here is the kind of fruit it produces. But the people living there are powerful, and their towns are large and fortified. We even saw giants there, the descendants of Anak!" (Numbers 13:27–28)

Our words reveal what's in our heart (Matthew 12:34–35). It is important that we monitor what we are speaking to assess what we truly believe. Sometimes we can deceive ourselves into thinking we believe one way, but we are speaking something completely different. This was the case with the children of Israel when they finally reached the Promised Land. They had struggled and complained for a number of years in the wilderness, and finally the day came when they arrived at their destination.

Moses appointed twelve leaders, one from each tribe, to go and scout out the land. When they came back, they reported that the land was just as Moses had described, a land flowing with milk and honey. Even though all twelve of the spies pointed out the facts, ten of them concluded their report negatively: "But the people living there are powerful, and their towns are large and fortified. We saw giants there, the descendants of Anak!" Their *but* nullified all the positive things they had said. We do the same thing when we speak negatively in the face of the promises of God.

How many times have we made a statement and then finished it with a *but*? Usually, that but was used to nullify everything we said before. When I hear someone say, "I know but…" it usually means they are going to either nullify or justify themselves. Have you ever heard someone say, "I know that this is wrong, but…"? You have probably said something like this yourself a couple of times. What we are doing when we use *but* in our statements is that we are giving ourselves permission to violate what we have said was wrong, making it okay. We essentially contradict ourselves, which causes inner turmoil and short-circuits our faith.

We need to be people who say only what we mean, and mean what we say! If we catch ourselves using a *but* in our statement, it is important to stop and correct ourselves. The more we correct ourselves, the less we will use *but* when we are making statements. We will also find that we will modify our behavior to reflect what we really believe. Get rid of the *buts* and change your life.

Scripture Readings:
Numbers 13:25–14:4

October 13

BE THE BEST YOU CAN BE

I knew you before I formed you in your mother's womb. Before you were born I set you apart and appointed you as My prophet to the nations. (Jeremiah 1:5)

One day I was listening to a Christian radio station, and after about an hour I turned the station because all the music began to sound the same. The music was good, but it was hard to distinguish one artist or group from the other. I later wondered what was wrong with me. Why didn't I find contemporary Christian music appealing? Then it came to me. There is no individuality in the songs. It's like a cookie cutter is producing the songs. This is the problem with many churches today. They are afraid to be what God called them to be. The world loves conformity because that is a good way to keep control. It keeps people in a box.

If we look at the characters in the Bible, they were willing to step outside of the normal status quo. They didn't comply to peer pressure. Jesus's peers didn't accept Him because He didn't fit and didn't conform to the ideology of His day. Because Jesus didn't bow to peer pressure, He was persecuted for it. The same is true in the secular world: anyone who chooses to step outside of the norm will face persecution. But if we are to be all that God called us to be, then we may have to step outside the boundaries society has made for us. I am not talking about doing something illegal here—God has not called us to be lawbreakers.

But there are many believers who have talents and gifts and are afraid to use them because of what someone may think. It might be outside the norm, but just because it is outside the norm doesn't make it wrong. The world has a stereotype view of the church for a good reason. Most churches have their rules and regulations; they only sing these types of songs and this many songs. There is no room for spontaneity or individuality.

If we are to live up to our true God-given potential, then we need to recognize the gifts and talents we have and use them. For only this will bring glory to the Kingdom of God. But we also have to know that we may face opposition along the way. Many of those people who are ridiculing us now will be on the bandwagon later. When the Beatles were first formed, many record labels rejected them. They said that they had no talent, and there wasn't a market for them. Well, those record labels that had the opportunity to sign them wound up eating their words. The same could happen for you too. Believe in yourself and cherish the gifts and talents God has given you. Follow your dream, because God has given you that dream for a reason. Be the best *you* you can be!

Scriptural Readings:
Jeremiah 1:5
1 Corinthians 12:11

October 14

LET GO AND LET GOD

For God wanted them to know that the riches and glory of Christ are for you Gentiles, too. And this is the secret: Christ lives in you. This gives you assurance of sharing His glory. (Colossians 1:27)

The apostle Paul contributed much to the advancement of the Kingdom of God throughout his life. He went from being an archenemy of the church to being responsible for writing the majority of the New Testament. It would be of great benefit for us to learn how this man was able to accomplish so much for the Kingdom of God. Luckily, Paul gives us the secret for his success: Christ lived in him (Colossians 1:29). He had to learn that it was not his own ability or knowledge that produced anything of significance, but it was the revelation of Christ living inside of him that allowed him to endure all the trials and tribulations he faced.

Many believers struggle with bad habits and are slaves to the cravings of their flesh because they try to exercise their will without relying on the power of God. They may succeed for a period of time, but most revert back to their old behavior and patterns. The apostle Paul wrote that it is God who gives us the desire *and* the power to fulfill His will (Philippians 1:13). If this becomes a revelation to believers, then there is nothing that can stop us from doing the will of God. We must rely on the power of God that resides within us, and when that is coupled with our will we will be able to go the distance with God.

This is what sets apart the average, mediocre believer from the one who is making a mark for the Kingdom of God. They have learned to let God work through them; they don't limit themselves to their own abilities, but they dare to believe God and stand on the promises of God until they are manifested in their life. Let God work through you, and dare to allow God to fulfill His desire and dreams through you. Don't be afraid of failing, because God knows no failure. If you are in one accord with Him, then you will not fail!

Scripture Readings:
Galatians 2:20
Colossians 1:26–29
Philippians 2:13; 4:13

October 15

Psalm 23

The Lord is my shepherd; I have all that I need. (Psalm 23:1)

This was one of the first Bible verses I memorized as a child. I remember how proud I was when I recited it in front of my parents and neighbors. It wouldn't be until years later that I started to grasp the true meaning of this psalm. As I said in an earlier lesson, there is no power in the memorization of a Scripture. The power of Scripture is released once we get the revelation contained in the Scripture. There are many precious promises contained in Psalm 23 that are just waiting to be gleaned. Let's look at some of them.

This psalm only contains six verses. The first verse states that the Lord is our shepherd, and because He is our shepherd He will take care of our wants. He will be Yahweh-Jireh in our life. Notice the verse didn't say that He would only give us what we need; it says He will take care of our *wants*. Needs are things that are necessary for survival, and the Lord will surely take care of these, but He will make sure our wants are taken care of as well.

Verse two states He will provide rest and peace for us. This means that we can expect to find peace in the midst of the storm. Others around us might be stressed, but we will find peace because the Lord will lead us to a quiet place to fellowship with Him. There is no stress in heaven, so why should we allow it here on earth?

The Lord promises to strengthen us in verse three, but He will also guide us along right paths. This is done to bring honor to Him. When we feel weak and discouraged, we can ask Him to not only strengthen us but to guide us in the right paths. It may mean that the Holy Spirit will lead us to meet someone who can assist us in our profession, or lead us to a better job, or to put us in contact with our future spouse.

Verse four says that even when we are experiencing hardships and troubles in life, we can walk in the assurance that God is right there with us, comforting and protecting. This is true even if the circumstances were brought on by our doing. There is no situation greater than God. He is still with us, right by our side.

Verse five promises us that we will live a prosperous life, and blessings will overflow. And this will take place even in the midst of our enemies. They will see how God has blessed us, and they will envy us. The anointing of God's presence in our life will be evident to all.

Finally, verse six states that God's goodness and unfailing love will follow us everywhere we go. No matter where we go, God's goodness and unfailing love will be with us. It will never leave us! I encourage you to take some time and meditate on this psalm, letting it marinate in your spirit until you can see the reality of it in your life. Then be it. Expect these promises to be true in your life. God is truly amazing.

Scripture Readings:
Psalm 23

October 16

CARELESS AND IDLE WORDS ARE DEAL BREAKERS

I said to myself, "I will watch what I do and not sin in what I say. I will hold my tongue when the ungodly are around me." (Psalm 39:1)

There is power in the words we speak, even those carless and idle words we say when we think no one is listening (Matthew 12:36). It is those careless and idle words that are the deal breakers. People take for granted the idle words they speak in casual conversations with others in the workplace or as they go about their everyday routine. But whether we realize it or not, those words can have an impact on whether or not our prayers are answered. Many believers will spend hours petitioning God for something, only to sabotage their prayers by careless and thoughtless words.

Jesus said that out of the abundance of the heart the mouth speaks (Matthew 12:33–35). Many believers deceive themselves into thinking they have faith, but their careless words reveal something entirely different. What they really have is faith that is only in the mental realm, not in their heart. The true force of faith is generated from the heart (Romans 10:9). If we have a faith that is just in the mental realm, it is nothing more than positive thinking, and it is thus limited.

It is easy to speak faith when we are in the company of other believers, but what we say when we are out in the world is what is really in our hearts. Do we speak the same way we do when we are at church, or does our conversation change? What do we say when we are watching the news? What do we say when we are around co-workers who are non-believers? Does our conversation change? How do we respond when the people around us start speaking negatively? Do we agree with them, or do we make a profession of faith?

If we are to expect God to work miracles in our lives and answer our prayers, then our speech must reflect what we believe all the time, not just at church. The words we speak outside church are what are truly in our hearts! Think about it today and watch your words.

Scripture Readings:
Psalm 1:1; 19:14; 39:1–5
Proverbs 17:27–28

October 17

What You Consider and the Hardened Heart

Then He climbed into the boat, and the wind stopped. They were totally amazed, for they still didn't understand the significance of the miracle of the loaves. Their hearts were too hard to take it in. (Mark 6:51–52)

When the disciples saw Jesus walking on the water, they were astonished and could not believe what they saw. The disciples couldn't comprehend this event because they failed to consider what had occurred previously, with Jesus feeding over five thousand people with just two fish and five loaves of bread. Had they considered this they would not be surprised to see Him walking on the water.

What we consider or focus on matters. It is hard to believe that God is going to take care of our needs when we are putting more focus on our bills and the economy than on the promises of God. James says that a double-minded man should not expect to receive anything from God (James 1:6–8). To be double minded means that we waver between opinions. One day we are full of faith, then we see something negative and we are back in doubt. People who focus only on the natural have a hardened heart toward the things of the Spirit (1 Corinthians 2:14).

One of the important things to remember is that everything we can see is only temporary and subject to change (2 Corinthians 4:18). But the things of the Spirit are eternal. The Word of God will never change. We can stand on it and know that it can be counted on. This is the difference between those who receive miracles and answered prayers and those who don't. It is all about what they consider and focus their attention on.

A perfect example of this is Abraham. He had no children, his wife was barren, and in spite of all this he chose to take God at His word, that he and his wife would produce a child. Instead of looking at the circumstances that were visible to his eyes, Abraham chose to focus on the promise God gave him. And at the age of a hundred, God blessed him with his son Isaac.

What are you considering today? Are you more focused on your circumstances than the Word and promises of God? If so, it's never too late to make a change. Remember that anything is truly possible for those who believe (Mark 9:23). So change your focus and only think of those things that are productive and what you want in your life (Philippians 4:8). This will ensure that your heart will not be hardened to the things of God.

Scripture Readings:
Mark 6:45–52; 9:23
Romans 4:18–25
2 Corinthians 4:18
James 1:6–8

October 18

Your Prosperity Brings God Honor

When the queen of Sheba heard of Solomon's fame, which brought honor to the name of the Lord, she came to test him with hard questions. (1 Kings 10:1)

God takes delight in seeing His people prosper (Psalm 35:27). In fact, when we prosper, it brings honor to God because He is being magnified when others hear and see what He has done for those who believe and trust in Him. This was the case with the queen of Sheba during Solomon's reign as king of Israel. The fame of Solomon had spread around the whole region, and governmental officials would travel great distances just to have an audience with him. Because they were so impressed with Solomon's wisdom and all that he achieved, they brought him gifts as a token of appreciation.

As believers we should have the same kind of influence around those in our lives. We should expect that God will prosper us in every area of our lives. There are many believers who think it is worldly to desire wealth and to enjoy the finer things in life. They have a mentality that barely getting by is holy. However, if we look in the Scriptures, we will see that God takes delight when His people are successful and prosperous. The world is not attracted to someone who is broke down on the side of the road telling them they need Jesus. They just scoff and say, "What can He do for me?"

There is no honor in being poor; in fact, that is part of the curse. And we know that Jesus bore the curse for us (Galatians 3:13). So why should we tolerate being poor any longer? People are more inclined to listen to someone they view as successful than someone who is not (Proverbs 14:20). If the church is going to make an impact on this world, then it's going to have to change its mindset in this area. We have the Spirit of the living God residing in us, which means that we should excel in every area of life. Like Solomon before us, people should seek us out for advice. The glory of God should be apparent to all who come in our presence. Our families should be blessed and prosperous (Psalm 112:1–3).

Don't settle for just being mediocre and let the world take your stuff. Aren't you tired of seeing the minions of darkness influence our young people with their moral filth and wanton behavior? They are influential in people's lives only because they are viewed as successful. If there were more believers who will step outside the box, they would have more influence in this world.

Scripture Readings:
Genesis 13:2
Proverbs 14:20; 19:4
Psalm 35:27; 112:1–3
1 Kings 10:1–27

October 19

The False Angel of Light

But I am not surprised! Even Satan disguises himself as an angel of light. (2 Corinthians 11:14)

What images come to mind when Satan or the devil is mentioned? Do you see some kind of monster with a pitchfork? Or do you see a red ugly creature with horns and a tail? This is the most common image people have when they imagine what Satan looks like. However, the Bible gives a good description of Satan, and it doesn't involve a pitchfork and horns. The apostle Paul described him as an angel of light. This is the enemy's greatest deception—he wants people to think he is some kind of ugly creature so that he can creep into their lives unawares.

Before his fall from heaven, Lucifer, who was later called Satan, was one of the archangels in heaven. He was responsible for bringing praises to God. He had access into the presence of God, something that not every angel had. He was described as being beautiful and magnificent—no other angel could compare to his beauty. But one day he forgot that he was a created being, and he wanted to be like God. So he decided to rebel against God, deceived himself into thinking that he could be like God, and was so convincing that he got a third of the angels to join him in his rebellion. Because of this he was expelled from heaven along with a third of the angels, never to return again. Satan was now an outlaw along with his band of fallen angels (Ezekiel 28:11–17).

Satan could no longer return to heaven, so he sought refuge on earth. God had created man to have dominion on the earth (Genesis 1:26–28), so Satan despised humanity; he wanted this planet to rule for himself (2 Corinthians 4:4). Satan devised a plan to usurp the authority of man. He would have to get man to willfully disobey God and follow him. He used a cunning deception in order to get Eve to disobey God, getting her to see the fruit in the Garden as something desirable, something she couldn't do without (Genesis 3:1–6). Eventually, she took the bait and convinced her husband to do the same. Once that happened, Satan became the god of this world. Man was now under Satan's control.

His strategy has not changed today. But Jesus has defeated him and has given the authority of this earth back to the church, His body. Satan tries to use his deceptions to keep believers from realizing who they are in Christ Jesus. If he is successful, then believers are not a threat to him. The best way for him to do this is by infiltrating the church with false doctrine, giving them religion that keeps people bound and separated from God. I invite you to look around and see all the atrocities committed by humans in the name of religion. Know your enemy and don't let him deceive you any longer.

Scripture Readings:
2 Corinthians 4:4; 11:13–15
Ephesians 2:1–3; 6:10–12
Revelation 12:9

October 20

Don't Let the Things of this World Take You Away

Do not love this world nor the things it offers you, for when you love the world, you do not have the love of the Father in you. (1 John 2:15)

One of the dangers of prosperity is that it causes a person to have a false sense of security, which causes them to disconnect from a God consciousness and become more connected to the things of this world. This was the case with King Solomon. He achieved many things during his reign as king. He expanded the kingdom of Israel, brought peace and prosperity to his people, and built a tabernacle for God to dwell in and a palace for himself. He was known all over the world for his wisdom; God had blessed him in every way. Not one of the promises God had made to Moses failed to come to pass (1 Kings 8:5–6).

Just when Solomon was at his zenith, he began to falter. Solomon loved many foreign women; in fact, he had seven hundred wives and three hundred concubines. These women were used to take his heart away from God (1 Kings 11:1–6). The king who once asked God for wisdom and understanding to rule the people was now building shrines to foreign gods to please his wives. God was not happy with Solomon because he committed spiritual adultery, so God took the kingdom away from him, only leaving him one tribe (1 King 11:9–13).

The events in the Old Testament are types and shadows of what is revealed in the New Testament. Solomon represents what happens to a people or a nation who turn their back on God because they have fallen in love with the world. They love the pleasures of this world more than they love God. There are many believers who started off loving the Lord, and when God started to bless them they fell in love with the stuff and turned their back on Him. The book of James says, "Don't you realize that the friendship with the world makes you an enemy of God?" (James 4:4).

God wants us to enjoy life and live in prosperity, but we must not forget who is responsible for all we have. Don't let the things of this world start to speak to you and lead you away from God. Keep in mind that you are only a steward of what you have, not the owner of it. God is the One who owns it all. He is only allowing us to enjoy it. If we keep this in mind, we will not allow our possessions to possess us, and we will walk humbly with our God.

Scripture Readings:
1 Kings 11:1–13
James 4:4–10
1 John 2:15–17

October 21

MAKE SEEKING THE KINGDOM A PRIORITY

Seek the Kingdom of God above all else, and live righteously, and He will give you everything you need. (Matthew 6:33)

Jesus told His followers that if they sought the Kingdom of God above all else, then all their needs would be taken care of. Do you believe this is true today—for *you*? Do you believe that if you were to follow God's principles, you would be prosperous? When we choose to follow God and exercise faith in doing things that don't make sense to our intellect, it pleases Him. This shows that we are more than listeners of the Word, but we are actually doers of the Word.

There are many believers who love the Lord but are so consumed with the cares and worries of this life that the Kingdom of God takes a backseat. Economic pressures can be draining when we are trying to make ends meet on our own. Some people take on side jobs and sacrifice time with their families. They are usually too tired to go to church, and studying the Word is no longer a priority. This is not God's best. According to the Scriptures, God promises to bless His people and bring no trouble with it (Proverbs 10:22). There are many who are blessed financially but have problems with their prosperity—they have problems with their family and health.

God wants to give you a prosperous life with none of the sorrows attached to it. Isn't that good news? All you have to do is believe and expect it. Make sure you follow God's financial plan, which is sowing and reaping. The more you give the more you will get back in return (Luke 6:38). If you have a need, then it's time to sow some seed. Just as a farmer plants seed in the spring for the harvest in summer and autumn, so we can sow seed for our financial harvest. This is the Kingdom's principle for a financial harvest.

When we start to reap our harvest, we must not be like Solomon and let our possessions possess us. The purpose of us being prosperous is not just for us to live in luxury for the rest of our life, but to be in a position to bless others. If we do this, we will not experience lack—ever.

Scripture Readings:
Job 22:21–30
Proverbs 10:22
Matthew 6:31–33
Luke 6:38

October 22

Spiritual Laws Supersede Natural Laws

For all who are led by the Spirit of God are children of God. (Romans 8:14)

We live in a world that has natural laws that govern it. However, we have been able to supersede these laws with higher laws. For example, a plane is able to fly because of the laws of lift, thrust, and drag. A large cruise ship weighing many tons is able to float in water because of the law of displacement. The same thing is true in the spiritual realm.

When a believer operates in spiritual laws, they are operating in Kingdom principles. Jesus referred to this as the Kingdom of God. He spoke on these spiritual principles often, imploring His followers to use these principles in their daily lives. These principles are:

- The law of faith. Faith is the currency of the Kingdom of God. We use faith to transfer the unseen into the seen. It is called "calling those things that are not as though they are" (Romans 4:17). Jesus taught that if we speak to a mountain to be removed and we don't doubt in our heart, then it would be done for us (Mark 11:23–24).
- The law of sowing and reaping. Jesus described the Kingdom of God like a seed that is planted in the ground. It will grow automatically without our assistance because God is responsible for the growth of the seed (Mark 4:26–29). A seed will produce after its kind (Genesis 1:12). If we are in need of something, then we need to plant a seed in order to get a harvest.
- The law of love. Love is the greatest power in the universe because it is the essence of who God is. Love would not exist without God. It is the power source of faith. If we are not operating in the power of love, supernatural faith is not possible (Mark 10:25). Love is the main fruit of the Spirit and it is the foundation of the Kingdom of God (Galatians 5:22).

These are the three main spiritual laws we need to know if we are to operate in the Kingdom of God on a regular basis. They are the essentials to live a successful and prosperous life, bringing honor to God. Take time to meditate on these laws and inculcate them into your thought process and you will see the glory of God being manifested in your life. Choose to live above the natural laws, and live on Kingdom principles.

Scripture Readings:
Genesis 1:1–26
Mark 4:26–29; 11:20–25
1 Corinthians 13:1–7
Galatians 5:22

October 23

Your Seed Is Enough to Meet Your Need

Then Andrew, Simon Peter's brother, spoke up. "There's a young boy here with five barley loaves and two fish. But what good is that with this huge crowd?" (John 6:8–9)

I want to give you an example of how using Kingdom principles to operate in the supernatural realm works from an account in the Bible. In this account we will see how all three of these laws were in operation to manifest the miracle of feeding five thousand people with just two fish and five barley loaves.

Jesus was in deserted place, which was far from town. Many people had followed Him to see the miracles and hear His teachings. It was getting late, and Jesus knew many of these people were hungry and probably wouldn't get back for lodging and food before nightfall. He had compassion on the people, which was the motivation for performing the miracle—it was not to gain fame. This was the principle of love in action.

Then Jesus asked one of His disciples where they could buy bread to feed the masses, but He was only asking to test His disciples (John 6:7). Andrew, Simon Peter's brother, pointed out that there was a boy with two fish and five barley loaves, but then realized that was surely not enough to feed everyone present (John 6:9). Once Jesus had something to work with (the seed), He instructed the disciples to have the people sit down. Jesus then took the two fish and five barley loaves (the seed), blessed it, and then passed it out to His disciples to feed all five thousand people. Everyone was fed and they even had leftovers. This was an example of planting a seed for a harvest.

All Jesus needed was something to work with to feed the multitude who were present that day. Once He got that, He could multiply it. The same principle works today. If we are in need, then we need to sow a seed, because this is how the Kingdom of God operates. How many people are in need financially, and instead of giving they hoard what they already have? This is the way the world's system works. The world teaches us that we need to put it away for a rainy day. There is nothing wrong with saving, as this is good stewardship, but we should put the Kingdom's financial plan before our own.

Many believers are overwhelmed with bills and other financial situations, which make it seemingly impossible for them to give—it is out of the question. They will try to reason intellectually, and try to solve their financial problems through natural means. They will get an extra job, work overtime, or take out a loan. Then there are those believers like Andrew who will entertain the idea of using the principle of sowing and reaping, but will talk themselves out of it because their focus is on the financial situation instead of on Kingdom principles.

Because Jesus was acquainted with the Kingdom of God and how it worked, He was able to use those principles to meet the needs of others. Love was the driving force behind everything Jesus did. Some might say that He was able to perform miracles like this because He was the Son of God. But I will remind you of two things: first, Jesus operated as a man anointed by God (Philippians 2:6–8), and second, Jesus said that all the things He did we could do also (John 14:12).

Scripture Readings:
John 6:1–15

October 24

A Word You Can Rely On

Praise the Lord who has given rest to His people Israel, just as He promised. Not one word had failed of all the wonderful promises He gave through His servant Moses. (1 Kings 8:56)

In today's world it's getting harder to trust what people tell us. Lies and deception seem to have become the norm for many. If we have to lie to get ahead in life, then the world suggests we do so. This is the philosophy of many in our society; in fact, in some circles this type of behavior is actually encouraged. Just take a moment and think about the most popular movies and television shows today, and we will see that lies and deceptions are the mainstay of the plot. Because of this, many people are skeptical of what they hear, and their hearts are hardened because of the disappointments they have experienced.

Unfortunately, this skepticism can be transferred in every area of life. Even believers can be skeptical about the things of God. Some believers have a hard time receiving the promises of God because of the doubt and unbelief they have. They have a hard time believing the goodness of God and His willingness to assist them to live a prosperous life. They look for a reason not to believe because they have been conditioned to do so. This is one of the reasons why most believers don't receive answers to their prayers—they are not expecting to receive.

We must understand that it is impossible for God to lie (Hebrews 6:18). The apostle Paul wrote that all God's promises are yes and amen in Christ Jesus (2 Corinthians 1:20). By renewing our mind according to the Word of God, we will be able to overcome the doubt and unbelief we have regarding God's willingness to fulfill His promises. We will learn to disregard the voice of the enemy when he tries to plant the seed of doubt in our mind. We will also learn to fight him with the Word of God, and watch him flee.

The promises of God are true and they can be relied on. We might not trust what the people of this world tell us, but we cannot let that affect our relationship with God. We need to believe and receive if we want God to manifest blessings in our life. The enemy knows that the only way he can stop that from happening is for us to doubt God's Word. Don't accept his truth, but receive God's truth.

Scripture Readings:
Numbers 23:19
Psalm 105:8–9
Proverbs 6:16–19
Hebrews 6:18–20

October 25

GIVE YOUR SEED TO JESUS TO MULTIPLY

Then Jesus took the loaves, gave thanks to God, and distributed them to the people. Afterward He did the same with the fish. And they all ate as much as they wanted. (John 6:11)

Several days ago I wrote about Jesus feeding the five thousand with just two fish and five loaves of bread. Well, today I received a revelation about this event that I would like to share with you. It's something that I have never thought about before today. It is truly amazing how the Word of God is alive and active, which means we can read the same Scripture and receive more understanding from it each time we read it. That is what happened to me when I meditated on this story.

When Jesus found someone who was willing to provide Him a seed (the two fish and five barley loaves), He took them, He blessed them, gave thanks to God, and then He distributed them to the people who were sitting around. From those two fish and five barley loaves, Jesus was able to feed over five thousand people. And everyone had more than enough to eat. As I thought about that incident, it dawned on me that because Jesus handled the fish and bread and blessed it, it caused the increase and multiplication to happen. In the hands of the disciples the fish and bread was insufficient, but in the hands of Jesus it multiplied.

What if we did the same thing when we sow a seed? What if we put that seed in the hands of Jesus and ask Him to bless and multiply it? We would get the same results. I know that some of us may think that this is a little out there, but it's in the Bible, and if Jesus is our example of how we are to live then why not do it? The next time we give an offering or a tithe, we should give it to Jesus to multiply it. Say to Jesus, "Take my seed and bless it, because I have a need."

If we have a need for something and we decide to sow a seed, we shouldn't look at the amount of the seed we are sowing and say it is not enough. We are only to give it to Jesus and let Him bless it and multiply it for us. Then we too will have more than enough.

Scripture Readings:
John 6:1–13
2 Corinthians 9:10–11

October 26

WHAT ARE YOU THE MOST MINDFUL OF?

Those who are dominated by the sinful nature think about sinful things, but those who are controlled by the Holy Spirit think about things that please the Spirit. (Romans 8:5)

If you have been reading this devotional every day, you should be at a point of spiritual maturity that I can move on to the solid meat of the Word of God. It is my goal to assist you in getting to your wealthy place in the Kingdom. Every child of God is entitled to all the privileges the Kingdom has to offer, but some will never experience it. We need to make sure that we are not one of those who fail to experience all God has for us. God is not a respecter of persons. Those who walk in the Spirit and follow the principles of the Kingdom are the ones who benefit the most. Those who don't will struggle like someone who is not a citizen of the Kingdom of God.

What are we led by, our senses and the natural realm or by the Spirit and supernatural realm? This is a question that we must ask ourselves on a regular basis. If we are walking in the natural or according to our senses, then we are under the domination of this world. We limit ourselves to the methods of this world's system, and exclude ourselves from the supernatural realm. However, if we choose to walk or be led by the Spirit, God is free to work in and through us. This means there are no limits or boundaries. One of the main reasons why we are not seeing the miraculous signs and wonders we read about in the book of Acts is that most of the body of Christ is operating in the natural realm, not the realm of the supernatural.

Being led by the senses doesn't mean we are involved in sinful behavior per say, but it does mean that we are living far below what God has for us. We are living in the natural realm and are governed by the laws of that realm. When a believer is ruled by his senses, reason and logic are in the front seat, and the spirit is in the back. This limits the ability of God to work through a believer because God is Spirit.

On the other hand, if the Spirit leads a believer, his or her spirit is in the front seat, and logic and reason are in the back. God is now able to work through that believer to perform miracles and to cause them to walk in the supernatural realm. Allowing ourselves to be led by the Spirit doesn't mean we completely ignore logic and reason. They have their place, but they do not rule us. When we are walking in the realm of the Spirit, we might be asked to do things that make absolutely no sense to our mind, but we have to decide whom we are going to follow. Who are we going to submit ourselves to, the Kingdom or to this world's system?

Scripture Readings:
Romans 8:1–14
1 Corinthians 3:1–4

October 27

GOING TO THE DOCTOR IS NOT A LACK OF FAITH

But for you who fear My name, the Sun of Righteousness will rise with healing in His wings. And you will go free, leaping with joy like calves out to pasture. (Malachi 4:2)

After reading so many books on faith and studying the lives of many great men and women of faith, I thought that it would be a lack of faith to go to the doctor when I was ill. Since these men and women of faith laid hands on people and they were healed, I thought I could do the same thing too. So when I had a headache or minor illness, I would lay hands on myself and would receive the healing. However, there came a time when this didn't work.

I had just learned I was suffering from a kidney disease, which was devastating to say the least. Up until this point I was healthy, I never had any serious medical issues happen to me. I was insensitive to anyone who was chronically ill, especially if they were a believer. I thought that if they had faith, they wouldn't be sick. So when I was informed of my diagnosis, I went to God in prayer and prayed for Him to heal me. The doctor encouraged me to take medication, but I refused. I thought it would be a lack of faith to take any kind of medication. For a while my condition got better, but then it got worse. I was retaining a great amount of fluid, my blood pressure was getting out of control, and my breathing was getting shallower. Even though I felt miserable, I refused to take the medication.

One day my ex-wife came by to see me, and she took one look at me and said, "You need to go to the hospital now!" In fact, she refused to leave until she took me. I thank God that she came by because I know I would have died if she hadn't stopped by. When I arrived at the hospital, my blood pressure was 210/120. I was immediately admitted into the emergency room and given medication to bring my blood pressure down, and also to get rid of the fluid in my body.

Later that night the Holy Spirit spoke to me and told me I shouldn't limit God in the area of healing. God can heal an individual in many different ways. He can use the hands of physicians as well as the hands of the clergy. It was my ego that almost killed me because I wanted God to perform a miraculous healing so I could boast about the great faith I had. If God had healed me the way I wanted Him to, it would had done more harm than good.

Some people have developed their faith in the area of healing, and have been graced in that area. Just because we are not yet at that level doesn't mean we failed at trusting God, it just means we need to develop our faith and mature more before we can be trusted with that kind of power. Until then, we should be content to ask God to heal us and work through the physicians He sends across our path.

Scripture Readings:
Jeremiah 8:22
Colossians 4:14

October 28

RECOGNIZE YOUR WEAKNESS AND ASK FOR GOD'S GRACE

Three different times I begged the Lord to take it away. Each time He said, "My grace is all you need. My power works best in weakness." (2 Corinthians 12:8–9)

Anyone who knows Bible history would agree that the apostle Paul was influential in the history of the early church. He was responsible for giving the gospel to the Gentile nations of that time and providing revelation and insights to the church that were beyond human reason. Paul received revelation from Jesus Himself (Galatians 1:15–17), and he endured great hardships such as shipwrecks, being imprisoned, beaten with whips, and stoned to death. But he was able to overcome all of it. Would you like to know how he was able to do this?

The secret to his success is found in 2 Corinthians 12. The apostle states he had learned to find glory in his weakness because when he recognized his weakness it allowed God to come in and make him strong (2 Corinthians 12:8–9). We all have areas of weakness in our lives. The natural tendency is to ignore or not recognize these areas. Though this may provide a sense of comfort, it is a false comfort that will eventually hinder us down the road. Instead, we are to recognize our weakness and ask God for grace in that area.

If you have a problem with substance abuse, then you should recognize that you have a problem in that area and not put yourself in a position where that weakness can be exploited. Instead, ask God for the grace to overcome. Recognize that it will take more than your willpower; you will require the assistance of God to overcome. This applies to any area of your life that you may have a weakness in. Remember that with God nothing is impossible, and all things are possible for those who believe (Luke 1:37; Mark 9:23).

Scripture Readings:
2 Corinthians 12:8–10

October 29

ARE YOU TOO FULL OF YOURSELF TO BE FILLED WITH GOD?

He must become greater and greater, and I must become less and less. (John 3:30)

If we want to walk in the Spirit and be used mightily by God, we will have to humble ourselves and become less while God becomes more. If we are full of ourselves, then there is no room for God to operate in our life. Pride is what turned Lucifer into a rebellious spirit (Ezekiel 28:13–15, 17). Many people who have been gifted by God have disqualified themselves from being used by Him because of their pride and lack of humility.

God requires that He be recognized as God. Any attempt to dethrone Him from this position will be dealt with. So it is to our benefit that we humble ourselves before God's mighty hand. When we read the account of Jesus's life, He always said that it was the Father in Him who did the work, and that He did nothing He didn't see His Father doing (John 5:30). This is the reason why Jesus was able to do such great exploits for God. It was not Jesus who was doing the work, but God working through Him. It wasn't because He was the Son of God that He was able to perform miracles; it was because God anointed Him and allowed the power of God to flow through Him (Acts 10:38).

Jesus said that everything He did we could do also (John 14:12). If this is to be true in our life, we will need to believe and receive this as truth. Then we will need to humble ourselves and make room for God to work in and through us. Our faith and power are limited, and we need God's faith and power to perform the miraculous and bring glory to Him.

When we look at the people God used in the Bible, most of them were overlooked by others and discredited. But God chose them anyhow because they were humble and recognized that they could not achieve what He wanted them to do without His assistance.

Being a believer can be humbling at times. This is especially true when we begin to study the Scriptures and see how flawed our thinking is compared to God's way of thinking. Some people, because of their pride, will reject the truths of the Bible because it is in conflict with what they believe. In their stubbornness, they walk away from the truth to seek their own version of truth. This is nothing more than a form of pride.

There are many people who are guilty of this. Don't be one of them. When you have conviction about something you may have said, done, or believed, humble yourself and correct it. Get aligned with God so He can do mighty works in and through you.

Scripture Readings:
Micah 6:8
John 3:30; 5:19
James 4:6–10

October 30

THERE IS A DIFFERENCE BETWEEN BEING CONFIDENT AND PRIDEFUL

But He gives us even more grace to stand against such evil desires. As the Scriptures say, "God opposes the proud but favors the humble." (James 4:6)

For many people today there is a misconception about being humble. Some think that being humble means they are a doormat to those around them, that a person cannot be confident and humble at the same time. This is simply not true. Moses was described as being meek or humble, yet God used him to deliver the children of Israel from the Egyptian's captivity. Egypt was one of the greatest nations at that time, with millions of people in it. A doormat couldn't boldly walk into Pharaoh's court and demand that he let God's people go! Moses was humble, but he was also confident.

There is a difference between being confident and being prideful. Many people think that it is a worldly trait to be confident, so they put on a façade of being humble while they are around certain people. Others will allow others to walk all over them and violate their personal boundaries because they will not stand up for themselves. Both of these examples are wrong. Because we are created in the image of God, we should have a sense of confidence, but the reason for our confidence is based on what God has done for us, not what we have done for ourselves.

The reason Lucifer fell from heaven was because he was so filled with pride that he forgot he was a created being. He allowed his pride to deceive him into thinking he could be like God (Isaiah 14:12–14). When Adam bowed his knee to Satan and allowed him to take dominion over this planet (2 Corinthians 4:4), humanity inherited a sinful nature that is inclined toward evil (Ephesians 2:2–3). That is why the world is in the shape that it is currently in. Pride is the sinful nature of humanity and our unwillingness to humble ourselves before God and repent (Acts 3:19).

Being prideful stems from not acknowledging God as the source of our success, which causes us to build a false sense of pride that needs to be fed. Prideful people demand that they be recognized and become egocentric in their thinking. They view people as less than them, and treat them that way. They refuse to admit that they are wrong and are difficult to get along with. On the other hand, a person who is humble or meek recognizes their uniqueness, realizing that the source of their uniqueness is from God. They are quick to make adjustments and change if they are convicted.

Jesus was a perfect example of being humble and confident. He was confident because He knew who He was, but He was humble enough to allow God to work through Him (John 5:19–21; 14:10–12). That is why God was able to manifest His glory through Him. Do you want God to manifest His glory in your life? Then learn what it means to be humble.

Scripture Readings:
John 5:19–21; 14:10–12
James 4:6–10
1 Peter 5:5–7

October 31

GOD HAS NOT APPOINTED US FOR WRATH

For God chose to save us through our Lord Jesus Christ, not to pour out His anger on us. (1 Thessalonians 5:9)

With all the unrest and turmoil in the world, there have been more and more people talking about the rapture of the church, the antichrist, and the tribulation. Some have turned to Bible scholars to determine how much time is left before the tribulation starts and the rapture begins. There are people who argue for a pre-tribulation rapture and some who argue for a post-tribulation rapture. Then there are those who are of the opinion that we are living in the tribulation right now. It can be confusing when we listen to all these varying opinions.

For me, I have found that if I just focus on what God has for me, then He will take care of me. So it really doesn't matter where we are on God's calendar, or when the rapture or tribulation will happen. Jesus said that no one knows the time of His return except God Himself (Matthew 24:36). So why spend time trying to figure it out? There are many people who predicted the end of the world, who were wrong, and their creditability has been called into question.

What I do know is this: God knows how to rescue His people from His wrath. This has been demonstrated in the Bible on several occasions. In the book of Genesis, God told Noah to build the ark to save him from the flood (Genesis 6:9–22). Later God rescued Lot from the destruction of Sodom and Gomorrah (Genesis 19:27–29). In the book of Exodus, God showed His power when He poured down hailstones from heaven, destroying all the crops and the landscape of Egypt, but nothing was touched in the land of Goshen, where the people of Israel lived (Exodus 9:26). When God brought darkness over the land of Egypt, so that no one could move, there was still light where the people of Israel lived (Exodus 10:23). Finally, God parted the Red Sea for the people of Israel, and He closed it once all the people had crossed (Exodus 14:21–26). These accounts clearly demonstrate God's ability to save His people from His wrath.

So whether you believe in the pre-tribulation or the post-tribulation rapture, know that God has not designated His children to suffer the wrath that is coming on this world. This can be found in His Word; it is not based on human opinion or conjecture. It is the truth of God. So don't spend too much time concerned with this topic. Our time and energy would be better spent focusing on the assignment God has given us to do today.

Scripture Readings:
Genesis 6:9–22; 19:27–29
Exodus 9:26; 10:23; 14:21–26
1 Thessalonians 5:9–10

November 1

WHAT YOU NEED TO DO TO RECEIVE GOD'S BEST

Now all glory to God, who is able, through His mighty power at work within us, to accomplish infinitely more than we might ask or think. (Ephesians 3:20)

It is God's desire that we live a prosperous life. To be prosperous is not just talking about how much money we have or make, but it means that we are whole in every area of our life. Being prosperous means that we and our family are healthy and happy. What good is it to have a lot of money if we can't enjoy it because of poor health or constant dissension within our family? There is nothing worse than someone who has wealth but is miserable. Many people grow up thinking money is the answer to life's problems, but that is not the case. The only answer to wholeness in one's life comes from a solid relationship with God. Only He can give us wealth without any of the other trouble that comes along with it (Proverbs 10:22).

Many in the body of Christ are not experiencing all that God has for them. God is delighted when His people are living a prosperous and happy life (Psalm 35:27). Living in God's abundance demonstrates His goodness and magnifies His glory to the world. So why aren't more believers tapping into the goodness of God? Some are just ignorant of God wanting to bless them, some are blinded by false doctrine they believe to be true, and others are stuck in unbelief and refuse to receive. If we don't fall into any of those categories, then we can go through the checklist below and see if we are lacking in any area.

- Do you give God's Word first place in your life? Do you make reading and studying the Word a priority (Psalm 119:11)?
- Do your words line up with the Word of God? Some believers will pray for something and then speak against what they had just prayed for. You need to watch your words all the time. It is those words you speak casually that reveal what is really in your heart (Matthew 12:34–37).

- How do you conduct yourself in your everyday life? Does it reflect what you profess to believe? If not, then repent and make the necessary changes in your speech and conduct. You are an ambassador of the Kingdom of God (2 Corinthians 5:20).
- Do you walk in love? God is love, which means that love would not exist without God. Love is the greatest power in the cosmos. If you are not walking in love, then the power of God cannot work through you (1 Corinthians 13:1–7).
- Are you keeping strife and unforgiveness out of your life? You cannot walk in love if you have unforgiveness in your heart. The enemy will bring people across your path for the purpose of keeping strife in your life. Choose to always walk in love (Mark 11:25).
- Do you have a heart of thanksgiving? Make it a practice to give thanks for everything God has done for you. This is a token of respect to God. It blesses Him when His people acknowledge His goodness. It also keeps worry and anxiety away.
- Make it your goal to be a blessing to others, for that is why you were blessed in the first place (Genesis 12:2).

If you go through this checklist and make a practice of doing all six of these things, then you will live a happy and prosperous life.

Scripture Readings:
Psalm 119:11
Matthew 12:34–37
2 Corinthians 5:20
1 Corinthians 13:1–7
Mark 11:25
Genesis 12:2

November 2

Don't Lose Hope because Nothing Is Impossible with God

Elisha replied, "Listen to this message from the Lord! This what the Lord says: By this time tomorrow in the markets of Samaria, five quarts of choice flour will cost only one piece of silver, and ten quarts of barley grain will cost only one piece of silver." The officer assisting the king said to the man of God, "That couldn't happen even if the Lord opened the windows of heaven!" But Elisha replied, "You will see it happen with your own eyes, but you won't be able to eat any of it!" (2 Kings 7:1–2)

No matter how dire our circumstances may be, we cannot give up our faith because nothing is impossible with God. God doesn't know what failure is and the word *impossible* doesn't even exist in His vocabulary. If we are children of God, then we have access to God's power to resolve any issues we may be facing. We have a covenant with God through Jesus Christ, and it states that God will never leave us nor forsake us (Hebrews 13:5). When things around us are falling apart and negative thoughts are flooding our mind, we only need to find promises in the Word of God and declare those promises, watching our circumstances change.

The king of Aram was besieging the city of Samaria. As a result, there was a great famine in the land. Things got so bad that people were eating donkey heads and dove's dung, paying top dollar for these items. Some women resorted to eating their children just in order to stay alive. Things were desperate for the people of Samaria. The king of Israel was upset with God, so he went to the man of God to make a complaint. Before the king could speak, however, Elisha told him that things would change and the famine would be over by the next day.

The officer who was assisting the king scoffed at Elisha, and because of his attitude of unbelief he would only witness what Elisha had spoken of but he would not enjoy what was prophesied. To make a long story short, the very next day God intervened in a change of events that caused the Aramean army to flee from what they thought was an approaching army. They abandoned their camps and left all their goods. Later that day, three lepers informed the king of Israel that they had been to the enemy camp and there was no one there. When the people heard the report, they rushed the city gate, trampling the king's assistant to death. The word of Elisha, the man of God, had come to pass (1 Kings 6:24–7:19).

What is the moral of the story? Well, there are several. The first thing is that we should trust the man or woman of God. If they give us a word from the Lord, then we need to accept it, no matter how outrageous it may sound. This should only be done if they are credible and what they are telling us is not in conflict with the Scriptures. Secondly, and, most importantly, is that we cannot limit the power of God with our human reasoning. Many people have talked themselves out of blessings because they thought it was too good to be true. We must not do that, believing God has our best interests at heart.

Scripture Readings:
1 Kings 6:24–7:19

November 3

Your Giving Will Provide for All Your Needs

If you will obey Me, you will have plenty to eat. (Isaiah 1:19)

In earlier teachings I discussed the importance of understanding the principle of sowing and reaping. This is the foundation of the Kingdom of God. If we have a need in our lives, then we need to plant a seed. A farmer understands the principle of seedtime and harvest. If he wants a crop, he plants a seed for the crop he wants to harvest. The same is true in life. If we want to be loved, then we need to give love. If we are in need of finances, then we need to be willing to plant financial seeds. This was the case with a widow who lived in the village of Zarephath (1 Kings 17:8–16).

Elijah had been instructed by God to go to the village of Zarephath because there was a widow there to feed him. When Elijah arrived, he approached a woman and boldly asked for some water and some bread to eat. The woman explained her dire situation. She had very little. In fact, she only had enough for her and her son to eat. Then Elijah encouraged her by telling her if she obeyed his request, then she would have more than enough flour and olive oil to eat. The word of the man of God proved true. The widow and her household had more than enough and never experienced lack for the rest of their lives.

We serve a God who is more than enough. In heaven there is no lack of provision. God does not know lack. If you are a child of God and a citizen of the Kingdom of God, the same should be said of you. However, many believers are not experiencing this in their lives—they are experiencing lack and are barely getting by.

One of the reasons believers experience lack in their lives is because of their lack of obedience in their finances. The widow had a choice when Elijah approached her and asked for some food and drink. She could have said that she didn't have enough to feed him, then walked away. Had she done that, she and her household would have eventually died of starvation. But she chose to obey the request of the man of God, which required faith on her part. As a result, the Lord blessed her entire family with abundance.

Many believers look at their finances and allow their financial situation dictate to them what they are to do, rather than the other way around. Many choose to live under the financial philosophy of the world rather than of the Kingdom of God. If you want to experience blessing in your finances, then be willing to use Kingdom principles of sowing and reaping, and you will experience an abundant harvest.

Scripture Readings:
Isaiah 1:19
1 Kings 17:8–16
Luke 6:38
2 Corinthians 9:6–15

November 4

PRAYER HAS POWER

The earnest prayer of a righteous person has great power and produces wonderful results. (James 5:16)

Prayer for many people has become a mere formality—it is something we do to show respect to God. But we really don't think that anything will come of it. Prayer for others is like making a wish—they are voicing what they would like to happen, but they don't believe it will actually happen. Because they don't have any expectation of their prayers being answered, they receive what they expect—which is nothing. Their words are powerless—they sound good but lack power.

The prayer of faith is the most powerful weapon a believer has in her or her arsenal. There is power in the prayers of those who have faith and believe they will receive what they have asked for. The prayer of faith will take from the unseen world and bring it into the seen. But the key to answered prayer is having the faith to believe what we have requested will actually come to pass. Jesus said that whatever we ask for in His name would be granted to us (John 14:13). He also said that if we prayed for anything, not doubting in our heart, then we would receive what we have asked for (Mark 11:24).

Don't mitigate the power of prayer; this is what the enemy wants us to do. He realizes the power of the believer and understands the power of prayer. Elijah was a human just like each of us, but he prayed that it would not rain, and it didn't for three and half years. Then he prayed again for it to rain, and it did. He prayed for fire to come down from heaven and it did on several occasions. Elijah was able to do this because he was a righteous man who prayed the prayer of faith.

We have the same standing as Elijah, so we should be able to have access to the same kind of prayer power Elijah had. What stops most believers is a lack of faith and doubt in their heart. They are not fully convinced that their prayers will be answered. They know what the Bible says concerning prayer, but they waver from belief to disbelief. This attitude will disqualify and nullify our prayer request. The Kingdom of God operates on the currency of faith; if we don't have that, then we cannot purchase what we desire.

If we are guilty of having wavering faith, then we need to renew our minds according to the Word of God. We should meditate on the Scriptures concerning prayer, then speak those promises to ourselves in order to build up our faith. This is something that has to be done continually; it's not a one-time thing. Remember that God will reward you for your diligence, and you will get results when you pray.

Scripture Readings:
1 Kings 18:1–46
Mark 11:23–24
John 14:13; 16:26
1 John 5:14

November 5

YOU ENTER GOD'S REST BY FAITH

So God's is there for people to enter, but those who first heard this good news failed to enter because they disobeyed God. (Hebrews 4:6)

Are you experiencing the rest of God in your life? God promises rest for His people, but to enjoy that rest we must enter it by faith. The children of Israel failed to enter into His rest because of their disobedience (Hebrews 4:1–3). They should be an example for us New Testament believers. If we do not mix faith with what we read and hear from the Scriptures, we too will not enter the rest of God.

God is pleased when His children come to Him in faith (Hebrews 11:6). There are many believers who go to church, listen to the sermon, and they don't mix faith with what they hear. As a result, they leave church with a sense of temporary relief, but by Monday morning they are stressed out again.

The only labor required to enter God's rest is faith and obedience: it is not just listening to the Word but doing what the Word instructs of us (James 2:20). If we only listen to the Word and not do what it says, our faith is dead and not good for anything. There are many believers who deceive themselves by being only a hearer of the Word and not a doer. Then they get angry with God because they have no fruit in their lives. It takes more than quoting Scriptures to reap a harvest.

For example, if you are in need of finances and you don't tithe or sow a seed, then you can't expect God to honor your decree, "He will meet all my needs according to His riches and glory!" You are wasting your time. There are spiritual laws that have to be followed, and to follow them requires faith. If you believe that God will meet your needs, then show it by sowing a seed. This is a demonstration of your faith.

Many believers give lip service to the things of God, and think that is enough. No, it takes more than that. We have to not only be willing but obedient to what the Spirit of God tells us to do. Jesus said that He would give rest to those who would take His yoke upon them and learn from Him (Matthew 11:28–29). What is the yoke of Jesus? It is to love God with all our heart and soul, and to love our neighbor as ourselves (Matthew 22:37–39). If every believer would make this his or her daily goal, the manifestation of the glory of God would be demonstrated through Christ's church. Let us labor to enter the rest of God.

Scripture Readings:
Matthew 11:28–29; 22:37–39
Hebrews 4:1–7; 11:6
James 2:14–20

November 6

ARE YOU EXPERIENCING INCREASE IN YOUR LIFE?

And may the Lord make you to increase and excel and overflow in love for one another and for all people, just as we also do for you. (1 Thessalonians 3:12 AMP)

Ever since God created the cosmos, it has been continually expanding. Scientists estimate that it is expanding at the speed of light. That is amazing when you think about it. When God said, "Light be!" the cosmos obeyed and has never stopped ever since. The God we serve is a God of increase, and He expects His children, who are made in His image and likeness, to increase as well. There are numerous examples of this contained in the Bible. God took Abraham and pronounced a blessing upon him for increase (Genesis 12:1–3), and, as a result of this blessing, the nation of Israel was born. From the nation of Israel, the Messiah was born, and through His death the church was born. And it all started with one man.

It's God's desire that believers increase in every area of their lives. We should be increasing in our knowledge and understanding of God (Ephesians 1:17–19), we should be growing in our faith, and we should be growing in our spiritual stature (1 Corinthians 3:2–3). Unfortunately, this is not happening for a majority of the church. Most believers have not progressed as they should. The enemy has done a good job of keeping most of the body of Christ treading water. Going to church has just become a ritual, something they know they should do to be a "good Christian." There is very little increase in their lives, and there is little distinction between them and non-believers.

Jesus came to show us what we are capable of doing when we follow the agenda of the Kingdom of God. He died so that we who believe in Him can share in His life. He was the seed of God (the Word of God) that was planted so that God could receive a harvest (Isaiah 55:11). God expects every one of us to increase and produce a harvest. This is the principle of seedtime and harvest (Mark 4:26–29).

If you are the same you were a year ago, then something is wrong in your life. You need to access your situation and find out what is keeping you from progressing further. If this is the case, you are no different than the steward who buried his talent in the dirt and did nothing with it when his master left (Luke 19:22).

Our God is a God of increase. Since we are created in the image and likeness of God, we should be increasing in every area of our lives and leaving an inheritance to our children (Psalm 112:1–3). If this is not your mindset, then you should consider changing it in order to reflect the desire of God.

Scripture Readings:
Genesis 1:1–2, 11; 12:1–3
Mark 4:26–29
Luke 13:37–39
1 Corinthians 1:17–19

November 7

ARE YOU OCCUPYING FROM A POSITION IN CHRIST?

"And you will be My kingdom of priests, My holy nation." This is the message you must give to the people of Israel. (Exodus 19:6)

God's desire is that He has a people who represent Him in the world. We are to be ambassadors of the Kingdom of God (2 Corinthians 5:20). If every believer were mindful of this, what an impact on the world we would truly have! God wants the church to manifest His glory to a dying and unbelieving world. This has been His desire all along (Isaiah 61:6–7). However, for a majority of believers, this is not the case. They don't understand who they are and they live and die like any ordinary person (Psalm 82:6–7). Don't let this be you.

Through the precious blood of Jesus, we have access to the Kingdom of God. By renewing our mind, we can change our paradigm and we can change our perception about the world and ourselves. We can have the same mindset Jesus had (1 Corinthians 2:16), and then we can do the works of Jesus (John 14:12). It is not impossible because nothing is impossible with God. Because we are citizens of the Kingdom of God, we have access to everything in that Kingdom. Through the blood of Jesus we can receive power, riches, wisdom, strength, honor, and glory (Revelation 5:12). It is there for those who believe and are willing to receive it.

The only thing God requires of us to access the resources of the Kingdom are faith and obedience. These are the keys to everything within the Kingdom. Jesus said the key to His success was that He did only what He saw His Father doing. In other words, He followed the principles of the

Kingdom. He was not occupied with His own agenda. His agenda was to do the will of His Father. God has a specific plan for each of us. It is our job to find out what that is and do it. The choice is ours. We can live as a king and priest, or we can live a mediocre life.

Scripture Readings:
Exodus 19:6
Psalm 82:1–8
Isaiah 61:6–7
Revelation 1:6; 5:12

November 8

KINGDOM PROTOCOL

Seek the Kingdom of God above all else, and live righteously, and He will give you everything you need. (Mathew 6:33)

If we are to be used by God in a mighty way, we need to understand the importance of following the protocol of the Kingdom of God. The first rule to understand is that the Kingdom is a theocracy, not a democracy. It has one ruler, and that is God Himself. He is to be trusted and not questioned. It was actually questioning God's motivation that got Adam and Eve in trouble in the Garden. We need to learn to trust God with all of our heart and soul if we are to walk in God's best for our lives.

In order to trust God in this way, we have to humble ourselves and surrender our will to do the will of the Father. This was the key for Jesus's success while He walked on this earth (John 5:19–20, 30). It is only when we submit our will to do the will of God, that we will be used by Him in a great way. To the degree that we submit ourselves to Him, that is the degree that we will be used.

The greater God uses the believer, the more humble that believer needs to become to keep them from being consumed with pride. Many men and women of God have fallen because of pride, eventually cutting themselves off from the power of God because of their prideful heart. Remember that this is what happened to Lucifer before he fell from heaven. He got so prideful that he was blinded and self-deceived into thinking that he could be like God (Isaiah 14:13–14). He forgot that he was a created being.

If we stay mindful of Kingdom protocol, we will position ourselves to be used by God in a powerful way. In order for this to happen, however, we have to renew our minds to a new way of thinking (Romans 12:1–2). We cannot understand the Kingdom of God with the knowledge we have of this world's system. The problem many believers have today is that they try to use worldly wisdom and logic to understand God's principles, and it doesn't work (1 Corinthians 2:13–14). So reeducate yourself to the protocol of the Kingdom of God today.

Scripture Readings:
Psalm 82:1–6
Matthew 6:33
John 5:19–20, 30
James 4:5–8
1 Peter 5:5–7

November 9

HOW TO KEEP YOURSELF UP WHEN YOU ARE FEELING DOWN

No, despite all these things, overwhelming victory is ours through Christ, who loved us. (Romans 8:37)

Have you ever had one of those days, weeks, or months where you feel like you are a target for the enemy? Maybe you receive bad news about a business deal, a trusted friend has disappointed you, or you just went through a break-up with a loved one. And maybe you had all of this happen to you in the same day. You feel forlorn and destitute. You feel forsaken and abandoned by God. And you immediately think to yourself, "What did I do to deserve this?" The more you ponder the situation, the more depressed you become. Just a few days ago everything was going so good and you were walking in the Spirit, but now you are dragging in the flesh.

Know that you are not alone. We have all gone through periods like this. The important thing is to not stay there. It is all right to grieve for a time because it is part of the healing process. Give yourself some time; get it out of your system. Once the grieving process is done, then it's time to move on.

It is completely natural to feel down when we experience a setback of some kind. It is important that we don't allow ourselves to stay in the soulish realm too long. As a believer, we should be walking in the Spirit and not the flesh (Romans 8:1).

So many believers are still allowing themselves to be controlled by their lower nature; it is not possible to walk in the supernatural realm if we are controlled by the lower nature. The enemy will use disappointments and hardships as a way to get us to leave our estate in the spiritual realm and descend to the natural realm. There are three principles to remember: resurrection, redemption, and renewal.

- Resurrection: The cross and what it represents is the power of the gospel, signifying the victory of Jesus and the defeat of Satan. It is an eternal defeat for Satan that can never be changed. Because of the death and resurrection of Jesus, we are assured the victory over life's circumstances. We are more than conquerors in Christ (Romans 8:37). No matter what life throws at us, we can overcome it because we are in Christ. We cannot let the devil tell us anything different. When he starts talking smack about how we are a loser, we only have to remind him of his pending fate. That will shut him up quickly.
- Redemption: We have been redeemed from the curse of this world. It is unacceptable to allow ourselves to stay under the curse of the law because Jesus bore the curse upon Himself (Galatians 3:13). If Jesus bore the curse, then why would we allow ourselves to continue to live under the curse? That just doesn't make any sense. But there are many believers who are living under the curse because they tolerate it and think it is normal.
- Renewal: In order for us to live in the realm of the supernatural, we will have to renew our mind and change our paradigm. We have to obtain the mind of Christ (1 Corinthians 2:16), which only comes though renewing our thought life (Romans 12:1–2) so that we are no longer conformed to this world's system. Instead, we are to let the Spirit renew our mind and attitude. If we do these things, then we will be back up where we belong.

Scripture Readings:
Romans 8:1, 37
Galatians 3:13
1 Corinthians 2:16
Romans 12:1–2

November 10

ADMITTING WHEN YOU HAVE WRONGED SOMEONE

Love does no wrong to others, so love fulfills the requirement of God's laws. (Romans 13:10)

Sometimes the hardest thing to admit is when we are wrong. We can get so caught up in looking at a person or situation a certain way that it becomes our truth, and we get hardhearted and see it from only one perspective. I have often wondered why Pharaoh didn't let the children of Israel go when Moses performed all those signs and wonders. I thought to myself, "If all that was happening to me, I would get the hint and let those people go." But that is what happens when we allow our pride to blind us. This is one of the reasons why it is important to be humble and teachable. No one has all the answers for life except God.

When someone confronts us about something in our lives, the natural response is to get defensive. When this happens, we are generally not receptive to what they are saying to us. Instead of listening to their opinion, we have a tendency to justify ourselves. Instead of seeking a solution to the issue, it becomes a war of the wills where someone has to win and the other lose. This is not the way believers should conduct themselves. God has called us to walk in love toward one another. Love does not behave in this manner. It is patient and it is kind. Love is not jealous, boastful, or proud. It does not demand its own way, nor is it rude. Love is not irritable and keeps no record of being wronged. Love does not rejoice about injustice but rejoices when the truth wins out. Love never gives up, never loses faith, is always hopeful, and endures through every circumstance (1 Corinthians 13:4–7).

If we made it a point to go through every day and ask ourselves if we are walking in love, the problems we experience in any kind of relationship would be greatly reduced. We might be asking ourselves, "How can I walk in love?" You can't, but God can through you. If you ask God to help you walk in love, He will. When you find yourself slipping from time to time, the Holy Spirit will bring it to your attention. When He does, don't resist or argue, just repent and agree with what He reveals. Make it your goal to walk in love every day. There is power in love, because God is love. It is actually the greatest power in the cosmos because it is the essence of God.

The quickest way to get out from under the power of God is to stop walking in love. Our prayers will not be answered if we have unforgiveness in our heart (Mark 11:25). So when we feel conviction about the way we handled a specific situation, take a moment to reflect and ask ourselves, "Am I walking in love?" If not, then humble yourself, admit you were wrong, and ask for forgiveness. It could be the difference in keeping a relationship or losing it.

Scripture Readings:
1 Corinthians 13:4–7
1 John 3:23; 4:7, 11–12

November 11

Whom Do You Identify with the Most, Adam or Christ?

The Scriptures tells us, "The first man, Adam, became a living person." But the last Adam—that is, Christ—is a life-giving Spirit. What comes first is the natural body, then the spiritual body comes later. Adam, the first man, was made from the dust of the earth, while Christ, the second man, came from heaven. (1 Corinthians 15:45–47)

One of the biggest hindrances I had in my early years as a believer was whom I identified with the most. You see, I was athletic and prided myself on my appearance and athletic skill. It is completely natural for any athlete to do this. This attitude is part of what causes them to excel in their sport. Once I accepted the Lord, I continued to work out regularly to maintain my fitness. I would be in the gym or out running six to seven days a week. I enjoyed working out and having the kind of physique that many admired.

I remember one day after a men's Bible study, the pastor came up to me and suggested that I spend less time in the gym and more time with God. At that time I didn't pay too much attention to his suggestion. I just thought he was jealous. I read my Bible almost every day, and I thought that was good enough. I didn't realize I was more consumed with my physical appearance than I was in developing my inner man. Time passed and I continued to work out as I normally did, developing bigger muscles and a trimmer waist. In fact, I started competing in bodybuilding contests, and even won a few shows. I was very proud of the way I looked and felt. I felt invincible; I was one of the biggest and strongest guys in the gym.

Well, all that came to an end with a series of illnesses. First, I had kidney failure and I lost a considerable amount of muscle. Then a couple of years later I had a spinal infection that left me paralyzed in both my legs and arms. In a matter of weeks, I lost over thirty pounds. The muscles that took over twenty years to build were gone. It was at that moment that the words of that pastor years ago rang in my ears. I realized my identity was in my physical appearance. I had grown so used to it that when it was gone I didn't know who I really was anymore.

The apostle Paul said that physical training was good, but training ourselves in godliness was far better (1 Timothy 4:7–8). Many believers will spend years developing the natural man through education, and becoming rich, successful, and beautiful to gain the esteem of the world. There is nothing wrong with that, but it can't be done at the expense of developing the inner man. If we focus our attention on developing the spiritual man, it will pay dividends not only in this life but in the one to come. It is important to have balance in our life. Exercise is good for us, both physically and mentally, but so is training our spiritual man. So who do we identify with the most—Adam, the natural man, or Christ?

Scripture Readings:
1 Corinthians 15:45–49
1 Timothy 4:7–8

November 12

Are You Prepared to Receive?

Now all glory to God, who is able, through His mighty power at work within us, to accomplish infinitely more than we might ask or think. (Ephesians 3:20)

We serve a God who is more than enough. There is no insufficiency in Him. No matter how dire the circumstances we find ourselves in, God has the ability to meet the need. But it will require faith and obedience in order to access His provisions.

I just read a story in the Bible about a widow, whose husband just recently died, and she was in financial need. The creditors had threatened to take away her two sons to satisfy the debt. Needless to say, she was distraught and went to the man of God for an answer to her problem. Elisha asked the widow what she had in her household. She told him that all she had was one jar of olive oil. Then Elisha told the woman to get as many empty jars as she could find, shut the door behind her and her sons, and start pouring olive oil into the empty jars. The widow and her two sons did just what the man of God said. To their amazement, they were able to fill all of the empty jars with olive oil. In fact, the only reason the oil stopped flowing was because they did not have any more empty jars to fill (2 Kings 4:3–6).

This story clearly illustrates that we have a God who is more than enough, El Shaddai. This story also shows the importance of having faith and obeying the instructions God gives to us. There are many believers who are willing to receive but are not obedient, so they disqualify themselves from receiving the provisions of God. Had this widow questioned the instructions the man of God gave her and tried to rationalize in her mind about what he said, she would not have experienced this miracle, and her family would have suffered as a result. How many believers are not experiencing the supernatural miracles of God because of doubt and unbelief?

Another point that we can take away from this story is that we control how much God will do for us. There are no limits with God. He will do for us as much as our faith will allow Him to do. The only reason the olive oil stopped flowing was because there were no more empty jars left to be filled. Had the widow had more jars, she could have received more oil. But the story indicates that she had enough to sell to pay off her debts with some left over. You see, we have access to El Shaddai, the God who is more than enough. He will meet our every need as we seek Him and seek to live in obedience to His will.

Scripture Readings:
2 Kings 4:1–7
Isaiah 1:19
John 6:1–15
Ephesians 3:20

November 13

THE POWER OF SOWING WHEN IN NEED

For God is the One who provides seed for the farmer and the bread to eat. In the same way, He will provide and increase your resources and then produce a great harvest of generosity in you. (2 Corinthians 9:10)

It requires faith to sow or give when we are in need. It goes against everything this world's system teaches. We are supposed to conserve our resources when times are tight. Well, the Kingdom of God has a different philosophy. God asks us to sow when tough times come, because this gives Him the opportunity to meet our need. Remember this: if we have a need, then we need to sow a seed. This will activate the principle of sowing and reaping in our life.

There are several examples in the Bible that illustrate this principle. I will use just one of them from the Old Testament, involving Elisha, a man of God. There was a famine in the land of Israel. One day a man gave Elisha a sack of fresh grain and twenty loaves of bread. It was the first grain harvest of the year. This man knew that if he gave from his first fruits, God would surely bless his next harvest. Elisha took the twenty loaves of bread and instructed his servant to feed the people. The servant questioned Elisha because of the number of loaves of bread and the number of people to feed didn't measure out. But Elisha told the servant again to feed the people, and only this time he told the servant, "This is what the Lord says: Everyone will eat, and there will even be some left over! So the servant gave out the bread, and everyone ate and there was some left over…just as the Lord had promised" (2 Kings 4:43–44).

Jesus was well acquainted with this story because He performed a miracle like this when He fed over five thousand people with just two fish and five barley loaves (John 6:1–13). We have access to this power of increase if we use our faith and are willing to receive. It takes faith and obedience to give when we are financially in need.

Many believers will talk themselves out of giving, and not allow God the opportunity to work on their behalf. Others will give but immediately speak doubt and unbelief and nullify what they have sown because it didn't happen as quickly as they thought it would. Others give but sow their seed in bad soil. This means we should scrutinize which ministries we give our tithes and offerings to. There are many wolves in sheep's clothing ready to take our money in the name of the Lord. We have to find ourselves a true man or woman of God and sow seed into their ministry. God will reward our faithfulness.

Scripture Readings:
2 Kings 4:43–44
John 6:1–13
2 Corinthians 9:6–11

November 14

FAITH IS THE KEY TO MAKING THE UNSEEN SEEN

Faith is the confidence that what we hope for will actually happen; it gives us assurance about things we cannot see. (Hebrews 11:1)

The difference between believers who receive the manifestation from God and those who don't is faith. Some people confuse mental assent with faith. They are similar, but in reality they are actually quite different. Mental assent to something means that we agree with something, but it is only in the mental realm. Therefore, it is easy to reason away what we think we believe. Faith, on the other hand, comes from the heart, or the inner man. It goes beyond the mental realm. This is why Jesus told His disciples that if they would believe what they had prayed for and would not doubt in their heart, they would receive it (Mark 11:23). It is possible to believe in our heart and have some doubt in our mind. Just because we have doubt in our mind doesn't mean our prayers will not be answered, unless we start speaking against what we have prayed for.

When we use our faith, we are taking something that already exists in the unseen realm and bringing it into the realm of the seen. As a citizen of the Kingdom of God, we have access to all the resources that are in heaven. There is no sickness or disease in heaven, so we can decree that we have received healing. There is no lack in heaven, so we can decree that all our needs are met. If we have a faulty body part, we can use our faith to replace it. Jesus said that whatever we bind on earth will be bound in heaven, and whatever we loose on earth shall be loosed in heaven (Matthew 16:19). Jesus has given us this power to use right now, not when we get to heaven.

There is an example in the Gospels of how the power of faith caused two blind men to receive their sight. After Jesus healed a woman with the issue of blood and raised a young girl from the dead, two blind men began to follow Him, shouting, "Son of David, have mercy on us." They even followed Jesus into the house He was staying at. Once Jesus was inside, He asked the two men, "Do you believe I can make you see?" They both answered yes. Then Jesus touched their eyes and said, "Because of your faith, it will happen." After He said that, their eyes were opened and they could suddenly see (Matthew 9:27–30). It was their faith that opened the door for their healing to occur. Faith is the currency believers use to purchase the resources of the Kingdom of God.

Scripture Readings:
Matthew 9:18–30
Mark 11:22–24
Hebrews 11:1

November 15

THERE IS A THIN LINE BETWEEN FAITH AND FOOLISHNESS

Don't wear yourself out trying to get rich. Be wise enough to know when to quit. In the blink of an eye wealth disappears, for it will sprout wings and fly away like an eagle. (Proverbs 23:4–5)

There are many scam artists who are targeting churches today, especially ones that teach faith and prosperity. The reason for this is because faith people are more willing to act without much physical evidence—they have learned to walk by faith (2 Corinthians 5:7). These people will come into the church with plans to make big money very quickly. They will paint false dreams and hope that their victims will get drunk on the dream so they can take advantage of them. They will pose as people of great faith and quote Scriptures to convince their victims that they are sincere. This should not be surprising because Satan will present himself as an angel of light to deceive believers (2 Corinthians 11:14).

We believe in miracles and the supernatural realm, which makes us prone to be risk takers. But there is a difference between walking in faith and walking in foolishness. Many have fallen prey to these conmen and women who got drunk on the dreams of being rich and having all their needs met. The Bible teaches that we are to prosper, and the wealth of the sinner is laid up for the righteous (Proverbs 13:22). They will often use these types of Scriptures to grease the wheels.

There is a story in the Old Testament that clearly illustrates what I am talking about here. There was a prophet who was on an assignment for God. He was instructed to rebuke King Jeroboam of Israel for burning incense at the altar of a foreign god. After the man of God rebuked the king, he tried to have the man of God seized, but He paralyzed the king's arm so he could not move it. The king then pleaded with the man of God to heal him. The man prayed to the Lord and the king's arm was restored. The king was so happy that he invited the man of God to the palace, but the man of God refused to go because God had instructed him to come back immediately after completing his assignment.

There was an old prophet who heard what happened and he wanted to meet the man of God. So he saddled his donkey and chased him down. He too wanted the man of God to come and stay with him. Initially the man of God refused and told the old prophet the same thing he told the king. But the old prophet told the man of God that God had told him to have him come to his house and have dinner, which we know was a lie. The prophet listened to the old prophet and wound up being killed by a lion because he disobeyed the order God had given him (1 Kings 13:1–33). This old prophet was a wolf in sheep's clothing, using his office to deceive the man of God. Beware of those wolves who pretend to be someone they are not.

Scripture Readings:
1 Kings 13:1–33
Proverbs 13:22

November 16

God Works in Mysterious Ways

Have you never heard? Have you never understood? The Lord is the everlasting God, the Creator of all the earth. He never grows weak or weary. No one can measure the depths of His understanding. (Isaiah 40:28)

I have learned not to put God in a box by expecting Him to answer my prayers in the way I think He should answer them. I know I have forfeited many blessing because of my tendency to do this. In fact, I almost died because I had made up my mind that God was going to heal me supernaturally without human means. It was not until I read the story about Naaman that I came to my senses and started taking the medication the doctor had prescribed for me. Don't limit God when you make a request of Him. Remember that God can get anything to you at any time, and it can come from anyone He chooses. This is perfectly illustrated in the story of Naaman.

Naaman was a commander in the Aramean army. He had won great favor with the king of Aram, but Naaman was a leper. A maid of Naaman's wife told her that there was a man of God in Israel who could heal Naaman. So his wife encouraged her husband to go see him. He got a letter of recommendation from the king of Aram, and Naaman brought gifts for the man of God. When Elisha found out that Naaman was coming, he told the king that he would heal him, and directed the king to send Naaman to him.

When Naaman arrived at the house of Elisha, Elisha's servant came out to meet him and instructed Naaman to dip himself in the Jordan River. He was upset because Elisha didn't come out to meet him. He had envisioned the man of God coming out and waving his hand over him, healing him. He reasoned that the instructions he received were foolish and didn't make any sense, so he was ready to walk away. Fortunately for Naaman, however, one of his men encouraged him to do what Elisha had told him to do. He reluctantly went down to the river and dipped seven times, just as he was instructed to do. On the seventh time, Naaman was totally healed of his leprosy.

In great gratitude Naaman went back to the man of God and thanked him. He offered to give gifts to Elisha, but he refused to take them. So Naaman requested that he take some piles of dirt back to his country so that he could worship the Lord. That day Naaman became a believer of the true God (2 Kings 5:1–19).

You see, Naaman had preconceived ideas about how God was going to heal him, and he almost walked away from his healing. Don't limit God, because He can answer your prayers any way He so chooses and through anyone He chooses. If you are sick, He can use the hands of a believer or the hands of a medical doctor or nurse. The bottom line is that we are to look to God for the remedy, even if He chooses to use a human to do His work.

Scripture Readings:
2 Kings 5:1–19

November 17

GOD HAS NO TIMELINE BECAUSE HE LIVES IN THE NOW

But you must not forget this one thing, dear friends: A day is like a thousand years to the Lord, and a thousand years is like a day. The Lord isn't really being slow about His promise, as some people think. No, He is being patient for your sake. He does not want anyone to be destroyed but wants everyone to repent. (2 Peter 3:9)

This is something I learned from the late Charles Capps, one of my spiritual fathers. Once I understood what I am about to share with you, it completely changed my prayer life and gave me a deeper understanding of why my prayers would be answered.

First, we must understand that God lives in a realm where time as we know it does not exist. We live in a world where there are four dimensions—time, length, width, and height. However, God has at least six other dimensions we are not aware of. There could be spiritual beings in our home or vehicle with us that we cannot detect. If you have not seen it, I suggest you rent the movie *The Matrix*, as this is a perfect example of what I am talking about. I would also invite you to read a book by Dr. Hugh Ross entitled *Beyond the Cosmos*. He goes into detail about all of the different dimensions that surround us.

For a long time, when I prayed for something I put it in the future tense. For example, if I was sick I would pray and say, "God is going to heal me." However, Jesus said that when we pray, we must believe that we have received it at the moment we pray (Mark 11:24). The reason He said this was because God lives in the now. There is no such thing as time in the realm of the Spirit. Faith is in the now. That is why we are instructed that when we pray we are to believe that we have received our request at the moment we prayed for it. Then we are to thank God for answering our prayers until we receive the manifestation.

Most people say that God is going to answer their prayer, putting it off into the future. But Jesus said that we are to believe that we have received it the very moment we pray. When we pray, we are doing a transaction in the realm of the Spirit. This means that it is beyond the sense realm.

Therefore, we cannot determine if our prayers are answered by what we see or feel. We have to base it on faith alone, which comes from the Word of God (Romans 10:17). So how do we know our prayers are answered? The Word says that if we ask anything according to the will of God, He will give it to us (1 John 5:14). We also need to remember that it is impossible for God to lie, and His will is found in His Word. So the next time we pray, we need to believe that we have received our request the moment we pray, and thank God for answering our prayer until we receive the manifestation.

Scripture Readings:
Mark 11:23–24
John 14:13–14; 16:23
1 John 5:14

November 18

USING THE EYES OF FAITH

For we believe by believing and not by seeing. (2 Corinthians 5:7)

If we are to live a victorious life, we need to learn that there is a spiritual realm we must operate in. Most people are so consumed with their life in the physical realm that they ignore the spiritual realm altogether. Because the spiritual realm is greater than the physical realm, it is easy to be manipulated by the prince of the power of the air. Satan is the god of this world's system and he will influence people to do his will (Ephesians 2:1–3).

We as believers have the ability to see beyond the material world and look into the spiritual realm through the eyes of faith. We can be in the midst of a storm and see peace. We can be in a desperate situation and see victory, because of who we are in Christ Jesus (Romans 8:37). But seeing in the realm of the Spirit only comes to those who believe and are willing to put in the work of renewing their minds. There are many believers who love the Lord but are living defeated lives because they focus only on the physical or material world. When we do that we are living in the carnal or fleshly realm, and we are subject to this world's system. But when a believer focuses on the Kingdom of God, their perception changes, and they begin to see things like Jesus saw them, because they have the mind of Christ (1 Corinthians 2:16).

There is a perfect example of this in the Old Testament. The prophet Elisha was in the city of Dothan, and the king of Aram wanted to capture him because Elisha would tell the king of Israel whenever the king of Aram was going to attack Israel. Someone had told the king of Aram that Elisha was the one who revealed his plans to destroy Israel. So the king of Aram sent his army and surrounded the city where the man of God was. Early in the morning, Elisha's servant went outside and saw the army and panicked. He went back inside and told Elisha what he saw. Elisha calmed him down, and said, "There are more with us than with them." Then he requested that

God open his eyes to see into the spiritual realm. When God answered Elisha's prayer, the servant saw chariots of fire surrounding the Aramean army (2 Kings 6:8–17).

Whether we realize it or not, we have access to angels. They assist all those who are children of the Kingdom of God (Hebrews 1:14). But many believers don't take advantage of their angels because of either ignorance or unbelief. Others speak things contrary to the Word of God and prevent their angels from acting on their behalf. Angels only listen to the Word of God or commands that come from God (Psalm 103:20).

If we are speaking negatively, instead of activating angels we open the door for the enemy to come in and do damage. This is why it is important to renew our mind and learn to see beyond the natural and begin to see with the eyes of our faith.

Scripture Readings:
2 Kings 6:8–23
Psalm 103:20
Ephesians 2:1–3; 6:10–12

November 19

ARE YOU A SLAVE OR AN HEIR OF GOD?

But when the right time came, God sent His Son, born of a woman, subject to the law. God sent Him to buy freedom for us who were slaves to the law, so that He could adopt us as His very own children. (Galatians 4:4–5)

There are many believers who are not enjoying the freedom of being a child of God. They have received Jesus into their hearts, but they don't fully comprehend the finished work of Christ. As a result, they have put themselves back into bondage by subjecting themselves to a program of works. They ask questions like, "Did I pray enough? Am I going to church enough?" or, "Am I reading my Bible enough?" In essence, they are trying to earn brownie points with God to gain His favor. What usually happens is that they will either get burned out or become so legalistic that their Christian experience is not enjoyable.

Have you ever been around a legalistic Christian? They look like they continually suck on a lemon. They are not fun to be around. You feel like you are walking on eggshells when you are around them. I have attended some churches with these types of believers. The whole service is full of rules and regulations, and it was so cold and rigid that the Holy Spirit had to put on an overcoat. That place was dead—no life at all. I got nothing out of the service but a cold.

The apostle Paul ran into this same problem with the Galatian church. He had started the church with the gospel of grace, which was well accepted, but when he found that false teachers had come in and was attempting to put these believers under the law again, Paul got upset (Galatians 4:1–19). Many churches today are trying to mix the gospel of grace with the law, and that does not work very well. All it does is discredit the finished work of Christ Jesus and puts believers back into bondage under the law. What eventually happens is that the flesh gets involved because our Christianity is based on self-effort, which then leads to pride instead of the grace of

God (Ephesians 2:8–9). When a believer falls back into the works of the law, they short-circuit their faith because faith operates by grace. Another problem that occurs is that, because the believer is operating under the law, they have put themselves back under this world's system, which can confine them from experiencing the fullness of God.

In order for a believer to live up to all God has for them, they must realize who they are in Christ Jesus. They are the seed of Abraham, and are entitled to everything God promised Abraham (Galatians 3:13–14). We are to rely of the finished work of Jesus and the grace of God in order to live the kind of life God has made available to us. Let the grace of God take away those bad habits, and not try to do it with self-effort only. Let the grace of God work with you instead. You are an heir, not a slave.

Scripture Readings:
Galatians 3:13–14, 29; 4:1–18
Ephesians 2:8–9

November 20

Your Righteousness Is Based on Faith Alone

But we who live by the Spirit eagerly wait to receive by faith the righteousness God has promised to us. (Galatians 5:5)

Jesus came to the earth for two reasons, to redeem humanity from the wrath of God (John 1:29) and to demonstrate what we could do if we walked as Jesus did (John 14:12). Jesus bore all the curses of humanity upon Himself so those who would believe and receive Jesus as their Lord and Savior could once again be in right standing with God, obtaining access to the Kingdom of God (Galatians 3:13). God's love for us is so great that He provided a way for us to get back into right standing with Him.

The only thing that God requires of us to receive this wonderful gift is faith. You see, it is impossible to please God without faith (Hebrews 11:6). It is the currency of the Kingdom of God, which means that anything we want to purchase from the Kingdom requires faith. Faith is the vehicle that transfers things from the spiritual realm to the physical realm. Those believers who understand this have far more purchasing power than those who don't. When believers attempt to obtain right standing with God through their self-effort only, they are destined to fail because their righteousness is but filthy rags to God (Isaiah 64:6).

It is an affront to God when a believer tries to depend on his or her efforts alone to achieve right standing with God. Jesus came to the earth to do this for us. He was the sacrificial lamb spoken of in the Old Testament (Isaiah 53:1–12). Don't be like the children of Israel who refused to receive from God and died in the wilderness because of their unbelief (1 Corinthians 10:1–5). Instead, enter the rest of God through faith (Hebrews 4:1–3). It is God's grace that has redeemed us and put us in right standing with God (Ephesians 2:8–9). So we need to allow the grace of God to work in and through us.

It is vital for us to understand that we are not to sit around doing nothing because we have been saved by grace through faith. God has given us His grace to do the works He has assigned for us to do. He has given each of us grace in different areas to build the Kingdom of God. Some of us He has given the grace to teach, others to preach and exhort. Some believers just love to serve or evangelize. We have to find what it is that God wants us to do, and then just do it. Then it will not be motivated by self-effort or the flesh, but by love for God. This makes a big difference as we seek to fulfill our destiny in Him.

Scripture Readings:
Isaiah 53:1–12
Galatians 3:13–14; 5:16–26
Ephesians 2:8–9

November 21

Don't Allow Your Emotions to Overrule God's Favor

Why am I discouraged? Why is my heart sad? I will put my hope in God! I will praise Him again—my Savior and my God! Now I am deeply discouraged, but I will remember You—even from distant Mount Hermon, the source of the Jordan, from the land of Mount Mizar. (Psalm 42:5–6)

God's favor is available to us, but it will take faith in order to obtain it. We should profess every day that the favor of God surrounds us (Psalm 5:12), as this will increase our faith in this area because faith comes by hearing the Word of God (Romans 10:17). But in order to do this, we need to define what the favor of God is. The best definition I have found is a demonstrated delight. The favor of God can be described as tangible evidence that a person has the approval of God. When we favor someone, we give them special treatment because we like or admire them. The same is true with God. Since God has no favorites and we are in Christ Jesus, we can all experience the favor of God in our lives.

A great example of someone who walked in the favor of the Lord was Joseph (Genesis 39–41). It didn't matter what happened to him, Joseph always wound up landing on his feet. He was betrayed by his brothers and thrown in a pit to die, he was lied about and thrown in prison, but through all of that God was with him, and he wound up being second in command in the greatest nation at the time. Joseph had the favor of God upon him.

Our current circumstances don't dictate the favor of God in our life. We might be going through a hard time right now, and it might not seem like the favor of God is working on our behalf. Our emotions cannot overrule the favor of God, and we cannot let our words talk us into having a negative attitude. If we start singing the blues, that is exactly what we will get.

Instead, be like the psalmist David and speak to your soul and ask it, "Why are you depressed?" Sometimes you need to speak to yourself and encourage yourself in the Lord. Your inner man needs to take over so that you get some "get right" in your thinking. You need to tell yourself, "I am highly favored of the Lord. So why am I feeling down?" That will increase our positive thoughts, which will produce hormones that are helpful to our mind and body.

Scripture Readings:
Genesis 39–41
Psalm 5:12; 23:5–6
Romans 8:28

November 22

THE GIFTS OF THE SPIRIT

God has given each of you a gift from His great variety of spiritual gifts. Use them well to serve one another. (1 Peter 4:10)

As believers in the body of Christ, we have been given gifts from the Holy Spirit to benefit others. The gifts of the Spirit and the fruit of the Spirit are different in nature. The fruit of the Spirit are the results of the Spirit of God living inside of us, producing His character within us. Because we have the Spirit of God living within us, we should be producing the fruit of the Spirit, which are love, joy, peace, patience, kindness, goodness, faithfulness, gentleness, and self-control (Galatians 5:22–23). These fruit of the Spirit should be manifested in every believer's life.

On the other hand, the gifts of the Spirit are more specific and not every believer will have the same gifts. Some believers have the gift of prophecy, and some have the gift of healing. Not everyone will have all the gifts of the Spirit. These gifts are the word of wisdom, the word of knowledge, the discernment of spirits, the gift of great faith, the gift of healing, the power to perform miracles, the ability to speak in unknown tongues, and the ability to interpret tongues (1 Corinthians 12:7–11). Each of these are given by the discretion of the Holy Spirit to equip the believer for the specific assignment they are to do. God will not ask us to do something He has not equipped us to do.

If God has called us to minister healing, He will anoint us with the power to heal. We will have a desire to lay hands on people and heal them— we will have a passion for that. Not everyone has that passion. Another believer might be called to counsel people. Well, God will give them the word of knowledge, the word of wisdom, and the discernment of spirits. Not every believer has that specific calling on their lives. These are just two examples of the gifts operating in believers' lives for the benefit of the body of Christ.

The best way to know what your gifts are is by finding out what you are passionate about. Usually, what you are passionate about will indicate what your gift is, but not always. I highly recommend you read *Gifts of the Holy Spirit* by Kenneth E. Hagin. It is an excellent book that goes into detail on each of the different gifts of the Spirit.

The apostle Peter encourages us to use our gifts for the benefit of others, because doing so brings glory to God. Remember, we will have to give an account for the gift God has given to us. Don't be like the foolish servant who buried his talent in the dirt (Matthew 25:24–26), because God was not happy with him. Instead, use the talents God has given you to bring glory to the Kingdom of God.

Scripture Readings:
1 Corinthians 12:7–11
1 Timothy 4:14
1 Peter 4:10–11

November 23

THE WORD OF WISDOM, THE WORD OF KNOWLEDGE, AND THE DISCERNMENT OF SPIRITS

One of them named Agabus stood up in one of the meetings and predicted by the Spirit that a great famine was coming upon the entire Roman world. (This was fulfilled during the reign of Claudius.) (Acts 11:28)

The word of wisdom, the word of knowledge, and the discernment of spirits are all revelation gifts. They are designed to reveal future and current events and provide insight into specific situations. Quite often in the Old Testament, the word of wisdom and knowledge operated together, them being the gifts Elijah and Elisha used quite often in their ministries (1 Kings 17:1–2 Kings 13:21). If we study these Scriptures, we will see how they used the word of wisdom and knowledge. Every story I read about these two men of God, I would make a point of discovery about which gift was operating in their lives. It was fun, and I also became more acquainted with these particular gifts.

In my opinion, these three gifts are the most functional and should be desired by every believer. Because of their functionality, they can be used in everyday life. Just think of the time we could save by using the word of wisdom and knowledge, the problems that could be avoided if we had the insight to see what was going to happen before it actually happened, thus causing us to choose what God desired rather than what we desired. Imagine the potential conflicts that could be avoided; just think of the benefit we could be to others using these gifts on their behalf.

The Bible says we are to covet the gifts of the Spirit, so it is all right to ask God for a specific gift that we desire. The very desire we have may be an indication of the gift God wants to give us. As I said yesterday, God has given all of us specific gifts. Some He has given more than one to, but we all have at least one of the gifts of the Spirit. It is possible to be given a gift for a specific task only, then that gift will not operate in our life ever again.

The gifts of the Spirit are specific—the only person who operated in all the gifts during His ministry on earth was Jesus (John 3:34). So ask God to reveal to you the gift He has for you, and then get to work!

I have an exercise for you to do today. I had mentioned reading in the Old Testament about the lives of Elijah and Elisha, two men who were greatly used by God. We can see how they operated in the spiritual gifts of the word of wisdom and the word of knowledge, as well as the gifts of great faith with the working of miracles and healings. Read the below Scriptures and pick out which gift was in operation at specific times. It may take some time to read through them all, but I guarantee that you will be blessed if you do.

Scripture Readings:
1 Kings 17:1–2 Kings 13:21

November 24

WATER YOURSELF WITH THE WORD OF GOD

I planted the seed in your hearts, and Apollos watered it, but it was God who made it grow. (1 Corinthians 3:6)

When we accepted Jesus Christ as our Lord and Savior, the seed of God was planted in our inner being. It was placed there so that through use and over time it would grow and flourish. But in order for that seed to grow, it needs the water of the Spirit. Like a seed in the natural, if we don't water and care for that seed, it will not grow and it will in fact eventually die. However, we have the incorruptible seed of God within us that can never die (1 Peter 1:23), but we can determine how much fruit we produce in our lives.

Some believers are producing a lot of fruit in their lives. They are increasing in every area and the favor of God is evident in all they do. But there are others who are producing very little fruit and are not experiencing increase at all. The reason for this is the amount of time they are spending watering the Word within them.

Jesus compared the seed to the Word of God (Mark 4:24–32). Much like a farmer knows that planting the seed is only the beginning of the process, and in order to produce a crop the farmer will have to make sure that the crop is watered regularly, it is the same in the spiritual realm. We have to make sure that we are watering the seed of God's Word if we are to get a harvest.

We can water the Word of God in several ways. The first is by hearing it. How much time do you spend hearing the Word? For some, the only time they hear the Word of God is when they go to church on Sundays. How physically developed would a child be if he were fed only once a week? That is why some believers are not increasing in their lives.

Another way to water the Word of God is through meditation, prayer, and decreeing. When we meditate on a Scripture, we are muttering over that Scripture in our minds. Then we are speaking what we have read, and we are making a formal decree to God. God will then make sure that the angels get involved because they harken to His commands (Psalm 103:20). It is important for us to continually give ourselves to watering the seed of God's Word that dwells within us. For as we do, God will give the increase and cause it to flourish.

Scripture Readings:
Mark 4:24–32
1 Corinthians 3:6
1 Peter 1:23

November 25

THE IMPORTANCE OF THE DECREE

You shall also decide and decree a thing, and it shall be established for you; and the light [of God's favor] shall shine upon your ways. (Job 22:28 AMP)

We hold a position in the Kingdom of God that allows us to use the authority of the Kingdom to speak forth God's will on this planet. When we speak the will of God over our lives and the circumstances surrounding us, we are making a decree. Since we were made to be kings and priests by Christ Jesus (Revelation 1:5), we have the right to make heavenly decrees. Jesus said, "Whatever you forbid on earth will be forbidden in heaven" (Matthew 16:19).

When we make a decree according to the will of God, we are speaking God's Word back to Him, which gives Him permission to perform His will in our lives. We can see a picture of this in Isaiah 55:10–11. God has given us His Word, and speaking His Word back to Him releases the angels to work on our behalf (Psalm 103:20). Many believers are unaware of the power of the decree, so they seldom use it. Instead, they will say something contrary to the will of God, which is a decree in the negative sense. This prevents the angels from doing anything on their behalf, because angels are only allowed to act on God's Word. It also gives the enemy license to bring upon the believer what they have spoken.

If we read through the book of Job, we will see one of the reasons the enemy targeted him. Job feared that what happened to him was going to happen (Job 3:25). He probably spoke negative confessions repeatedly, which gave the enemy license to kill his children and steal his herd and flocks. Once he realized what he had done was wrong, however, he repented and started making statements that agreed with God's Word. In the end, Job got back all he had lost.

Like Job before us, we can change our decree from a negative one to a positive one. We need to be aware of the power of our words and only speak things that we want to see happen. We also need to find the promises of God that pertain to our situation and start to speak them back to Him. You see, this was the key to Jesus's success—He only said what He saw His Father saying (John 5:19–20). Each one of us has been commissioned to do just that (John 14:12)—so start decreeing the will of God in your life today!

Scripture Readings:
Job 22:28
Psalm 103:20
Isaiah 55:10–11
Matthew 16:19
John 5:18–20, 30; 14:12

November 26

YOU ARE GOD'S ULTIMATE DESIGN

Then God blessed them and said, "Be fruitful and multiply. Fill the earth and govern it. Reign over the fish in the sea, the birds in the sky, and all the animals that scurry along the ground." (Genesis 1:28)

When God created man in the Garden of Eden, He wanted someone He could fellowship with. He wanted someone He could communicate with, so He created a being in a similar class as Himself. Now, don't think that I am saying that humans are equal with God. There is only one God, but we are in the same class as God. He gave enough of His characteristics to us so that we could communicate with Him in an intimate way.

God wanted a family here on earth. He created this planet specifically for the habitation of humanity. We have the perfect blend of oxygen and hydrogen so that we can exist in our day-to-day lives. We are just far enough away from the sun to have a perfect climate for habitation, and the earth has been perfectly aligned with the other planets in our solar system to provide protection from meteors that could to great damage to our planet.

God created all of this for humans to exist. The original design for the earth was to be a replica of heaven. God placed us on this planet, blessed us, and gave us dominion over all of it. He even gave us something that was not given to the angels—the right to make choices. Angels have the ability to make choices, but not the right to do so. There is no redemption for Satan and his fallen angels because they stepped outside the bounds set for them. Unfortunately, Adam and Eve failed to exercise their dominion over Satan and were deceived into giving their authority over to him. Because they chose to listen to Satan and disobeyed God, the enemy became the lord of this earth.

Their disobedience not only affected all humanity, but the animals and the environment were affected as well (Romans 8:19–20). The entire planet was placed under the curse. Even though this planet was designed to be a paradise, it was now under a curse with a new god reigning over it. Adam was reborn. He went from life to death. He could no longer receive direct revelation from God because he was spiritually dead. He could only rely on his physical senses to guide and direct him. His soul was in the driver's seat. But God immediately put a plan into place to redeem humanity. It took over four thousand years, but what God promised finally came to pass—the Messiah was born to redeem all of humanity (Galatians 3:13–14, 29).

Now those who have accepted Jesus as their Lord and Savior can live the life originally designed for humanity in the Garden. We still have that old nature to contend with, but with the Spirit of God living within us, we have the choice to walk after the Spirit, our higher nature, or follow after our flesh, which is our lower nature. We are faced with the same choices Adam faced, with the only difference being that we have the Bible to guide us as well as the Holy Spirit. We can still fulfill God's plan. We can use the gifts God has provided and do exploits for the glory of God and the Kingdom of God—Jesus said we could (John 14:12). But do we believe Him?

Scripture Readings:
Genesis 1:26–28
Romans 5:12–17; 8:1–30
Galatians 3:13–14, 29

November 27

Jesus: The Last Adam

The Scriptures tell us, "The first man, Adam, became a living person." But the last Adam—that is, Christ— is a life-giving Spirit. (1 Corinthians 15:45)

I love the Word of God because it is alive and active (Hebrews 4:12), which means that we can read the same Scripture every day and still see something different each time. This happens because it is not the words but the Spirit in those words who speaks to our spirit. There is revelation to be found, and it never stops flowing. I saw something today I never grasped before. I have read this Scripture countless times, but this time the Holy Spirit gave me an understanding I would like to share with you. I know that some of you will not completely understand what I am about to share, but I encourage you to read with an open mind.

Jesus came to the earth for two reasons: The first, as most believers know, is to save humanity from our sins and restore us to the position that we once held before the fall (Galatians 3:13–14). The other reason that is not as much recognized today, or at least not talked about, was to show us what Adam was like before the fall. To take that idea even further, Jesus wanted to show us what we are capable of doing while on the earth. Just think about some of the statements Jesus made to His disciples.

For example, when Jesus walked on water and Peter asked Him to do the same, Peter stepped out of the boat and walked on water for a short period of time. He only began to sink when he allowed doubt and fear to enter his mind (Matthew 14:22–33). Jesus later rebuked Peter for his doubt.

Another time Jesus and the disciples were in a boat in the middle of a lake when a great storm arose, and the disciples were afraid that they were going to drown because of the intensity of the storm. When they woke Jesus up from sleep, He spoke to the wind and the waves, and they became still. Jesus asked them where their faith was (Mark 4:35–41). Finally, He told

His disciples that all the things they witnessed Him doing, they could do also (John 14:12). Why would Jesus say something like that if it were not true?

When I read Genesis 1:26, that God created man in His image and likeness, and then I read in Colossians 1:15 that Jesus was the visible image of the invisible God, a light bulb came on in my head. I suddenly saw it! Adam, in his original state, was the visible image of God on the earth. God wanted humanity to be the physical representation of Himself, just like Jesus was thousands of years later.

What Jesus did we are capable of also doing. It will require we change our paradigm to the mind of Christ, which means we have to renew our minds to a new way of thinking about our faith (Romans 12:1–2). The apostles and the early church understood this and that is why we read about the great exploits they did in the book of Acts. Through false teaching and traditions of religion, the power of the church has been greatly diminished. It's time that it came back!

Scripture Readings:
Genesis 1:26–28
Colossians 1:15
1 Corinthians 15:45–49

November 28

Jesus Wants to Give You Life in Abundance

The thief's purpose is to steal and kill and destroy. My purpose is to give them a rich and satisfying life. (John 10:10)

Jesus was rich and became poor on our behalf (2 Corinthians 8:9). Therefore, every believer has the right to live an abundant life if they live that life in Christ. God made this possible through Christ Jesus. Unfortunately, there are many believers who are not experiencing that kind of life. Some are just ignorant and think Jesus only died for their sins, and they will experience the abundant life when they get to heaven. These types of believers only have a plantation faith.

When slavery was legal in this country, the plantation owners would handpick the preacher because of the influence he had on the other slaves. They wanted someone to preach about submission to the master because the slave would be rewarded when he got to heaven. It was a form of brainwashing. So many slaves just accepted their position, thinking God would be happy with them and they would receive their reward when they got to heaven. This can be plainly seen by just reading some of the old-time spiritual songs.

Satan was behind that strategy, and he is employing the same strategy against the church today. Most of the churches are having a hard time financially. They have resorted to rummage sales, having raffles, selling chicken dinners, and having car washes in order to raise money. Some have avoided this dilemma by compromising the message of the gospel to please their audiences rather than pleasing God. They have become user-friendly churches that have a form of godliness but denied the power of God (2 Timothy 3:5).

Jesus died not only to save us from our sins, but to also make it possible for us to live a life of abundance. This doesn't mean we will not go through challenges from time to time, because we live in a fallen world. But we should have the confidence to know that we will overcome anything that comes against us (Romans 8:37).

Jesus demonstrated to us what we are capable of doing if we commit to living according to the Word of God and Kingdom principles. He showed us the kind of life Adam lived before the fall. Adam didn't sweat or toil; he just used his faith and his words to get things done. The angels were there waiting for the Word of God to come out of his lips, ready to perform what he commanded (Psalm 103:20).

We have been restored by Jesus to the position Adam had before the fall, where we are just below God Himself (Psalm 8:5). Yes, it is true! Read the Scriptures for yourself. This means that Satan should be under our feet.

Scripture Readings:
John 10:10–21
2 Corinthians 8:9
Ephesians 3:20

November 29

Jesus Sowed His Seed to Get a Harvest

Jesus replied, "Now the time has come for the Son of Man to enter into His glory. I tell you the truth, unless a kernel of wheat is planted in the soil and dies, it remains alone. But its death will produce many new kernels—a plentiful harvest of new lives." (John 12:23–24)

The Bible is the most amazing book I have ever read. It is like a big puzzle, and through revelation we can put the pieces together in order to get the whole picture. I started reading the Bible again from the beginning, and before I even got halfway done, what I imagined would be boring turned out to be the opposite. God has shown me things this time I had not seen the last time I read through the Bible. We have two sets of eyes, our natural eyes that we physically see with, and our spiritual eyes that we see in the spiritual realm with (Ephesians 1:17–19). I have been asking God to open my spiritual eyes to give me insight into His Word, and He has been doing just that.

Jesus is the Word of God with a physical body. And we know that the Word of God is also the seed of God (Luke 8:11). Therefore, we can say that Jesus is the seed of God. He said that if we are to understand how the Kingdom of God works, we need to understand the principle of seedtime and harvest (Mark 4:26–29). The Kingdom of God operates on this principle, so if we want to get anything out of the Kingdom of God we must acquaint ourselves with this system.

Jesus's assignment was to plant His seed into the earth so He would receive a harvest. He sacrificed His life in the natural to get a harvest in the spiritual. Just like a farmer plants seeds into the soil to later reap a harvest, so Jesus planted His seed into the soil of our hearts to get a harvest. Every seed produces after its kind, so Jesus planted Himself to get more people like Himself.

When a farmer plants a kernel of corn in the ground, he expects to get back more than one kernel of corn. Likewise, when Jesus died, it was for the purpose of multiplication. There are countless believers who have the potential to walk and act like Jesus. Because we are in Christ Jesus, when Satan looks at us he sees Jesus because we are in Him (John 17:20–24). Let that marinate in your inner man. You are more powerful than you think. The whole strategy of the enemy is to keep you ignorant of this fact so that you will stay in the natural realm where he can dominate you. You are the replica of Jesus! Don't ever forget that.

Scripture Readings:
Mark 4:26–29
John 12:23–24; 17:20–24
Ephesians 2:10

November 30

YOU ARE GOD'S MASTERPIECE

For we are God's masterpiece. He has created us anew in Christ Jesus, so we can do the good things He planned for us long ago. (Ephesians 2:10)

Do you realize how unique you truly are? You are God's masterpiece! This is hard to believe sometimes, but that doesn't make it untrue. Many people suffer from an inferiority complex. They have failed to see their uniqueness or have been told by loved ones that they are no good. Many believers are walking around today with the emotional bruises of yesterday. They see themselves as failures because of poor choices they may have made in the past. Others condemn themselves because of moral weaknesses and bad habits. Then there is the accuser of the brethren who likes to point out every mistake we make.

But when God looks at us, He sees a masterpiece—He sees what we are capable of being, not how we see ourselves. Many of us are too hard on ourselves, and speak negatively about ourselves and the circumstances we are in. Instead of doing that, we should speak what we want to see happen. Too many people are quick to tell what is happening in their lives, instead of what they want to happen. God has given us the power and the ability to speak His promises over any circumstance we encounter. We only need to use our spiritual eyes to see what God has planned for our life. Then we can tell ourselves that we are God's masterpiece and He has created us to fulfill His purpose on the earth.

Your life might not be reflecting what God has planned, but nothing is impossible with God. He can take any negative circumstances and turn them around for good. You may have made a poor choice and acted foolishly, but that does not nullify the power of God from working in your life. You only have to acknowledge your mistake and move on. You might have to face some consequences for your actions, but that doesn't mean God is punishing you; you are just reaping what you have sown (Galatians

6:7). Don't allow your feelings to dictate who you are. They can change like the weather, but the Word of God remains the same. You are God's masterpiece, no matter how you feel, what you say, or what you do. Don't let this world or others define who you are, for you are God's masterpiece, the apple of God's eye (Zechariah 2:8).

Scripture Readings:
Psalm 17:8
Zechariah 2:8
Ephesians 2:10

November 31

You Are to Be Holy

I am a special messenger from Christ Jesus to you Gentiles. I bring you the Good News so that I might present you as an acceptable offering to God, made holy by the Holy Spirit. (Romans 15:16)

Most people think being holy means that we are upright in the way that we conduct ourselves. Though this is true, *holy* means so much more that. A better definition of being holy means that we are set apart. When we hear some people say that the Bible is a *holy* book, they are really saying that it is set apart from all other books. It is special and unique. When a person makes Jesus their Lord and Savior, they are immediately set apart from all the non-believers in the world. He or she becomes a new creation is Christ Jesus (2 Corinthians 5:17).

It has always been God's desire to have a family. That is why He created Adam in His image and likeness, and He blessed him and told him to multiply on this planet (Genesis 1:26–28). God wanted a family of beings created in His image and likeness. He later told Abram to separate himself from his relatives and then promised to make him into a great nation (Genesis 12:1–3). And God later took the children of Israel out of Egypt in order to make them a nation of priests (Exodus 19:5–6). His desire was always to have a people who are set apart for Him.

Peter echoed this thought throughout his writings. He said that we are a chosen people, royal priests, a holy nation, and God's own possession (1 Peter 2:9–10). We are a people separated out of the kingdom of darkness and called into the Kingdom of Light (Colossians 1:13). Jesus purchased us through His death and resurrection so that God could have the family He longed for. He has made us to be kings and priests so that we can represent Him. We are to be ambassadors of the Kingdom of God (2 Corinthians 5:20).

Only thinking of holiness as a way we conduct ourselves is myopic. It is so much more than that. A person is not holy because of the way they conduct themselves, but because of what Jesus did on the cross on their behalf. We are holy because of the finished work of Christ Jesus (1 Corinthians 1:30)—nothing else. When God gave me this revelation not too long ago, it became easier for me to conduct myself in a holy manner because I realized it was not based on my self-effort, but on the grace of God. I still have my struggles; however, I overcome them because I am the holiness of God.

Scripture Readings:
Genesis 1:26–28; 12:1–3
Exodus 19:5–6
1 Corinthians 1:30
1 Peter 2:9–10
Revelation 1:6

December 1

LET JESUS LIVE IN AND THROUGH YOU

For in Him we live and move and exist. (Acts 17:28)

If we are to live above the average Christian experience and see the supernatural manifested in our lives, we are going to have to go beyond the traditions and doctrines of the status quo. That may mean some of our "Christian friends" might think we are completely crazy. This should not surprise us, however, because people thought the same about Jesus. It is recorded in the book of Mark that Jesus's family thought He was out of His mind (Mark 3:21). So if we want to do the things Jesus did, then we have to be prepared to be marginalized by others. If Jesus went through it, what makes us think that we won't have to go through it too?

Many believers hear a message of faith and get excited—they are fired up and ready to set the world on fire. In their zeal they tell their best friend or family about what they learned, and then the looks and negative reports come flooding in. They will hear story after story about how faith didn't work for so and so, thus they should be more reserved in their faith. The believer then gets confused because these are Christians telling them this. At that point, a choice has to be made: Will they play it safe and stay in the boat by listening to them, or take a step out of the boat in order to follow Jesus?

If they choose to stay in the boat, they will never experience the supernatural realm, ultimately relegating themselves to a mediocre Christian existence. However, if they choose to step outside the boat, they will open themselves up to experience the fullness of God, witnessing and doing remarkable things for the Kingdom. Unfortunately, many believers choose the former over the latter. For those who choose to believe God's Word and follow the teachings of Jesus, they will do exploits for the Kingdom of God.

For those of you who have decided to step out of the boat, you are to be congratulated. It takes strength and conviction to go against the grain in our society. It is much easier to go with the flow, which is why so many choose that path. One thing to remember is that it will always be Jesus within us who does the work. We can't rely on how many times we attend church, how much time we spend in prayer, fast, or read our Bibles. All these things are good and should be done, but it is not about self-effort and works. It's about grace through faith. It's about living a life where you are God conscious and will do what you are led to do and say what you are led to say (John 5:19–20, 30)

This was the secret to Jesus's success. And this is what the apostle Paul meant when he said, "For in Him we live and move and exist" (Acts 17:28). It is in Christ Jesus that our power is generated to be more than overcomers and experience the supernatural in this world.

Scripture Readings:
Acts 17:28
Ephesians 2:10
Philippians 2:13; 4:13

December 2

BE PATIENT: CHANGE IS A PROGRESSION

Now we see things imperfectly, like puzzling reflections in a mirror, but then we will see everything with perfect clarity. All that I know now is partial and incomplete, but then I will know everything completely, just as God now knows me completely. (1 Corinthians 13:12)

Our walk with the Lord is a journey. Along the way we will have ups and downs, we will make mistakes and fall short. *When* this occurs—not *if*—there will be opportunity for condemnation to come, trying to drag us down even further. But we cannot let it. Rather, we must realize that this is all part of the growth process. God will not let us fail. He will never give up on us. Will we give up on ourselves? That is what the enemy wants from us. He will try to discourage us and plant seeds of doubt in our minds, telling us how much of a failure we are, but we have to know that's not how God feels about us.

When a person accepts Jesus as their Lord and Savior, they become a new creation in Christ (2 Corinthians 5:17). Their spirit becomes filled with the Spirit of God, and they are perfect in God's sight. However, their soul, which is made up of the mind, will, and emotions, continues to be the same. And their body is still the same too. So it is up to the believer to get his soul and body aligned with the born-again spirit within him. This is a process that will take some effort. A paradigm shift will have to take place through renewing the mind (Romans 12:1–2).

The more time we spend reading and studying the Word of God, the clearer we will see who we really are in Christ Jesus. We will develop our spiritual eyes and not rely on the natural eyes to tell us who we are. The more revelation we get from the Word, the more we become like Jesus, because we will become what we think most about. If we think fearful thoughts, then we will become afraid; if we think positive thoughts, then we will become more positive. The same principle applies here as well. The

Kingdom of God is based on the principle of sowing and reaping. If we want to reap a harvest, then we are going to have to sow a seed.

The Word is the seed of God (Luke 8:11). So if we sow the Word into our heart, it will produce a crop. Every seed will produce after its kind, so if we sow the Word we can expect to reap the Word in our life. It will produce—it has no choice. This is why Jesus admonished His disciples to pay attention to what they hear, because the more attention they gave to what was said the more understanding they would receive (Mark 4:24–25). Don't be discouraged when you miss the mark and stumble and even fall, because God will pick you up again (Psalm 37:23–24).

Scripture Readings:
Psalm 37:23–24
Romans 12:1–2
2 Corinthians 5:17
Philippians 2:13

December 3

From Doctrine to Glory

There is much more we would like to say about this, but it is difficult to explain, especially since you are spiritually dull and don't seem to listen. You have been believers so long now that you ought to be teaching others. Instead, you need someone to teach you again the basic things about God's word. You are like babies who need milk and cannot eat solid food. (Hebrews 5:11–12)

The writer of Hebrews rebuked the believers this letter was address to for their lack of spiritual progress. I wonder if this same rebuke could be used for many of us today. There are many believers who are stuck. They have the routine of attending church service regularly, even bringing their Bibles, but they don't even open their Bibles; and there are others who only open them when they attend church. There are some believers who rely totally on what is being taught from the pulpit. This could be dangerous.

I met a woman while on vacation in Maui that professed to be a Christian. She was complaining about being depressed. I asked her what she was depressed about, because she was on vacation in one of the most beautiful places in the world. She owned her own business and was healthy. When I pointed all this out to her, she just nodded her head.

Somehow during our conversation the topic of hell came up. She exclaimed that she didn't believe in hell. I then told her that hell is spoken of in the Bible, and that Jesus spoke of hell too. She then looked at me and said she didn't believe that the Bible was the Word of God, and that men, who weren't inspired by God, wrote it. Once she said that, I quickly changed the subject. I realized why she was depressed. On another occasion, I was in a conversation with a person who said she was a Presbyterian. She prided herself on the work her church did in the community, but she confided in me that she didn't read the Bible.

These are just two examples I can think of that illustrate the point I am making here. The reason why the church is not experiencing the miraculous signs and wonders that can be found in the book of Acts is because of the lack of revelation a majority of the believers have in the church today. It takes revelation knowledge to acquire the things of God. The apostle Paul prayed for the Ephesian believers that God would give them the revelation knowledge to gain understanding into the things of God (Ephesians 1:17–19).

Some believers read their Bibles without revelation, and they don't experience the riches that can be found in the words. Teachings have become a formula to them, which is why they seldom work. God is a rewarder of those who diligently seek Him (Hebrews 11:6). How does He reward? By giving us revelation and insight into how the Kingdom of God works. With this we can receive anything we ask for. If we want to see the glory of God manifested in our life, then we need to be diligent in seeking the revelation of God. Just ask and you will receive (Matthew 7:8).

Scripture Readings:
1 Corinthians 3:1–4
Hebrews 5:11–14

December 4

You Need Revelation to See the Manifestation

He reveals the deep and secret things; He knows what is in the darkness, and the light dwells with Him! (Daniel 2:22 AMP)

It's is God's desire that His people magnify His glory in the earth today. We have the potential to live a life that resembles the life Jesus lived (John 14:12). But this type of life is not automatic; it will take some diligence on the part of the believer so they can renew their mind and change their paradigm to the mind of Christ (1 Corinthians 2:16).

When a person accepts the Lord as their Savior, their spirit is immediately reborn from death to life, but their flesh, which includes the soul and the body, remains the same. A person can be a believer but live the rest of their life being ruled by their flesh. People like this are referred to as "carnal Christians"—they are saved but they live as though they were still in the world. The principles of the Kingdom of God are foreign to them.

Too many believers today fall into this category. Being carnal doesn't necessarily mean that you are not living what some would consider a moral life; to be carnal means that you are living a life that is ruled by the senses, not by the Spirit (Romans 8:1). A believer can live a very upright life, follow all the rules, and still be carnal. Why is this? If their behavior is based only on their self-effort, without being led by the Holy Spirit, then the flesh generates their conduct. There are many believers who are religious, basing their righteousness on following rules and regulations. But in reality their righteousness should be based on the finished work of Christ Jesus alone (Romans 3:12–22).

As believers we are to walk in the Spirit, which means we are to look to the Holy Spirit to reveal God's truths to us. One of the functions of the Holy Spirit is to lead and guide us into all truth (John 16:13). It is through revelation that the Kingdom of God is opened to us.

In the book of Mark, Jesus gave the parable of the sower sowing the Word. After He taught the people, He pulled His disciples away and explained what the parable meant, which means not everyone who heard the parable understood what it meant (Mark 4:11–12). A person can read their Bible regularly and not completely understand what they are reading because they lack revelation knowledge.

When I was attending Bible college and seminary for my master's degree, I had professors who had great knowledge of the Scriptures. They could tell you all about the historical facts that went along with the Bible stories, but most of them had little or no revelation knowledge. Their knowledge was in the mental realm alone.

If we look at every person whom God has used to do mighty works, we will see that they had revelation knowledge that separated them from the rest. In order to be used by God in a significant way, we need to ask God to give us revelation knowledge and open the eyes of our understanding (Ephesians 1:17–19). This is so that we can see what God wants us to do in our life.

Scripture Readings:
Daniel 2:22
Mark 4:11–12
John 16:13

December 5

ARE YOU ALLOWING CHRIST TO LIVE IN YOU?

My old self has been crucified with Christ. It is no longer I who live, but Christ lives in me. So I live in this earthly body by trusting in the Son of God, who loved me and gave Himself for me. I do not treat the grace of God as meaningless. For if keeping the law could make us right with God, then there was no need for Christ to die. (Galatians 3:20–21)

For a long time I struggled in my walk with the Lord. I was like the person the apostle Paul wrote about in Romans 7. I knew what I was doing was wrong, but I kept doing it anyway. I wanted to stop and would ask for forgiveness, and I would swear I wouldn't do it again, but I did (Romans 7:14–24). This went on for many years. Thank God for His immense patience with me! Sometimes I would just give up and give in to the pressure to please the desires of my fleshly appetite. And I would rationalize my behavior by telling myself that there are people who do far worse than me. Then I would go out and do something "good" to make myself feel better.

It was not until I received the revelation of the finished work of Christ that I realized I could live a life pleasing to the Lord, and not bow my knee to the desires of my flesh. I could do this by letting Christ live His life in and through me. When I allowed Christ to live in me, I didn't desire to do those things that plagued me before. I didn't have to struggle at all. In fact, I wanted to live a life that was pleasing to Him. Jesus said that we should take His yoke upon us and learn from Him, for His yoke is easy and His burden is light (Matthew 11:28–30).

If we will learn to walk in the Spirit and not the flesh, then we open ourselves up to allow Jesus to live the Christ life through us. It is then Jesus giving us the desire and the will to do His will (Philippians 2:13). We no longer have to rely on our self-effort but the life of God within us. And it is at this point where we understand what Acts 17:28 means, for we live and move and have our being in Christ Jesus.

This was the secret to the power the early church had. They trusted in the finished work of Jesus and allowed the power of God to flow through them. God wants His church to do signs and wonders once again before His coming. It will happen, but only those who are prepared and ready will manifest the glory of God. Will you be one of them? If so, then start today by allowing Jesus to live His life through you.

Scripture Readings:
Matthew 11:28–30
John 14:12; 17:21–24
Galatians 3:20
Philippians 2:13; 4:13

December 6

BALANCE IS THE KEY

So don't be too good or too wise! Why destroy yourself? On the other hand, don't be too wicked either. Don't be a fool! Why die before your time? Pay attention to these instructions, for anyone who fears God will avoid both extremes. (Ecclesiastes 7:16–18)

What I have found is that having balance in our life is one of the most important things we can do for our growth in Christ. There are people who are workaholics—they work all the time. They neglect their family and loved ones because they are totally focused on their profession or making money. Then there are those who just want to party and have fun all the time. This also is not good.

There are believers who live for nothing but the church. Their life revolves around church activities, and they consider it worldly to be involved in any secular entertainment. They wouldn't dare go to a movie unless it was biblically based. Then on the other hand, there are those believers who live on the edge—we wouldn't even know they were Christians by the way they live their life.

Neither one of these lifestyles are healthy. God created this planet for us to enjoy. He gave us His Spirit to guide us, so if we entrust ourselves to the guiding of the Holy Spirit, what is wrong with enjoying some of the pleasures this life has to offer? If we enjoy music, what is wrong with going to see a talented artist? Just because they may not be "Christian" does mean that listening to their music is a sin. I know that there is a lot of trash they call movies, but good movies are still being made, and they are in fact "secular." So what's wrong with going to see a movie from time to time?

I know some believers don't drink alcohol, and that is good. However, there are some who don't think it is wrong to have an occasional drink from time to time. When Jesus was on the earth, He was accused of being a glutton and a drunkard because He drank and ate at various feasts (Matthew

11:19). Jesus was far from being either a drunkard or a glutton, but He enjoyed Himself while He was under the control of the Holy Spirit.

There are many people who get turned off by the church because of the rules and regulations they impose upon their members. Many children turn away from the faith as soon as they are old enough to get out on their own because of the restrictions imposed on them while growing up. A friend of mine wouldn't let his son play football in high school because he thought it was worldly. His son really wanted to play and was actually talented. He knew he might have even gotten a scholarship to play college ball. Instead, he played flag football in some church league with his dad. Now this kid has had several run-ins with the law and has nothing to do with church. What the father feared is what actually happened to him. Maybe it would have been a different story if he weren't so extreme in keeping his son from "worldly" sports.

Scripture Readings:
Ecclesiastes 7:16–20
Matthew 11:18–19

December 7

If You Really Love Jesus, You Will Obey Him

Those who accept My commandments and obey them are the ones who love Me. And because they love Me, My Father will love them. And I will love them and reveal Myself to each of them. (John 14:21)

The best way to tell Jesus you love Him is by obeying His commandments and teachings. There are many who profess how much they love Jesus, but their actions tell a completely different story. They listen to the words of Jesus but will not do what they have been taught. It is like children who tell their parents how much they love them, but they refuse to do anything their parents ask. After a while the parents start to wonder how sincere the children are. If a child really wanted to show love to his or her parents, then they would obey what their parents asked them to do. Obedience is the best way to show someone love and respect.

Many believers worship God with their lips but their hearts are far away (Matthew 15:8–9). True worshippers will show Jesus how much they love Him by obeying His commandments. James says that the individual who is not a doer of the Word but just a listener is only deceiving oneself (James 1:22). But they are not deceiving Jesus!

Jesus's love for us is unconditional. He loves all His children regardless if they love Him back. But we must realize there are rewards for those who are obedient. One of the rewards is that the believer will have the confidence to ask for anything in Jesus's name and know they will receive what they have asked for (John 14:15–16). The second reward is that Jesus will reveal Himself to the believer who obeys what He says. Some believers have more insight and revelation knowledge than others because they are more obedient to Jesus.

The disciples were privileged to have more insight and revelation than others because they were more obedient to His commands and teachings. The same is true today. Those believers who are making more of an effort to follow Jesus are the ones who are getting the revelation and insight into the nature of God. I used to ask myself about why God speaks to Kenneth Hagin, Kenneth Copeland, Charles Capps, and Bill Winston but He doesn't speak to me. I wondered how these men of God got their insight and revelation. But then I began to understand that they got it because of their obedience to the teachings of Jesus. God is not a respecter of persons; He will reward anyone who diligently seeks Him (Hebrews 11:6). So show your love for Jesus today by doing what He says.

Scripture Readings:
Matthew 15:8–9
John 14:15–21
James 1:22–25

December 8

THE LOVE WALK

Jesus replied, "'You must love the Lord your God with all your heart, all your soul, and all your mind.' This is the first and greatest commandment. A second is equally important: 'Love your neighbor as yourself.' The entire law and all the demands of the prophets are based on these two commandments." (Matthew 22:37–39)

If a believer is not walking in love, then they are short-circuiting the power of God from operating in their lives. They are only left with the principles of faith, and thus will get limited results. The world has secularized many of the principles contained in the Bible, and they have been fairly successful in doing so. They have taken Scriptures on faith and watered them down, and then called it positive thinking. In fact, many of the principles of cognitive behavioral therapy are principles that come straight out of the Bible. The principles of God will work for anyone who will apply them; without the power of love, however, the results will be limited.

Believers have to realize that "God is love" is more than a religious cliché; it is a foundational truth of our faith. Love is the power source of faith because it is the essence of who God is. It is the most powerful force in the universe because God is love! That is why we want to keep strife out of our life—strife takes us out of our love walk. Unforgiveness will take us out of our love walk too. Many prayers are not answered because of the unforgiveness in a believer's heart. Jesus said that when we pray, we should forgive anyone we have a grudge against (Mark 11:25). Many will just quote Mark 11:22–24, but they will forget to include Mark 11:25. They are designed to work together.

Jesus also taught that before we offer praise and worship to God, we are to reconcile our disagreements we have with others. This means if a husband and wife were arguing on their way to church, their prayers and worship will be hindered if they don't reconcile because they are not walking in love (Matthew 5:22–24).

The enemy likes to create circumstances that would cause us to walk in strife and create grudges against others. He knows that if we have unforgiveness in our hearts, we lack the power of the love of God working in our life. So we need to be quick to forgive those who have offended us. We also need to be quick to reconcile differences we have with others and come to terms with them quickly. We cannot be so easily offended and defensive with others, because that is not the way of love.

Scripture Readings:
Matthew 5:22–24; 6:14; 22:37–39
Mark 11:25
Ephesians 4:31–32

December 9

Your Treasure Will Determine Your Destiny

Wherever your treasure is, there the desires of your heart will also be. (Matthew 6:21)

Temptation is something we will encounter on a regular basis. Some are successful in their encounters, while others are not. If you are a believer, there should be no reason for you to fall into temptation, unless of course you want to. I say this because, according to the Word of God, "greater is He who is within me than he who is in the world" (1 John 4:4). When temptation comes our way, we have the power to overcome it by the power of Christ residing within us. The reason why we give into temptation is because we fail to use the right strategy.

If you know that you have a weakness in a specific area, why would you put yourself in a position where you are exposed to that temptation? I remember one case I had where the person had a serious substance abuse problem. This man had a successful contracting business, but he lost his license and the business because of his addiction. After losing his business, he got clean and eventually started another business. He was clean for five years and was doing really well.

But one Friday after work he went down to a local bar with some of his friends. At first, he would drink a Coke while the others drank beer, which went on for about a month. Then he decided he was tired of explaining why he would just drink a Coke while the others drank beer. So he allowed himself to have one beer. In a matter of a few weeks, however, he was drinking pitchers of beer and was back on drugs again. This time he wound up in jail and later went to prison.

I could tell you about many stories of people falling into temptation because they refused to exercise their power to say no. How many men and women have left their families because they loved drugs and alcohol more than they loved their family? Jesus said it best, "Wherever your treasure is, there your heart will be also" (Matthew 6:21). If a person's treasure is on the golf course, then that person will make playing golf their priority.

John admonishes us not to love the world, because if we love the world the love of God would not be in us (1 John 2:15–16). Many Christians have abandoned their faith to return back to the world because they love the world more than they love God. It is impossible to serve two masters because we will love one and hate the other, or we will be devoted to one and despise the other (Matthew 6:24).

You will treasure most what you put your attention on. If you consume yourself with reading auto magazines and going to car shows, then your treasure will be set on cars. If you read cooking books and magazines, and then spend several hours a day watching cooking shows on television, your treasure will be set on food and cooking. If you spend your time reading and watching pornography, then your treasure is going to go into pornography. If our treasure is in the things of God, however, that is where our heart will be also. Where our treasure is will determine our destiny.

Scripture Readings:
Matthew 6:21–24
1 Corinthians 10:13
1 John 2:15–16

December 10

THERE IS NO NEED TO BE IN A HURRY

The earth produces the crops on its own. First a leaf blade pushes through, then the heads of wheat are formed, and finally the grain ripens. (Mark 4:28)

Many believers today make the mistake of acting on presumption when they use their faith. They act prematurely and sometimes get themselves into trouble. They read Mark 11:22–25 and get fired up in their faith, then they'll pray for something and believe they have received it, just like the Scriptures say. Off they go in presumption and use their self-effort to make it come to pass instead of waiting for God to make it happen. They started out with God, but then they left God behind and took matters into their own hands. Many well-meaning pastors have jumped the gun and started churches they were not ready for. Now they are struggling financially. Many business ventures have been started and failed because it was not the right time. God wants us to be successful, and the principles of faith do work, but we must remember there is a process and a time for everything.

Like the analogy of the seed Jesus spoke of, how a seed has to grow to maturity before it can be harvested (Mark 4:26–29), so the same is true with the things we pray for. God might have given us a vision of something He wants us to do. That vision was the seed that needed to be planted in our inner man or subconscious mind, germinating and marinating. As we meditate on that vision, it will grow inside of us. In fact, every day that seed is growing until the day it is ready for harvest.

The problem that some believers have is that they will get impatient and take matters into their own hands, trying to help God. Like Abraham and his wife, they will manufacture their own manifestation instead of letting God bring it to pass. What they wind up with is an Ishmael instead of an Isaac. Then they wonder why they are struggling in their daily lives. It is because they did it on their own without the blessing of God.

We have to realize that God knows what is best for us. He knows when we are ready for what He has placed in our heart. We might think we are ready, but we don't have the ability to see into the future. We might think that it is the right time for us to start that business or buy that house, but we didn't know the housing market was going to crash.

Surely you remember the housing crisis in 2008. How many people lost their houses and lost money because of acting on presumption and speculation? We must discipline ourselves to trust God and not act prematurely. Faith and patience work together in order to perfect us, so there is no need to worry or be in a hurry.

Scripture Readings:
Genesis 16:1–15
Ecclesiastes 3:1–8
Mark 4:26–29
James 1:3–4

December 11

Your Decisions Will Open the Door to Your Future

Today I have given you the choice between life and death, between blessings and curses. Now I call on heaven and earth to witness the choice you make. Oh, that you would choose life, so that you and your descendants might live! You can make this choice by loving the Lord your God, obeying Him, and committing yourself firmly to Him. This is the key to your life. And if you love and obey the Lord, you will live long in the land the Lord swore to give your ancestors Abraham, Isaac, and Jacob. (Deuteronomy 30:19–20)

God has given every human being the ability to make choices. When God created humanity, He gave them a will that was designed to make choices, either good or bad. It was God's design to create a being He would be able to fellowship with, so He created humans a little lower than Him. In humanity's original state, we were elevated above the angels (Psalm 8:5–9). That is why Satan hated us and plotted how to usurp our authority. And that's why God didn't intervene when Adam and Eve disobeyed His commandment.

Your will is the key component in making decisions in your life. Your mind, your human spirit, and your physical body can all influence it. If you are a believer, the Holy Spirit can be an influence through your human spirit. All these are just influences; the ultimate decision resides with your will. This means that you have the final say in your destiny and the direction your life will go.

One thing I have noticed by working in corrections is the number of inmates and juveniles who didn't understand the connection between their will and their actions. They were quick to blame others for their problems and troubles in life. They had a "victim mentality," and it's my belief that many cannot break the cycle of incarceration. This issue motivated me to write my first book, *RAP Therapy for Your Prosperity*.

This dilemma is not limited to those in the penal system, however. Many others in our world suffer from the same malady today. Unwilling to take responsibility for the choices they make, they continue to blame others for their misfortune. All this does is exacerbate the problem more and more while providing a false sense of comfort to the alleged victim. A person with this mentality will never live up to their God-given potential and will probably self-sabotage every effort to get ahead.

Some people are afraid to make a decision for fear of making the wrong choice. All this does is keep a person stuck where they are. They will stay in the same miserable situation until they make a decision to change their circumstances. For me, when I am in a position of indecision, I feel uneasy. I have learned to seek God's guidance and trust that Christ within me will direct me. I also know that if I make a decision in faith, God has my back, even if it was the wrong decision (Psalm 37:24). Knowing this takes the pressure and fear off of making the wrong decision.

Even with the assistance of the Holy Spirit, there will be times when we will make the wrong choice. When this happens, we need to acknowledge that we made a poor choice and plead the blood of Jesus over our lives. One thing we cannot do is beat ourselves up over it. All that does is bring on self-condemnation. So cherish the gift that God has given you and use it wisely.

Scripture Readings:
Psalm 37:24
Proverbs 20:27; 21:1

December 12

GOD'S WORD NEVER FAILS

It is the same with My word. I send it out, and it always produces fruit. It will accomplish all I want it to, and it will prosper everywhere I send it. (Isaiah 55:11)

I don't know how people can live in this world today without the Word of God. The world is so unstable and it seems that every day there is a new crisis that has just happened, or one that is impending. I was watching the news last night and it was the civil unrest between Israel and Palestine, then the Malaysian plane that was shot down, and the typhoon that hit Thailand and China. We live in a small and fragile world. I understand why people would seek escape through drugs, alcohol, and other various forms of entertainment. But those solutions will only provide temporary relief.

If you are a believer in the Lord Jesus Christ, then you can witness all the chaos in the world and know that it is not your home, and God will always provide for and protect His people. I was reading in the Old Testament about the nation of Judah and King Hezekiah. Hezekiah was a godly king who honored the Lord. During his reign, a neighboring nation, Assyria, threatened to attack them and force its citizens to leave their land. Hezekiah fortified his nation from attack, but the Assyrians surrounded the capital city so that the people could not get any food or water. Then the Assyrian king sent messengers telling the people to give up. He taunted their God and said He could not and would not save them (2 Kings 18:19–27).

Once Hezekiah heard the threats of the king of Assyria, he called on the prophet Isaiah to seek the guidance of the Lord on Israel's behalf. Isaiah told King Hezekiah that the Lord would deliver Judah from the Assyrians. This promise seemed impossible in the natural realm—their army was no match for the Assyrian army. They had no money to pay allies to assist them. All they had was the Word of the Lord. Hezekiah believed the words of the prophet and he prayed and gave thanks to God. That night an angel of the Lord killed 185,000 Assyrian soldiers (2 Kings 19:35). The Word of God was fulfilled just as the prophet had said.

Like King Hezekiah, you might be looking at situations and circumstances that look hopeless. You might be feeling outside pressure that makes you want to give up and quit. But if you are a believer, that is not an option you want to take. Instead, strengthen yourself in the Lord, look at the Word of God, and find promises to strengthen you. Speak those promises back to God so that He can send angels to assist you (Psalm 103:20). We are to walk by faith and not by what we see in the natural realm (2 Corinthians 5:7). Things in the natural are subject to change, but things in the spiritual realm are eternal.

Scripture Readings:
2 Kings 18:19–19:37
1 John 4:4

December 13

ARE YOU LOOKING WITHIN OR WITHOUT?

This message was kept secret for centuries and generations past, but now it has been revealed to God's people. For God wanted them to know that the riches and glory of Christ are for you Gentiles, too. And this is the secret: Christ lives in you. This gives you assurance of sharing His glory. (Colossians 1:26–27)

There are many people who don't feel good about themselves. Maybe they have a poor self-image because of the way they look, or maybe it might stem from something that was told to them when they were younger by their parents, teachers, or someone in authority; or it could be some bad decision they made in the past they have not let go of—any number of things could cause a person not to feel good about themselves. But all of these are based on external forces alone.

We as believers have the choice of allowing the world to define our reality, or the Word of God can define it. If we are a believer in Christ Jesus, we are a new creation in Him (2 Corinthians 5:17). This means the old us has passed away, and we have become a new being who has never existed before. Our family and friends might look at us the same and try to keep us in that same old mold, but in the eyes of God we are perfect. This is because of the life of Christ Jesus who resides in us (Galatians 2:20). All that is needed is to renew our minds.

We don't have to compare ourselves to others because God created us with unique talents and abilities that no other person possesses. This world likes conformity, promoting it because it is easier to control people when they all think and act the same. We cannot let others define our reality, but the Word of God must define who we are. We are citizens of the Kingdom of heaven. We are God's chosen people and belong to a royal priesthood, God's own possession (1 Peter 2:9). We need to tell ourselves that the next time we are feeling depressed or discouraged. We are the workmanship of

Jesus, so why should we not feel good about ourselves? The only reason we wouldn't is if we are looking without rather than within.

We need to realize the real us is not who we see in the mirror. The real us is a spirit being. What we see in the mirror is the earth suit we have to wear while we are on this planet (2 Corinthians 4:6–7). Most non-believers identify with their physical body and with things in the physical realm only. However, we should identify with the things in the spiritual realm first, then the physical realm, with an emphasis on the spiritual side because that side is eternal. The physical realm is temporal and will eventually fade away.

Scripture Readings:
2 Corinthians 4:6–7; 5:17
Galatians 2:20
1 Peter 2:9

December 14

GOD'S WORD IS THE ULTIMATE TRUTH

Jesus told him, "I am the way, the truth, and the life. No one can come to the Father except through Me." (John 14:6)

Jesus made this statement to His disciples in preparation for His departure. It is something we too should be mindful of as well. Jesus was the Word of God manifested in a physical body (John 1:14). The Word of God is the highest form of reality that exists; it supersedes any other reality in this world. What a person believes to be true will become their reality. If a person believes that things never work out for them, then that will become their reality and will come to pass in their life. If a person believes the diagnosis of the physician, that they have cancer and will eventually die, that will become their reality unless they believe in a higher form of reality.

The report of the physician is truth—their diagnosis is correct. They have factual evidence to prove that the cancer exists in the patient's body. However, there is a higher form of truth that says, "By the stripes of Jesus you have been healed" (Isaiah 53:5). Now the patient has the choice as to which truth they will put their faith in. If the patient puts their faith in the truth of their physician, they will limit the power of God to heal them, relying only on the methods of the physician. However, if the patient puts their faith in the truth of the Word of God, they will allow God to heal them. God may choose to heal them miraculously, or He could use the hands of the physician to do so—it is all according to the faith of the patient.

I am speaking from my own personal experience here. When I had a spinal infection that left me paralyzed from my shoulders down, the physicians thought I would be wheelchair bound for the rest of my life. But I had a Word from God that told me I would recover. I had to make a choice as to what I was going to put my faith in. I chose the Word of God, and from that point on it didn't matter what the doctors or the therapists told me. God said I would walk again and that I would fully recover from this illness. He also told me that it would not be a miraculous healing, but it would happen over a period of time. I didn't ask why, I just received His Word.

Today I am walking and doing practically everything the medical experts said I would not be able to do. I am not fully recovered in the natural, but I know that I will be very soon because I have faith in the ultimate truth, God's Word. The choice is up to us as to which truth will become our reality: God's truth or the world's truth?

Scripture Readings:
Isaiah 55:10–11
John 1:14; 14:1–14

December 15

It's Not According to God's Faith but Yours

They went right into the house where He was staying, and Jesus asked them, "Do you believe I can make you see?" "Yes, Lord," they told Him, "we do." Then He touched their eyes and said, "Because of your faith, it will happen." (Matthew 9:28–29)

I recently attended a church service where the guest speaker was known for healing people through the power of God. The people were excited to hear this man of God speak. He spoke of some of the miracles of healing he had witnessed during his services. With every story, the crowd would cheer and give praise to God. Finally, he called people up to receive healing. I watched as one by one people came up to have hands laid on them. Many fell under the power of the Holy Spirit, but there was no immediate healings that occurred.

I thought to myself, "Why wasn't anyone immediately healed?" I remembered the stories of Jesus healing people, and most were healed immediately. I recalled the stories in the book of Acts where the apostles performed signs and wonders and brought many to the Lord as a result. This wasn't the first time I had witnessed something like this. In fact, it has become commonplace in many churches today. Where does the fault lay? Is it in the man of God? In some cases it is. Many profess to have the power to heal, but it is only fabricated in order to get money. Others *want* the power to heal—they know the principles of how it should work, but they are relying on self-effort, not on the power of God. But there are those who have been anointed to heal, and they act as conduits to channel the healing power of God to the people.

For those who have the anointing to heal, sometimes healing doesn't take place, but it has nothing to do with the person administering the healing. It has more to do with the recipient. The recipient has to be willing to receive in faith. If there is any question in the person's heart about being healed, they won't receive the healing.

There is a story in the book of Mark where Jesus could not heal anyone because of unbelief. In fact, the Scripture says that He marveled at their unbelief (Mark 6:5). But in the previous chapter, Jesus performed several miraculous healings. After two blind men followed Jesus into a home requesting to be healed, Jesus asked them if they believed He could heal them. They both answered yes! Then He touched their eyes and said, "Because of your faith you will be healed." Jesus said a similar thing to the woman with the issue of blood (Matthew 9:22).

It is our faith that determines if we will receive healing! Some people have the faith and the insight to receive a complete healing immediately, while others will receive their healing the moment they make contact with the person anointed to heal, but even that might manifest itself several days later. Ultimately, God is responsible for the power to heal, and He will determine how it will come about. Our job is to believe and receive it, maintaining a spirit of thanksgiving until the manifestation comes. We have to cooperate with God to make it happen.

Scripture Readings:
Matthew 9:18–30

December 16

THE POWER OF THE PRAYERS OF THE RIGHTEOUS

Confess your sins to each other and pray for each other so that you may be healed. The earnest prayer of a righteous person has great power and produces wonderful results. (James 5:16)

Don't underestimate the power of prayer, because prayer can open the windows of heaven. For many believers, prayer has become a ritual, something that we are supposed to do in order to be a Christian. However, prayer is much more than that. It is a spiritual exercise that requires faith and a form of communication that God has established for His people to communicate with Him. Prayer is God's method for allowing His will to be done on the earth. When a believer prays the promises of God back to Him, it allows God to act on their behalf.

We must be careful how we pray. Many people will pray about their circumstances rather than praying the Word concerning their circumstances. When a person prays about the problem, they are just complaining and that is why their prayers are seldom answered. However, when a person prays the promises of God, they have activated the power of God to act on their behalf. It is a way of reminding God of His Word, and God's Word will never fail to produce results (Isaiah 55:10–11).

In the Old Testament, there is a story about King Hezekiah. The prophet Isaiah told him that he was going to die. Once King Hezekiah received this report, he immediately went before God and earnestly prayed that he would be healed. He prayed in faith and reminded God of how faithful He had been. Before Isaiah left the palace, the Lord told him to go back and tell Hezekiah that his prayer had been heard, and he would live for another fifteen years (2 Kings 20:1–10). The doctors may tell you that your condition is terminal and there is no hope, but they are looking at the situation from the natural perspective. You have access to the spiritual realm where nothing is impossible.

Because we are the righteousness of God in Christ Jesus (Romans 3:21–22), we can go into the throne room of God and make our request known to Him, and we can have the confidence to know that we have received what we have asked for (1 John 5:14–15). Prayer is not a waste of time, nor is it something that we do as a last resort. No, it is a way to communicate our needs and desires to God, obtaining the results we desire. We cannot mitigate the power of the prayers of the righteous.

Scripture Readings:
2 Kings 20:1–10
Isaiah 55:10–11
Mark 11:22–24
James 5:16

December 16

How Committed Are You?

Commit everything you do to the Lord. Trust Him, and He will help you. He will make your innocence radiate like the dawn, and the justice of your cause will shine like the noonday sun. Be still in the presence of the Lord, and wait patiently for Him to act. Don't worry about evil people who prosper or fret about their wicked schemes. (Psalm 37:5–7)

One of the reasons why some believers are not experiencing more of the goodness of God is due to a lack of commitment to God's Word. Many will grasp the promises of God with great joy, but all that joy and enthusiasm quickly dissipates when they face hardships and troubles. They are like the seeds planted on the rocky soil, where the seed quickly sprouted, but when the hot sun hit the plant it wilted away (Mark 4:17). Their faith couldn't stand the test of time because of their lack of commitment to the Word of God.

Your commitment to God's Word will indicate how much faith you have in something. Many people will make a New Year's resolution to lose weight and get in shape. They will go to the local gym and even buy a membership. They will go out and buy the shoes and workout clothing, and they are motivated to get in shape. At first they are excited about going to the gym, and they get engaged in their new fitness routine, getting even more excited when they start to notice a difference in their physique. But after a couple of months they hit a plateau—they are not seeing the same results they once did, and they begin to get frustrated. Before long they are missing days and making excuses for not working out. And by April they stop working out altogether.

Many believers are the same way in the spiritual realm. They will hear a speaker who motivates them to believe God and His promises, and they are on fire for a short time. When the problems come with trials and tribulation, they let go of their faith. This happens because of their lack of commitment. If we are truly committed to something, we don't let go or give up.

Thomas Edison was committed to the invention of the light bulb. He had faith that it would work. He didn't get discouraged when his experiments failed. In fact, it is said that he had approximately 9,999 failures before it finally worked. On the 10,000th time he finally got it right. Imagine if he had said, "I've had enough of this. I quit!" after the 9,999th time. Somebody else would have come along and invented the light bulb. This is a small example, but we can see how faith and commitment work together.

There will be times in life when the odds are stacked against us, and the promises of God seem so far away and so unrealistic that we want to throw in the towel and quit. When that happens, we need to remind ourselves that it is impossible for God to lie (Numbers 23:19), and His Word will not return to Him void but will accomplish what it was designed to do (Isaiah 55:10–11). Do like David did and strengthen yourself in the Lord your God!

Scripture Readings:
1 Samuel 30:1–7
Mark 4:13–20
2 Corinthians 1:20

December 17

WHAT YOU FOCUS ON WILL DETERMINE YOUR ATTITUDE

Your eye is a lamp that provides light for your body. When your eye is good, your whole body is filled with light. (Matthew 6:22)

Do you know that what you choose to focus on will have an effect on your attitude and behavior? It's true. What we regularly put before our eyes we will constantly think about. Moses admonished the children of Israel before they entered the Promise Land to tie the commandments to their foreheads so that they would be mindful of them as they went to bed at night and woke up in the morning (Deuteronomy 11:18–20).

There are many people who are caught in the addiction of pornography by looking at some provocative magazine. And that image that was created in their minds produced a craving for more. Next thing you know, they are going to strip clubs and watching hardcore pornography. How did this happen? It happened by them not regulating what they put before their eyes. How did Adam and Eve fall into temptation? It happened by not regulating what they put before their eyes. According to Scripture, Eve was not tempted to eat from the tree of knowledge of good and evil until she focused on the tree and saw how beautiful and desirable it was (Genesis 3:6).

What we focus on makes a difference. When the twelve spies went to scout out the Promise Land, ten came back with a negative report while only two had a positive one. Why was that? All the scouts saw the same thing with their eyes. Ten of those spies focused on the environment and the people, while the other two put their focus on the promise of God and His Word (Numbers 13:25–33).

What we focus on will determine our attitude. Some people have negative and cynical attitudes because their focus is on negative problems. Many believers go before God in prayer and spend a majority of the time discussing the problem rather speaking the promises of God so that He could assist them in doing something about the issue.

We have the control to determine what kind of attitude we will have by what we choose to focus on. Are we going to choose to complain about our problems and talk ourselves into having a negative attitude, or are we going to speak the promises of God and put our focus on the Word? If we do the former we are guaranteed to have some type of aggravation and anxiety; if we do the latter, then our situation probably won't change immediately but we will have a good attitude until it does. So take responsibility of your mindset and don't allow the external situations of life to dictate your mood any longer.

Scripture Readings:
Genesis 3:6
Deuteronomy 11:18–20
Numbers 13:25–33
Matthew 6:22

December 18

ARE YOU LETTING YOUR GLORY SHINE?

But you are not like that, for you are a chosen people. You are royal priests, a holy nation, God's very own possession. As a result, you can show others the goodness of God, for He called you out of the darkness into His wonderful light. (1 Peter 2:9)

Through the finished work of Jesus Christ, we have been made to be royal priests in the likeness of Jesus. I know that we may not feel like it, but we are. Jesus not only came to this planet to die for our sins, but He also came to show us what we are capable of doing if we would fully believe in Him (John 14:12). The apostle Peter described us as a chosen people, royal priests, and God's very own possession. This is a pretty lofty description for those who have made Jesus their Lord and Savior.

Every believer has the potential to be all of the above; however, few will actually achieve it. The two main reasons for this are unbelief and ignorance. Some believers reject this message and rationalize it away, allowing their sense knowledge to override the spirit, so they walk through life never achieving what God has planned for them. The bad thing is that one day they will appear before the judgment seat of Christ and will be shown what they could have done if they only believed (2 Corinthians 5:10). The second group is those believers who have never heard this message before. Maybe they attend a traditional church where only salvation is taught, or they feel comfortable with the elementary things of God.

Through the Scriptures it has always been God's plan to have a group of people who would demonstrate His glory in this dark world. In Exodus 19:5–6, God spoke through Moses and told the children of Israel that if they would obey His commandments then they would be a holy nation and His special treasure. The apostle Paul said in 2 Corinthians 5:20 that we are to act as ambassadors for Christ, being His representatives. If people want to see what the Kingdom of God is all about, then they should look at us. The power of God should be flowing in and thorough us in a way that others notice.

God wants to bless us so that we can be a blessing to others (Genesis 12:1–3). This is an awesome assignment! We have to be honest with ourselves and make the corrections in our thought life to make this a reality. It will require changing our paradigm of thinking and separating ourselves from those who are not of the same mindset. Everyone God used mightily in the Bible had to go through a period of separation. You and I are not exceptions. Are you willing to be all that God has called you to be?

Scripture Readings:
Genesis 12:1–3
Exodus 19:5–6
2 Peter 2:9
Revelation 1:6

December 19

THINKING, BELIEVING, AND SAYING

Yet we have the same spirit of faith as he had who wrote, I have believed, and therefore have I spoken. We too believed, and therefore we speak. (2 Corinthians 4:13 AMP)

What we think, believe, and say is instrumental in our walk with the Lord. To the degree that we cooperate with God through our thoughts, words, actions, and decisions is the degree that the glory of God will shine in our life (Hebrews 11:6). We can learn a lot about a person by just listening to what they say. They tell us everything we need to know by just listening to them speak. As a therapist, I get paid to assist people in dealing with issues that are hindering them. The best way for me to assess them is to ask questions and listen to their responses.

This reveals their cognitive thought process, which includes thinking and believing, the culmination of which are the words they speak to convey their thoughts, perceptions, and beliefs. This internal process will determine what the individual will experience externally. God has designed us like Himself (Genesis 1:26–28), so we have the ability to use our words to change the world. God spoke into the darkness of the deep and created the earth (Genesis 1:1–25). He internally created what He wanted, and He spoke what He believed and it was.

We have the same ability within us. There are some people who go from one disaster to another, and very little of that comes from our background. I say *very little* because what a person has experienced in the past does have an impact on their life if the individual believes what is true. But there are plenty of stories of how people have overcome horrible situations and are living healthy and happy lives. What was the difference? It was in what they thought, believed, and spoke. These were individuals with a strong internal locus of control. They understood that the power on the inside of them was greater than the power on the outside (1 John 4:4).

After church service one day, I was talking to one of the brothers at church. I asked him about how his business was going. He shrugged his shoulders and said, "Okay." Then he told me, "I am hanging in there, just trusting the Lord to get by." He continued, "God seems to find me enough work just to get by." I thought to myself, "I now know why you are in the financial position you're in. It is what you think, believe, and say." This brother loves the Lord, is faithful in attending services, and even has a notebook with him which means he is a student of the Word. But, with all that he is only getting by. If anyone should be walking in the full blessings of the Lord, it should be him.

The reason why he is not is simple: It is because of the things he thinks, believes, and says. We cannot rise above our thought life, for they have an effect on our perceptions, and our perceptions will dictate what we say. We need to renew our minds and then we will change our beliefs; then and only then will our speech change. Once this happens, our life will change too. But everything begins with our thoughts.

Scripture Readings:
Genesis 1:1–28

December 20

HOW WOULD YOUR RELATIONSHIP BE DESCRIBED?

He has made us a Kingdom of priests for God His Father. All glory and power to Him forever and ever! Amen. (Revelation 1:6)

Since the beginning of the year, I have been reading through the Bible, which has been a tremendous blessing to me. I started off in Genesis and I am now in the book of 2 Kings. God has given me revelation and insight I was not expecting. I thought some of the books like Leviticus would be boring, but I was surprised to discover the revelation I got from that book. In reading the books of Kings, each king who reigned in either the nation of Judah or Israel is described in detail. Some kings are described in a good light, and some are described in a bad one. For example, King David was described as "a man after God's heart" (1 Samuel 13:14), and he is the template for every king in Judah who would follow after him.

After the death of King David, his son Solomon became king of Israel and Judah. The kingdom experienced peace and prosperity while Solomon was king (1 Kings 5:25). However, at his death, the Bible says, "In Solomon's old age, they turned his heart to worship other gods instead of being completely faithful to the Lord his God, as his father, David, had been" (1 Kings 11:4). Because of Solomon's compromise, the kingdom of Israel was divided into the northern and southern regions. The northern region was called Israel and the southern was called Judah.

Jeroboam was the first king of Israel. He made two golden calves and instructed the people to worship these calves instead of going to Jerusalem to worship God. He erected buildings at the pagan altars and ordained common people as priests as an alternative for the people to worship God. Jeroboam set the stage for a series of evil kings who would come after him, like Ahab, who was described as doing evil before the Lord (1 King 16:29–31). The kings in Judah varied from King Abijam, who was described as not being as faithful as David was (1 Kings 15:3–4), to Manasseh, who was described as doing evil in the sight of the Lord, following the detestable practices of the pagans around him (2 Kings 21:2).

Since we are a Kingdom of priests and kings, how would the Bible describe your reign? Would you be described as a king in the mold of David, fully committed to the Lord? Or would you be described as a king who was like David, falling short in some areas in your life that caused conflicts? Or would you be described as an evil king, as Ahab was described? It is something to think about. It might just motivate you to make some changes in your life.

Scripture Readings:
1 Samuel 13:14
1 Kings 15:3–4
2 Kings 15:3; 18:3; 21:2, 20–21

December 21

ARE YOU LIVING UNDER THE CURSE AND DON'T KNOW IT?

But Christ has rescued us from the curse pronounced by the law. When He was hung on the cross, He took upon Himself the curse for our wrongdoing. For it is written in the Scriptures, "Cursed is everyone who is hung on a tree." (Galatians 3:13)

There are many believers who are living under the curse of this world because of either ignorance or unbelief of the finished work of Christ Jesus. I want to focus on those believers who are unaware that they are living under the curse pronounced on this earth. The first thing we need to do is understand what the curse is. If we don't know what the curse is, then we won't have the wherewithal to get out from under it. In Genesis 3:14–19, God pronounced a curse on the serpent, the woman, and the man. I want to focus on the curse God put on the woman and man because this pertains to us today.

The first curse for the woman was that she would experience pain during childbirth. This is part of the curse, so Jesus paid the price for that curse. The second curse would be the conflict in the relationship between the man and woman—there would be a power struggle. That is also part of the curse Jesus paid the price for not to exist in our marriages.

For the man, God pronounced that the ground would be cursed, and he would have to struggle to get it to produce for him. It would take much effort to get crops to grow and produce. And the final curse was spiritual and physical death that would take place in the heart and lives of the people in the world. Well, Jesus paid the price for those curses too. This means we don't have to struggle to make a living. Some people are working two to three jobs to make ends meet while others are relying on overtime to get by. This is the world's remedy for finances, not God's.

In Romans 8:19–20, it says that the creation eagerly waits with longing for God to reveal the children of God so that it can be relieved from death and decay. We as children of God have the power to speak blessings over this world. Instead of taking advantage of our royal position in Christ Jesus, some are waiting for someone else to come along and do it for them. As a result, these believers will die like any other man or woman who is not a part of the Kingdom of God (Psalm 82:6–7). They fail to realize that Christ paid the price for them to live as kings and priests in the Kingdom of God. We should be living such a lifestyle that the glory of God is magnified and the world takes notice (1 Peter 2:9).

It is important to take some time and educate yourself on the curse of the law. Read Deuteronomy 28:15–68, and if you see any of those things going on in your life, command it to go in the name of Jesus. Christ died on the cross to take that curse from you. Don't live with those curses any longer. Take authority over those curses in Jesus's name, telling them to leave you and your family.

Scripture Readings:
Genesis 3:14–19
Deuteronomy 28:1–68
Galatians 3:13

December 22

It's Time to Wake Up

But their evil intentions will be exposed when the light shines on them, for the light makes everything visible. This is why it is said, "Awake, O sleeper, rise up from the dead, and Christ will give you light." (Ephesians 5:13–14)

God wants to do mighty works in your life, but it requires that you do your part in order to see those mighty works take place. Many in the body of Christ are asleep while walking through life. They have allowed this world to lull them into a spiritual slumber. Believers, who don't know who they are in Christ Jesus, are going to church and it has become more of a ritual to make them feel good about themselves than anything else. They don't understand what the finished work of Christ did for them, and they are ignorant of the authority they have access to through Christ Jesus (Philippians 4:13).

There are some believers who are content keeping their light covered. They are not willing to put their light out for the world to see (Luke 12:35–40). They keep their beliefs to themselves because of the fear of offending someone; they have allowed this world's system to confine them within the boundaries that have been established. They have a form of godliness but they reject the power that could make them godly (2 Timothy 3:5). According to the apostle Peter, God has given us everything we need to live a godly life (2 Peter 1:3), but we have to wake up to receive it. We have to renew our minds to this truth (Ephesians 4:23).

Accepting Jesus as your Lord and Savior means so much more than being saved from the wrath of God and going to heaven. God has people who need to be reached, and He will reach them through us. He has called us to be a Kingdom of priests to represent the Kingdom of God to this dark world (1 Peter 2:9). Jesus has given us the authority to use His name to perform signs and wonders (Mark 16:15–18). What is happening today in most churches is that they are giving the message of the gospel but there is no power accompanying it (1 Corinthians 2:4–5). We must make a decision to be what God has called us to be, which is Christ's ambassadors representing the Kingdom of God.

Scripture Readings:
Isaiah 61:6–8
Luke 12:35–40
Ephesians 4:23
2 Peter 1:3–4

December 23

THE KINGDOM OF GOD IS WITHIN YOU: WILL YOU LET IT OUT?

One day the Pharisees asked Jesus, "When will the Kingdom of God come?" Jesus replied, "The Kingdom of God can't be detected by visible signs. You won't be able to say, 'Here it is!' or 'It's over there!' For the Kingdom of God is already among you." (Luke 17:20–21)

When the Pharisees asked Jesus about the coming of the Kingdom of God, they didn't realize it was standing right in their midst. According Colossians 1:9, Jesus is the fullness of God in a human body. The apostle Paul continued to explain that those who accept Jesus into their lives are in union with Him, so the fullness of God also resides in them. Jesus Himself prayed to His Father that all those who would believe in Him would be one with the Father and with the Son (John 17:21–24).

This is a revelation the body of Christ needs to grasp in order to manifest the glory of the Kingdom. We need to develop a Kingdom consciousness. In the book of Ephesians, the apostle Paul tells us that we have been adopted into the family of God; we have received an inheritance from Him (Ephesians 1:4–5, 11). Right now the fullness of God resides within us in the person of the Holy Spirit (John 16:13).

In Matthew 25:1–13, Jesus told the parable of the ten bridesmaids, who represent the body of Christ. Jesus described five of the bridesmaids as being wise, and five as being foolish. What was the difference between the wise and foolish bridesmaids? The wise bridesmaids made sure they had enough oil, which is a type of the Spirit of God. They spent time cultivating their spiritual life. The foolish ones didn't—they settled for having just enough to get by. The foolish bridesmaids got drowsy and went to sleep. Then suddenly the bridegroom came, and they were not prepared when He showed up. So they asked the wise bridesmaids for some of their oil, but the wise ones told them to go to the store and buy some of their own. By the time they came back, it was too late—the wedding feast had started without them.

Why did Jesus tell this parable? It was a warning of what could happen to believers who are not building themselves up spiritually. We have to feed our inner man with the things of God in order to build ourselves up. Jesus has provided us with everything we need to let our light shine in this dark world, but we have to exercise our will to allow that to happen. Will we be like the wise or foolish bridesmaids? The choice is ours today.

Scripture Readings:
Matthew 25:1–13
Luke 18:20–21
John 16:13
Ephesians 1:1–11

December 24

Spiritual Ignorance No More

My people are being destroyed because they don't know Me. Since you priests refuse to know Me, I refuse to recognize you as My priests. Since you have forgotten the laws of your God, I will forget to bless your children. (Hosea 4:6)

One thing I ask God for every day is for spiritual wisdom, knowledge, and insight, which is a necessity if we are going to walk in the full manifestation of the finished work of Christ. As I have said before, there are many believers who love the Lord and who are not walking in the fullness of what God has for them because they are spiritually ignorant. I am reminded of Psalm 82:6–7, where the psalmist wrote, "I say, 'You are gods; you are children of the Most High. But you will die like mere mortals and fall like every other ruler.'" Many believers are living lives just like this—they are not taking advantage of all the precious promises God has made available to them.

As I write this book, my eyes have been opened to see my spiritual ignorance. I knew what I read in the Scriptures was true, but I wondered why it was not happening in my life. Then I realized how spiritual ignorant I am about certain things. I thought that if I had just memorized enough Scriptures, that was the key. I was completely wrong. It was not in the memorization of Scripture but what is inside those Scriptures that release the power of God. There are many people who can quote Scriptures, but the power of God is absent from their lives.

We have to go deeper and allow the Spirit of God to reveal His truth to us. The apostle Paul prayed a prayer in the book of Ephesians that I pray almost every day: "Asking God, the glorious Father of our Lord Jesus Christ, to give you spiritual wisdom and insight so that you might grow in your knowledge of God. I pray that your hearts will be flooded with light so that you can understand the confident hope He has given to those

He called—His holy people who are His rich and glorious inheritance" (Ephesians 1:17–18).

This is a powerful prayer I would suggest everyone who is serious about his or her walk with God should pray regularly. As we engage in this prayer, our spiritual eyes will be opened to see what the world cannot see (John 14:19). In the days ahead, this world will become darker and darker, which means we have the opportunity to shine brighter and brighter. Will we wake up, or will we remain asleep in our spiritual ignorance?

Scripture Readings:
Psalm 82:6–7
Hosea 4:6
John 14:19
Ephesians 1:17–19; 3:17–20

December 25

WHAT YOU THINK MATTERS

We use God's mighty weapons, not worldly weapons, to knock down the strongholds of human reasoning and to destroy false arguments. We destroy every proud obstacle that keeps people from knowing God. We capture their rebellious thoughts and teach them to obey Christ. (2 Corinthians 10:4–5)

Our thought life is extremely important to our success. Our thoughts have an influence on our will, mood, and behavior. Believers should not mitigate the mental aspect of their lives. Many believers make the mistake of thinking that since they are born again, their minds will be automatically renewed as well. This is simply not true. We have to renew our mind because it is still tied to the flesh. That is why the Bible says that we are no longer to be conformed to this world, but we are to be transformed by renewing our minds (Romans 12:1–2). If we don't renew our minds, then we will remain carnal in our thinking as we live our Christian experience on a low level.

The only access the enemy has to us is through the mental realm. If he can influence our thoughts, he has an inroad to control us. There are believers who are oppressed by the enemy because they have given him access through their minds. He will introduce a thought into their minds, and if that thought is not dealt with, it will remain in their mind and grow like a cancerous seed. That thought will slowly become an imagination and enter their unconscious mind or inner being. From that point on, the fruit of that thought will be manifested in that person's life.

How can a person prevent this from happening? It starts by stopping the thought when we first have it. We have a choice to accept or reject what comes into our minds. It has been reported that the average person will have anywhere from three to ten thousand thoughts per day. Most of those thoughts are fleeting thoughts, like birds that fly over our head. But when a person chooses to focus on a thought, it will remain with them. It is like a bird landing on our head and making a nest. In order to prevent this from happening, we have to exercise our authority, speak to that thought, and tell it to leave. I know that sounds a little extreme, but it is something that must be done. Had Adam and Eve used their authority in the Garden of Eden and told that serpent to go, he would have had to leave.

Our battle is not just in the natural realm, but in the spiritual realm as well. The enemy and his cohorts will use the mental realm to hold people in bondage and oppress them. We as believers need to know the authority we have in our words to do battle and win when we speak the Word of God. We need to meditate on the Word of God so that we are armed to do battle with the enemies of our soul.

Scripture Readings:
Matthew 4:1–11
Romans 12:1–2
2 Corinthians 10:4–5
Ephesians 6:10–17

December 26

It Is Not the Amount of Faith, but the Amount of Unbelief that Makes the Difference

The father instantly cried out, "I do believe, but help me overcome my unbelief!" (Mark 9:24)

There are many believers who will pray for something and not get their prayer answered. Has that ever happened to you? It has happened to me more times than I care to remember. When this happened to me, I immediately rationalized that I must have done something wrong. Maybe I should have prayed longer or quoted more Bible Scriptures. Maybe I have some unconfessed sin in my life. Or just maybe it was not God's will to grant my request. Well, maybe it was none of the previously mentioned things.

The Scriptures clearly state that the amount of faith we have is not the problem. Jesus told His disciples that if they had faith the size of a mustard seed, they could tell a mulberry tree to be uprooted and cast into the sea (Luke 17:6), and it would obey them. If we have ever seen a mustard seed, it's tiny—one of the tiniest seeds in the world. The apostle Paul said in the book of Romans that every believer has been given *the* measure of faith (Romans 12:3), and the apostle Peter described our faith as being more precious than gold that perishes (1 Peter 1:3–5). It is not an issue on the amount of faith, or the quality of faith we possess.

The problem is the amount of unbelief we have in our heart (Mark 11:23). Unbelief will nullify our faith from working, especially if that unbelief is in our heart. Because our mind is not reborn, we have to work to get our mind in line with our reborn spirit. So it is not unnatural to have unbelief in our mind while having faith in our heart. The risk we have with the unbelief in our mind is that it could eventually get to our heart if we spend too much time meditating in unbelief. That is why it is important to spend time in the Word to get that unbelief out of our minds.

To illustrate this point, there was a situation where the disciples couldn't heal a man's son. Jesus had given them authority to heal the sick and cast out demonic spirits (Matthew 10:6); they even had a history of casting out demonic spirits and healing people (Mark 6:12–13). But for some reason they could not heal this boy. When Jesus was told about this, He became frustrated with the disciples and told them to bring the boy to Him. He then healed the boy. Afterward the disciples asked why they couldn't heal him, and Jesus said, "Because of your unbelief" (Matthew 17:14–20). So keep this in mind the next time your prayers go unanswered. Check to see if you have some unbelief that needs to be dealt with today.

Scripture Readings:
Matthew 17:14–20
Mark 11:23
Romans 12:3
Galatians 2:20

December 27

THE GOD KIND OF FAITH

Peter remembered what Jesus had said to the tree on the previous day and exclaimed, "Look Rabbi! The fig tree You cursed has withered and died!" Then Jesus said to the disciples, "Have faith in God." (Mark 11:21–22)

When a believer receives Christ as their Lord and Savior, God gives them *the* measure of faith. This is the God kind of faith, the kind of faith that will never fail. However, if we don't have understanding about the God kind of faith, we might confuse it with our natural faith. Faith is not a commodity that is exclusive to believers only—every one of us uses faith in our everyday lives. There are even non-believers who have demonstrated great faith. The problem with natural faith is that it has its limits, whereas the God kind of faith does not.

When Smith Wigglesworth was asked how he was able to perform the miracles of healing that he did, he said he did not rely on his faith but on the faith of God. He explained that when he relied on God's faith, he had no doubts that what he prayed for would not happen. He had this confidence because nothing is impossible with God (Luke 1:37). Jesus said the same thing when He explained how He performed miracles—it was the Father in Him doing the works (John 5:19–20). Faith is not just a formula that we can use to get what we want. Yes, there are principles that are used with faith, and we can get results by just applying the principles of faith, but there is no guarantee it will work every time.

When the disciples were unable to heal the demon-possessed boy (Matthew 17:14–20), it was because they had faith in the principle of faith, not faith in God's ability to heal the boy through them. Many believers have reduced faith to a mere formula. If I make sure that I make a positive confession a certain number of times, give an offering, and pray, then God will grant my prayer. One thing is missing. Where is God in this process? What has happened is that this formula of faith has taken the place of God.

When I was paralyzed, I heard God tell me that I would recover. It was my faith in God's spoken Word that healed me. It was not my faith, but faith in God working in me that actually healed me. God's Word is the ultimate reality. If God said it would happen, then it will! It does not matter what our environment says to us. If we put our faith in the sense realm, we open ourselves up to doubt because everything in the natural realm is subject to change. But the Word of God does not change, and it can be relied upon (2 Corinthians 4:18).

Scripture Readings:
Matthew 17:14–20
Mark 11:21–24
2 Corinthians 4:18

December 28

Your Circumstances Won't Change God's Word; God's Word Will Change Your Circumstances

For I have come down from heaven not to do My own will and purpose but to do the will and purpose of Him Who sent Me. (John 6:38 AMP)

If we want to know the will of God, we can go to His Word. Jesus was the Word of God encased in a fleshly body (John 1:14). So we can say that Jesus and the Word of God are the same. Many of us don't realize the power of the Word of God, but it was that same Word that caused the universe to be created and caused the unseen to be seen that is still with us today. When we accept Jesus into our hearts, we have the Word of God residing within us because Jesus is the Word of God made flesh. Say to yourself, "The Word of God resides within me!"

With this awareness we can go to the Word of God and find promises to correct any situation we are facing. This is what Abraham learned when God promised him an heir. He had to wait almost twenty-five years, and during that time he became impatient and tried to help God fulfill the promise (Genesis 16:1–5). But he finally got it right. He learned to have faith in the ability of God and His faithfulness. Abraham learned to look beyond the circumstances and to put his faith in the Word of God (Romans 4:17–21). Abraham was fully convinced that God would come through on His promises.

We might be facing situations that seem insurmountable. We have no one to encourage us; in fact, those who are closest to us seem to be an enemy to our faith rather than an ally. It is in times like this that our fleshly nature starts talking to us, planting seeds of doubt and discouragement. When this happens, it is important that we strengthen ourselves in the Word of God. Take that opportunity to do what Abraham did; his faith grew stronger as he focused on the promise of God. Abraham knew that no matter what his circumstances were, God's Word doesn't change. It will change the circumstances. Abraham recalled all of the promises God fulfilled in his life. God said that He would bless him so that he could be a blessing to others, and He did (Genesis 12:1–3). In fact, the Scriptures say that Abraham was very rich in livestock, silver, and gold (Genesis 13:2).

So we can do the same thing today. Is all we need to do is recall all the promises of God that have come to pass in our life. We can think of all the times God has come through for us, and we can read all the Scriptures pertaining to our situation, realizing that God's Word is the ultimate truth. What the doctors are telling us is the truth—they have factual evidence to prove it. But God's Word is the ultimate truth; all other truth has to bow its knee to the truth of the Word of God.

Scripture Readings:
Isaiah 55:10–11
Romans 4:17–21

December 29

LEARN TO SEE WITH YOUR SPIRITUAL EYES

Soon the world will no longer see Me, but you will see Me. Since I live, you also will live. When I am raised to life again, you will know that I am in My Father, and you are in Me, and I am in you. (John 14:19–20)

This is part of the speech Jesus told to His disciples while preparing them for His departure. He was about to go from the physical realm back to the spiritual realm: "The world will see Me no longer." But He said that His disciples would in fact see Him. What this means is that we have the ability to see things non-believers cannot see. Through the Word of God, we can see victory when the world sees defeat. We can see abundance when others see famine.

This is because we are not citizens of this world's system—we are citizens of the Kingdom of God. In God's Kingdom there is no such thing as lack or fear. Once a person accepts Jesus as their Lord and Savior, they are automatically given citizenship to God's Kingdom (John 17:21). Yes, it is true! Jesus has made a way for anyone who will accept Him as his or her Lord and Savior to escape from the kingdom of darkness into the glorious Kingdom of God (Colossians 1:13). There is hope available, but we won't find it in this world's system. All they can give us is a temporary solution to our problems, which only delays the indelible.

The Bible is more than a book; it contains the will and life of God. It is alive and active, and it has the power to speak to our inner man and bring life to our spirit (Hebrews 4:12). It is through the Scriptures that revelation is given so that we have vision into the spiritual realm. Jesus said that His words are spirit and they are life (John 6:63). This means that there are two ways a person could read the Bible: They could just read the words without spiritual insight and get very little out of it, or they can read the Bible with assistance from the Holy Spirit and receive spiritual wisdom and insight that we can't imagine.

I started reading the Bible earlier this year. I knew I would enjoy reading Genesis and Exodus, but Leviticus? Well, I am less than halfway done and I can say that I have been pleasantly surprised. The books of the Bible I thought were going to be boring have given me the most insight. I can see Jesus through the entire Bible! I feel like I know the character of God better from this study. I would encourage anyone who is serious about their walk with the Lord to do the same. The spiritual rewards will be well worth the time. Learn to see with your spiritual eyes.

Scripture Readings:
John 6:63; 14:19–21
Colossians 1:13
Hebrews 4:12

December 30

MAKING GOD'S THOUGHTS YOUR THOUGHTS

"My thoughts are nothing like your thoughts," says the Lord. "And My ways are far beyond anything you could imagine. For just as the heavens are higher than the earth, so My ways are higher than your ways and My thoughts higher than your thoughts." (Isaiah 55:8–9)

Since the fall of humanity, man's spirit has been disconnected from the Spirit of God. Humanity has only had our sense knowledge and fallen nature to guide us. However, Jesus came to make it possible for us to be reconnected to the Spirit of God so that we could receive revelation knowledge about God and His Kingdom. Everyone who accepts Jesus as their Savior and Lord, their spirits are reborn, but their minds are still in a carnal state. They have to reeducate their minds to the things of God (Romans 12:1–2).

This is the process every believer who wants to experience the fullness of God has to go through. There are many believers who have accepted the Lord into their hearts, but their minds are not renewed. The apostle Paul described this type of believer as being infants in their Christian walk (1 Corinthians 3:1–4). They are still carnal in their thinking because they had not renewed their minds. We must realize the importance of renewing our cognitive thought processes so they come into agreement with our born-again spirit. When this is done, then we will have the mind of Christ (1 Corinthians 2:16) and will be able to do what Jesus did (John 14:12).

Our thoughts dictate our attitude and our behavior, so it is important we guard the thoughts we allow into our mind and heart, because we ultimately serve our thoughts. What we believe we will perceive, and what we perceive we will act upon. This is the cognitive process that is common to us all. So if we want to change our life, we must change our thoughts! If we want to be more like God, then we must learn to think the way God thinks.

How do we do that? We do it primarily by reading His Word. Just like our words convey our thoughts and meaning, so God's words convey His thoughts. Jesus was the Word of God personified (John 1:14). He walked out the will of God and showed us what the Kingdom of God was like (Luke 17:20). When a person's mind is renewed to the things of God, they can manifest the Kingdom of God in their daily lives. So what is stopping us from doing so?

Scripture Readings:
Isaiah 55:8–11
Romans 12:1–2
John 1:14
1 Corinthians 2:16; 3:1–4
Ephesians 4:23

December 31

WHOSE TRUTH WILL YOU FOLLOW?

Jesus told him, "I am the way, the truth, and the life. No one can come to the Father except through Me." (John 14:6)

Congratulations! You made it through the year. This is the last day of our journey to the Promise Land. If there is one thing that I want to emphasize throughout this devotional, it is the power to choose. God has given each of us the ability to make choices in life. If an individual realizes this one fact, it can transform them from being a victim to an empowered individual. We can be changed from someone who is being controlled by our external environment to someone who has a strong internal locus of control. This is something all successful people have in common.

Our last lesson is truth. There are many versions of truth in the world today. However, it was not always that way. When God created man and placed him in the Garden of Eden, he lived in a perfect paradise. The earth at that time was a replica of heaven. Man had access to God and enjoyed unbroken fellowship with Him. All that changed when Satan, in the form of a serpent, introduced his version of the truth. This was the first time another truth besides God's truth was introduced. At that point, Adam had a choice to make: which truth was he going to believe? God had established clear boundaries regarding the trees in the Garden. God had said that if they ate the fruit of the knowledge of good and evil, they would die. However, Satan gave his version of the truth—the serpent said they would not die (Genesis 3:3–4).

Then the serpent gave the woman a reason for disobeying God's truth. Slowly, God's truth was fading away as the woman's truth that was influenced by the serpent became stronger. As the truth became stronger within her, she began to imagine Satan's version of truth in her mind, and got her will involved. Suddenly, the truth of the serpent became her truth and she acted on it (Genesis 3:5–6). Ever since that day, humanity has had the task of deciding which truth they will follow. When following the truth of this world, we are following the truth of Satan because he is the god of this world (2 Corinthians 4:4).

We have been led to believe that Satan is this evil monster with horns and a pitchfork. But the Bible describes him as portraying himself as an angel of light (2 Corinthians 11:13–15). This means that Satan can appear to be truth, and that's how so many people are deceived with false religions and doctrines. When Satan approached Eve in the Garden of Eden, he appealed to her reasoning and desire. He capitalized off her desire to be more godlike. And he uses the same tactic today to deceive people. He uses their desire for wealth, power, and prestige to deceive humanity into doing his will.

We have to be able to discern between the deceptions of Satan and the truth of God. It can be hard at times, because Satan can be very convincing. But with the power of the Holy Spirit we will be guided into all truth (John 16:13). For this coming year make a quality decision to make God's truth your truth. Seek to know the truth of God through studying His Word, and seek the guidance of the Holy Spirit. Have a Happy New Year!

Scripture Readings:
Genesis 3:1–6

Final Thoughts

It has been a pleasure to write this book. I never thought that God would use me for such an endeavor. I hope that you have learned as much through reading it as I did through writing it. The Holy Spirit gave much of this material to me on the day I sat down to write. It is amazing to see what comes out of your spirit when you give yourself to God. I surprised myself at times. I don't expect that everyone will agree with some of the lessons in this book. That's all right. We are all at different levels of our spiritual walk. And on some subjects we can agree to disagree.

I have tried to keep away from giving my opinions, and instead have given scriptural references to back up my opinions and thoughts. God designed this book to be a tool to empower the individual who reads it. It can be read from year to year, because every time you read it you will see something different. That's because the words are Spirit-inspired, which makes the words alive and active. God wants His children to represent Him; we are to be lights in this dark world. We are to be His ambassadors for the Kingdom of God. We are priests and kings of the Most High, and our lives should reflect that truth.

God has given each of us an assignment for the Kingdom, and it is our job to find out what that assignment is and fulfill it to the best of our ability. True happiness comes when we can say that we have done the will of God. So make it your goal to do the will of God in everything you do. Don't compare yourself with anyone else because that is a big mistake. You can't be happy living someone else's revelation. You need to find your own, and it may not be as glamorous as you would like, but that doesn't matter. All that matters is that are you doing the will of God from the heart.

I pray that God's hand would be upon you and bless you in all your endeavors. If you don't know Jesus as your Lord and Savior, all it takes is believing in your heart and confessing with your mouth that Jesus is God's gift sent to the world to redeem humanity from the wrath of God (Romans 10:7–10). Jesus paid the price for all the sins of humanity so that all those who believe in Him can go boldly before the throne of God to find mercy in their time of need (2 Corinthians 5:21). It is a free gift from God. All that is required is that we believe and receive this gift, and then we will become a child of God (John 1:12–13). So if you have not made Jesus your Lord and Savior, or you are not sure if you have done that, what's stopping you from doing so right now? Don't wait until tomorrow, for tomorrow is not guaranteed to anyone.

Be strong in the Lord and the power of His might always,
Keith E. Jackson, MA, MFT

About the Author

Keith E. Jackson, MA, MFT, received his undergraduate degree from the University of Arizona—a bachelors of arts degree with a major in psychology and minor in sociology and history. He was also a member of the football team, where he played running back. After he graduated, he had a brief career in the NFL with the San Diego Chargers. He later worked in the field of criminal justice. He worked as a juvenile probation officer for over twenty years with San Diego County, and eight years for the San Diego County Sheriff's Department as a correctional counselor. After he retired, he obtained his master's degree in counseling psychology from Southern California Bible College and Seminary. He was later licensed as a marriage and family therapist in the State of California. He currently resides in Portland, Oregon, and is the founder of One Last Chance Outreach. He does motivational speaking and song writing. For more information please go to his website www.olcoutreach.com.

Bear Down!

Edwards Brothers Malloy
Oxnard, CA USA
November 4, 2014